Study Guide

Contemporary Marketing
TWELFTH EDITION

Louis E. Boone

University of South Alabama

David L. Kurtz

University of Arkansas

THOMSON
™
SOUTH-WESTERN

Australia · Brazil · Canada · Mexico · Singapore · Spain · United Kingdom · United States

THOMSON

SOUTH-WESTERN

Study Guide to accompany Contemporary Marketing, 12/e

Louis E. Boone & David L. Kurtz

VP/Editorial Director:
Jack W. Calhoun

VP/Editor-in-Chief:
Dave Shaut

Publisher:
Melissa Acuña

Executive Editor:
Neil Marquardt

Developmental Editor:
Rebecca von Gillern

Marketing Manager:
Nicole Moore

Senior Promotions Manager:
Terron Sanders

Production Editor:
Margaret M. Bril

Technology Project Editor:
Kristen Meere

Media Editor:
Karen Schaffer

Manufacturing Coordinator:
Diane Lohman

Printer:
Darby Printing
Atlanta, GA

Art Director:
Michelle Kunkler

Cover and Internal Designer:
Liz Harasymczuk Design

Cover Images:
© Getty Images and © Corbis

Photography Manager:
John Hill

Photo Researchers:
Darren Wright and Annette Coolidge

CONTENTS

INTRODUCTION

I am happy to present you with the *Study Guide for Contemporary Marketing – Twelfth Edition.* There have been a number of changes in the order of presentation and content of this edition. As always, such changes were made only when I felt they would improve the essential function of this book – to help you, the student, develop greater understanding of the marketing profession as it is practiced and studied today. The *Study Guide* is closely coordinated with the textbook and each of its parts is structured as a learning unit exploring a particular area of the marketing field.

Coverage of each chapter of the *Study Guide* begins with a detailed outline of the material in the chapter. This outline, when used in concert with the textbook, is designed to serve as a memory refresher to assist in recalling significant points in the text as you work through the exercises in the guide.

Other features include a section on each chapter's **Key Concepts**, a matching of important topics in the chapter to their definitions; a **Self-Quiz** for each chapter's material – fifty questions exploring the material in the chapter in detail; **Applying Marketing Concepts**, a series of illustrations of how the techniques and principles described in the text are put to use; and **Surfing the Net**, including the addresses and commentaries on some Internet Web sites of particular interest to the marketing student

In **Creating a Marketing Plan**, an episode of which appears in each of the parts of the guide (with one left as a free-standing closing episode at the end) you are given information to develop by following the adventures of three young entrepreneurs. Each of the parts of the guide also contains a brief synopsis of the part to supplement to chapter outlines.

As always, I earnestly solicit and welcome your comments and those of your teachers. Though I have made every effort to make sure that the questions and answers match and that it all makes sense, I know that there are errors scattered here and there through the *Study Guide.* For these I apologize and request that if you find any, please tell me about them and they will be changed in the next printing of this work. I can be reached at toconnor@uno.edu.

My very best wishes to you for success in your studies and in the use of these materials

Acknowledgements and Thanks

I have now been the author of the *Study Guide to Accompany Contemporary Marketing* since the sixth edition of the text back in 1989. During that time, my relationship with the authors of the text, the editorial staff of its publisher, and a whole bunch of other people, including a number of students all over the U. S., has been nothing but extraordinarily pleasant.

I would, therefore, like to thank all of them from the beginning, but since that would take too much time and space, I will express my heartfelt appreciation to those who were directly involved in this edition. I cannot say too many good things about professors Boone and Kurtz. Two more gentlemanly gentlemen are unlikely to exist anywhere. They and the *Contemporary Marketing* text, in all its many editions, have made a very substantial contribution to the understanding of marketing by thousands upon thousands of students over the years.

The editorial staff at Thomson Business and Professional Publishing has been most helpful in the development of this edition's *Study Guide*. My thanks go first to Rebecca Von Gillern, the Developmental Editor on the project, and the person with whom I have worked most directly. Thanks also to Executive Editor, Neil Marquardt, Marketing Manager, Nicole Moore, and Production Editor, Marge Bril.

As always and every day, I thank my secretary, Renee Cox Kern, an old hand at dealing with the trials, tribulations, foibles and failings of academics of all stripes. Her efforts have smoothed the way to fitting this project in among all the other tasks incumbent on a professor.

And finally, I thank my family for all the help and understanding they have, as usual, brought to this project. My sons, Brian and Terrence, who were in grade school when all this started, are now adults and men of their own but still have something to say when I start revisions. They have, over the years, provided a lot of close-up insights for me into the behavior of pre-teenagers, teenagers, and post-teenagers that appear in the *Guide*. My wife of 31 years, Valerie, has always been extraordinarily tolerant of the unusual demands on my – and hence her – time that a project like this involves, for which I say thanks yet again.

Thomas S. O'Connor
The University of New Orleans

Part 1
Designing Customer-Oriented Marketing Strategies

In the early twenty-first century, marketing has realized the necessity of transition from transaction-base marketing to relationship marketing. The marketing process creates time, place, and ownership utilities for consumers. Marketing itself is defined as the process of planning and executing the conception, pricing, promotion, and distribution of ideas, goods, services, organizations, and events to create and maintain relationships that satisfy organizational and individual objectives. Today's marketplace is global in scope. Firms can no longer limit their activities to a single or even several nations. Products and services have both been affected.

Marketing arises out of the exchange process. The emphasis on marketing activities increases as firms progress through the four eras of: (1) production orientation, (2) sales orientation, (3) marketing orientation, and (4) relationship orientation. Long-run success does not happen unless firms adopt a company-wide consumer orientation. This realization has been called the marketing concept. The desirability of the development of positive long-term relationships between vendors and customers of all sorts must be recognized. In recent years, the marketing concept has called managers' attention to avoidance of "marketing myopia," a too-narrow definition of the firm's market, and has been broadened to include the activities of not-for-profit organizations. In the area of nontraditional marketing, we find people, places, causes, events, and organizations now being treated as though they were goods or services. Critical thinking and creativity are concepts that define how marketers validate and use information.

There has been a revolution in the technology of marketing, which has resulted in interactive marketing in which the customer controls the information received from a marketer. The development of the Internet, broadband technology, wireless Internet connectivity, and interactive technology have opened new vistas on market access to both marketers and consumers. The traditional view of marketing is being replaced by a different orientation.

Given the high cost of marketing, effective relationships confer significant competitive advantages. For marketing to take place, it is usually necessary that a firm or some combination of firms perform the eight universal functions of: (1) buying, (2) selling, (3) transporting, (4) storing, (5) standardization and grading, (6) financing, (7) risk-taking, and (8) securing marketing information.

Ethics and social responsibility are important aspects of the role of the modern marketer. They have to do with the perception and actions required by one's moral standards.

Planning is the basis for strategy and tactics. One of the marketing manager's primary responsibilities is to create plans to facilitate the achievement of marketing objectives. Marketing planning focuses on relationships between vendors and customers. Marketing management addresses strategic issues through long-range planning and tactical issues in the planning of shorter-term programs. Central to marketing planning is identification of strategic windows B short periods of time when company resources optimally match environmental conditions.

Top managers are responsible for strategic planning; lower level managers have a greater degree of involvement with the development and implementation of tactical plans. Planning begins with objectives stated in the firm's mission statement. SWOT analysis identifies strengths, weaknesses, opportunities, and threats related to the firm. Opportunity analysis culminates in the formation of marketing objectives designed to achieve overall organizational objectives.

Marketers use operating plans to put the marketing strategy into action. Having picked a target market whose needs they intend to satisfy, marketers plan and coordinate the four strategic areas of product, distribution, promotion, and pricing in a marketing mix designed to satisfy the wants and needs of a specific target market, a group of people to whom the firm directs its marketing effort.

The marketer must be aware of the five interacting environments, which affect marketing activities: the competitive, the political-legal, the economic, the technological, and the social-cultural. Each of these has its own complexities and rules, written or unwritten, that affects what, how, when and where certain activities may be acceptable, necessary, or prohibited. Globalization of business has expanded the necessity to be aware of the differences between environmental components from one place to another.

The competitive environment includes all those organizations competing for the purchasing power of customers. A firm chooses its competitive environment when it chooses its markets and may face direct competition, competition from substitutes, and competition from all other organizations that seek to sell to consumers.

Marketing strategies must be adjusted in response to changes in the political-legal environment. Early antitrust legislation was aimed at maintaining a competitive environment. Later legislation arising out of the depression conditions of the 1930s was designed to protect small competitors from discriminatory practices. Since the 1950s, a number of laws have been designed to protect consumers from harmful marketing practices and unsafe products or services. Beginning in the 1970s, it became common to "deregulate" industries which were formerly under substantial government control, yet there still exist many regulatory agencies charged with implementing existing laws. In addition, public and private consumer interest groups have an effect on this environment.

The rate of inflation, stage of the business cycle, level of unemployment, national income, and availability of critical resources all influence the likelihood of individuals parting with discretionary income. If resources are in short supply it becomes difficult to satisfy consumer demand.

Technology is changing with incredible speed. There are competitors in this environment, too, and technological breakthroughs by others may take market share away from those who don't keep up the pace.

The social-cultural environment is a significant factor to marketers. This area includes all relationships marketers have with society. Rising educational levels and better communications have lead to greater public involvement and consumer activism in this area. Moreover, changing dietary habits and greater consciousness of cultural diversity have presented opportunities and challenges in the marketplace. Finally, the question of ethical conduct is a very serious issue in this context c many would say that marketing's role in society now hinges on the moral/ethical issue. Ethical considerations are an intrinsic part of operating within an environmental structure. Ethics has to do with moral values and standards of conduct. Social responsibility places increased weight on the well-being of society in its relationship to a firm's desire for profits and the consumer's wish to be satisfied. Ethical issues affect each of the components of the marketing mix.

Electronic commerce (e-commerce) consists or targeting customers by collecting and analyzing business information, conducting customer transactions, and maintaining customer relationships using communications networks. Electronic marketing (e-marketing) is the narrower concept of presenting a marketing mix through the facilities of e-commerce. Online marketing is the pursuit of e-marketing through interactive computer systems. The Internet is the primary vehicle for online marketing through its World Wide Web of interlinked computers functioning within the Internet. To access it, one must use the services of an internet service provider. The Web provides communication, entertainment, information, and e-commerce opportunities to its users. E-commerce impacts the economy through its business-to-business and business-to-consumer marketing resources, offering lower prices, convenience, and personalization of service often lacking elsewhere. Durable goods and business products dominate the B2B segment of the online market. B2B online marketing allows marketers to discover new markets and customers and provide cost savings to themselves and their customers. Online consumers save money, obtain convenience, and receive a level of personalization not available elsewhere. From the vendor's point of view, it contributes to relationship building, increased efficiency, cost reductions, and a more level playing field for all players. The Internet's effect on marketing has been significant, with a large number of new commercial sites being added every month. But marketing has also impacted the Internet, creating new promotional techniques and channels of distribution for goods and services. Online consumer buyers tend to be affluent, urban consumers while online vendors sell everything from auto parts to fresh vegetables delivered to your door. Big sellers on the Net are airline tickets and computer hardware. Security and privacy are still issues among Internet users on both the buying and selling ends of the transaction. Interactive marketing channels include company Web sites, electronic store fronts and cybermalls, advertising on other Web sites, online communities, and a number of other links such as Web kiosks, smart cards, virtual coupons and online samples, and "blogs."

Creating an effective Web presence for the marketer means more than just being there. The objective of marketing on the Web is to create a sustainable Web presence generating profit, new customers, and related benefits to the firm. The Web site must help build relationships between the firm and its customers. Managing the Web site and measuring its effectiveness become crucial activities in this context. Strategically, interactive marketing is expected to increase in importance and complexity during the next several years.

Chapter 1
Marketing: Creating Satisfaction through
Customer Relationships

Chapter Outline

You may want to use the following as a guide in taking notes.

I. Chapter Overview

Customer loyalty is the watchword of twenty-first century marketing. The technology revolution continues to change the rules of marketing. Sophisticated technologies create new types of products and demand new approaches to marketing existing products. Rapidly changing business landscapes create new challenges for firms both small and large, whether operated for profit or not. Companies don't necessarily have to be devoted to high technology, though, to attract and create loyal customers – it's the ability to create customer satisfaction through customer relationships that determines a firm's success.

II. What is Marketing?

A. Production and marketing of goods and services are the essence of economic life in any society.
   1. Utility is the want-satisfying power of a good or service. Its four forms are utility of form, time, place, and ownership.
   2. Marketing creates utility of time, place, and ownership.
   3. ALL organizations must create utility to survive, and to do this they must convince potential customers that their products have utility.
   4. To create customers, organizations must identify needs in the marketplace, determine which needs they can profitably serve, and develop an offering that will convert potential buyers into customers.

B. A Definition of Marketing – Marketing is the process of planning and executing the conception, pricing, distribution, and promotion of ideas, goods, services, organizations, and events to create and maintain relationships that will satisfy individual and organizational objectives.
   1. This definition reflects the expanded concept of marketing, an idea that permeates the whole organization and assumes that marketing will be conducted ethically and will effectively serve the interests of society and the organization.
   2. The concept recognizes identifies the marketing variables of product, price, place, and distribution that combine to produce customer satisfaction.
   3. The customer, client, or public determines the nature of the marketing program.
   4. Emphasis is placed on creating and maintaining long-term relationships with customers and suppliers.
   5. These concepts are recognized as applying to not-for-profit as well as profit-oriented businesses.

C. Today's Global Marketplace provides a worldwide customer base of 6 billion people.
   1. International agreements are increasing the volume of international trade.

5

2. Electronic commerce and related technology brings formerly isolated locations into the world marketplace.
3. Modern nations are interdependent because none can produce everything it needs. Events in one country can produce results in a number of others.
4. Services, including skilled labor and technology, are marketable internationally.
5. The U. S. is an attractive market for foreign firms because of its size and high standard of living. .
6. Domestic strategies may work well unchanged or need modification to work in the international sphere.

III. Four Eras in the History of Marketing

A. The Production Era – Before 1925, most firms were oriented toward production as a goal.
   1. The prevailing attitude was that a quality product would sell itself.
   2. The idea was to produce more and produce it better and faster. Output was the measure of success.
   3. Neglected was the realization that a product must fill a marketplace need.

B. The Sales Era – Output increased while demand remained roughly the same so manufacturers sought customers for their goods, and personal selling and advertising were viewed as means to overcome sales resistance.
   1. The basic assumption of this era was that customers would resist buying products not deemed essential and that selling and advertising were the keys to convincing them to buy.
   2. Once again, marketers overlooked the idea that selling is only one part of the marketing task.

C. The Marketing Era – A new point of view appeared as organizations developed a company-wide consumer orientation to satisfying customer needs as a means of achieving long-term success.
   1. At the end or World War II, a shift in market conditions from a seller's market – one in which there were more buyers than goods and services available to them – to a buyer's market – one in which there were more goods and service available that people who wanted them – occurred.
   2. Marketing took its place as a leading player in product planning.
   3. Firms embraced the marketing concept – a company-wide consumer orientation designed to discover and satisfy consumer wants and needs.
   4. The strength of a firm's market orientation related and continues to relate directly to market success.

D. The Relationship Era – Firms learned to focus on establishing and maintaining long-term relationships with customers and suppliers
   1. The concept of relationships rather than simple exchanges became central to marketing thinking.
   2. Long-term, value-added relationships with customers and suppliers create strategic alliances that benefit everyone.

E. Converting needs to wants is achieved by focusing on the benefits resulting from the acquisition of goods and services
   1. The need for clothing is translated into a market for designer clothing.
   2. Easier to use – "user-friendly" – software and low prices make computers accessible to "non-techies"
   3. Firms adopting the marketing concept focus on solving consumer problems such as security and privacy on the Internet.

IV. Avoiding Marketing Myopia – Recognizing the Scope of One's Business.

   A. There have been mis-steps along the way to general use of the marketing concept. Levitt identified marketing myopia as management's failure to recognize the scope of its business.
      1. Firms should define their goals broadly and in terms of satisfying consumer needs.
      2. AT&T isn't a telephone company – it's a communications firm.

V. Extending the Traditional Boundaries of Marketing – For-profit and Not-for-profit organizations can both successfully apply the marketing concept.

   A. Marketing in public-sector and private-sector not-for-profit organizations
      1. Not-for-profit organizations are big business – there are more than 1.6 million of them generating more than $620 billion in revenues every year.
      2. Not-for-profits are present in both the public and the private sectors.
      3. The private sector has a greater array of not-for-profits than does the public.
      4. Adopting the marketing concept often means partnering between a not-for-profit and a for-profit firm.

   B. Characteristics of not-for-profit marketing
      1. Not-for-profit organizations lack an orientation toward "the bottom line" – the profitability that is so important to for-profit firms. On the other hand, they need just as much money to do the things they do as do for-profits.
      2. Recent history has not-for-profits developing more cost-effective ways to render their services and better ways to compete for donor dollars.
      3. Not-for-profits differ from for-profits in having multiple "publics" – typically at least their clients and sponsors, but sometimes others as well.
      4. Not-for-profits' customers often have less control over the organization's destiny than do customers of profit-making firms.
      5. Sometimes resource contributors attempt to interfere with not-for-profit marketing programs to advance their own agendas.

   C. Nontraditional marketing – marketing persons, places, causes, events, and organizations
      1. Person marketing involves attempting to cultivate the attention, interest, and preferences of a target market toward a celebrity or authority figure.
         a. Professional athletes are major endorsers of products and services.
         b. Celebrity endorsers need not be real – Spongebob Squarepants promotes Kraft Macaroni and Cheese.
         c. Singers, actors, and musicians are important endorsers.
      2. Place marketing is the attempt to attract customers to a particular place, such as a city, state, country, or other attraction.

    3. Cause marketing refers to the identification and marketing of a social issue, cause, or idea to selected target markets.
      a. Fairly common is linkage between a profit-seeking firm and a cause, such as Crest toothpaste's relationship with the Boys' and Girls' Clubs of America.
    4. Event marketing refers to marketing of sporting, cultural, and charitable activities to selected target markets.
      a. The Super Bowl and the Olympics are sold as advertising venues long before they are scheduled or the competitors are chosen.
    5. Organization marketing is the attempt to influence others to accept the goals of, receive the services of, or contribute in some way to an organization.

VI. Critical Thinking and Creativity – Source of New Concepts and Ideas

  A. Creativity is an activity that produces original ideas or knowledge, frequently by testing combinations of concepts or data to produce unique results.
    1. Age is no barrier to creativity

  B. Critical thinking is the process of determining the authenticity, accuracy, and worth of information, knowledge, claims, and arguments.
    1. Critical thinking by James Lindsay resulted in the introduction of Rap Snacks, inexpensive bagged snacks carrying the images of famous rap artists.

VII. The Technology Revolution in Marketing

  A. Technology is the business application of knowledge based on scientific discoveries, inventions, and innovations
    1. Interactive multimedia technologies have revolutionized the way we store, distribute, retrieve, and present information.
    2. The Internet and interactive online services comprise new media over which products and customer services can be marketed.

  B. Interactive marketing includes buyer-seller communications in which the customer controls the amount and type of information received from a marketer.
    1. Based on interactive media technologies that combine computers and telecommunications to create software that consumers can use themselves, people can choose from a wealth of marketing opportunities for themselves and vendors.
    2. Interactive marketing allows the customization of communication.
    3. Airlines, such as Delta, are major uses of interactive marketing with their e-ticket vending operations.

  C. The Internet is a global network that includes some 50,000 sub-networks around the globe that lets anyone with a personal computer send and receive text and images practically anywhere.
    1. The World Wide Web (WWW) is an interlinked collection of information sources within the larger Internet.
    2. The Web offers advantages over traditional media of speed of communication, interactivity, ease of navigation, currency of information, and multimedia capabilities.

  D. Broadband technology is an always-on Internet connection operating at a very high rate of speed (200 Kilobytes/second or higher) that can deliver large amounts of data at once, making online marketing even faster and easier than it was previously.

E. Wireless Internet connections eliminate the need for a physical connection between computer and connector, increasing the mobility of access to the Internet.

F. Interactive television is, as the name implies, a package that allows viewers to interact with programs or commercials by using their remote controls.

G. Marketers use the Web in four general ways
   1. Virtual storefronts allow customers to view and order merchandise.
   2. Interactive brochures provide company and product information.
   3. Online newsletters provide current news, industry information, and contacts and links for internal and external customers.
   4. The Web is a customer service tool through which one can order catalogs, get information, place orders, and question the company.
   5. The key to success in cyberspace is convincing potential customers to visit one's site.
   6. More firms have failed in marketing efforts on the Net than have succeeded.

VIII. From Transaction-Based Marketing to Relationship Marketing

A. The traditional view of marketing is being replaced by a different view
   1. Traditional – transactions-based – marketing focused on attracting customers and closing deals.
   2. Relationship marketing is oriented toward creating and maintaining long-term, cost-effective relationships with customers and suppliers.
   3. Relationship marketing expands the definition of the terms customer and supplier to include people within the firm.
   4. Ultimately, the objective is to convert indifferent customers into loyal ones, generating repeat sales.
   5. Relationship marketing often relies on information technologies such as databases but also incorporates good manners, a valuable skill in developing relationships.

B. One-to-One Marketing seeks to build long-term relationships with individual customers
   1. Methods of one-to-one marketing may include technology such as the Hypersonic Sound emitter or Sbarro's LidRocks
   2. Other methods of reaching individuals may include customized products or low-tech customization like Build-a-Bear Workshops that let customers build their own stuffed bears from the ground up.
   3. Finally, customer service can be an important part of the one-to-one marketing program.

C. Developing Partnerships and Strategic Alliances.
   1. A strategic alliance is a business-to-business partnership between supplier and customer that creates a competitive advantage for both.
   2. The use of strategic alliance sis not limited to for-profit organizations.

VIII. Costs and Functions of Marketing – It costs money to produce utility

A. The exchange functions
   1. Buying has a number of implications for marketers, both in terms of their customers and themselves.

2. Selling, the "other half" of the exchange process, involves advertising, sales promotion, and personal selling as tools to effect its success.

B. The physical distribution functions
1. Transporting creates utility of place by getting products where they are wanted.
2. Storing involves warehousing goods until they are needed.

C. The facilitating functions
1. Standardizing and grading reduce the need for purchasers to inspect every item they buy to assure that it meets their specifications.
2. Financing provides buyers with access to funds to pay for inventories between time of purchase and time of sale. Marketers at all levels of distribution may provide such services.
3. Risk-taking is an inherent function of business which recognizes the uncertainties involved in being in the marketplace.
4. Securing marketing information meets the need for decision-oriented input about customers.

IX. Ethics and Social Responsibility: Doing Well by Doing Good

A. Ethics are moral standard of behavior expected by a society.

B. Most firms adhere to an ethical code, but there have been transgressions in recent years.

C. Ethics training may help in improving behavioral standards, but sometimes public or media pressure is the most persuasive tool.

D. Social responsibility involves marketing philosophies, policies, procedures, and actions whose primary objective is the enhancement of society.

E. Social responsibility never hurts, often producing improved customer relationships, employee loyalty, marketplace success, and improved financial performance.

48. The marketing functions of transportation and storage are most closely related to the utilities of
    a. time and place.
    b. form and time.
    c. ownership and place.
    d. ownership and form.
    e. time and ownership.

49. Legend Computer, China's largest personal computer manufacturer,
    a. commands more of the U. S. market than Hewlett-Packard.
    b. holds a seven percent share of the world PC market.
    c. serves the world's wealthiest market and most populous nation on earth.
    d. sells more PCs than Dell and IBM put together.
    e. commands less than two percent of the world market.

50. The idea that customers will resist purchasing products and services not deemed essential and that the task of personal selling and advertising is to convince them to buy is typical of the
    a. production-oriented company.
    b. sales-oriented company.
    c. marketing-oriented company.
    d. relationship-oriented company.
    e. none of the above.

Name_____   Instructor_____

Section_____   Date_____

Applying Marketing Concepts

Rob McGillicudy, a former star player on the football team, has opened a sporting goods store near the campus of Southwest State University. The store sells team sports, hunting, and fishing equipment, accessories, and supplies. The brands of equipment McGillicudy's store carries include Daiwa, Pflueger, Browning, Remington, Teamsport, Spalding, Ritter, and Louisville Slugger, among others. In addition to sales of new equipment, Mr. McGillicudy provides an extensive repair and service facility capable of restoring even the most sophisticated and well-used sports equipment to first-class condition.

In a recent interview, Rob explained his business strategy: "I am convinced there is tremendous interest in sports among the students, faculty, and staff of Southwest State. I want to satisfy their need for products and services suited for all areas of sporting activity. Generally, I stock the products and brands that they ask for as long as I can get them and make a profit on the sale. Some manufacturers, like Mountain Munitions, from whom I used to buy shotgun shells, make this a problem. I have had to stop dealing with them because they acted very independently, sometimes not filling orders for up to six months. On the other hand, I also have to deal with people like that salesman from Sweetwater Jerseys. That guy won't take no for an answer. He keeps trying to sell me what he's got to sell, rather than what I know my customers want."

"Some of the products I stock are purchased from wholesalers because we order in small quantities. I like dealing with most of them, though, because they ship our orders very quickly, so my customers don't have to wait long for special order items. If I ordered from the manufacturers, it would take forever to get some products. I'm also lucky because this old building has lots of display and storage space, so I can have a pretty good stock of most standard products for my customers to choose from. A lot of my business is people who buy stuff the day before fishing season, take it home right then, and use it the next day."

"I think I'm doing all right. My relationship with the bank lets me borrow money at a very good rate, so I can buy inventory for cash. Of my two employees, one is a local outdoorsman in his fifties who knows what the "seasoned" sportsmen in town like, the other is a student who has a good grasp of what's hot with her fellow students, so the locals like us because we've got the older styles of products they like, while the kids generally like us because we have things that some of the older stores in town don't stock yet. Don't get me wrong about them; they're good merchants and tough competitors and it takes work to compete with them. I sometimes stick my neck out by buying a particular item, but I haven't been stuck with much unsellable inventory yet. I think I'll keep doing this for a while."

True or False?

_____ 1. Rob McGillicudy appears to have adopted the marketing concept.

_____ 2. The Mountain Munitions Company may be production oriented.

_____ 3. McGillicudy's Sporting Goods Store faces a seller's market.

_____ 4. Sweetwater Jerseys is definitely a marketing oriented firm.

_____ 5. Rob McGillicudy's decision to locate his store near his market created time utility for his customers.

Choose the best answer.

6. Repairing sporting goods equipment creates
    a. form utility.
    b. place utility.
    c. ownership utility.
    d. time utility.
    e. none of the above.

7. Mr. McGillicudy's use of quick-acting wholesalers for special orders helps provide his customers with
    a. space utility.
    b. time utility.
    c. ownership utility.
    d. place utility.
    e. good prices.

8. The availability of storage and display space in McGillicudy's store provides
    a. space utility.
    b. place utility.
    c. form utility.
    d. financial utility.
    e. an interest factor.

9. Mr. McGillicudy's relationship with the bank facilitates performance of the marketing function of
    a. standardization.
    b. acquiring marketing information.
    c. financing.
    d. selling.
    e. transportation.

10. Mr. McGillicudy's willingness to "stick his neck out" when buying certain items is evidence of his performance of the marketing function of
    a. financing.
    b. grading.
    c. acquiring marketing information.
    d. risk bearing.
    e. storage.

Wilhelmus Gottfriedson, who recently graduated from university in Salzburg with a degree in music (but with a minor in business), has returned home to Linz to help his father run the family business, Heimatland Harpsichord Enterprise. Begun in 1703, the Heimatland Company has long since had a reputation for making the very finest in home and performance harpsichords. These keyboard instruments, usually used by chamber music performers, are typically crafted with decorative details that represent mythic creatures like trolls and gnomes and animals such as elk, swans, and reebok.

The first thing Wilhelmus (Willi) did upon reporting for work was to apply his business training to an analysis of the firm's financial records. He was surprised to learn that, during the last ten years, there had been a dramatic decline in sales of the company's in-home line. When he asked his father about this, the elder Gottfriedson replied, "Gee, son, I don't really know why that's happening. Our instruments are the very best that can be bought. We're still making them exactly the same way we have for the last three hundred years, using the same designs and with the same materials. I can't really understand why sales are off so badly. But I have taken steps to do something about it. Just last month, I hired a young man to go out and try and find us some new customers. We really do have to do something to try and increase sales volume."

Willi was now disturbed. He knew his father believed he had done the right thing, but Willi thought that more needed to be done. His thinking was that the company needed to look more carefully at the marketplace. He felt that Heimatland Harpsichord had lost touch with its customers and with harpsichord styles. Though he hesitated to do it, he felt that he had to suggest to his father that they invest in some research to find out what was happening in harpsichord "looks" and to adapt their products to what was currently popular. He though it might even be possible that the firm would find it desirable to expand or even change the nature of their product line. Perhaps pianos, organs, or even electronic harpsichords could be a possibility.

11. Willi's father, judging from his distress at the decline in his company's fortunes and the fact that he can't understand why the company's figures aren't selling, is probably a victim of
    a. his inability to produce a product of the required quality.
    b. the "better mousetrap" fallacy (production orientation.)
    c. a general decline in the economy about which nothing can be done.
    d. too much of a commitment to a marketing orientation.

12. Gottfriedson the elder's retention of a salesman may well be evidence that he has been converted to
    a. a philosophy of company-wide consumer orientation.
    b. a mere figurehead in his son's presence.
    c. an attitude typical of the sales era of marketing history.
    d. a belief that he's in a seller's market.

13. Willi's idea of investigating the nature of the market reveals that
    a. he is at least aware of the marketing concept.
    b. he shares his father's attitude toward the changes in the company's sales performance.
    c. his college education has been largely wasted; he should be able to analyze the problem from internal company records.
    d. he, too, is a victim of "marketing myopia".

14. "Marketing myopia" refers to
    a. defining the scope of your business too broadly.
    b. failing to define the scope of your business
    c. defining the scope of your business too narrowly.
    d. making comparisons between your business and businesses not much like the one you're in.

Name_____   Instructor_____

Section_____   Date_____

Surfing the Net

Keeping in mind that addresses change and what's on the Internet as this is being written may have changed by the time you read this, let's take a look at some of the places on the Net that reflect aspects of marketing. We are not endorsing or recommending any of these sources, merely making note of the information and services that people have elected to offer through the Internet.

In this initial episode, let's mention the fact that there are many Web browsers out there, and what you see when you access the Net depends to some extent on your Internet Service Provider (ISP) and the way your browser works. We suggest you use the most recent version of Netscape Navigator or MicroSoft's Internet Explorer that is available to you. Older browsers may produce odd-looking displays when used to access sites written with newer versions in mind. You can usually "short-cut" the address when accessing these sites, leaving off the http:// in many cases. Nonetheless, we've given the entire address for each site. So! Let's get started!

Feeling Consumed? It's supposed to be the other way around. You're the consumer! For consumer information on all sorts of products and services, order the *Consumer Information Catalog* from Uncle Sam. Just fill out the order form at **http://pueblo.gsa.gov/** It's a free service of the General Services Administration of the Federal Government.

Thinking about changing schools? There are several Web sites that offer information of one sort or another about college rankings, costs, and even how good certain programs at certain schools are supposed to be. The most comprehensive of these appears to be one at the University of Illinois Champaign-Urbana that can be accessed at **http://www.library.uiuc.edu/edx/rankings.htm.** Alternative sites include **http:nces.ed.gov**, another of those federal government sites that provide so much information about so many things. Finally, we suggest **http://www.collegeboard.com** as a general-purpose site oriented more to the high school senior than the individual already in college, buy still worth a look see. Alternatively, you can experiment by seeking the web sites of schools whose names you know. Interested in the University of Massachusetts at Amherst? Try **http://www.umass.edu**. Interested in the University of Louisiana? Yes, there is such a place. Try http://www.ull.edu and you'll get the University of Louisiana, Lafayette, the flagship school of the UL system. On the other hand, sometimes these searches don't work out exactly as you'd expect. Search for South Dakota State University at **http://www.sdsu.edu** and you'll get San Diego State University. South Dakota State is at **http://www3.sdstate.edu**. Curious about Australian education? Try **http://www.unsw.edu.au** and you'll access the University of New South Wales in Sydney.

Thirsty? Unless you drink only water, take a look at all the topics available on the beverage network. Devoted to information on commercially available nonalcoholic beverages, there's something there for everyone. We'd be willing to bet you haven't heard of almost all of the beverages on this site. It's at **http://www.thebevnet.com**

Into sports? Professional sports is all over the Net! Just for starters, can we not mention the *Sports Illustrated* site at **http://sportsillustrated/cnn.com** for an incredible array of current scores, standings, and articles on what's happening NOW in the world of sports. Alternatively, for something a little less slick but definitely for the fan, try **http://www.sportznutz.com** if what you want is to get your sports info from the fan's point of view. On the other hand, if lifestyle is your bag, especially southern lifestyle, take a look at **http://www.southernliving.com**, the Web site of the very popular magazine of the southern way of doing things. You might find something that you'll enjoy – even if you're in Minneapolis. Lest we be accused of being regionist, be also advised that other regional magazines exist and can be accessed via the Net, such as *Midwest Outdoors* at **http://www.midwestoutdoors.com** and the magazine of New England is available at **http://www.Yankeemagazine.com**.

Sites verified August 10, 2004

Chapter 2
Strategic Planning and the Marketing Process

Chapter Outline

You may want to use the following outline as a guide in taking notes.

I. Chapter Overview

The marketplace changes continually in response to changes in every aspect of the environment. The causes of these changes lie outside the control of the marketer, but planning can anticipate many of them. Planning involves matching company strengths with developing opportunities.

II. Marketing Planning: The basis for strategy and tactics

   A. Planning is the process of anticipating future events and conditions and of determining the best way to achieve organizational objectives.
      1. It plays an important role in both small and large companies.
      2. Marketing planning, which involves implementing planning activities devoted to achieving marketing objectives, establishes the basis for any marketing strategy.
         a. An important trend in marketing planning centers on relationship marketing, the firm's effort to develop long-term, cost-effective links with individual customers and suppliers for mutual benefit.

   B. Strategic planning versus tactical planning – it's a matter of time and timing.
      1. Strategic planning is the process of determining an organization's primary objectives and adopting courses of action that will achieve these objectives.
      2. Tactical planning guides the activities specified in the strategic plan.
      3. Mistakes made at either level can be very costly.

   C. Planning at different organizational levels – the roles of managers in the planning process.
      1. All managers plan but the amount of time devoted to the process varies with the level of management involved.
      2. Top management has a longer-term view of the planning process and spends more time on it than lower-level decision makers.
      3. Effective planning seeks input from a wide range of sources within and outside the firm.

III. Steps in the Marketing Planning Process – Definition of the firm's mission, determination of its objectives, assessment of its resources, evaluation of environmental risks and opportunities.

   A. Defining the organization's mission
      1. A firm's mission is the essential purpose that differentiates the company from others.
      2. The company's mission is spelled out in its mission statement.

   B. Determining organizational objectives
      1. The term objective is synonymous with the term goal when applied to a company's activities.

    2. Soundly conceived objectives should state specific intentions along with time periods required to meet those intentions.

  C. Assessing organizational resources and evaluating environmental risks and opportunities
    1. It is in this step that a firm identifies its strengths, weaknesses, and available opportunities, as well as the threats it faces.
    2. A firm's resources include its ability to produce, market, and finance activities and to apply technology and obtain and keep capable employees.
    3. Environmental factors may accentuate the firm's resources or act as threats to its success.

  D. Formulating, implementing, and monitoring a marketing strategy
    1. The output of the steps that have gone before becomes the basis for formulating the firm's marketing strategy, an overall, company-wide program for selecting a particular target market and satisfying consumers in that market through a careful balance of the elements of the marketing mix.
    2. The process of implementation involves two steps.
      a. Use of operating plans to put the strategy into action and
      b. Monitoring of performance to ensure that objectives are achieved.
      c. The results of this process may reveal that modification of the strategy is necessary.

IV. Successful Strategies: Tools and Techniques – An Examination of Porter's Five Forces Model, first and second mover strategies, SWOT analysis, and the concept of the strategic window. All these are designed to provide s firm with a sustainable competitive advantage.

  A. Porter's Five Forces Model examines the effect of potential new entrants, the threat of substitute products, bargaining power of buyers, bargaining power of suppliers, and rivalry of competitors on the strategies companies use. Porter has recently added the effect of the Internet as a mediating variable.
    1. Potential entry into a market is sometimes blocked by the cost or difficulty of entry.
    2. If customers have considerable bargaining power, they can significantly affect a firm's strategy.
      a. The Internet can affect this power by providing information that might not otherwise be conveniently available.
    3. The number of suppliers available to a manufacturer or retailer can affect its bargaining power. A larger number of suppliers available to a manufacturer or retailer strengthen its bargaining power with them.
    4. The availability to customers of products or services from competing firms that can replace those they currently use (substitutes) may require the original firm to find new markets, change its prices, or develop a new competitive strategy to maintain its advantage.
    5. All the above influence the intensity of the rivalry among competitors.

  B. First mover and second mover strategies refer to the decision either to attempt to capture the greatest market share and develop long-term relationships by being the first to enter the market with a product (first mover strategy) or observing closely the actions of first movers and then improve on them to gain marketplace advantage (second mover strategy).

1. Each strategy has its advantages and its disadvantages.
    a. The mistakes of first-movers can be valuable to second-movers.
    b. Second-movers may find it difficult to develop a market against an entrenched first-mover.

C. SWOT – Strengths, Weaknesses, Opportunities, and Threats – analysis provides managers with a critical view of the firm's internal and external environments and helps them evaluate whether it is fulfilling its basic mission.
    1. A company's strengths reflect its core competencies – what it does well. Matching a core competency with an external opportunity produces leverage for the firm.
    2. When planners face environmental threats to their organizational weaknesses, a problem exists.
    3. It is not unusual for an opportunity to be perceived as a threat by risk-averse managers.

D. A strategic window is a limited period of time during which the key requirements of a market and the core competencies of a firm best fit together.
    1. A strategic window may be detected by comparing current and future environmental conditions, current and projected internal company capabilities, and how, whether, and when the firm can favorably implement one or more marketing strategies.

V. Elements of a Marketing Strategy include the target market chosen by firm and the marketing mix variables of product, distribution, promotion, and price that meet the needs of the target market.

A. The target market is the group of people toward whom the firm decides to direct its marketing efforts and ultimately its goods and services.
    1. Targeting markets involves dividing them into segments, a process which will be discussed in a later chapter.
    2. The diversity of the U. S. population and its changing characteristics are important variables in the targeting of markets.

B. Marketing Mix Variables of product, price, distribution, and promotion are blended to fit the needs and preferences of the target market subject to the constraints imposed by the environment.
    1. Since products are more broadly defined than merely as goods, services, or ideas, but also as the satisfaction of wants, product strategy also has a broader interpretation than just what goods or services the firm should offer and to whom.
        a. Wyndham Hotels targets female business travelers with a product strategy having special features such a skirt hangers in the rooms.
    2. Distribution strategies are designed to ensure that consumers find products in the proper quantities and in the right places at the right times.
        a. These strategies involve transportation, warehousing, inventory control, order processing, and selection of marketing channels.
        b. Technology is having a distinct effect on channels of distribution in many industries.
        c. Business alliances have become common occurrences in distribution because of the advantages they offer.

    3. Promotional strategy defines the communication link between buyers and sellers.
      a. The communication process may be direct through salespeople or indirect through advertisement and promotion.
      b. Marketers blend the elements of promotion to communicate most effectively with their target market.
      c. Integrated marketing communications (IMC) is used to coordinate promotional activities so produce a unified, consistent message.
    4. Pricing strategy is one of the most difficult areas of marketing decision making because it is closely regulated and subject to public scrutiny.
      a. Competition has a significant effect on setting prices – increased competition has driven personal computer prices down significantly in recent years.
      b. A good pricing strategy should create value for customers, building and strengthening their relationship with the firm.

V. The Marketing Environment – decisions cannot be made in a vacuum. The competitive, political-legal, economic, technological, and social-cultural dimensions of the environment are dynamic and affect marketing planning.

  A. Competitors enter and leave the market, discontinue old products and offer new ones on a regular basis. The hybrid automobile, combining gasoline and electric power, has begun to change the competitive nature of that market.

  B. Foreign markets have become increasingly attractive to American firms in recent years.

  C. Technology, partly because of the Internet, has significantly changed the marketing environment in recent years.
    1. As technology changes the way firms do business, the legal environment must respond to situations that couldn't have existed until recently.
    2. The legal environment has, according to some, lagged the technological, resulting in situations that damage some competitors, particularly in the area of protection afforded to intellectual property (such as patents).

  D. Competition is a serious environmental issue, particularly because the most effective competitors in any industry usually capture from 70 to 90 percent of the market.
    1. The United States was the first nation to recognize the dangers of unregulated competition (which often leads to monopoly) and still polices the competitive environment.

  E. Cultural diversity and ethics constitute significant areas of concern in marketing planning.

VI. Methods for Marketing Planning – among the methods that are presently used for marketing planning, the strategic business unit concept and the market share/market growth matrix are of greatest significance.

  A. Strategic Business Units (SBUs) are key business units within diversified firms.
    1. Conceptually growing out of portfolio analysis, the evaluation of a company's products and divisions to determine which are strongest and which are weakest, SBUs have become a commonly-used structure among diversified firms.
    2. Each SBU has its own managers, resources, objectives, and competitors.

3. SBUs, also called "categories," focus the attention of company managers to respond effectively to changing conditions of demand.

B. The market share/market growth matrix is also a tool to measure portfolio performance.
    1. This tool places SBUs in a chart that plots market share against market growth potential and provides four possible categories. It is also known as the "Boston Consulting Group" Matrix.
        a. Stars possess high market shares of high growth markets, producing significant income but requiring considerable financial support.
        b. Cash cows command high market shares of low-growth markets, generating considerable income but requiring little financial support.
        c. Question marks hold low shares of high-growth markets and must be watched carefully because they usually produce less income than they consume.
        d. Dogs are in the position of holding low shares of low-growth markets and are excellent candidates for removal from the firm's product line.

Name_____   Instructor_____

Section_____   Date_____

Key Concepts

The purpose of this section is to allow you to determine if you can match key concepts with the definitions of the concepts. It is essential that you know the definitions of the concepts prior to applying the concepts in later exercises in this chapter.

From the list of lettered terms, select the one that best fits in the blank of the numbered statement below. Write the letter of that choice in the space provided.

Key Terms

a. planning
b. marketing planning
c. strategic planning
d. tactical planning
e. mission
f. marketing strategy
g. Porter's Five Forces
h. first mover strategy
i. second mover strategy

j. SWOT analysis
k. strategic window
l. marketing mix
m. product strategy
n. distribution strategy
o. promotion
p. pricing strategy
q. strategic business units (SBUs)

_____ 1. Implementing planning activities devoted to achieving marketing objectives.

_____ 2. Limited period of time during which the "fit" between the key requirements of a market and the particular competencies of a firm are optimal.

_____ 3. Determining an organization's primary objectives and adopting courses of action to achieve those objectives.

_____ 4. The essential purpose that differentiates one company from others.

_____ 5. Blending of products, pricing, distribution, and promotion to fit the needs of a specific target market.

_____ 6. Model identifying five competitive conditions that influence planning strategies.

_____ 7. Strategies to insure that consumers find products in the proper quantities at the right times and places.

_____ 8. Process of anticipating future events and conditions and determining the courses of action necessary to achieve organizational objectives.

_____ 9. The communication link between buyers and sellers.

_____ 10.   Its basic elements are the target market and the marketing mix variables of product, distribution, promotion, and price.

_____ 11.   Study of organizational resources and capabilities to assess the firm's strengths and weaknesses and scanning its external environment to identify opportunities and threats.

_____ 12.   In a multi-product firm, a division built around related product groupings or business activities with specific managers, resources, objectives, competitors, and structure for optimal independent planning; a key business unit.

_____ 13.   Methods of setting profitable and justifiable prices.

_____ 14.   Consists of being the first to enter the market with a product in the attempt to capture the greatest market share and develop long-term relationships.

_____ 15.   Planning the implementation of activities specified in the strategic plan.

_____ 16.   Decisions about what goods or services, customer service, packaging, brand names, and the like a firm will offer its customers.

_____ 17.   Accomplished by observing the innovations of first movers and then improving on them to gain a market place advantage.

Name_____ Instructor_____

Section_____ Date_____

Self-Quiz

You should use these objective questions to test your understanding of the chapter material. You can check your answers with those provided at the end of the chapter.

While these questions cover most of the chapter topics, they are not intended to be the same as the test questions your instructor may use in an examination. A good understanding of all aspects of the course material is essential to good performance on any examination.

True/False

Write "T" for True or "F" for False for each of the following statements.

_____ 1. Strategic plans focus on adoption of courses of action necessary to achieve very short-run organizational objectives typically designed to be achieved within two to three months.

_____ 2. A customer-driven organization begins its overall strategy with a detailed description of its marketing mix – the blend of product, price, distribution, and promotion it intends to offer its target market

_____ 3. Middle-level managers – general sales managers, for example – tend to focus their efforts on operational planning such as daily and weekly plans.

_____ 4. The starting point for the marketing planning process begins at the corporate level with the definition of the firm's mission.

_____ 5. SWOT analysis does not involve any consideration of organizational resources or environmental factors.

_____ 6. The view through a strategic window shows planners a way to relate potential opportunities to company capabilities.

_____ 7. A firm's product strategy typically includes making decisions about communicating most effective with their target market.

_____ 8. Internal weaknesses in a company can create vulnerabilities within it – environmental threats to its organizational strength.

_____ 9. Organizations may communicate with their target market directly through salespeople or indirectly through advertisements and promotions.

_____ 10. The Boston Consulting Group Matrix provides a method top executives can use to identify promising SBUs that warrant investment of additional resources as well as those that should be pruned from the company's product portfolio.

_____ 11. As conceptualized in the market share/market growth matrix, "question marks" generate considerable income while requiring little cash inflow to provide further growth.

_____ 12. The "rule of three" states that in any industry the three strongest, most efficient companies dominate between 70 and 90 percent of the market.

_____ 13. Marketing channels are made up of institutions such as wholesalers and retailers – intermediaries involved in a product's movement from producer to final user.

_____ 14. An effective marketing strategy reaches the right buyers at the right time, convinces them to try the product, and develops a strong relationship with them over time.

_____ 15. Pricing strategy is one of the most difficult areas of marketing decision making because the objective is to set prices as high as the maximum the consumer is willing to pay.

_____ 16. The distribution component of the marketing mix calls for such specialized expertise that it is seldom possible for firms in distribution to form alliances.

_____ 17. The market share/market growth matrix identifies a firm's business units as cattle, cookies, carriers, and cart horses – the four Cs.

_____ 18. A "first mover strategy" is the strategy of attempting to capture the greatest market share by being the first company to offer a product in a market.

_____ 19. Targeting markets requires a knowledge of and recognition of the importance of population diversity in the United Sates.

_____ 20. Even when a firm's marketing strategy does not result in the expected performance, that never constitutes sufficient reason to change the strategy.

_____ 21. An organization lays out its basic objectives, or goals, in its promotion program.

_____ 22. Matching an internal strength with an external opportunity produces a situation known as "vulnerability to constraints" for the organization.

_____ 23. In Porter's Five Forces Model, it is rivalry among competitors that is the focus of the influence of the other four forces.

_____ 24. Wyndham Hotels targets women business travelers by, among other things, providing these customers with jogging partners and chilled bottled water, fresh fruits and plush towels on a return from a run.

_____ 25. Sustainable competitive advantage for a firm is a condition in which other companies simply cannot provide the same value to their customers that the advantageous firm does – no matter how hard they try.

Multiple Choice

Circle the letter of the word or phrase that best completes the sentence or best answers the question.

26. Strategic planning is best described as
    a. decisions related to the pricing of the firm's output for the current year.
    b. actions taken based upon review of monthly and quarterly sales data.
    c. planning designed to attack and systematically solve short-term company problems
    d. determining primary objectives of an organization and adopting courses of action that will achieve them.
    e. the responsibility of middle-level managers within the firm.

27. Which of the following differentiates correctly between strategic and tactical plans?
    a. tactical–10 year plan; strategic – next year
    b. tactical—current and near-future activity; strategic – broad in scope, long-term in orientation
    c. tactical–top management responsibility; strategic–supervisory responsibility
    d. tactical–total company budgets; strategic–unit or division budgets
    e. tactical–plans for new product development in the next 20 years; strategic–advertising plan for a new product to be introduced next year

28. Which of the following is an example of strategic planning?
    a. Northern Telecom raises its rates in response to an increase announced by Pacific Bell.
    b. The Anaheim Mighty Ducks offer the first 15,000 fans into the arena for their next game a free padded seat cushion.
    c. Transtar International plans to phase out its tractor division over the next five years and to purchase several manufacturers of major household appliances to expand its product base.
    d. The May Company, a retailer, decides to switch the bulk of this year's advertising from television to newspaper ads.
    e. Panasonic offers a $10 rebate to everyone who purchases one of its cordless phones during the next month.

29. Electromotive Corporation is preparing its new strategic plan. Who, of the following people, should be given the greatest responsibility (and spend the most time) on this planning process?
    a. district sales managers
    b. the marketing research director
    c. the director of advertising
    d. sales representatives
    e. the vice-president of marketing

30. Marketing planning usually begins with which of the following?
    a. a program for selecting a particular target market and then satisfying consumers in that market
    b. determining the basic overall goals or objectives of the firm for the next several years
    c. selection of appropriate production techniques for the firm's output
    d. deciding whether or not to reorganize the company and how to do it
    e. testing to ascertain whether products meet engineering-related standards

31. Which of the following statements is an example of use of the concept of the strategic window?
    a. Transcripts of the meetings of the board of directors are made required reading for middle-level managers at Wilton Standard Engine and Pump Company.
    b. The law firm of Anderson, Villere, and Jones decides to open a labor relations department because several of the firm's partners have developed an interest in the area.
    c. Diamond Community Antenna Company (a cable TV service provider) has decided to expand its service from Diamond to the nearby town of Westphalia because it has done a study that showed a need for the service before Westphalia's previous service provider has closed. In addition, Diamond has the resources to provide the service.
    d. The Gates Tire and Rubber Company has decided to produce and market hip boots because they feel there is a market for hip boots. The company does not have adequate resources, however, to fund the production and marketing of this new product line.
    e. The Watrous Valve Company has decided to lower the prices of its products by 20 percent across-the-board.

32. Which of the following selections is not a planning method usually used in marketing planning (Some of the selections may refer to essentially the same things?)
    a. the SBU concept
    b. the market share/market growth matrix
    c. portfolio analysis
    d. the BCG matrix
    e. a Jury of Executive Opinion

33. The blending of the four strategic elements of product, pricing, distribution, and promotion forms
    a. the marketing concept.
    b. an analytical tool for deriving formulae to use in spreadsheet analysis.
    c. the marketing plan.
    d. the marketing mix.
    e. the basis of Blavatski's analogy.

34. A business executive that you know tells you she can't go to the basketball game Tuesday because she will be involved in corporate planning meetings helping puttogether her firm's next "five-year plan." She is probably
    a. a middle manager: she's probably working on some tactical plan to be applied locally.
    b. a top management member: they are usually the ones who do the strategic planning for the firm.
    c. supervisor: her job involves planning sales events and other special promotions.
    d. an assembly-line worker who is there simply to make it look like management cares
    e. just trying to avoid going to that particular game

35. American Kitchen Products, a firm that produces and sells kitchen implements to food processors, has decided to reorganize its business into a number of Strategic Business Units. Which of the following questions should be used in deciding on how to create the SBUs?
   a. Will defining this particular area of the business as an SBU focus managerial attention so they can respond effectively to changing consumer demand within limited markets?
   b. Does this particular area of the business produce mechanically similar products using a coherent technological base?
   c. Can this area of the business use the same production lines and distribution facilities to handle the products it sells and markets?
   d. Do the entities to be brought under this SBU use the same raw materials from the same sources?
   e. Do the activities of the components of the proposed SBU use basically the same quality control personnel?

36. If the framework provided by the market growth/market share matrix is used as the guideline, an SBU that holds a low market share in a high growth market would be a
   a. cash cow.
   b. dog.
   c. star.
   d. question mark.
   e. skunk.

37. You are using the market share/market growth matrix approach to adjust your company's product portfolio. A usually correct action when using this approach is to
   a. eliminate all question marks; they're hopeless, anyway.
   b. invest heavily in promotion and production capacity for cash cows.
   c. find funds to finance the future growth of stars.
   d. continue to fund question marks under all conditions; they're bound to become stars.
   e. hold on to dogs for as long as possible; they might still make some money.

38. Making decisions about customer service, package design, brand names, trademarks, patents, and warranties is part of
   a. distribution strategy.
   b. promotion planning.
   c. distribution analysis.
   d. product strategy.
   e. the pricing process.

39. Distribution strategy involves decisions involving
   a. warehousing and inventory control.
   b. communication between sellers and buyers.
   c. managing the product life cycle.
   d. the length and character of warranties.
   e. whether or not to participate in price wars.

40. Technology has a tendency to move faster than
    a. people's ability to adapt, creating a competency gap in the marketplace.
    b. patenting procedures, that can leave some businesses behind.
    c. history's ability to document its progress.
    d. management's ability to adapt to the new rules technology brings with it.
    e. the normal rate of speed of the transportation system, slowing its adoption.

41. "We create solutions to problems involving the leading-edge technology needs of major industrial corporations." This quote is an example of
    a. a mission statement.
    b. a strategic plan.
    c. an operational plan.
    d. a tactical appraisal of conditions.
    e. wishful thinking: it is obviously not attainable.

42. Which of the following is one of the identified strengths of Malden Mills, maker of Polartec and Polarfleece?
    a. the cost of being a U. S. manufacturer
    b. increasing competition
    c. customers in more than 50 countries
    d. a conservative, noninnovative management team
    e. the fire that destroyed their factory

43. When a firm possesses internal weaknesses or limitations that create threats to its organizational strength, it is said to suffer from
    a. leverage.
    b. vulnerabilities.
    c. a problem.
    d. constraints.
    e. core competency.

44. The term SWOT as used in "SWOT analysis" stands for
    a. struggling with older technology.
    b. standards, work orders, and techniques.
    c. seasonal, weekly, and orderly transmission (of data).
    d. sequences and workovers of organization and territory.
    e. strengths and weaknesses, opportunities and threats.

45. One of the strategic business units in your company's portfolio is a cash cow. The best set of actions to take with that SBU would be to
    a. allocate substantial advertising money and new equipment to it to stimulate future growth.
    b. withdraw from this market by selling or closing the SBU as soon as possible.
    c. reallocate resources away from this marginal SBU; allow it to wither on the vine.
    d. maintain this status for as long as possible, using the funds generated by this SBU to finance the growth of other SBUs with higher growth potential.
    e. make a "go" or "no go" decision as soon as possible; then either get out of that market or aggressively pursue development of the SBU.

46. Strategic Business Units are sometimes known as
   a. categories .
   b. audit systems; they are used by accountants to test the financial stability of firms.
   c. elements of the firm's product portfolio being tested with the Persian Messenger Rule.
   d. sales programs used in connection with the Delphi technique..
   e. qualitative sales forecasting methods.

47. A product is, in the broad sense,
   a. a good, service, or idea that can be manufactured or conceptualized very simply.
   b. the goods or services a firm decides to offer to its customers.
   c. satisfaction of all consumer needs with respect to a good, service, or idea.
   d. an alliance between two firms that results in a market entry.
   e. whatever the communication between seller and buyer says it is.

48. Which of the following is generally considered to be a tool or technique used for marketing planning?
   a. Farnsworth's Syllogism
   b. Tandoor's altered trend analysis
   c. exponential plaster smoothing
   d. the Saloniki technique
   e. Porter's Five Forces Model

49. One of the weaknesses of Malden Mills, maker of Polarfleece and Polartec fabrics, as revealed by a SWOT analysis, is
   a. its low rate of growth during the last decade.
   b. the cost of manufacturing in the U.S.
   c. negative public relations impact because of appearances on *Dateline* and in *People Magazine.*
   d. its rate of customer and employee retention.
   e. the fact that it has customers in more than 50 countries.

50. Of the following, which would typically come first in the marketing planning process?
   a. the assessment of organizational resources
   b. evaluation of environmental risks and opportunities
   c. monitoring and assessing strategy based on feedback
   d. implementing strategy through operational plans
   e. development of organizational objectives.

Name_____ Instructor_____

Section_____ Date_____

Applying Marketing Concepts

Albert Nickel of GlobaPharm was pleased with his company's prospects. The recent forest fires in Brazil had left a number of cities and towns in isolated areas with damaged or destroyed hospitals and other healthcare facilities. GlobaPharm rushed in its personnel and truck-borne clinical pharmacies to provide emergency service as a humanitarian gesture, but Mr. Nickel knew that many of the facilities which his personnel had brought in on a temporary basis needed to be replaced soon – their capacity was significantly less than the facilities they had replaced. He knew he had the advantage over his two closest competitors to build the replacements. The competitors were Ethical Services, Ltd., from Great Britain, and Pharmaserv, another U.S. firm.

Ethical Services had recently run into financial difficulties and was unable to send anyone into the area to help out or to solicit business. Pharmaserv, despite building a good facility and being financially sound, had only recently gotten into foreign markets and still made equipment with all U.S.-type screw threads and fasteners – very different from the ISO metric fasteners used in the typical South American application and hard to interface with existing equipment. Even their scales were calibrated in grains rather than in milligrams. GlobaPharm was able to supply basic units with either U.S. or ISO fittings and calibrations and a wide range of special adaptors from inventory.

Mr. Nickel was worried about one thing. He knew that his success doing business in Brazil depended on being associated with the right people locally – the ones with the most power and status. Prior to the forest fires, his firm had worked closely with the Sao Paolo/Nacional group and had been quite successful. Rumor had it, though, that the Sao Paolo/Nacional consortium, because of some unpopular political positions they had recently taken, might be eased out by the Companhia Janeiro, who represented EuroPharma St. Etienne, a French provider of clinical pharmacies and equipment.

Circle the letter of the word or phrase that best completes the sentence or best answers the question.

1. Because of its ability to be there when needed and to supply the products to meet local interface needs. GlobaPharm finds itself
    a. with considerable leverage in the Brazilian market.
    b. with a problem doing business in Brazil.
    c. vulnerable to competitive pressure, particularly from Ethical Services.
    d. constrained by staff shortages.
    e. lacking a strategic window to develop its opportunity.

2. Ethical Services
    a. is vulnerable in Brazil.
    b. suffers from constraints in this market.
    c. has real problems with product quality.
    d. probably has as much leverage as does GlobaPharm.
    e. has shown more wisdom than any of its competitors so far; it is staying away until the dust settles.

3. Pharmaserv's entry into the Brazilian market
    a. is hampered by a problem.
    b. is hampered by constraints.
    c. depends on its leverage in the market.
    d. seems particularly vulnerable.
    e. goes without saying.

4. GlobaPharm's relationship with the Sao Paolo/Nacional group
    a. could never constitute a problem for them.
    b. places a high level of constraint on them.
    c. may make them vulnerable, particularly if the Companhia Janeiro accedes to power.
    d. has no effect on the amount of leverage they are able to employ.
    e. is irrelevant to their marketing effort.

5. Every town in the region that has a healthcare facility also has a clinical pharmacy. If GlobaPharm succeeds in dominating the market for replacement equipment, it will hold a very large share of the market, but the market probably will not grow very rapidly, if at all. From a market share/market growth matrix point of view, the Brazilian clinical pharmacy market would appear to be
    a. a question mark.
    b. a cash cow.
    c. a dog.
    d. a star.
    e. a rocket.

The Südtirolische Bergsbahn (South Tyrolean Mountain Railroad or STB, for short) has been involved in an analysis of its operations in the aftermath of EC-2000, the complete abolition of barriers to travel in Europe that occurred that year. Despite its name, STB is a diversified transportation company offering coordinated rail, autobus, and river and coastal steamship passenger and cargo service all through Northern Italy and much of western Austria. An individual traveling through the region can book a trip to do exactly what he or she wants it to do – be scenic, quick, or even exciting if one of the more mountain-hugging train routes is selected.

Aldo Vitterini, the firm's chief executive officer, is concerned about his firm's future, however. He is, in fact, considering moving his firm's headquarters from Innsbruck, Austria, to Bolzano, in Italy, to take advantage of the availability of lower costs of newspaper, magazine, and radio advertising when booked from an Italian source. He is also concerned that the appearance on the rivers of the area of vessels from Switzerland, Slovenia , and even Hungary may negatively impact his business.

Circle the letter of the word or phrase that best completes the sentence or best answers the question.

6. Signore Vitterini's idea of moving his corporate headquarters to Bolzano is motivated by a desire to
    a. escape the extraordinarily high taxes charged to transportation companies by the Austrian government.
    b. live in a location where his native language is spoken.
    c. develop a promotion program that will do the same things that hc's doing now – or more – for less money.
    d. move into an area somewhat less mountainous than western Austria.

7. The fact that STB operates a number of different types of transportation media and routes in a relatively small area of the world, offering a wide range of choices for the traveler, indicates that
    a. the company is attempting to satisfy the needs of its customers for not just travel but something more – Mr. Vitterini conceptualizes his product broadly.
    b. it must be terribly difficult to get from some of these places to others of them – otherwise why would it get so complicated.
    c. the firm hasn't got a clear grasp of what it is about and apparently is still living in the nineteenth century.
    d. Signore Vitterini realizes that all he has to do is get people from where they are to where they want to be and they will be satisfied.
    e. STB is in trouble due to overexpansion of its facilities and routes and hasn't created a viable marketing mix.

8. Sr. Vitterini's concern about the presence of Swiss, Slovenian, and Hungarian vessels in his native waters is motivated by considerations of which of the following components of the environmental framework of marketing?
    a. the technological
    b. the social-cultural
    c. the technological
    d. the competitive
    e. the political

The Widgeon Sound Publishing Company has been producing a broad line of books for over 100 years. Its product portfolio includes hardbound fiction for adult readers, books for younger readers, hardbound nonfiction , and even a line of trendy paperbacks aimed at male and female teenagers. The line of hardbound novels for grown-ups, which was the first line the company published beginning back in 1882 and is anchored by a stable of well-known, popular writers, remains a sound, steady performer in the marketplace, with a substantial share of a slowly growing but quite loyal market segment.

In recent years, the performance of the hardbound nonfiction line has been disappointing. Sales have been declining every year despite a determined effort by the company to offer an attractive, well-researched and topical product at a reasonable price. A recent analysis by the Widgeon Sound marketing team indicates that there has been an industry-wide reduction in the demand for nonfiction books and that Widgeon Sound's share of the market in this area has been shrinking as well.

The books for younger readers are the company's present pride and joy. The dominant entry in a rapidly growing segment, the "Widgeon Sound Wonders" stories for the 16-and-under crowd have proven themselves the company's big profit-producer for the new millenium. The results are still out on the teen paperbacks. Only recently introduced, they have not yet captured a large share of the market. Widgeon Sound management feels the line is an "in product" and will ultimately capture a substantial share of this rapidly growing market.

Circle the letter of the word or phrase that best completes the sentence or best answers the question.

9. According to market share/market growth analysis, the "Widgeon Sound Wonders" are
   a. a cash cow.
   b. a star.
   c. a dog.
   d. a question mark.
   e. a duck.

10. Using the market share/market growth matrix as a base, Widgeon Sound's adult fiction line would be a
    a. dog.
    b. star.
    c. cash cow.
    d. question mark.
    e. dreamer.

11. Widgeon Sound's new line of teen paperbacks
    a. is obviously a loser and should be dropped as soon as possible.
    b. shows every evidence of being a question mark offering and should be carefully watched and nurtured.
    c. is undoubtedly a star right now and should be treated as such.
    d. will probably become a cash cow before it becomes a star.
    e. will never beat out the Hardy Boys and Nancy Drew.

12. If you had to make the decision to drop one of the Widgeon Sound lines of products right now, it would be
    a. the teen paperbacks; the market is too uncertain and the risk too great to stay in it.
    b. the adult fiction; resources could be better allocated to developing the teen paperback line.
    c. the books for younger readers; sales have undoubtedly peaked and the end is in sight for this line.
    d. the hardbound nonfiction; a declining share of a declining market makes this product a dog and a prime candidate for deletion.

Name_____   Instructor_____

Section_____   Date_____

Surfing the Net

Keeping in mind that addresses change and what's on the Web now may have changed by the time you read this, let's take a look at some of the places on the Net that reflect aspects of marketing planning. We are not endorsing or recommending any of these sources, merely making note of the information and services that people have elected to offer through the Internet.

It's worth knowing about *Hoover's Business Profiles* of some 2,000 of the largest and fastest-growing public and private companies in the United States and the rest of the world. You have to subscribe to use this service, but the coverage of the competition is exhaustive. To inquire, access the Hoover Web site at **http://www.hoovers.com/free**. If you don't want to fork over to use the Hoover's database, you might try a look at the *Fortune 500*. This refers to America's 500 largest corporations ranked by sales volume. You can also click for a company profile. That's at **http://www.fortune.com/fortune/fortune500**. Feel inclined to look at British businesses? Their profiles can be found at the BizEd site. Check the following: **http://www.bized.ac.uk/compfact/business_profiles.htm**.

Among the research oriented publications related to determining some of the characteristics of target markets to be found on the Net are the periodical *American Demographics,* whose site is located at **http://www.demographics.com/main.html**. You can review current articles from the magazine or even subscribe if you're of a mind.

If segmentation is your interest, try accessing this site, devoted to examination of all sorts of issues related to marketing segmentation. It's **http://www.atwebo.com/marketing_segmentation.htm**. Its main focus is on outsourcing. Nearby, you can also find a somewhat more technical discussion of the process of segmentation research. That's at **http://www.nationalanalysts.com/marketing/market-segmentation-research/Marketing-segmentation-models.asp**

Feeling really professional? The American Marketing Association, which many regard as the definitive organization for marketers worldwide, is on-line at **http://www.marketingpower.com**. You can browse their publications, including the *Journal of Marketing,* decide which marketing conferences to attend, and there is even a section that offers support (moral, we assume, as opposed to financial) to students of the discipline.

Want to know more about SWOT analysis? There are three handy sites that may provide you with useful information. The first is **http://www.mindtools.com/pages/article/newTMC_05.htm**. The second is to be found at **http://www.quickmba.com/strategy/SWOT**. And finally, if you're interested in using SWOT analysis to plan your career, go to **http://www.quintcareers.com/SWOT_Analysis.html**.

And finally, who or what is or are this Boston Consulting Group thing? Well, try this site on for size if the though interests you: **http://www.bcg.com**. That's short and easy.

Verified August 12, 2004

Chapter 3
The Marketing Environment, Ethics, and Social Responsibility

Chapter Outline

You may want to use the following as a guide in taking notes.

I. Chapter Overview – Firms and the Impact of External Forces

    Change is inevitable. Sometimes it is the result of crisis, but more often it is gradual. Change can be planned for, and many groups are concerned with its occurrence. The five forces that drive change are the environmental components of competition, political-legal considerations, economics, technology, and the social-cultural sphere.

II. Environmental Scanning and Environmental Management

    A. Environmental scanning is the process of gathering information about the external environment to identify and interpret potential trends.
        1. During the "mad cow" scare, vendors of organic beef, noting the fear of the public over even the remote possibility of illness, took the opportunity to promote the safety of eating their beef, a fact that appealed then – and does now – to many consumers.

    B. Environmental management is the effort to achieve organizational objectives by predicting and influencing the competitive, political-legal, economic, technological, and social-cultural components of the environment.
        1. Joining or forming political action committees (PACs) may be a way managers can affect the political-legal environment.
        2. Competing with industry leaders may involve forming *strategic alliances* with other firms to create competitive advantages in a new market.
        3. Strategic alliances are especially important in the international market where local firms can provide regional expertise for companies expanding their business abroad.
        4. Research and development efforts may successfully impact the technological environment, creating superior products or lowering production costs.
        5. Successful research and development may cause changes in the technological environment.

III. The Competitive Environment – Firms seeking to satisfy customers create interactive exchanges.

    Firms operating as monopolies have historically found themselves regulated by government entities. The last three decades have seen a reduction in regulation (deregulation) of formerly highly   regulated industries. Possession of a patent may create a temporary – and legal – form of monopoly. Other industries are dominated by just a few firms of large size. These industries are oligopolies.

    A. Types of competition – Competition may be direct, indirect, or general.
        1. Direct competition is competition between marketers of similar products, such as competition between MacDonald's and Burger King in fast foods or between Nokia and Motorola in the cell phone market.

2. Indirect competition involves competition between products that are easily substituted, such as pizza and hamburgers as alternative foods or mountain climbing versus going to the beach as forms of vacation. New technologies or a drop or increase in the price of an existing product may also create a new type of competition, such as that between oil fuel and solar energy.

3. General competition describes the concept that a vast number of organizations of different types ultimately compete for the consumer's dollar. A cruise may be an alternative to the purchase of a new heating system in this context.

B. Developing a competitive strategy – It's a matter of choices.
  1. Creating a competitive strategy depends on the answers to three questions
     a. Should we compete? The answer depends on the firm's resources, objectives, and expected profit potential.
     b. If so, in what markets should we compete? All firms' resources are limited, so the possible alternatives must be matched to the available resources.
     c. How should we compete? This requires that answers be given to the question of how to produce a marketing mix that will give the firm an advantage in the marketplace.
  2. Time-based competition is the strategy of developing and distributing goods and services more quickly than competitors. It is a crucial component of consumer electronics and computer marketing.

IV. The Political-Legal Environment

This area includes the laws and their interpretations that require firms to operate under certain competitive conditions and protect consumer rights. The U.S. legal system was constructed piecemeal, and is composed of regulations enacted at the federal, state, and local level that affect marketing.

A. Federal government regulation of business in the United States can be divided into four historical phases.
  1. The first is the antimonopoly period of the late nineteenth and early twentieth centuries. During this phase the Sherman Act, Clayton Act, and Federal Trade Commission Act were passed. These laws remain in force and have resulted in such situations as the recent Microsoft case.
  2. The second phase occurred during the Great Depression of the 1930s and had the objective of protecting competition.
  3. Between the end of World War II and the early 1970s, the focus of most federal legislation was on consumer protection.
  4. Finally, beginning in the late 1970s, the tendency was to discontinue many regulations – the phase of deregulation.
  5. At present, government is attempting to cope with problems brought about by the development of online services – attempting to regulate cyberspace.
     a. E-fraud, or scams related to the use and sale of Internet access, is quite common.
     b. Privacy and child protection constitute serious cybermarketing related issues.
     c. The "do-not-call" registry is the most recent regulation affecting vendor-customer interaction through communication.

B. Government regulatory agencies
1. Federal, state, and local governments have all established regulatory agencies to enforce laws.
2. Among the federal agencies are the Federal Trade Commission and Federal Communications Commission, as well as the Food and Drug Administration, Consumer Products Safety Commission, and Environmental Protection Agency.
3. The Federal Trade Commission uses several procedures to enforce the law.
   a. A consent decree may be issued in which an alleged offender agrees to voluntary compliance without admitting guilt.
   b. The agency may issue a cease-and-desist order demanding that an illegal practice be stopped.
   c. Cease and desist orders are often challenged in court.
   d. Other specific actions may be required of offenders by the FTC.
4. Deregulation has changed a number of industries, particularly through the dismantling of legal monopolies such as the telephone company, requiring closer monitoring of competitive firms.

C. Other regulatory forces
1. Public and private consumer interest groups have an influence on the legal environment.
2. Self-regulatory groups represent industries' attempts to set guidelines for responsible business conduct.
   a. The Council of Better Business Bureaus is a national organization devoted to consumer service and business self-regulation.
   b. The Direct Marketing Association, an industry group, polices unwanted mail and telephone solicitations.

D. Controlling the political-legal environment
1. Most businesses fight regulations they feel are unjust through lawsuits.
2. Other firms create new opportunities allowed by changes in the laws.
3. Consumer groups and political action committees influence which laws are passed and which are not.

V. The Economic Environment – The forces that influence consumer buying power and marketing strategies constitute the economic environment. These include the stages of the business cycle, inflation, unemployment, income, and resource availability.

A. Business cycles consist of four stages: prosperity, recession, depression, and recovery.
1. During prosperity, spending maintains a brisk pace and buyers are willing to spend more for premium versions of well-known brands.
2. When recession hits, buying patterns shift to basic, functional products with low price tags.
3. During a depression, consumer spending sinks to its lowest level. The last U.S. depression was during the 1930s and it is unlikely that another will occur.
4. The advent of recovery shows increases in consumer purchasing power but there is often a reluctance to spend the available money until people are convinced that prosperity is on the way. In the recovery of the early twenty-first century, however, spending increased quickly due to the wealth effect.
5. The most recent recession began in 2001, but by 2004 recovery was well under way.

B. Inflation is best described as rising prices caused by some combination of excess demand and increases in the costs of the factors of production. High rates of inflation make consumers aware of prices and they may decide to buy now, postpone the purchase, or change their buying patterns entirely.

C. Unemployment is the proportion of people in the economy who do not have jobs and are actively looking for work.
  1. Unemployment is a function of the business cycle.
  2. High rates of unemployment are present during recession and depression, while those rates decline significantly during recovery and prosperity.

D. Income, especially discretionary income – the money left over to the consumer after buying necessities such as food, clothing, and housing – is an important environmental factor because it influences consumer buying power
  1. Periods of major innovation are typically accompanied by dramatic increases in living standards.

E. Resource availability can be affected by shortages of raw materials, component parts, energy, or labor.
  1. A common reaction to shortages is demarketing, the process of reducing consumer demand to a level that can be reasonably supplied.
  2. For certain products, such aluminum, recycling may be the solution to a shortage that goes back to the raw material.

F. The international economic environment must be monitored because changes in one part of the world don't always reflect changes occurring elsewhere.

VI The Technological Environment – The application to marketing of knowledge in science, inventions, and innovations.

A. Technology is revolutionizing the marketing environment, changing the way companies promote and distribute goods

B. Technology can improve manufacturing operations and even address social concerns.

C. Industry, government, colleges, universities, and other not-for-profits play roles in the development of new technology.
  1. Private industry represents a major source of innovation including dramatic medicines for humans and animals such as those produced by Pfizer.
  2. The federal government produces significant innovations such as the technology on which the airbag for cars is based, digital computers, and the microwave oven.
  3. Foreign countries such a Japan and Germany also produce new technology.

D. Applying technology with skill and creativity can result in a competitive edge for the firm and may even benefit society. Customer service can also be improved.
  1. The use of Voice over Internet Protocol (VoIP) telephone service allows a new standard of telephone service at reduced cost through technological innovation.

VII. The Social-Cultural Environment – The U.S. population is becoming older, more affluent, and more culturally diverse, and as it does the relationship between marketing and society and its culture – the socio-cultural environment – changes.

    A. The importance in marketing decisions of this environmental factor relates to the demographic shifts within and changing values embraced by society.

    B. Cultural diversity, which deals with the changing ethnic aspects of the society, is a major issue in the early twenty-first century.

    C. Consumerism, that social force within the environment that aids and protects the buyer by exerting moral, legal, and economic pressures on business, has increased its level of activity in recent years.
        1. Can and should the demands of the consumer always be met? Many firms say they can't do   everything consumers demand and still stay in business.
        2. Consumers should have certain rights, and President John F. Kennedy summed them up.
            a. Consumers should have the right to choose freely.
            b. Consumers should have the right to be informed.
            c. Consumers should have the right to be heard.
            d. Consumers should have the right to be safe.

VIII. Ethical Issues in Marketing

Marketers should have standards of conduct and moral values. Ethics have to do with issues of what is right and what is wrong. In some instances, ethical abuses such as the corporate fraud and conflicts of interest on Wall Street during the last decade result in the passage of new laws to regain control of the situation. Earlier, the actions of the tobacco companies and the issue of cigarette promotion when the hazards of smoking were known had illuminated the problem. Marketers have developed ethical standards to guide their behavior.

    A. Ethical problems in marketing research have become chronic because the digital age has produced a plethora of databases, mailing lists, and an ease of gathering data about individuals never seen before.

    B. Ethical problems in product strategy include such things as product quality, planned obsolescence, brand similarity, and questions of misleading, deceptive, or unethical packaging practices.

    C. Ethical problems in distribution strategy can be summed up in two questions: first, "What is the appropriate degree of control over the channel?" and second, "Should a company distribute its products in marginally profitable outlets that have no alternative source of supply?" The answers are not so clear.

    D. Ethical problems in promotional strategy constitute the majority of the ethical problems faced by marketers.
        1. Is it right to target artificial sweeteners to diabetics? Are cakes and cookies really appropriate for this market segment?

2. Is it right to advertise prescription drugs to the consumer? Does the consumer know enough about his or her ailment to prescribe to the physician on the basis of an advertisement?
   a. Is the lavish promotion aimed at physicians to get them to prescribe certain pharmaceuticals right? Are they prescribing the best choice of medication or the one with the deepest pockets?
   b. How much disclosure is necessary to protect consumers from their own ignorance? An anyone really understand what that fast-talking radio announcer is saying about the detailed terms of the automobile lease and does that constitute sufficient information to act upon?

E. Ethical problems in pricing are fewer than in the other areas of marketing because pricing is the most regulated aspect of the marketing mix, but they do occur, usually in the realm of the cost of   distribution. Should people who live where distribution costs are high really pay more than those who live where they are low?

IX. Social Responsibility in Marketing – Marketers have an obligation to give equal weight to profits, consumer satisfaction, and social well-being in evaluating the firm's performance. It is easier to measure social responsibility than marketing ethics because responsibility can be mandated while ethics cannot.

A. Marketing's responsibilities historically have concerned relationships with customers, employees, and stockholders. Today the scope of responsibility has been expanded to cover the entire societal framework.

B. Marketing and ecology have become a driving force influencing the way in which businesses operate.
   1. Planned obsolescence is no longer acceptable as a product characteristic.
   2. Pollution is not the inevitable consequence of business operation.
   3. Recovery of wastes created by high levels of technology has become an ecological issue – lead and other toxic materials but also gold, silver, and platinum can be salvaged from computer and cellular telephone equipment.
   4. A policy of marketing "ecology-friendly" products, called "green marketing," was popular during the 1990s but was not well supported by consumers.

Name_____   Instructor_____

Section_____   Date_____

Key Concepts

From the list of lettered terms, select the one that best fits each of the numbered statements below. Write the letter of that choice in the space provided.

Key Terms

a. environmental scanning
b. environmental management
c. competitive environment
d. time-based competition
e. political-legal environment
f. economic environment
g. demarketing

h. technological environment
i. social-cultural environment
j. consumerism
k. consumer rights
l. marketing ethics
m. social responsibility
n. green marketing

_____ 1. Laws and their interpretations that require firms to operate under competitive conditions and serve to protect consumer rights.

_____ 2. Standards of conduct and moral values under which marketers operate.

_____ 3. Producing, marketing, and reclaiming environmentally sensitive products.

_____ 4. Reducing consumer demand for a product or service to a level that the firm can supply.

_____ 5. Attainment of organizational objectives by predicting and influencing the competitive, political/legal, economic, technological, and social/cultural environments.

_____ 6. Social force that aids and protects the consumer by exerting legal, moral, and economic pressure on business and government.

_____ 7. Strategy of developing and distributing goods and services more quickly than competitors.

_____ 8. The relationship between the marketer and society and its culture.

_____ 9. Interactive process occurring in the marketplace among marketers of directly competing products, marketers of substitutable products, and other marketers competing for consumer purchasing power.

_____ 10. Includes the state of the business cycle, inflation, unemployment, resource availability, and income.

_____ 11. Marketing philosophies, policies, procedures, and actions intended primarily to enhance society's welfare.

_____ 12. Application to marketing of knowledge based on discoveries in science, inventions, and innovation.

_____ 13. Collecting information about the external marketing environment to identify and interpret potential trends.

_____ 14. The right to choose freely, to be informed, to be heard, and to be safe.

Name_____   Instructor_____

Section_____   Date_____

Self-Quiz

You should use these questions to test your understanding of the chapter material. Check your answers against those provided at the end of the chapter.

While these questions cover most of the chapter topics, they are not intended to be the same as the test questions your instructor may use in an examination. A good understanding of all aspects of the course material is essential to good performance on any examination.

True/False

Write "T" for True and "F" for False for each of the following statements.

_____ 1. Environmental scanning involves detailed examination of the firm's internal structure to affect and control the use of resources.

_____ 2. One aspect of environmental management is strategic alliances – partnerships with other firms in which the partners combine resources and capital to create competitive advantages in a new market.

_____ 3. The first decision a company must make with respect to competition is whether it will compete or not.

_____ 4. Unable to compete directly with its cruise ship and airline competitors, Amtrak decided to team up with them and become the means by which people can make travel arrangements to get where they want to go by air, land, and sea.

_____ 5. The most striking aspect of the existing legal framework for marketing in the U.S. is the clear organization of the legal framework and its consistent enforcement.

_____ 6. Government regulation of business in the United States has passed through four historical phases: the antimonopoly phase, the protecting competitors phase, the protecting consumers phase, and the industry deregulation phase.

_____ 7. The newest regulatory frontier is cyberspace. The policing of the Internet and online services has proven more difficult than have regulatory efforts directed at business in the past because of the absence of the federal government from the arena.

_____ 8. Deflation, devaluation of the money through persistent price increases, can occur at any stage in the business cycle.

_____ 9. The Federal Trade Commission and state regulators cannot do anything to stop firms from using fraudulent and deceptive advertising, especially in cyberspace.

_____ 10. Deregulation of the utility industry has improved its efficiency and increased competition as firms have expanded their service offerings to new markets.

_____ 11. Discretionary income is the amount of money people have left to spend after they've paid for food, clothing, housing, and other necessities.

_____ 12. Historically, periods of major innovation have been accompanied by dramatic declines in living standards and rising inflation.

_____ 13. Technological innovations often bear a fairly stiff price. The cost of insulating aircraft cabins to protect against fire, for example, would amount to $300,000 for each life saved.

_____ 14. America's cultural diversity has historically had little effect on consumers' reactions to different products and marketing practices.

_____ 15. The Chinese market for cell phones has been growing at a rate of 50 percent per year while the European market for the same product has been slowing down.

_____ 16. The federal government is a major source of technology, among its products being air bags for automobiles, digital computers, and the microwave oven.

_____ 17. Consumerism is a radical, reactionary movement that resists and contradicts the societal demand that organizations adopt the marketing concept.

_____ 18. President Kennedy's statement of consumer rights includes "the right to be safe." This means that products and services must be designed in such a way that they will be absolutely safe for anyone to use in all circumstances.

_____ 19. It is seldom necessary to redesign packages and modify products and advertising messages to suit the tastes and preferences of different cultures.

_____ 20. One issue that seldom comes up in the consideration of ethics in marketing research is invasion of personal privacy.

_____ 21. In addition to individual and organizational ethics, individuals may also be influenced by a professional code of ethics that transcends both organizational and individual value systems.

_____ 22. The new wave of "hybrid" automobiles provide interesting examples of how technology can address social concerns such as greater fuel efficiency and lowered exhaust emissions.

_____ 23. The practice of "green marketing" involves letting people know that products are made from all-new materials, thus encouraging the growth of new trees for making paper and other products and the development of new sources of metals, plastics, and similar materials.

_____ 24. Lobbying groups frequently enlist the support of consumers, employees, and suppliers to assist their efforts to influence the passage of proposed legislation.

_____ 25. Business cannot successfully please ALL consumers and still generate the profits necessary to remain viable.

Multiple Choice

Circle the letter of the word or phrase that best completes the sentence or best answers the question.

26. Microsoft's recent difficulties with the U.S. Justice Department grew out of the operation of which of the environments of marketing?
    a. the social-cultural environment
    b. the economic environment
    c. the political-legal environment
    d. the technological environment
    e. none of the above

27. Which of the following orientations toward the marketing environment is most useful for the marketer?
    a. Practice environmental management, seeking to achieve organizational objectives by predicting and influencing the firm's environmental framework.
    b. Ignore it and maybe it will go away.
    c. Realize that an individual firm cannot have any effect on the marketing environment.
    d. Do not change marketing strategies until substantial losses result from environmental forces.
    e. Make sure marketing strategies satisfy legal requirements but ignore other aspects of the marketing environment because there are no legal penalties for such behavior.

28. The speed at which changes occur in the Internet arena is so great that marketers count time in "Internet years" which are actually periods of only weeks or months. This would lead one to believe that Internet innovators are facing
    a. time-based competition.
    b. price-based promotional action.
    c. space-based competition.
    d. sour grapes marketing.
    e. a deceptive advertising practice.

29. Major reasons why a firm may choose NOT to compete in a particular market include
    a. inadequate resources available to the firm.
    b. a lack of fit between the market and the firm's objectives.
    c. low profit expectations.
    d. a, b, and c above.
    e. only a and b above.

30. A correct match of a specific law and its primary objective is
    a. Robinson-Patman Act – protect consumers
    b. Sherman Act – protect the competitive environment
    c. Wheeler-Lea Act – protect the consumer
    d. Staggers Rail Act – regulation of competition
    e. Consumer Product Safety Act – deregulate industry

31. All of the following are parts of the economic environment except
    a. resource availability.
    b. inflation and deflation.
    c. income and its distribution.
    d. the stage of the business cycle.
    e. falling birth rate.

32. Firms such as public utilities that once held a monopoly position in the market enjoyed, at the cost of considerable regulation, protection from the forces of the
    a. economic environment.
    b. competitive environment.
    c. political-legal environment.
    d. technological environment.
    e. social-cultural environment.

33. This most-recent phase in the regulation of American business has seen government working to increase competition in such industries as telecommunications, utilities, transportation, and financial services. This is the
    a. antimonopoly period.
    b. era of protecting competitors.
    c. phase of deregulation of industry
    d. consumer protection times.
    e. environmental development phase.

34. Which of the following methods is used by the Federal Trade Commission to protect consumers?
    a. The FTC takes hostages from firms believed to be violating the law and holds them for ransom.
    b. Injunctions are issued requiring that firms prove themselves innocent or pay large fines.
    c. Public service announcements identifying all firms that have used deceptive selling practices are broadcast.
    d. A cease and desist order is issued, demanding that a firm stop an illegal practice.
    e. A closure order to shut down an accused firm's operations is issued.

35. An example of an ethical problem related to product strategy would be
    a. whether automobile dealers should be required to purchase repair parts from the manufacturer of the cars they sell.
    b. the exaggeration of product merits or outright deceit in product descriptions.
    c. whether marketers have an obligation to warn consumers of impending discount or returns policy changes.
    d. whether there is an obligation to serve areas where there are few users of the firm's product.
    e. whether packages should be kept to some standard size, rather than made extra-large or odd-shaped.

36. Historically and traditionally, the socially responsible manager has been concerned with
    a. providing quality products at reasonable prices.
    b. providing workers with adequate wages.
    c. making acceptable profits for stockholders.
    d. creating decent working conditions for employees.
    e. All of the above.

37. A correct statement about the economic environment is that
    a. during periods of recession, consumers tend to purchase lower-priced brands of grocery and household items and more private-label goods.
    b. consumer spending rises to its highest overall level during periods of economic recovery.
    c. the last economic depression in the United States occurred in the 1950s.
    d. the rate of inflation since the year 2000 has been well over eight percent per year.
    e. unemployment does not affect marketing because consumer behavior remains the same.

38. Which force in the marketing environment is noted for improving existing products, offering better customer service, and even creating entirely new industries?
    a. the economic environment.
    b. the competitive environment.
    c. the political-legal environment.
    d. the social-cultural environment.
    e. the technological environment.

39. Which of the following is an example of a demarketing strategy?
    a. Offering a second gallon of milk for half price if a first gallon is purchased at full price.
    b. Providing consumers with tips on how to make a product last longer or use less energy.
    c. Advertising the convenience of owning more than one car.
    d. Telling consumers that they should stock up on a product in abundant supply.
    e. Making substantial reductions in a firm's advertising budget.

40. Which of the following is an accurate statement about the social-cultural environment?
    a. The United States, as a nation, is becoming younger and less affluent.
    b. Marketing strategies that have proven themselves in the United States will work anywhere.
    c. Most marketers do not need to take the social environment into consideration.
    d. Consumer activism, because so many industries are now protected from it, has been declining for a number of years.
    e. Changing social values have led to the social force called the consumerism movement.

41. A person's standards of ethical behavior based on their own, personal system of values would be called
    a. organizational ethics.
    b. corporate ethics.
    c. individual ethics.
    d. professional ethics.
    e. coded ethics.

42. Given their limited resources, which of the following would most likely NOT be an appropriate strategy for a small retailer to use to survive when faced with competition from a Wal-Mart Supercenter or similar megadiscount store?
    a. Offer a more complete selection of a single line of products like hardware or building materials than does Wal-Mart.
    b. Stock more up-scale merchandise than the discounter competitor.
    c. Extend operating hours and liberalize returns policies.
    d. Offer the same products as the discounter at the same prices.
    e. Deliver purchases for free and have an on-site repair department.

43. Which of the following situations best reflects the competitive condition of substitution (or indirect competition)?
    a. Tide, Cheer, Surf, Oxydol, and Fab in the detergent section of the supermarket
    b. gypsum board (sheetrock), wood paneling, Masonite sheet, and plaster as wall finishing materials
    c. rock concerts, video rentals, dining out, and wind surfing for an evening's entertainment
    d. Delta, Continental, and Southwest Airlines all offering cut-rate fares between their major destinations
    e. None of the above are examples of substitution; all represent direct competition.

44. The most critical ethical issue related to marketing research has to do with
    a. alleged invasion of personal privacy.
    b. planned obsolescence.
    c. product testing issues.
    d. the danger inherent in automotive air bags.
    e. the degree of corporate distributional control.

45. The Federal Food and Drug Act and the Childrens' Online Privacy Protection Act are examples of laws that
    a. are designed to help maintain a competitive environment.
    b. regulate the conditions of competition in some way.
    c. have as their objective the protection of consumers.
    d. deregulate particular industries.
    e. serve to create a new class of criminal where none existed before.

46. George, Howard, and Louis are the only three real estate brokers in the town of Pierre Part. They have the informal habit of getting together for lunch once a month to "talk things over." At their most recent meeting, George proposed that they divide the town up into sections, with each realtor taking one part as his exclusive territory. If they carry out their plan, they can be accused of violating the
    a. Consumer Goods Pricing Act.
    b. Federal Trade Commission Act.
    c. Robinson-Patman Act.
    d. Celler-Kefauver Act.
    e. Federal Election Commission Act.

47. The Federal Regulatory Agency that wields the broadest powers of any agency to influence marketing activities is the
    a. Air Transport Commission.
    b. Transportation Regulatory Commission.
    c. Federal Power Commission.
    d. Federal Trade Commission.
    e. Federal Communications Commission.

48. Production of disposable diapers, ballpoint pens, razors, and cameras may lay firms open to charges of
    a. taking a cavalier attitude toward social responsibility.
    b. practicing planned obsolescence.
    c. attempting to control the channel of distribution for corporate gain.
    d. violating the National Quality Standards Act.
    e. avoiding deregulation efforts by their industries.

49. That phase of the business cycle during which consumer spending is brisk and buyers are willing to spend more for premium versions of familiar brands is
    a. recession.
    b. depression.
    c. recovery.
    d. prosperity.
    e. exclusion.

50. During the recovery phase of the business cycle,
    a. consumers' ability to buy increases, but their willingness to buy often lags behind.
    b. consumer buying power declines and marketers should consider increasing promotional outlays.
    c. consumer spending is brisk, and demand for premium versions of well-known brands is strong.
    d. consumer spending readies its lowest level.
    e. marketers may increase prices or extend their product lines to take advantage of brisk consumer spending.

Name_____   Instructor_____

Section_____   Date_____

Applying Marketing Concepts

Sandy Willis was thinking about her problems with her printing business. They all began when she first decided to go into business for herself. Having found the "perfect" location for her firm, she was dismayed when the city wouldn't give her a business license on the grounds that the local zoning ordinances didn't allow a facility of that type in the chosen location.

After much effort, Sandy found a new location and was successful in getting a license to operate. She experienced trouble getting some minor renovations to the building done because of a "building boom" the city was experiencing. She also had trouble hiring technicians and other workers because unemployment was at an all-time low and good people were at a premium.

At long last the renovations were complete, a staff had been hired, and Sandy's Printing Company was ready to open. But almost the minute the dustsheets were taken off the outdoor signs, Sandy received a visit from a neighborhood committee objecting to one of her window displays. It seems the display featured a rather large poster of which Sandy was quite proud. It had taken a lot of time for her and her technicians to get the color just right. It featured a semi-nude couple in a rather suggestive pose on a sofa that was to be used as the cover of a forthcoming edition of *Lifestyle* magazine. In an effort to be accommodating, Sandy removed the poster.

Soon Sandy was faced with two new problems. The building she had rented was equipped with an incinerator, which she intended to use to dispose of waste and paper trimmings from the business. The first time it was lighted, however, the police appeared and presented her with a citation for a violation of a section of the city sanitation code. On top of that, Sandy discovered that the cost of materials used in her business was going up so fast that she could barely cover the cost of paying for what she'd sold from what she was able to get for it.

The straw that broke the camel's back, however, was Sandy's discovery, only sixty days after she'd opened for business, that Mergenthaler Industries, a national chain of giant printing facilities, was about to open a plant only two blocks away. Sandy knew that they could, because of their enormous buying power, undersell her by thirty percent on practically every piece of work she'd be likely to get.

Realizing that the handwriting was on the wall, Sandy held an auction sale to dispose of her equipment and supplies and closed her plant.

Write "T" for True and "F" for False for each of the following statements.

_____ 1. Sandy's difficulty in getting a business license was due to the social/cultural environment.

_____ 2. Sandy seemed able to adapt her marketing strategy to the constraints of the environment.

_____ 3. Sandy's problems getting a business license could have been avoided if she had checked the appropriate environmental constraints before she decided on her first location.

_____ 4. The actions of a company like Mergenthaler Industries – buying in bulk and selling at low delivered prices – are likely a violation of the Robinson-Patman Act.

_____ 5. Sandy may have been shortsighted in going out of business. It's possible that she may have been able to develop an appeal to a different target market than people who would choose to deal with Mergenthaler Industries.

Circle the letter of the word or phrase that best completes the sentence or best answers the question.

6. Sandy had problems with the
   a. economic environment.
   b. political-legal environment.
   c. competitive environment.
   d. social-cultural environment.
   e. environments in a through d above.

7. Sandy's citation was probably issued by the police because she
   a. was in violation of an air pollution regulation.
   b. was destroying valuable recyclable materials.
   c. used an excessive amount of natural gas firing her incinerator.
   d. had failed to get a city inspection of her store before opening.
   e. was a particular target of a "get-tough" administration.

8. Sandy's problems in getting her facility renovated were probably due to the fact that
   a. her city was experiencing a period of recession and lots of workers had left town.
   b. the city was experiencing a prosperous period of the business cycle.
   c. she was in competition with other employment opportunities for the services of the available labor.
   d. all of the statements above are true.
   e. the statements in b and c above are true.

9. Sandy's inability to purchase new supplies for what she'd paid for the old was due to
   a. her inability to manage her money so as to make sure that she'd have enough to buy new goods.
   b. low sales volume and a high proportion of fixed costs in her plant's operation.
   c. inflation which made today's dollar less valuable than yesterday's and drove up merchandise costs.
   d. unemployment at the national level which increased the cost of government services to businesses like Sandy's.

10. From Sandy's point of view, Mergenthaler Industries is part of the
    a. social-cultural environment.
    b. competitive environment.
    c. political-legal environment.
    d. economic environment.
    e. ethnic environment.

Malonce Eldebert was tired, lonely, and a little confused. When she left her home in East Northhall to move to Baja Sierra, she was sure it was the right thing. After all, the job she'd been offered had been a real opportunity and her prospective employer had a fine reputation. But she couldn't seem to get used to Baja Sierra. It was so <u>different</u> from East Northhall. For one thing, just getting around town involved dealing with traffic that was unbelievably frustrating. Left turns at divided intersections were against the law, and the speed limit was 25 miles an hour – even in industrial neighborhoods. This didn't seem to bother the local population, nor did the fact that their lives revolved around whether or not Electrotechnical Industries Corporation, one of Baja Sierra's major employers, or a Japanese firm which was also bidding for it, got the order for those 10,000 integrated predicting anti-aircraft radar units for air-to-air missiles from Consolidated Aircraft.

Malonce couldn't believe how hard it was to make friends in Baja Sierra. It seemed as if everyone she met had been there all their lives and wasn't interested in anything or anyone not a Baja Sierra native. All in all, though, it wasn't so bad for Malonce. Her employer was great to work for and her job let him use the latest equipment in her field of supersubminiaturized electronics. She did all the magnetometric and X-ray testing of the mini-integrated circuits that Light Flight, her employer, made for Electrotechnical. She felt she was on the very leading edge of technology in her job at Light Flight, and that made up a lot for having to live in Baja Sierra. Now if she could only find some friends who thought that it took more than a six-pack of beer and a bug zapper to equal quality entertainment, she'd be just fine.

Circle the letter of the word or phrase that best completes the sentence or best answers the question.

11. Malonce's perception of the traffic in Baja Sierra being frustrating was very largely due to
    a.   her own rather bad driving habits.
    b.   differences in the political-legal environment between Baja Sierra and Northhall.
    c.   her general dissatisfaction with Baja Sierra itself.
    d.   her dislike of her job.

12. Malonce's job appears to have been deeply involved with the
    a.   economic environment.
    b.   social-cultural environment.
    c.   competitive environment.
    d.   technological environment.
    e.   development of railroad hardware.

13. Malonce's comments about Baja Sierra people being unconcerned with anyone or anything not from Baja Sierra is really a statement relating to the
    a.   social-cultural environment.
    b.   ethnic environment.
    c.   competitive environment.
    d.   political environment.

14. The relationship between Electrotechnical Industries and the Japanese company that is also bidding on the missile contract is
    a.   part of the legal environment.
    b.   a condition of direct competition.
    c.   a sort of indirect competition
    d.   nonexistent; there is no relationship, direct or indirect, between the two firms.

Name_____   Instructor_____

Section_____   Date_____

Surfing the Net

Keeping in mind that addresses change and what's on the Web now may have changed by the time you read this, let's take a look at some of the places on the Net that reflect aspects of ethical, social, or environmental influence. We are not endorsing or recommending any of these sources, merely making note of the information and services that people have elected to offer through the Internet.

If it sounds too good to be true . . . you may have run afoul of a fraud. To check it out, try the U.S. Postal Service's site at **http://www.usps.gov/websites/depart/inspect/**, a long but informative web label belonging to the Department of Postal Inspection, for information on the legal aspects of fraud at the consumer level.

The economic environment is accessible. Why not check out the idea of credit and how to use it? There are four Websites you might find interesting. The first is very personal, with an extensive array of frequently asked questions (FAQs) dealing with what's on a credit report, how to establish and maintain good credit, and what a credit rating's all about. It's at **http://www.cdiaonline.org/consumers.cfm**, and is operated by the Consumer Data Industry Association, the organization for people who evaluate the worth of individual credit. The other sites are devoted to more specific issues concerning credit. The first is at **http://www.nacm.org**; it's the site of the National Association of Credit Managers and discusses issues related to their work. A third site can be found at **http://www.truecredit.com/** and deals with how to get a copy of your own credit report and how to repair credit which may have been damaged by a credit report that is in error. If you find yourself with a sudden serious need to read the text of the Fair Credit Reporting Act – go to **http://www.ftc.gov/os/statutes/ fcrajump.htm**. That's the Federal Trade Commission's site and the file "fcrajump.htm" discusses the law.

Technology up close and personal – it's the NASA homepage. A lot of this is about the space program, but NASA has a lot more than that on the burner (so to speak), and some of it's on their Website. Try **http://www.nasa.gov/home** for the overview. For the current hot topic from those good folks, look at **http://nasa.gov/externalflash/apollo11/index.htm**. It's all about the flight of Apollo 11, with moving pictures and sound. It also has links to other Apollo missions. Neat.

The social-cultural environment's worth a look. What movies are worth seeing? Try **http://www.imdb.com**. for the largest database of movie reviews, analysis, and commentary around.

Prefer your economic environment in larger doses? You can always go straight to the Securities and Exchange Commission at **http://www.sec.gov/edgar.shtml** for access to all the filings firms wishing to make initial public offerings (IPOs) of their stocks. For more general economic information, try Washington University at St. Louis' Economics Homepage at **http://econwpa.wustl.edu**.

Just curious about federal agencies? Most of them are fairly forthcoming with stuff about what they do and how they do it. The Federal Communications Commission is, as one might expect, at **http://www.fcc.gov**. The site is clean and easy to navigate – hey, they're communicators, after all. The Tennessee Valley Authority is at **http://www.tva.gov**. This interesting agency is in charge of the flood control and power generating facilities all along the river of the same name and provides electricity to a large area of the East Central U.S. Finally, when everything goes wrong, there's always the Federal Emergency Management Administration. These people swing into action when disasters have struck. Now, use your imagination and find your favorite agency. Watch out, though! The site is sometimes not quite as you might imagine. **http://www.fpc.gov** does NOT get you the Federal Power Commission.

Sites verified August 12, 2004

Chapter 4
E-Commerce: Electronic Marketing in the Digital Age

Chapter Outline

You may want to use the following as a guide in taking notes.

I. Chapter Overview

Marketing now holds the key to creating a competitive advantage in an era of change as it has become the cutting-edge tool for success on the Internet. The Internet has revolutionized every aspect of life. Consumers like e-commerce so much that entire industries have changed the way they conduct their marketing and business practices. Internet marketers can reach individual consumers or target organizations worldwide through a vast array of technologies. This chapter differentiates e-commerce and e-marketing, discusses the Internet and World Wide Web, explains the transition from industrial to electronic economies, and describes recent e-successes and failures.

II. What Is Electronic Commerce? It consists of targeting customers by collecting and analyzing business information, conducting customer transactions, and maintaining online customer relationships using telecommunications networks.

A. E-marketing is the strategic process of creating, promoting, distributing, and pricing goods and services to a target market over the Internet or using digital tools such as tablet PCs and wireless LANs that create short-range radio connections between desktop and notebook computers and the Internet.
    1. The technology involved may reduce costs and increase customer satisfaction by increasing the speed and efficiency of marketing interactions.
    2. Online marketing is marketing activities that connect buyers and sellers electronically through interactive computer systems.
    3. E-commerce offers countless opportunities for marketers to reach consumers.
        a. Global reach eliminates the geographic protections of local business.
        b. One-to-one marketing (or personalization) is possible because production can wait until orders are received.
        c. Interactive marketing allows consumers and vendors to negotiate prices online.
        d. Right-time marketing allows vendors to provide products when and where customers want them.
        e. Integrated marketing on the Internet enables the coordination of all promotional activities and communications to create a unified, customer-oriented promotional message.

III. Interactivity and E-commerce – involves two-way back-and-forth communications between marketers and their customers and precise tailoring of products to desires. Interactive marketing is buyer-seller communications in which the customer controls the amount and type of information received from a marketer. Tools include point-of-sale brochures, coupon dispensers, and the Internet. The customer's computer and the Internet facilitate shopping, price comparisons, and ultimately the purchase of a desired product without ever leaving home.

A. The Internet is a global collection of computer networks linked together for the purpose of exchanging data and information.

1. Internet use in the U.S. has grown, in just over ten years, from 20 million Americans to over 132 million.
2. Intranets are internal corporate networks that allow employees within a firm to communicate with each other and gain access to corporate information.
3. Extranets are corporate networks that allow communications between a firm and selected customers, suppliers, and external business partners.

B. The World Wide Web was "invented" by Tim Bernes-Lee at the European Laboratory for Particle Physics in Geneva to be an internal document management system but grew to be an interlinked collection of hundreds of thousands of linked computers that function together within the Internet.
   1. The Web is now the premier means for marketers to reach consumers in their target markets because it allows them to reach consumers in their target markets and provide two-way communications between sellers and potential customers.

C. The Four Primary Web Functions – communication, information, entertainment, and e-commerce
   1. Communication includes the following:
      a. use of e-mail. This now outnumbers regular mail 10 to 1 and is easy, quick, and convenient.
      b. instant messaging, which allows real-time communication between senders and recipients.
      c. chat rooms and bulletin boards that are essentially forums in which groups of people can share information.
   2. Information can be obtained by consulting commercial "search engines" – Google or Dogpile, for example, or by visiting the online sites of publications such as the *New York Times* or *Business Week*. There are also government sites and sites providing online educational information.
   3. Entertainment on the Web includes games, radio programming, movies, and music clips.
      a. Copyrights and other protections of intellectual property rights may be at hazard due to infringement on the Web. Downloading of files of all sorts has been a particular area of concern.
   4. E-commerce has become the primary function of the Web with almost 80 percent of all sites devoted to some aspect of it.
      a. The Web facilitates marketing activities including buying and selling, building relationships, increasing market size, and reducing the costs of intermediaries.
      b. Both goods vendors and service providers can successfully use the Web for e-commerce.
      c. Even matchmaking, bringing together the lovelorn scientifically, is a fast-growing area of Web commerce
      d. Business-to-business (B2B) commerce facilitated by using the Web now accounts for over $2 trillion a year in sales volume.

D. The Internet is accessed through Internet Service Providers (ISPs) such as Earthlink, America Online, or Microsoft Network.
   1. Individuals can access the Internet using dial-up connections or broadband connections, which are much faster.
   2. Cell phones, called smart phones, are now capable of connecting with the Internet.
   3. Wireless Fidelity, also called the "wireless local-area network," is becoming more popular, and Verizon Wireless is offering a new high-speed technology that will automatically connect a number of different devices to the Internet.

IV. E-commerce and the Economy ʙ a leading force in changing the way the world lives and breathes. An Internet-based economy is supplanting the century-old industrial economy and fueling growth in the twenty-first century. It is an economy based on information, the Internet, and other online technologies. It is estimated that by 2006 e-commerce will generate productivity gains of $450 billion. But a pretty Web site does not automatically spell success. The Web site must facilitate communication between organizations, customers, and suppliers.

A. Business-to-business online marketing interactions involve professional buyers and sellers involved in transactions in which large sums of money and quantities of products and services change hands. Electronic exchanges, Web-based marketplaces that cater to the needs of a specific industry, are popular in the B2B arena. The volume of B2B commerce is now $2.4 trillion per year. Durable goods are the biggest B2B sellers on the Net, followed by business products (office supplies, electronics, scientific equipment); service providers are active as well. New systems and software have been created to make B2B online marketing work. Going online has let a number of businesses find entirely new markets for their goods and services. Distinguishing one's firm from competitors is a major objective of online (and offline) marketers. The use of search engine and Internet yellow pages listings is a good start. Successful online B2B marketers serve their customers by thinking like a buyer.

B. The true advantages of B2B online marketing over traditional methods are only beginning to be realized.
   1. Online marketers can discover new markets and customers.
   2. Online marketing can produce cost savings in every aspect of marketing strategy.
   3. The number of new Web sites increases daily; the bulk of these are commercial.
   4. Many firms, as well as government agencies, have begun save time and money using e-procurement to purchase needed items.

C. Online Consumer Marketing is inherently interactive marketing. It expands the reach of marketers in connecting with consumers as part of an overall marketing strategy. There are two types of B2C Web sites: shopping sites and informational sites. Consumers shop online primarily for one or more of three reasons:
   1. Many products cost less online. Examples are airfares and hotels, but other products and services are often similarly cheaper on the Net.
   2. Going online can be very convenient because one can shop globally twenty-four hours a day, register credit card numbers, even shopping information like clothing sizes.
      a. Customized products can be made to match individual customer requirements.
   3. Personalization, or one-to-one marketing, is possible because the vendor creates a database of each customer's preferences and tastes and what they have purchased in the past and uses the information to create the personal relationship.

D. Benefits of Online Consumer Marketing – relationship building, cost reduction, increased efficiency, a more level playing field, and achievement of a global presence are all possibilities.
   1. Databases allow the online marketer to create a relationship with shoppers by "remembering" them and what they like to buy and creating the digital equivalent of a one-on-one shopping experience.
      a. Small businesses can find customers in unsuspected places and build relationships with them.
      b. Customer service is the key to building strong customer relationships in online as well as offline marketing.

2. Increased efficiency means much higher profit margins for online retailers than on sales made through traditional channels.
3. Going online can reduce the costs of starting and operating a business.
4. Being online can level the playing field for members of minorities who go into business there because online shoppers don't know their race, age, national origin and other such characteristics.

E. Online Marketing is International Marketing
1. The global reach of the Internet allows inexpensive communication with consumers is faraway places.
2. Culture is a barrier that hampers online marketing overseas.
3. The 100 million online Europeans shop much less online than do Americans. For them, it's a way of working at home, catching up on local politics, choosing a vacation destination, or taking courses.
4. Online commerce in the U.S. still leads global online commerce in volume and will for years to come.

F. Security and Privacy Issues of E-Commerce – consumers still worry about revealing information that may come into the hands of others without their permission, so much so that it may be an impediment to the growth of e-commerce.
1. Passwords and electronic signatures offer means of authenticating that an online presence is who they say they are.
2. Automatic data collection methods leave trails of information behind every individual who surfs the Net. In addition to *cookies* that record sites that one has surfed, there is also *spyware* that looks at all the interactions between an individual's PC and the Internet and makes that information available to the spyware owner. Promises to not use such information to invade Web users' privacy are the only ways in which many Web vendors will keep their customers happy.
3. Many customers want assurances that their names and other information about them will not be sold without their permission.
4. Assurances are only as good as the firms providing them, so privacy software has become available to prevent the unwanted revelation of identity.
5. Privacy software may ultimately become legally required of site operators if consumer concerns about online privacy continue to grow.

G. Online Buyers – who's actually out there spending their money on the Internet?
1. Online buyers differ, but the heaviest users make more than $75,000 per year and live in urban areas.
   a. Evidence indicates that online demographics are changing, moving toward an older and less affluent group.
2. On the other hand, the Internet itself is changing customers. Online marketing reaches people who don't usually watch TV and read magazines. It offers more information than traditional marketing efforts, as well.

H. Online Sellers – the pioneers were book and music vendors, followed by discounters of airline tickets.
1. The most popular online items today are apparel, toys and video games, and consumer electronics.
2. According to a recent study, apparel, prescription drugs, and home products will be the online sales leaders of the future.

V. Interactive Online Marketing Channels – used by manufacturers and marketing intermediaries to offer their products because they provide cheaper, faster, and more efficient alternatives to traditional channels.

    A. Company Web sites
        1. Corporate Web sites are designed to increase firm visibility
        2. Marketing Web sites' goals are to increase purchases by site visitors.

    B. Electronic store fronts and cybermalls
        1. Electronic store fronts are virtual stores where customers can view and order merchandise just like shopping at a bricks-and-mortar outlet.
        2. Electronic storefronts may replace or supplement existing bricks-and-mortar stores.
        3. Firms attempting to operate solely as electronic storefronts have had less than great success.
        4. Cybermalls link as many as 400 electronic storefronts into a virtual shopping mall.

    C. Advertising on other Web sites
        1. Banner ads are strip messages placed in high-visibility areas of frequently-visited Web sites.
        2. Pop-up ads are separate windows that suddenly appear on the screen.
        3. Many online marketers combine online and offline advertising with other forms of interactive promotion.

    D. Online communities
        1. Online forums are Internet discussion groups located on commercial online services. They may appear as electronic bulletin boards, libraries for storing information, or as classified ad directories.
        2. Newsgroups are noncommercial Internet versions of forums.
        3. Online communities are not limited only to consumers, but may also be used by business-to-business marketers.

    E. Other interactive marketing links
        1. Web kiosks are freestanding computers, often located in retail showrooms or shopping centers, that deliver information on demand. Some can even function as virtual storefronts.
        2. Smart cards are plastic cards similar to credit cards embedded with computer chips that store personal and financial information. They are viewed as a possible first step toward electronic currency.
        3. Some traditional direct marketing firms have gone online with virtual coupons and online samples. These require that the computer user download and print the paper certificate needed.
        4. A blog is a Web page that serves as a publicly accessible personal journal for an individual. Blogs can be used as forums for complaint, asking questins, or just plain stating one's opinions.
           a. Blogs can also be used for *stealth marketing* at low cost.

VI. Creating an Effective Web Presence – Involves a process: first, research the market to make sure that any e-commerce venture will cut costs, improve customer satisfaction, and increase revenues. Then appraise the effect of the action on competition to determine that it is positive, determine that profits will be increased, growth accelerated, product time-to-market reduced, customer service improved, and a more positive public perception of the organization created. If all of these are true, go ahead with the e-commerce activity.

A. Building an effective Web site
   1. The focus should be on building relationships through the company's Web presence.
   2. The first step is to define the mission of the site.
   3. Second, the purpose of the site must be identified. Marketers should be clear about how the purpose of the site fits in with the company's overall marketing strategy.
   4. Finally, customer needs and wants must be clearly identified by marketers. They must remember that there are differences between offline and online customers.
   5. Set about satisfying the needs and wants identified above.

B. Managing a Web site – often requires frequent updates, constant attention to content and technical presentation, frequent software updates to take advantage of new technology, and careful examination of site costs and benefits. Even merchandise assortments may need radical alteration to assure success.

C. Measuring the effectiveness of online marketing can be accomplished several ways.
   1. The profitability of the site may be calculated, and if it meets or exceeds the desired level, it may be called successful.
   2. Another way to measure site effectiveness is by measuring the traffic the site draws by using visitor counters simply to count the number of people that access the site.
   3. Slightly more sophisticated is a measure called the click-through rate, the number of people exposed to a banner ad that click on it, linking to the ad's source.
   4. Conversion rates measure the percentage of visitors to a Web site that make purchases from it.
   5. Finally, formal marketing research studies can be done to explore Internet site performance.

Name_____   Instructor_____

Section_____   Date_____

Key Concepts

The purpose of this section is to allow you to determine if you can match key concepts with the definitions of the concepts. It is essential that you know the definitions of the concepts prior to applying the concepts in later exercises in this chapter.

From the list of lettered terms, select the one that best fits each of the numbered statements below. Write the letter of that choice in the space provided.

Key Terms

a. electronic commerce (e-commerce)
b. electronic marketing (e-marketing)
c. digital tools
d. interactive marketing
e. Internet (Net)
f. intranet
g. extranet
h. instant messaging
i. Internet service provider (ISP)
j. Wi-Fi (wireless fidelity)
k. bot

l. electronic signature
m. corporate Web sites
n. marketing Web sites
o. electronic storefront
p. cybermall
q. electronic bulletin board
r. Web kiosk
s. smart card
t. blog
u. click-through rate
v. conversion rate

_____ 1. This new technology "cuts the Internet plug-in cord" by offering the mobile online user wireless Internet access.

_____ 2. E-mail service that allows for the immediate exchange of short messages between online users.

_____ 3. Web sites that seek to build customer good will and supplement other sales channels rather than to sell goods and services.

_____ 4. Organization that provides access to the Internet via a telephone, satellite TV service, or cable TV network.

_____ 5. Worldwide network of interconnected computers that lets anyone with access to a personal computer send and receive images and data anywhere.

_____ 6. Internal corporate network that allows employees within an organization to communicate with each other and gain access to corporate information.

_____ 7. The strategic process of creating, distributing, promoting, and pricing goods and services to a target market over the Internet or through digital tools such as tablet PCs and Bluetooth technology.

_____ 8. Electronic technologies used in e-commerce, such as fax machines, personal digital assistants, and smart phones.

_____ 9. Targeting customers by collecting and analyzing business information, conducting customer transactions, and maintaining online relationships with customers by means of computer networks.

_____ 10. Multipurpose card embedded with computer chips that store personal and financial information such as credit-card data, health records, and driver's license number.

_____ 11. Web sites that often include information about company history, products, locations, and finances.

_____ 12. Small, free-standing computer, often located in a store, that provides consumers with Internet connections to a firm and its goods and services.

_____ 13. Search program that checks hundreds of sites, gathers and assembles information, and brings it back to the sender.

_____ 14. The percentage of people presented with a Web banner advertisement who click on it.

_____ 15. Buyer-seller communications in which the customer controls the amount and type of information received from a marketer through such channels as the Internet, CD-ROMs, interactive toll-free telephone numbers, and virtual reality kiosks.

_____ 16. Electronic approval of a document that has the same status as a written signature.

_____ 17. The percentage of visitors to a Web site who make a purchase.

_____ 18. Secure network accessible through a Web site by external customers or organizations for electronic commerce, providing more information than a public site.

_____ 19. Online store where customers can view and order merchandise much like window shopping at traditional retail establishments.

_____ 20. Group of virtual stores planned, coordinated, and operated as a unit for online shoppers.

_____ 21. Specialized online service that provides information on a specific topic or area of interest.

_____ 22. Web page that serves as a publicly accessible personal journal for individuals and, in more and more instances, for marketers.

Name_____   Instructor_____

Section_____   Date_____

Self-Quiz

You should use these questions to test your understanding of the chapter material. Check your answers against those provided at the end of the chapter.

While these questions cover most of the chapter topics, they are not intended to be the same as the test questions your instructor may use in an examination. A good understanding of all aspects of the course material is essential to good performance on any examination.

True/False

Write "T" for True and "F" for False for each of the following statements.

_____ 1.   Ordering a computer mainboard from the "Computer Components 'R' Us" Web site with overnight delivery by Federal Express is an example of electronic marketing.

_____ 2.   The Internet improves the geographic protection of local businesses by demonstrating that they can usually meet or beat the terms of sale offered by distant vendors.

_____ 3.   Creating products to meet customer specifications B even to the extent of starting production after an order has been placed B is an example of interactive marketing.

_____ 4.   Through his or her control of the amount and type of information received from a marketer, the customer using interactive marketing normally experiences a better result.

_____ 5.   What we now know as the World-Wide Web was originally developed as an internal document-management system at the European Center for Nuclear Research in Geneva, Switzerland.

_____ 6.   The primary function of the World Wide Web in the early twenty-first century is provision of entertainment to its users.

_____ 7.   At present, over 300 million people are users of the World-Wide Web.

_____ 8.   Most of the users of Internet Service Providers such as MSN and Earthlink still use dial-up connections.

_____ 9.   To be successful, Web sites must provide platforms for communication between organizations and their customers and suppliers.

_____10.   Business-to-business online marketing has come to have even more glitz and glamour than the business-to-consumer segment.

_____ 11.   It is expected that business-to-business e-commerce will amount to $1.3 trillion in 2007, or almost ten percent of total worldwide business sales.

_____ 12. A business-to-business site on the Web needs to be listed with the major search engines and with Internet yellow pages such as Verizon's SuperPages.com to position itself so corporate buyers notice it, though even that may not be enough.

_____ 13. Successful online business-to-business marketers serve their customers by thinking like a vendor.

_____ 14. Price is seldom a major benefit one receives from shopping on the Web because prices there tend to be higher than store prices to offset the convenience of using the Web.

_____ 15. The emphasis of consumer-oriented e-commerce has turned to one-to-one marketing, creating loyal customers who are likely to make repeat purchases.

_____ 16. Brand loyalty, a part of many off-line relationships, does not transfer well to online sites.

_____ 17. Though customer service is the key to building strong customer relationships, improvements are needed in online consumer marketing — it now takes online merchants an average of 25 hours to send personalized responses to e-mail questions.

_____ 18. Web-based marketplaces that cater to a specific industry's needs in B2B e-commerce are called electronic exchanges.

_____ 19. Asian consumers are more familiar and comfortable with catalog and telephone buying than are shoppers in North America, thus are willing to accept online shopping as safe and secure.

_____ 20. Issues of infrastructure, economy, legal restrictions, and politics all come into play when marketers try to enter international markets.

_____ 21. The good thing about cookies and spyware is that they always give themselves away when they download to a person's PC.

_____ 22. Blogging, the creation of hybrid diary/guide Web sites, has recently become a new vehicle of "stealth marketing" with Dr. Pepper's use of the technique to promote its new flavored milk drink, Raging Cow.

_____ 23. Americans of Asian and Pacific Island origin are the most likely racial groups to use the Internet, while African-Americans and Hispanics are only one-third as likely to do so.

_____ 24. Smart cards, pioneered in the United States, have finally found their way to Europe and Asia, where they are slowly catching on.

_____ 25. Marketing Web sites seldom attempt to increase purchase by site visitors, but attempt to build customer good will and assist channel members in their marketing efforts.

Multiple Choice

Circle the letter of the phrase or sentence that best completes the sentence or answers the question.

26 The strategic process of creating, distributing, promoting, and pricing goods and services to a target market over the Internet or by using other digital tools is called
  a. electronic marketing.
  b. electronic commerce.
  c. digital business.
  d. virtual commerce.
  e. an out-of-body experience.

27. The fact that customers on the Internet may negotiate prices online in much the same way as customers do at a local flea market or car dealership is an example of
  a. integrated marketing communications.
  b. what is called "right-time marketing."
  c. interactive marketing.
  d. personalization of transactions.
  e. global reach.

28. The Internet is best defined as
  a. an organization of computer users who use telephone lines to communicate with each other.
  b. a government-run database interfacing the nation's personal computers by satellite link.
  c. a conspiracy of hackers and computer geeks to obtain information from other computer users.
  d. an entirely commercial endeavor designed to change the shape of the market place.
  e. a worldwide network of interconnected computers that lets anyone with a personal computer send and receive images and data anywhere.

29. The primary function of the World-Wide Web is
  a. as a communications device providing the capacity to send electronic mail to anyone with a known address.
  b. as a source of information about an enormously broad range of subjects.
  c. for purposes of entertainment including games, movies, and a wealth of other attractions.
  d. e-commerce for businesses ranging from multinational corporations to local entrepreneurships.
  e. military, providing a secure means for the armed forces of allied nations to communicate with each other.

30. Corporate networks that allow communication between a firm and selected suppliers, customers, and business partners outside the firm are called
  a. extranets.
  b. internets.
  c. intranets.
  d. outernets.
  e. undernets.

31. Building an effective Web site begins with
    a. designing state-of-the-art graphics and cool copy to attract attention.
    b. satisfying customer needs and wants through clear site design.
    c. establishing a mission for the site.
    d. offering products at hard-to-believe prices in a glitzy, flashy format.
    e. identifying the purpose of the site.

32. The basic pathway for accessing the Internet (going online) is
    a. through a Web gate accessed by cursor link.
    b. by linking with a government agency such as NASA or the CIA.
    c. through satellite feed direct to an off-planet source.
    d. by using an Internet Service Provider like Earthlink or the Microsoft Network.
    e. on your own through a domain established for the purpose.

33. Durable goods manufacturers are the leading category of business-to-business vendors on the Internet, followed by
    a. professionals such as attorneys and accountants offering their services on the Net.
    b. wholesalers of business products such as office supplies, electronic goods, and scientific equipment.
    c. makers of commercial small appliances like clothing irons, hair dryers, and similar items.
    d. computer software companies.
    e. firms offering personal and business security.

34. Many business writers have begun to label e-commerce
    a. edgy commerce because it makes competitors nervous when they see what each of them is doing to assure themselves a place on the Net.
    b. environmental commerce because it has to be examined from an environmental point of view.
    c. elementary commerce because of its resemblance to chemical processes.
    d. extensive commerce because of its rapid rate of growth and the involvement of so many buyers and sellers by comparison with other markets.
    e. easy commerce because online marketing tools allow the direct interchange of information such as order fulfillment and customers service in seamless fashion without the intervention of intermediaries.

35. In a recent survey cited in your textbook, the perceived benefits for online shoppers were led by
    a. To save money.
    b. Because it is fun.
    c. Better selection of merchandise available.
    d. For reasons of convenience.
    e. To avoid crowds and pesky salespeople.

36. The fact that cybershoppers can order goods and services from around the world any hour of the day or night is illustrative of cybershopping's
    a. privacy and security in use.
    b. convenience.
    c. demonstrative capacity.
    d. warmth and friendliness.
    e. ease of navigation.

37. An example of effective personalization on the Web would be
    a. having to search through several categories of merchandise on a Web vendor's site to reach the kinds of items you sought.
    b. finding an impressive array of size and color choices from a number of name brand manufacturers of fashion merchandise on a site selling casual clothing.
    c. having to use a password to charge a purchase to your credit card at a Web vendor's site.
    d. being welcomed back to a vendor's site by name and offered a choice of several new CDs by your favorite artists.
    e. being dumped from a Web vendor's site because it was too busy to handle your queries.

38. For large and small businesses alike, using the Web as a consumer market place can
    a. build strong relationships with customers.
    b. reduce both start up and operating costs.
    c. increase operational efficiency.
    d. level the playing field against discrimination.
    e. do all of the above.

39. Cultural differences can prove to be a barrier that hampers online marketing abroad, especially
    a. if the local government legislates against use of the Internet.
    b. in Australia, where on the entire continent only 12 percent of all homes are Internet users.
    c. in nearby Canada, where an abundance of local stores cater to every need and the Internet is seldom used.
    d. in Asia, where language problems and less familiarity with catalog and telephone buying cause reluctance on the part of consumers to buy.
    e. in the United States, where people in general are distrustful of anything foreign.

40. The rapid growth of e-commerce in the United States has not been matched in Europe, in part because of infrastructural differences such as
    a. the governments' tendencies to eavesdrop on the telephone calls placed by their citizens to prevent them from avoiding paying taxes on foreign Internet purchases.
    b. lack of availability of telephone and cable systems compatible with Internet connections.
    c. the custom of charging for even local telephone calls by the minute, making Internet use through dial-up connections very expensive.
    d. language barriers even within countries that made dealing with Web sites a matter of confusion and misunderstanding.
    e. difficulties in using charge cards issued in one country to pay for goods bought from another.

41. Among the steps being taken to address security and privacy concerns on the Internet,
    a. eBay now requires purchasers to pay vendors in full in cash before the goods are shipped.
    b. all Web sites are now required to obtain permission from parents by e-mail or Fax before collecting personal data from children under the age of 13.
    c. online shopping malls are requiring that their customers read explicit policies that make them responsible for the quality of the products they buy.
    d. the Federal Trade Commission requires that all information obtained by commercial Web sites from their customers be published on the Internet.
    e. Amazon.com has stopped accepting credit cards. All payments to them must be made in cash or by a cash-equivalent method.

42. Some estimates place the proportion of e-commerce activity that involves B2B transactions at
    a.   thirty-five percent.
    b.   forty percent.
    c.   fifty percent.
    d.   sixty-five percent.
    e.   eighty percent.

43. Which of the following is NOT something an effective Web presence ordinarily does?
    a.   improves public perception of the organization
    b.   reduces profits
    c.   accelerates company growth
    d.   reduces time-to-market for products
    e.   improves customer service

44. Web-based marketplaces that cater to a specific industry's needs are called
    a.   electronic exchanges.
    b.   e-brokerages.
    c.   online exploratoreums.
    d.   traditional market sites.
    e.   electronic bazaars.

45. Which of the following statements about online buyers in the American consumer market is true?
    a.   There are more than 85 million online buyers.
    b.   On an average day, 11 million Americans buy a product online.
    c.   Around 58 percent of Hispanic American Internet users buy online.
    d.   Men are more likely to shop online than are women.
    e.   small children (under age 6), with their parents' permission, spend an average online of $400 each per year.

46. Online marketing in the United States is more likely to reach people
    a.   who ordinarily do not watch television or read magazines.
    b.   of low income, regardless of where they live.
    c.   who live in rural areas and lack telephone service.
    d.   with lower-than-average educational attainments.
    e.   who are currently unemployed and did not graduate from college.

47. The most popular class of products purchased by consumers on the Internet is
    a.   consumer electronics.
    b.   toys and video games.
    c.   computer software.
    d.   concert and event tickets.
    e.   apparel.

48. A small, strip message placed in a high-visibility area of a frequently-visited Web site is a
    a.   headline.
    b.   footnote.
    c.   banner ad.
    d.   capstone.
    e.   sidebar.

49. A Web page that serves as a publicly accessible personal journal for an individual is a
    a. budgerigar.
    b. journaux de jour.
    c. valpack.
    d. blog (Web log)
    e. chat room.

50. A smart card is a
    a. credit card that refuses to be charged for a foolish or extravagant purchase.
    b. plastic card similar to a credit card containing a microchip storing personal and financial information.
    c. common sight in the U.S. but a fairly rare item in Europe as yet.
    d. credit card which will mail itself home if lost or stolen.
    e. credit card that can only be scanned when it is in the possession of its authorized owner.

Name_____   Instructor_____

Section_____   Date_____

Applying Marketing Concepts

The Web sites which may be named and discussed in the following exercises do not, to the best of our knowledge, exist, and if they do, they have nothing whatsoever to do with any of the fictitious people who may be named in association with them.

Treasure Hunt Antiques of Natchez, Mississippi, is a hundred and fifty year-old establishment that specializes in antebellum (which means "pre-war," and we KNOW which war they mean) household furnishings. But just because they're old doesn't mean they're slow. The Tarleton family, Reggie, Muffy, and their daughter (wait for it!) Buffy, owners of Treasure Hunt, know well the tastes of antique buyers and have developed a Web operation they think is as good as anything out there.

Every employee of the firm is computer-literate as well as being "antique-literate." They are all interconnected through their computers and can send and receive messages among themselves and use the company's inventory database to match what they have on hand to the desires of potential customers. Beyond that, employees can send and respond to queries from the other members of the antiqueNet, a computer-based linkage of a number of firms specializing in the same general categories of antiques as Treasure Hunt.

Treasure Hunt accesses the Internet through DeepSouth.net, a firm that provides this service to several hundred thousand subscribers in southern Mississippi, southwest Alabama, and part of Louisiana. They are also listed as antique dealers with Google, Yahoo!, and HotBot.

Just recently, the company began to solicit people who access the Treasure Hunt Web site for information about their interests and preferences, even their tastes in antebellum antiques. This information is entered into a database and if that person ever accesses the Treasure Hunt Web site again, they are greeted with a reference to an antique presently in stock that will probably appeal to them.

The Tarletons have been amazed at the number and diversity of the people who have visited the Treasure Hunt Web site. "Yes, indeed," says Buffy Tarleton, daughter of the present owner and shipping manager of the firm, "we have people from all over the world signing in all the time – and buying stuff to be shipped to the most outlandish locations."

1. The interconnection of Treasure Hunt employees through their computers and their access to the inventory database is provided by an
   a. internet.
   b. infranet.
   c. intranet.
   d. extranet.
   e. overbite.

2. The "antiquenet" is an example of an
   a. overnet.
   b. undernet.
   c. net ball.
   d. extranet.
   e. venturenet.

3. DeepSouth.net is Treasure Hunt's credit department.
   b. Internet service provider (ISP).
   c. search base.
   d. security service.
   e. engine driver.

4. Being listed with Google, Yahoo!, and HotBot is important to Treasure Hunt because
   a. it vastly increases the prestige of the firm to be listed with these rating services.
   b. being listed on these search engines means that Treasure Hunt's name will automatically be forwarded to the computer of anyone who types in that they are searching for an "antique dealer."
   c. it's the thing to do on the Internet these days.
   d. it is the only way that Treasure Hunt can gain access to the lists of potential customers these services have compiled in the several years that they have been in business.
   e. it's the only way Treasure Hunt will get invited to the Google, Yahoo!, and HotBot antique dealers' Christmas parties every year.

5. Treasure Hunt's solicitation of its potential customers for information about their tastes in antiques is most likely part of an attempt to
   a. lower prices industry-wide by getting as many people as possible interested in different kinds of antiques.
   b. compile a mailing list of likely prospects to be sold to other antique dealers.
   c. reduce costs by limiting people's access to only those kinds of antiques they really like.
   d. personalize Treasure Hunt's relationship with potential and existing customers by catering to them as individuals.
   e. find and develop a new pool of vendors to sell antebellum antiques to Treasure Hunt.

6. Buffy's comments about the customers who have bought from Treasure Hunt's Web site are
   a. evidence of the global reach of electronic commerce.
   b. very unusual; most internet business is done within a very few miles of the Web site's home.
   c. well stated, but obviously quite confused; you can't ship antiques out of the country.
   d. strongly worded indications of the interactive nature of the e-commerce experience.
   e. fairly irrelevant; they're typical of most business today.

7. Bonus question for web surfers! The domain suffix Treasure Hunt's Web site is most likely to bear is
   a. .gov
   b. .edu
   c. .com
   d. .org
   e. .web

Odile Buchet is an Internet freak, a true Webhead and certified geek. Everything she buys, she buys on the net. She even has custom software to search for the lowest price on the best products in their classes on the Internet. Odile is such a well-known figure to many of the sites she visits that they welcome her by name and tantalize her with offers of her favorite products. Despite this, Odile spends only twenty to thirty minutes a day shopping on the Net.

She spends almost four hours a day taking distance learning classes from a university almost a thousand miles away, and another hour-and-a-half surfing the Web looking for needed data and preparing homework assignments to be e-mailed to her professors. Odile will receive her bachelor's degree in electrical engineering in December from a university she's never seen.

On an average day, Odile will spend between an hour and two hours at MusicCity.com or possibly at the French music site **fnac.com.fr**, listening to concerts by her favorite new wave groups. She will occasionally log on to a game site and play for a while. Sometimes she even takes a plunge and pays for the privilege of playing on the Web.

But Odile's day is not over. At least twice a day she reads her e-mail, much of which comes to her through his own Web site from firms who wish to buy one of her unique software packages or even to have her design a software array just for them. She always responds promptly, perhaps confirming the order and stating payment terms or providing an initial estimate of the cost of any special requests for programming a firm may have. Odile, it appears, is well known in the business world as Skylark Software. She can be found listed as a "serious software developer and publisher" on every search engine and in the Internet Yellow Pages and her Web site features a broad array of testimonials and references from satisfied clients.

But wait. Lest ye think that Odile never leaves her home or interacts with other real human beings, be advised that it is not so. A lovely young woman, she has a large group of friends and a fiancé with whom she goes out at least three times a week. How can she do so much? It's simple. The time she saves using the Internet efficiently gives her an abundance of free time to enjoy life.

8. The custom software Odile uses to get the best deal on the things she wants to buy is a
    a. dot. It seems that everything on the Internet has a dot in it.
    b. bot. This is one of the newest e-commerce tools.
    c. portal. It opens the doors to e-buying.
    d. gnome. That's what these little exploratory programs are called.
    e. lot. This stands for what the program can do.

9. The fact that Odile only spends twenty to thirty minutes a day doing her shopping is evidence of the net's
    a. convenience. When she's done, he's done.
    b. entertainment value. Odile has to seek other stimulation
    c. price structure. She obviously can't afford to buy much.
    d. complexity. Odile probably becomes confused and quits.
    e. dedication to businesses rather than consumers. She can't find anything to buy.

10. Odile's time spent "in class" and researching demonstrate this function of the Internet. The function is
    a. entertainment.
    b. providing information.
    c. e-commerce.
    d. government business.
    e. travel planning.

11. Odile's time spent at MusicCity.com and at the FNAC online is time spent using the Internet for
    a. entertainment.
    b. providing information.
    c. e-commerce.
    d. government business.
    e. travel planning.

12. Odile's Web site is devoted to
    a. consumer-to-consumer commerce.
    b. business-to-consumer commerce.
    c. consumer-to-business commerce.
    d. business-to-business commerce.
    e. idle gossip and flighty conversation.

13. That Odile's software is so well-known testifies not only to its quality but to
    a. Odile's luck in getting so many people to use it.
    b. the inaccessibility of good software so that people will seek her out.
    c. Odile's success in distinguishing her firm and its products from competitors and theirs.
    d. the power of word of mouth in getting the word out about such products.
    e. Odile's scintillant personality and firm cocktail-party handshake.

Name _____   Instructor_____

Section _____   Date_____

Surfing the Net

Keeping in mind that addresses change and what's on the Web now may have changed by the time you read this, let's take a look at some of the places on the Net that reflect aspects of global marketing. We are not endorsing or recommending any of these sources, merely making note of the information and services that people have elected to offer through the Internet.

Well, considering that your textbook is just loaded with Internet addresses that lead to interesting Web sites about the Internet and the World Wide Web itself, we were hard put to go that one better – but we tried. Cranking up our array of search engines – you could hear them a block away, the noise was so deafening – we looked for obscure but significant sites and believe we've found some

In the business-to-business sphere, we were surprised (we don't know why) to discover that the global reach of the Internet evident. Looking at the search string "electrical wholesalers," we suddenly found ourselves presented with sites for firms located in France – **http://www.sonepar.com** – Sonepar Distribution, a firm with a world-wide presence, including subsidiaries in Canada and the United States; on a smaller scale, there was a site for an Irish firm – **http://www.schneiderelectric.ie/** and even one in Iceland – **http://www.volti.is/indexenska.htm** – but of course you have to read Icelandic to do much with that one. (Seriously, there is an English-language version of the site: **http://www.volti.is/english_index.htm**. Finally, we encountered old faithful, the firm originally founded as the supply unit for the Bell System to its outside customers, the American Gray and Barton Electric Company at **http://www.graybar.com**.

Then we went railroading, and found some biggies, among them French ALSTOM, which, in addition to producing heavy rolling stock for the TGV train (Tres Grande Vitesse – Very High Speed), is also involved in the development of the Supertrain, builds ships at its Chantiers de l'Atlantique and ALSTOM Leroux Naval locations, and seemingly has a finger in every transportation pie around. They're at **http://www.alstom.com**. We also discovered a German company, Contec Groupe, which specializes in switching apparatus, at **http://www.contecgroupe.com**. In the United States, the locomotive industry is dominated by two firms: The Electromotive Division of General Motors, Inc., and General Electric Corporation. They can be found, respectively, at **http://www.gmemd.com/en/home/locomotive** and **http://www.getransportation.com/homepage**. Sadly, the classic firms of the steam age are no longer with us. Firms like Baldwin, Lima, and Hamilton, even ALCO (American Locomotive Company) have disappeared, victims of technology.

In the retail sphere, it really wasn't hard to find a few unusual, yet interesting locations simply by searching the string "major retailers." We discovered a site at **http://www1.bottomdollar.com** that acts like a bot, reporting the lowest prices from a significant array of vendors on all sorts of home entertainment and other electronics. A similar site is **http://www.overstock.com**, but we did notice that the products offered there appeared to be a little "out of date." We also stumbled on the site of a firm called MVP, owned by John Elway, Michael Jordan, and Wayne Gretsky, which, as you might suspect, features an incredible assortment of sporting goods. Try **http://www.mvp.com** for this one. We also discovered Coconuts Music and Movies, at **http://www.coconuts.com**, that features new and used Cds and claims to have over 500,000 items on hand at really low prices. And finally, there's Zale's, the jewelry store, except that it's also Gordon's, Bailey, Banks, and Biddle, and in Canada, People's Jewelry. The corporate Web site, where you can find out all about this stuff, is at **http://www.zalecorp.com**.

Finally, we looked at some alternative hardware – aircraft, and we found some interesting things. Northrop Grumman still lives at Grumman's old Web site, **http://www.grumman.com**, but when one invokes **http://www.mdc.com**, the McDonnell-Douglas site, we discover that we have actually accessed Boeing's Web site. (Boeing absorbed McDonnell- Douglas several years ago, but apparently recognize the importance of preserving at least the recognition effect of this fine old company.) Want to go to Boeing direct? I'll let you figure that one out for yourself. And don't forget Lockheed-Martin. This firm contains the history of two of America's oldest aircraft companies. See **http://www.lockheedmartin.com**.

Sites verified August 15, 2004

Part 1
Creating a Marketing Plan: A Continuing Exercise

Introduction

At this location in each section of this Study Guide, you will be presented with new facts in a continuing narrative designed to give you experience in the gathering of information, relating of abilities to opportunities, and matching of the needs of the marketplace to the desire for success of three young entrepreneurs. You will create for this threesome a marketing plan that will pave their way, if carefully followed, to the realization of their dreams.

The narrative will outline the abilities, aspirations, and strengths of our dynamic trio as well as their shortcomings. You will be given some information about conditions in the real world, but it is expected that you will have sufficient motivation to go beyond what is given, especially when it is presented as an opinion of one of the participants. At the end of each of the narrative parts, questions will be posed to help you stay on the right track. Before beginning this exercise and as you are presented with new facts at the end of each section of this book, you should review the appendix to Chapter 2, "Creating an Effective Marketing Plan," which can be found in *Contemporary Marketing*. The information which you will be given in any one section of this exercise will not necessarily follow the same order as the outline of the marketing plan in your textbook, but will be designed to help you complete a particular section of the plan. By the time you have completed all of the parts of "Creating a Marketing Plan" you will have a document which should serve the needs of the three young people for whom you have prepared it and which will contain all of the essential information required for the entry into the marketplace of their marketing mix.

Meeting the Cast

Mel Sandoval and Sandy St. Etienne were cousins, and with their friend Suzette O'Malley were considering their future. The three had known each other since childhood, but had not thought that their careers might bring them together until recently. After graduating together from Cal Poly, where Mel had majored in electrical engineering and Sandy in Industrial Management (specializing in communications applications), the two young men had decided to attend the Electrotechnical Development Corporation's NeoProducts Institute in Chicago to become more familiar with the hands-on side of digital wireless telephony and its application in business and in the home. They felt that their undergraduate education had given them an excellent preparation for dealing with the technology, but wanted to know more about how people interacted with the "intelligent machines" of the twenty-first century. Their plan was to use this extra information to get jobs at some communications company where Mel could design new circuits which would enhance the usefulness of digital wireless telephony and Sandy could work with software and its applications to make the equipment more "user friendly."

Imagine their surprise when, on reporting with the new class to the Institute, they met their life-long friend, Suzette. She had recently graduated with a degree in Business Administration from the University of Western New Mexico and was attending the Institute because her family used a large number of wireless communications units (digital wireless phones and the more sophisticated mobile personal radios) in the operation of their wholesale automobile parts distribution business and all of the family members had attended the Institute to learn the details of modern communication for use by the firm. Suzette had not yet made a commitment to enter the family firm, and was not being pressured to do so, but her mother had pointed out to her that the information she would receive at the Institute certainly wouldn't hurt her job prospects anywhere, and should she ever decide to join the family firm she would have to attend the Institute, anyway. Looking at the experience as an extension of her college training, Suzette enthusiastically decided to go.

The three old friends quickly renewed their acquaintance, and soon recognized that among themselves they possessed a unique combination of talents and interests that might well be put to good use. Mel and Sandy had a real desire to improve communications itself, Sandy through improvements in software systems and Mel through improvements in the available hardware. Suzette, as it turned out really had little interest in distributing spark plugs and distributor caps, and wanted to do something on her own, something interesting, different, and challenging.

All three of the friends did well at the Institute, mastering the details of current thinking on circuit design, software development, and communication system applications with reasonable facility. Needless to say, each was a bit stronger than the others in his or her own specialty. Mel whizzed through the circuit design part of the course, helping the others when they found themselves in difficulty. Sandy found the software logic, even the newest and most esoteric systems, a breeze, and Suzette thrived on systems applications, particularly on applications where economy of configuration was important. Soon the course was over, and all of them received the diploma that certified them to be graduates of the Neoproducts Institute.

Now they were sitting around a table in a small neighborhood restaurant they had all come to know and enjoy, relaxing over a friendly repast of healthy cheese fries with gravy and beast-burgers and discussing their plans for the future. None of them really wanted to break up the set, as they had come to think of themselves, and soon the conversation turned to the possibility of the three starting their own company in a communications-related field. Each felt that he or she could raise enough money to support the developmental cost of one-third of a firm in some aspect of the communications industry.

Questions and Instructions:

There are no questions for this part. Read the information, which appears above two or three times and try and absorb the nature of the strengths and weaknesses of each of the three partners in this venture, whatever its nature turns out to be. After you have completed the material in Part 2 of your text, the development of the marketing plan for Sumesa Enterprises will begin in earnest. (Sumesa, of course, is the first two letters of Suzette and Mel and Sandy strung together.)

Guidelines for Marketing Plan Construction:

Your textbook contains general guidelines on the construction of Business and Marketing Plans in Appendix A. (Page A-1 et seq.) To facilitate the construction of the parts of this exercise, I have included immediately following an outline you can refer to for specific components such a plan should contain.

Components of the Marketing Plan

I.   Situation Analysis: Where are we now?

   A. Historical Background
      1. Nature of the firm, sales and profit history, and current situation
   B. Consumer Analysis
      1. Who are the customers this firm is attempting to serve?

      2. What segments exist?
      3. How many customers are there?
      4. How much do they buy and why?

   C. Competitive Analysis
      1. Given the nature of the markets – size, characteristics, competitive activities, and strategies – what marketing opportunities exist for the firm?

II. Marketing Objectives: Where do we want to go?

   A. Sales Objectives
      1. What level of sales volume can we achieve during the next year? The next five years?

   B. Profit Objectives
      1. Given the firm's sales level and cost structure, what level of profits should it achieve?

   C. Customer Objectives
      1. How will we serve our market customers?
      2. What do we want present and potential customers to think about the firm?

III. Strategy: How can we get there?

   A. Product Strategy
      1. What goods and services should we offer to meet customers' needs?
      2. What is their exact nature?

   B. Pricing Strategy
      1. What level of prices should be used?
      2. What specific prices and price concessions are appropriate?

   C. Distribution Strategy
      1. What channels will be used in distributing the product offerings?
      2. What physical distribution facilities are needed?
      3. Where should they be located?
      4. What should be their major characteristics?

   D. Promotional Strategy
      1. What mix of personal selling, advertising, and sales promotional activities is needed?
      2. How much should be spent using what themes and what media?

   E. Financial Strategy
      1. What will be the financial impact of this plan on a one-year pro forma (projected) income statement?
      2. How does projected income compare with expected revenue if we do not implement the plan?

Part 2
Understanding Buyers and Markets

A key consideration in the design of marketing mixes is the behavior of customers. Customers include both consumers who buy goods and services for their own use and organizational buyers who purchase business products.

The acts of consumers as they obtain and use products and services depend on both personal and interpersonal influences. Culture (the values, beliefs, preferences, and tastes handed down from generation to generation), social influences (the Asch phenomenon, reference groups, social classes, and opinion leadership), and the family are important interpersonal determinants of consumer behavior. Cultural influences are particularly important for international marketers because there are so many different cultures on the face of the earth. In the domestic market, understanding subcultures is necessary. In the U.S., the three largest and most rapidly growing subcultures are Hispanics, African-Americans, and Asians.

Important personal determinants of consumer behavior are needs, motives, perception, attitudes, learning, and the self-concept. Consumers do not act until they realize they have a need. Motivation depends on which needs have already been satisfied, as is developed in Maslow's hierarchy, and the consumer's perception of those stimuli which have passed through perceptual screens. Attitudes are enduring evaluations, emotional feelings, or action tendencies to an attitude object. Marketers often seek to change attitudes through altering their affective, behavioral, or cognitive components. Learning is the result of experience, while the self-concept is a person's multifaceted picture of himself or herself. The consumer decision process involves problem or opportunity recognition, search, evaluation of alternatives, the purchase decision and purchase act, and post-purchase evaluation The amount of time and effort spent on consumer decision making varies for the three categories of (1) routinized response behavior, (2) limited problem solving, and (3) extended problem solving.

The business market is made up of four components: (1) the commercial market, (2) trade industries (wholesalers and retailers), (3) government organizations, and (4) public and private institutions. The business market is typically segmented demographically, by customer type, by end-use application of bought goods, and/or by purchasing situation. Several characteristics differentiate business markets from consumer markets. These include geographic market concentration, a relatively small number of large buyers, a formal decision-making process, and the nature of the relationships between buyers and sellers. A unique classifying system -- the - new North American Industrial Classification System (NAICS) – is simplifying market evaluation in the NAFTA countries. Global sourcing means that companies purchase needed products from sources all over the world.

Demand in organizations is different from consumer demand due to such influences as derived demand, volatile demand, joint demand, and inventory adjustments. Multiple buying influences – environmental, organizational, and interpersonal – are common in organizational purchasing because many individuals may be involved in the purchase of a single item. In addition, the question of whether a firm makes, buys, or leases products may have to be answered. Outsourcing – buying from other firms goods and services formerly produced in-house – has become an issue in the business market. Organizational buying, though similar to consumer decision-making, is an eight-step process. Like consumers, business buying situations also differ, running the gamut from the straight rebuy through modified rebuying to new-task buying in terms of complexity. Understanding the role of the professional buyer and how the buying center concept works is vital to the understanding of business buying behavior. Government, institutional, and international markets each offer their own set of challenges to the marketer seeking to serve them.

The United States is deeply involved in international trade. Such trade accounts for 25 per cent of U.S. GDP, up from 5 percent thirty years ago. American exports have grown at an average rate of ten per cent per year for the last twenty years. Entering the global market involves understanding the differences in the marketing environment as one moves from culture to culture. Failure to do this can mean disaster. The global market is a huge and diverse one, including over 6 billion people who are expected to number 8 billion by 2025.

The international marketing environment includes economic environments, social-cultural environments, technological environments, political-legal environments, and the possibility of trade barriers, all unique to each of the countries the firm might consider as trading partners.

A nation's size, its per-capita income, and its stage of economic development determine its prospects as a host for business expansion. Its infrastructure, monetary stability, cultural and technological capacities, as well as the working of its legal system and view on the desirability of being a trading partner or market for foreign goods all have an effect. One of the more significant influences on a firm's activities in the global sphere is the trend toward multinational economic integration. Multinational economic integration has added a new dimension to the international market. Today, a firm may find that several countries have bonded together to form an economic union for purposes of foreign trade. Treaties such as GATT and NAFTA have altered the relationships among cosignatory nations, and Free Trade Areas and ultimately the European Union – now composed of 25 nations, have created coherent markets where chaos used to reign.

Entry into the world market may be by importing or exporting, contractual agreement, or international direct investment. Entry strategies for marketing may be global, multi-domestic, or multinational. Product and promotional strategies include straight extension, promotional adaptation, product adaptation, dual adaptation, and product invention. Distribution and pricing may have to be modified for different target markets around the globe. American firms must also recognize that the United States is an attractive market for international entrepreneurs.

Chapter 5
Consumer Behavior

Chapter Outline

You may want to use the following outline as a guide in taking notes.

I. Chapter Overview

Customer behavior includes both individual consumers who buy goods and services for their own use and organizational buyers who purchase business products. It is the process by which consumers and business buyers make purchase decisions. These people are affected by a variety of influences on their behavior. Consumer behavior is the process by which ultimate buyers make purchase decisions. Kurt Lewin, a psychologist, has developed two functional relationships to explain buying behavior. The first states that behavior is a function of the interactions of personal influences and pressures exerted by outside environmental forces B = f(P,E). The second carries the analogy into consuming behavior by noting that consumer behavior is a function of the interactions of interpersonal influences such as culture, friends, classmates, coworkers, and relatives and personal factors such as attitudes, learning, and perception B = f(I,P).

II. Interpersonal Determinants of Consumer Behavior include the influence of the individual's culture, social relationships, and family.

A. Cultural influences include the values, beliefs, preferences, and tastes handed down from one generation to the next. Because cultures differ from one country to another, marketing strategies and business practices that work in one country – or even in a particular location in a country – may be offensive or ineffective in another. Ethnocentrism, the tendency to view your own culture as the norm as it relates to consumer behavior, is a concept with which marketers should be familiar.
    1. The core values in culture are those that do not change over time.
        a. The work ethic and desire to accumulate wealth are U.S. core values, as are the importance of family and home life.
        b. Other core values include education, individualism, freedom, youthfulness, activity, humanitarianism, efficiency, and practicality.
        c. Values that do change over time also have their effect, as has familiarity with the Internet on the present generation of teenagers.
    2. An international perspective on cultural influences quickly reveals that the number of cultures is very large, in Europe alone amounting to numerous (four in Switzerland alone) languages and many lifestyles and product preferences. Cultural differences can work to the marketer's advantage, as for example the preference for American brands among young Chinese because they are perceived to be "trendsetting."
    3. Subcultures B cultures within a larger culture – are groups with their own distinct modes of behavior. Subcultures in the United States differ by ethnicity, nationality, age, rural versus urban location, religion, and geographic distribution. America's ethnic mix is changing and by 2050 the changes will require that marketers be very aware of differences in shopping patterns and buying habits. Today, nearly one-third of Hispanic Americans are under age 17, and are both bilingual and bicultural. By 2050, Hispanics will compose 24 percent of the U.S. population. Marketing concepts do not always cross cultural boundaries without changes. America's three largest and fastest-growing subcultures are Hispanics, African-Americans, and Asians.

    a. Hispanic-Americans are not a homogeneous group, coming as they do from a number of countries each with its own culture. Hispanics themselves do not agree on what they are to be called, some preferring the term "Latino" to the conventional "Hispanic." The degree of acculturation of the individual is quite important.

        i. Some Hispanics are largely unacculturated, having been in the U.S. for less than ten years and still speaking Spanish exclusively;

        ii. others are partially unacculturated, the majority having been born in the U.S. and being bilingual;

        iii. a last group is highly acculturated, born and raised in the United States and speaking English but retaining many Hispanic values. The Hispanic population is young, numerous, and concentrated in relatively few states. The typical Hispanic household is larger than the non-Hispanic, so their purchasing tends to be in bulk.

    b. African-American buying power rose 73 percent during the last ten years. African-American families are younger than are white families resulting in different tastes and preferences, and tend to be headed by women. Approaching the African-American market calls for a number of different techniques. Though the African-American community has certain internal similarities, not all African-Americans can be treated or appealed to the same way.

    c. Asian-Americans, like Hispanics, come from many countries with diverse cultures. The two dozen ethnic groups in the subculture possess their own languages, religions, and value systems. Regardless of the group targeted, one should attempt to avoid sounding patronizing when marketing to Asian-Americans. By mid-century, there are expected to be 40 million Asian-Americans.

B. Social influences arise out of group membership. Every consumer belongs to a number of social groups, beginning with the family into which he or she is born. Group membership influences an individual's purchase decisions and behavior in both overt and subtle ways through <u>norms</u>. Differences in group <u>roles</u> and <u>status</u> also affect buying behavior. The Internet allows individuals to form and be influenced by new types of groups.

    1. The Asch phenomenon refers to the theory of social psychologist S. E. Asch that group influences can be strong enough to override even the individual's own beliefs.

    2. Reference groups are groups whose value structures and standards influence a person's behavior.

        a. Group values typically influence purchase decisions when the purchased product is visible and identifiable and stands out as unusual, a brand or product that not everyone owns.

        b. Reference groups may be classed as membership groups, aspirational groups, or dissociative groups based on the individual's relationship or degree of desired relationship with them.

        c. Children are especially vulnerable to reference group influences.

        d. Reference group influences appear in other countries as well as in the U.S.

    3. Social classes in the United States are determined by one's occupation, income, education, family background, and residence location.

        a. Six social classes have been identified, largely through the work of W. Lloyd Warner, a sociologist; in ascending order, they are the lower class, the working class, the lower middle and upper middle classes, and the lower upper and upper upper classes.

      b. Family characteristics have historically been the primary influences on social class.

      c. People in a given social class may aspire to a higher class and exhibit buying behavior common to that class rather than their own.

  4. Opinion leaders are trendsetters who are likely to purchase new products before others in their group and then share their experiences and opinions by word of mouth.

      a. Generalized opinion leaders are rare, people tending to act as opinion setters for goods and services that they know about and are interested in.

      b. Information may flow from the Internet, radio, television, and other mass media to opinion leaders then to others or from the mass media direct to all consumers – or even in multistep fashion from the original source to the general public.

      c. Some opinion leadership is based on the actions of the leaders rather than what they say.

C. Family influences come from two families in the course of one's life – from the family into which one is born and the one that one forms later in life.

  1. The traditional family structure consists of a husband, a wife, and children, but this is changing in the U.S.

  2. Even in the traditional family, the nature of buying decisions for specific products fall into one of four categories.

      a. autonomic – an equal number of decisions are made independently by each of the spouses;

      b. husband-dominant – the husband makes most of the decisions;

      c. wife-dominant – the wife makes most of the decisions

      d. syncratic – both partners jointly make most decisions.

  3. The two-income family has changed the role of women in family purchasing behavior, giving them increased power.

  4. The roles of men in family purchasing has also changed and become more "domestic."

  5. Shifting family roles have created new markets for time-saving goods and services.

D. Children and teenagers have become more important in family purchasing, especially the teenagers.

  1. These groups represent a market of some 50 million people who influence what their parents buy from cereal to automobiles.

  2. Advertisers use Nickelodeon cable network as a prime advertising outlet for marketers trying to reach parents through their children.

  3. The purchasing power of children is also quite large, with kids between 4 and 12 years old spending $29 billion of their own allowances in a recent year.

III. Personal Determinants of Consumer Behavior – the internalized, personal factors influencing buying decisions

A. Needs and motives are two different things. Needs are imbalances between the consumer's actual and desired states that marketers seek to use to create a sense of urgency that will influence people to attempt to satisfy a need. Motives are inner states that direct a person toward the goal of satisfying a felt need.

  1. Maslow's hierarchy of needs is the result of the efforts of psychologist Abraham H. Maslow to characterize needs and arrange them in a hierarchy to reflect their importance. According to Maslow, a person must at least partially satisfy lower-level needs before attempting to satisfy those of higher order.

      a. Physiological needs are the most basic needs in Maslow's hierarchy and consist of things essential for survival.

      b. Safety needs are the second level of needs and relate to protection from physical harm and avoidance of the unexpected.

      c. Social needs refer to the desire to be accepted by people and groups important to the individual.

      d. Esteem needs are the desire for a sense of accomplishment and achievement, to gain the respect of others, even to exceed the performance of others.

      e. At the top of Maslow's hierarchy are the needs for self-actualization – the desire to reach one's full potential and find fulfillment.

2. Maslow noted that a fulfilled need no longer motivated a person to act, but that the condition was not permanent. One is not hungry immediately after a meal, but will ultimately be hungry again at a later time.

3. The hierarchy is not perfect – some needs, for example, fit more than one level – but it is useful for explaining consumer behavior

B. Perceptions are the meanings that a person attributes to incoming stimuli gathered through the five senses – hearing, sight, smell, taste, and touch. Perceptions are based on two types of factors: stimulus factors that are characteristics of the physical object such as its size, color, weight, and shape; and individual factors, unique characteristics of the individual including not only sensory processes but also experiences with similar inputs and basic motivations and expectations.

1. Perceptual screens are mental filtering processes through which all sensory inputs must pass, and are very important to marketers because of the very large number of promotional messages to which people are exposed every day, so much so that the term "marketing clutter" has been coined to describe the condition.

      a. Marketing clutter has caused consumers to ignore many promotional messages.

      b. Marketers struggle to determine which stimuli evoke responses from consumers in the effort to hold their attention long enough to get them to read an ad..

      c. One way to break through clutter is to run large ads, another involves using color as a contrast to the usual black and white treatments in print ads.

      d. Closure, the tendency for the viewer to perceive a complete picture from incomplete stimuli, also helps to create a message that stands out.

      e. Word-of-mouth messages can effectively break through consumers' perceptual screens.

      f. Virtual reality offers some possibilities as a hard-hitting tool to crack clutter.

2. Subliminal perception is defined as the subconscious receipt of incoming information.

      a. Subliminal advertising is aimed at the subconscious level of awareness to circumvent the audience's perceptual screens.

      b. Though the practice has been condemned as manipulative, it is unlikely that it can induce purchasing except by people already inclined to buy. The reasons for this are

          i. Strong stimulus factors are required to get a prospective customer's attention.

          ii. Only a very short message can be transmitted.

          iii. Individuals vary greatly in their thresholds of consciousness.

3. At present, subliminal communication is in use in self-help tapes.

4. There is little, if any, evidence that subliminal advertising or any other form of subliminal communication has any real effect on individuals.

C. Attitudes are a person's enduring favorable or unfavorable evaluations, emotions, or action tendencies toward some object or data formed over time. Attitudes may be measured using any of a number of scaling devices.
   1. Attitude components include the cognitive, which measures an individual's information and knowledge about an object or concept; the affective, which deals with feelings or emotional reactions; and the behavioral, that involves tendencies to act in a certain way. Taken together, these components form one's overall attitude toward the object or idea.
   2. Changing consumer attitudes is one of the choices marketers must address in the effort to appeal to target markets.
      a. Marketers may attempt to produce consumer attitudes that will motivate purchase of a particular product or
      b. evaluate existing consumer attitudes and then make product features appeal to them.
      c. If an existing product is viewed unfavorably, the seller may choose to redesign it or offer new options.
   3. Modifying attitude components may become necessary if inconsistencies have developed among the three attitude components, most commonly when new information has changed the cognitive or affective components.
      a. Marketers can attempt to modify attitudes by providing evidence of product benefits and correcting misconceptions.
      b. Sometimes new technologies can encourage consumers to change their attitudes.
      c. Marketers may rely on new innovations to help change components of consumer attitudes.

D. Learning refers to immediate or expected changes in consumer behavior as a result of experience. Drive is any strong stimulus that impels action – such as fear, pride, desire for money, thirst, pain avoidance, or rivalry. A response is an individual's reaction to a set of cues and drives. Reinforcement is the reduction in drive that results from a proper response.
   1. Applying learning theory to marketing decisions consists of attempting to develop a desired outcome, such as repeat purchase behavior, gradually over time.
      a. Shaping is the process of applying a series of rewards and reinforcements to permit more complex behavior to evolve over time.
      b. Promotional strategy and the product itself both play a role in the shaping process.
         i. The first step in getting consumers to try the product could be to offer a free sample of it along with a coupon for a substantial reduction on the price of a purchase.
         ii. The second step is to entice the consumer to try the product at little financial risk.
         iii. The third step is to motivate the individual to buy the item again at moderate cost.
         iv. Finally, the consumer will decide whether to buy again at the product's regular price without coupons or discounts.

E. Self-concept theory, which is a person's multifaceted picture of himself or herself, plays a significant role in consumer behavior.
   1. Self-image emerges from an interaction of personal and interpersonal influences that affect buying behavior.

2. The self concept has four components:
   a. The real self is an objective view of the total person.
   b. The self-image is the way a person views him or herself, and may not be objective
   c. The looking-glass self is the way an individual thinks others see him or her, and may also lack objectivity.
   d. The ideal self serves as a personal set of objectives as the image to which the individual aspires.

IV. The Consumer Decision Process is a complete step-by-step process through which people pass in making purchasing decisions. Purchase decisions with high levels of social or economic consequences are *high-involvement purchase decisions*. Routine purchases are *low-involvement decisions*. The consumer decision process has six steps.

A. Problem or opportunity recognition takes place when the consumer becomes aware of a significant discrepancy between the existing situation and a desired situation.

B. Search is the process of gathering information about the attainment of a desired state of affairs, identifying alternative means of problem solution.
   1. Search may cover internal or external sources of information.
   2. Search identifies alternative brands for consideration and possible purchase, those being considered for purchase being called the evoked set.
   3. The range of possible choices is now larger than ever before.
   4. Marketers affect the search process by providing persuasive information about their goods and services in a format useful to consumers.

C. Evaluation of alternatives involves comparing the members of the evoked set identified during the search process for relative effectiveness in problem solution.
   1. The outcome of the evaluation stage is the choice of a brand or product or the decision to renew the search for additional possibilities.
      a. Evaluative criteria – features of the product being considered in choosing among alternatives – must be developed to guide the selection.
      b. Three methods are available to marketers to affect the choice process during this stage – education of consumers about the important attributes of particular product classes, identification of significant evaluative criteria and attempts to convince consumers that a specific brand meets those criteria, and trying to induce consumers to expand their evoked sets to include the products being marketed by that firm.

D. Purchase decision and purchase act eventually take place as a result of the stages that have previously occurred.
   1. First, the consumer decides on the product or service.
   2. Then, the consumer chooses the purchase location.

E. Postpurchase evaluation produces one of two results: satisfaction at the removal of the discrepancy between existing and desired states or dissatisfaction with the purchase.
   1. Consumers may experience some postpurchase anxieties called cognitive dissonance if their knowledge, belief, and attitudes are discrepant concerning their purchase.
   2. Dissonance tends to increase
      a. as the dollar value of the purchase increases,

      b. when the rejected alternatives have desirable features that chosen alternatives do not,

      c. and when the purchase decision has a major effect on the buyer.

F. Classifying consumer problem-solving processes essentially involves placing them into one of three categories

    1. Routinized response behavior occurs when consumers choose a preferred brand or one of a limited group of acceptable brands.

    2. Limited problem solving takes place when the consumer, who has previously set evaluative criteria for a particular kind of purchase, encounters a new, unknown brand.

    3. Extended problem solving results when brands are difficult to categorize or evaluate.

Name_____   Instructor_____

Section_____   Date_____

Key Concepts

The purpose of this section is to allow you to determine if you can match key concepts with the definitions of the concepts. It is essential you know the definitions of the concepts prior to applying the concepts in later exercises in this chapter.

From the list of lettered terms, select the one that best fits each of the numbered statements below. Write the letter of that choice in the space provided.

Key Terms

a. customer behavior
b. consumer behavior
c. culture
d. subculture
e. reference groups
f. opinion leader
g. need
h. motive
i. perception

j. attitudes
k. learning
l. self-concept
m. evoked set
n. evaluative criteria
o. cognitive dissonance
p. routinized response behavior
q. limited problem solving
r. extended problem solving

_____ 1. Number of brands that a consumer actually considers before making a purchase decision.

_____ 2. Buying behavior of individual consumers as well as organizational buyers.

_____ 3. Situations in which the consumer knows the evaluative criteria for a product, but has not employed the criteria to assess a new, unknown brand.

_____ 4. Groups with which individuals identify enough so that the groups' value structures and standards affect their behavior.

_____ 5. Meaning that an individual attributes to an incoming sensory stimulus.

_____ 6. Features that a consumer considers in choosing among alternatives.

_____ 7. Buyer behavior of ultimate consumers.

_____ 8. One's enduring favorable or unfavorable evaluations, emotional feelings, or pro or con action tendencies.

_____ 9. Inner state that directs a person toward the goal of satisfying a felt need.

_____ 10. Situation that results when brands are difficult to categorize or evaluate, and usually involves lengthy external searches.

_____ 11. Values, beliefs, preferences, and tastes that are handed down from generation to generation.

_____ 12. Subgroup of a culture with its own distinctive modes of behavior.

_____ 13. Type of quick consumer problem solving in which the consumer has already set evaluative criteria and identified available options.

_____ 14. Discrepancy between a desired state and the actual state; lack of something useful.

_____ 15. Postpurchase anxiety that results when an imbalance exists among an individual's knowledge, beliefs, and attitudes.

_____ 16. The real self, self-image, looking-glass self, and ideal self; mental conception of one's self.

_____ 17. Individual within a group who serves as an information source for other group members.

_____ 18. Changes in behavior, immediate or expected, that occur as the result of experience.

Name_____   Instructor_____

Section_____   Date_____

Self-Quiz

You should use these objective questions to test your understanding of the chapter material. Check your answers with those provided at the end of the chapter.

While these questions cover most of the chapter topics, they are not intended to be the same as the test questions your instructor may use in an examination. A good understanding of all aspects of course material is essential to good performance on any examination.

True/False

Write "T" for True and "F" for False for each of the following statements.

_____ 1. Cultural values that change over time have no effect on the members of the culture.

_____ 2. The three largest and fastest-growing ethnic subcultures in the United States are Hispanic-Americans, Mormons, and Asians.

_____ 3. Cultural influences can work to a marketer's advantage. The perceived "trendiness" of Western brands among young Chinese gives the brands a significant advantage.

_____ 4. The personal determinants of consumer behavior include attitudes, learning, and perception.

_____ 5. Asian-Americans are a homogeneous group because their origins are a number of different cultures and many retain their own languages, religions, and value systems.

_____ 6. It has been demonstrated, especially in the case of the Hispanic subculture, that the degree of acculturation has little effect on consumer behavior.

_____ 7. The formula B= f(I,P) may be interpreted to mean that the behavior of consumers (B) is a function of the interaction of personal determinants (P), such as attitudes, learning, and perception, and interpersonal determinants (I), like reference groups and culture.

_____ 8. The Asch phenomenon suggests that most consumers tend to adhere in varying degrees to the general expectations of any group they consider important, often without being aware of the motivation.

_____ 9. Consumers may be influenced by groups they belong to, groups they desire to associate with, and by groups with which they do not want to be identified.

_____ 10. Generalized opinion leadership is rare; people tend to act as opinion leaders for specific goods and services based on their knowledge of and interest in those products.

_____ 11. The success of Chinese basketball players in the NBA has created a surge of interest in professional basketball among Asian-Americans because of the superstar status of the Chinese players within that community.

_____ 12. Studies of family decision-making have shown that households with two wage-earners are less likely than others to exhibit joint purchasing decision-making.

_____ 13. Behavior members of a group expect of individuals who hold specific positions within that group are those individuals' roles.

_____ 14. The primary determinants of a person's social class are the person's occupation, income, level of education, family background, and location of the dwelling in which he or she resides.

_____ 15. Some opinion leaders influence purchases by others merely through their own actions, particularly in the case of fashion decisions.

_____ 16. The role of children and teenagers in family purchases has diminished in recent years due to advances in technology that have made it more important for adults to decide what to buy.

_____ 17. Within the household, syncratic decision making occurs when an equal number of decisions is made independently by each partner.

_____ 18. Perceptual screening B the human tendency to perceive an incomplete picture from a complete stimulus B helps marketers to create a message that stands out and breaks through the clutter and junk.

_____ 19. Motives are inner states of tension that direct a person toward the goal of satisfying a felt need by taking action to reduce the tension and return to a condition of equilibrium.

_____ 20. A person who flies "Upper Class" on Virgin Atlantic Airlines so that he or she will be admired and respected by his or her friends is satisfying a need to be _accepted_ by people and groups important to the individual, according to the hierarchy of Abraham Maslow.

_____ 21. The affective component of attitude refers to the individual's information and knowledge about an object or concept.

_____ 22. When a marketer attempts to apply *shaping* to achieve a desired consumer behavior, both promotional strategy and the product itself play a role in the process.

_____ 23. One's self-concept grows only out of the interaction of interpersonal influences that affect one's behavior.

_____ 24. The statement "My friends see me as an outstanding coach and manager," is an example of the component of self-concept known as the ideal self.

_____ 25. The marketing of products such as smoke detectors, insurance, burglar alarms, and safes for valuables appeals to the need for safety characterized by Maslow's hierarchy.

Multiple Choice

Circle the letter of the word or phrase that best completes the sentence or best answers the question.

26. Customer behavior includes
    a. the design of marketing strategies and business practices.
    b. the study of organization theory and practice.
    c. analysis of pricing policies and procedures.
    d. looking at how goods get from the producer to the marketplace..
    e. the way people purchase goods and services for personal use or for use by a business.

27. The typical lifestyle of the U.S. southwest emphasizes casual dress, outdoor entertaining, and active recreation. This is an example of
    a. how climate and weather affects the way people do things.
    b. the effect of genetic predispositions B southwesterners naturally prefer the outdoors.
    c. how a geographic subculture develops its own distinctive mode of behavior.
    d. the result of a lack of education about how things should be done.
    e. the youth of the market in the southwest.

28. Which of the following generalizations about the African-American, Hispanic, and Asian-American subcultures in the U.S. is correct?
    a. There are over 50 million Hispanics now living in the United States.
    b. The African-American population is less conservative in its investments than other groups.
    c. The average Hispanic household is smaller than that of the average non-Hispanic.
    d. Neither African-Americans nor Hispanics tend to be younger than other groups in U.S. society.
    e. The Asian subculture in the United States is marked by its diversity, actually including more than two dozen different ethnic groups.

29. For a reference group to significantly influence a person's buying behavior
    a. the person must belong to the group.
    b. the group must be composed of opinion leaders.
    c. the product purchased must be in common use; it must not be conspicuous or different.
    d. the product purchased must be one that can be seen by others.
    e. the person has to have daily physical or electronic contact with the group.

30. When they decide to purchase a product that's new to them, consumers
    a. usually rely solely on advertising to provide them with significant information.
    b. often rely for information on opinion leaders who share their experiences and opinions by word of mouth.
    c. seek out professional experts on the product to get the most reliable information about what's current.
    d. probably buy a specialized shopper's guide and read every product review.
    e. put it off for a while, knowing that as time goes along, they'll become more knowledge-able about the product and can make a better decision.

31. Self-help cassette tapes which feature relaxing music or the sound of the ocean audible at a conscious level and, at a level imperceptible to the ear, messages such as "Quit smoking," or "Work smarter, not harder," use
    a. perceptual screening to keep out the lower-level messages; the ocean sounds, however, are very nice.
    b. our need, according to Maslow, for self-actualization to cause us to take some desired action.
    c. selective perception as a cue which allows us to choose to listen to the music or the lower-level message.
    d. the concept of subliminal perception to impress the desired message on the listener's subconscious; such messages, however, have little real effect
    e. the Asch effect as a basis for their operation.

32. Learning, from a marketing point of view, is
    a. immediate or expected changes in consumer behavior which come about as the result of experience.
    b. the individual's market reaction to motives, perceptions, actions, and drives.
    c. any object in the environment that determines the nature of the response to a drive.
    d. the reduction in drive that results from an appropriate response to it.
    e. the gradual, cumulative intellectual process by which consumer decisions change over time.

33. Which of the following is a correct description of a specific need?
    a. safety need – enrollment in an investment program to provide for your retirement.
    b. social need – joining an exclusive club to achieve recognition and respect
    c. self-actualization need – taking a sea cruise to be with your friends
    d. physiological need – enrolling in an adult education class to develop unrealized potential
    e. esteem need – Enrolling in a local health club to increase personal longevity

34. Which of the following is a good way to ensure that customers will receive an advertising message?
    a. Decrease the size of ads in newspapers and magazines – increase their "boutique" nature.
    b. Use black and white rather than full-color in newspaper ads.
    c. use the principle of closure, filling some part of a word with a different object to break through perceptual screens.
    d. Make the presentation less intense – avoid the use of virtual reality devices.
    e. Do everything you can to circumvent word-of-mouth promotion – it never helps.

35. Which of the following is an example of a comment reflecting the cognitive component of attitude?
    a. "I just LOVE going to Steak DelRio to buy take-out. It always smells SO good!"
    b. "I intend to buy a new red BMW when I get my next promotion."
    c. "Light blue is my favorite color."
    d. "It must be a good movie – the stars are my favorites."
    e. "The best food value for the money is at Rouse's Supermarkets."

36. Ariadne Nusselmeyer is distressed. She has heard that Mitzi Kandelmann is coming to the Fall Dance in a dress that Ariadne wishes she could buy but that's over her budget.   The rivalry between her and Mitzi is turning Ariadne green with envy and frustration. From a learning point of view, the rivalry between the two girls constitutes a
    a. cue.
    b. variole.
    c. response.
    d. reinforcement.
    e. drive

37. "Be all that you can be – in today's Army" is the U.S. Army's appeal to you to make your
    a. real self more like your ideal self.
    b. looking-glass self more like your real self.
    c. utopian self more like your looking-glass self.
    d. ideal self more like your utopian self.
    e. none of the above.

38. Which of the following correctly describes a stage in the consumer decision making process?
    a. postpurchase evaluation – read newspaper ads to find dealers who sell the desired product.
    b. problem or opportunity recognition – discover that any of several brands would be satisfactory for your intended use.
    c. search – buy the desired product at the nearest store.
    d. evaluation of alternatives – create a set of evaluative criteria with which to analyze possible choices
    e. purchase act – discover that you don't have any toothpaste.

39. The marketing implications of cognitive dissonance are that
    a. buyers do not re-evaluate their purchases after they've paid their money.
    b. the postpurchase evaluation process only occurs for products of low dollar value.
    c. it may be desirable for the vendor to provide information that supports the chosen alternative.
    d. dissatisfied customers do not change their behavior in the future.
    e. consumers will be dissatisfied regardless of the quality or price of the product.

40. Which of the following would be a likely factor on which a subculture might be based?
    a. the average age of a group of people – teenagers, for example, versus elderly persons
    b. the type of location in which a group of people live – rural versus urban dwellers
    c. religious affiliation of a group of people – Catholics versus Moslems
    d. the national origin of a group – Guatemalans versus Hondurans
    e. all of the above may be bases for a subculture

41. In the consumer decision process,
    a. the most common cause of problem recognition is usually a change in the consumer's financial status.
    b. subjective impressions of a product should have no role at any level.
    c. the alternatives are narrowed to a single option after the choice of purchase location is made.
    d. the search identifies alternative brands for consideration and possible purchase.
    e. consumers are seldom satisfied even if the purchase exceeds their every expectation.

42. You are attending a party at the home of a friend and are introduced to Lieutenant Commander Cheryl Harrison of the U.S. Coast Guard. From this introduction, you know
    a. Commander Harrison's role within an aspirational group.
    b. Commander Harrison's status within a membership group.
    c. Commander Harrison's social class position in society.
    d. Commander Harrison's role within a dissociative group.
    e. very little about the Commander; certainly none of the above.

43. Being an opinion leader
    a. goes with the territory – A person who is an opinion leader in one situation will probably be an opinion leader in all situations.
    b. is product and service specific. Knowledge of and interest in the item under consideration motivates leadership.
    c. tends to induce one to delay purchasing new products so as not to make mistakes which will be visible to your followers.
    d. is generally a role that goes with high visibility and upper social class status.
    e. means that your followers expect you to take information from them and to use that information to make decisions for them.

44. When the flow of information about products, retail outlets, and ideas passes from the mass media to the general public without the intervention of any opinion leaders,
    a. you have an example of a "Texas two-step" process of communication.
    b. the flow is what is known as "direct."
    c. the process can be characterized as a "hypodermic needle" communications system.
    d. you have a typical "multistep flow of communications."
    e. none of the above is a good description of what's happening.

45. In the consumer decision process, the stage that sometimes results in the choice of a brand or product from the evoked set but which may instead result in a decision to renew the search for alternatives is
    a. the stage of problem or opportunity recognition.
    b. attitude modification – changes that have to take place before action results.
    c. the third step in the decision process – evaluation of alternatives.
    d. the purchase decision – actually committing resources to one's choice .
    e. the search process – identifying alternative means of solving the problem.

46. When an individual joins an elite country club, buys a "prestige" automobile, or takes a course in opera appreciation to know more than others about the subject, he/she is probably seeking to satisfy his/her
    a. social needs.
    b. safety needs.
    c. esteem needs.
    d. self-actualization needs.
    e. physiological needs

47. If a marketer were to seek to shape a consumer's response pattern to the marketer's product by reinforcement, a good program to follow might be
   a. first, to distribute cents off coupons of moderate value; then, if a purchase resulted, to include in the bought goods a higher value coupon.
   b. first, to distribute free samples of the product accompanied by a substantial cents off coupon; if a purchase resulted, to include in the bought goods a coupon of lower value.
   c. first, to advertise the product heavily to the target market; then, if a purchase resulted, offer free merchandise by mail to responding buyers.
   d. first, to redesign the product package; then, promote heavily to a new, untapped market segment.
   e. first, to require of all retailers who wished to stock the product that they buy at least ten cases in their first order; then, insist that stock levels be maintained at least at that level in all subsequent orders.

48. When a group defines the values, attitudes, and behaviors that it deems appropriate for its members, it has set the group's
   a. norms.
   b. status criteria.
   c. role relationships.
   d. proprietary values.
   e. membership.

49. In the problem solving process, the "evoked set" includes
   a. those brands and types of product which the consumer actually considers in making a purchase decision.
   b. those brands and types of product suitable for the desired purpose whether the shopper is aware of them or not.
   c. a list of products and brands provided by a trade organization that might be something the consumer might want.
   d. only one product – the one that's ultimately chosen by the consumer.
   e. a prioritization of the various problems which the consumer seeks to solve.

50. Mel Jacobs has decided it's time to buy a new high resolution TV. To help him in his efforts, he has bought several issues of *Home Electronics* magazine, visited several electronics specialty stores, and carefully read all the sales literature with which they have provided him. He is ready to make his choice from the four models which he believes meet his needs. Mel's problem solving behavior exemplifies
   a. routinized response behavior.
   b. limited problem solving.
   c. extreme problem solving.
   d. extended problem solving.
   e. outrageous problem solving.

Name_____   Instructor_____

Section_____   Date_____

Applying Marketing Concepts

As the plane began to make its descent toward the airport, Angelina Torricelli was glad, in a way, to be coming home. After eight years away, first at college in the northeast, then for graduate study at a large southern university, it was nice to know she'd soon be seeing her parents, grandparents, and great-grand-parents again. To herself she admitted, though, that she was going to have to readjust to her family's way of doing things. During her years away from home, she'd gotten used to doing things pretty much her own way, keeping her own hours, and making decisions for herself. She knew that some of that would have to change if she wanted to stay on good terms with the Torricelli/Mangiapanni clan.

One of the first things that Angelina knew was going to cause difficulty was her intention to have her own apartment near the medical facility where she was to be employed. She was concerned that great-grandfather might want her to live at the Torricelli compound in what was loosely known as "Little Italy," really an enclave of the homes of the earliest Italian settlers almost two centuries old in the middle of Albertville Center, her home town. It would be "just for a while" so that the family could reintroduce her to the local Italian-American community – but might end up being forever. Angelina knew that, even if great-grandfather Alberto Torricelli approved of her decision to live away from the family center, which was unlikely, he was going to want to go with her (possibly even bringing along a number of other members of the family) when she went apartment hunting. And Angelina was concerned that her great-grandfather would try and bargain with the landlord over the rent or as to who would pay the utilities. Angelina had seriously considered taking a position far away from home, being quite concerned about the levels of influence she was sure her family was going to bring to bear on her, but she had always felt comfortable in the Central Valley and, after all, there certainly were a lot more young, traditional Italian-Americans there than there had been in Pottstown or Lake Vista.

Wondering a little bit about how long it would take for her to brush up on her Italian so she could keep up and hold her own in her family's mile-a-minute conversations and then breathing a small sigh, Angelina gathered up her possessions and left the plane.

_____   1.   Part of Angelina's interest in the number of traditional Italian-Americans in the Central Valley may have had something to do with the fact that Italian-Americans like to operate in an environment that preserves their ethnic identity.

2.   Angelina's thoughts about there being "more young Italian-Americans in the Central Valley than in Pottstown or Lake Vista" reflects the idea that
   a.   Italian-Americans who live in the east and south have tended to be assimilated into the general population.
   b.   Angelina thought of herself as an Italian-American and wished to remain related to that culture.
   c.   Angelina didn't really know where to look to find persons of her own ethnic group. Pottstown and Lake Vista have large ethnic Italian populations.
   d.   Angelina was an unusual young woman, having a much higher level of education than is typical of Italian-Americans.

3. Angelina's worries about apartment shopping stemmed from the Italian custom(s)
    a. of shopping as a family group.
    b. of allowing buying decisions to be made by a family elder.
    c. of bargaining over almost any purchase.
    d. all of the above were part of her concern.

4. Angelina realized she'd have to brush up on her Italian because
    a. her family, like many Italian-American families, spoke the language at home and when dealing with other ethnic Italians.
    b. it's always a good idea to have working knowledge of a second language.
    c. she knew that her work would require her to use Italian a lot.
    d. Italian is such a complex language that it must be used constantly or you forget it.

For several years, Kelly Andersen has been a successful amateur tennis player. Ranked seventh in her home state, she had long favored Dunlop racquets. Recently, though, she had been having problems with her old racquet (she was improving and it wasn't) and had decided to invest in a new one. Though she wasn't fabulously wealthy, her standing in the sport meant that she felt that she had to buy the best equipment for this special activity, so she started looking for the best racquet money could buy.

She spoke with friends at her country club about their preferences in racquets and became convinced that she would be more credible on the court and would have a psychological advantage if she switched to the Prince Pro racquet. Kelly's brother, golf pro at a nearby club, opposed the change because he thought the Prince racquets weren't as durable as the Dunlops. Kelly continued to read golf magazines, talk to friends, and check advertisements for the Prince line. Ultimately, she decided to buy the Prince Pro.

Next, she had to decide where to buy her new racquet. The alternatives available were two local dealers and a mail-order firm located only 100 miles away in Capital City. All three of these dealers stocked the racquet Kelly wanted, but the mail-order house's price was substantially lower than the other two outlets. Kelly finally ordered her racquet from the mail-order house, "AllSports Direct."

The following week, Kelly's racquet arrived. She immediately drove over to the country club to show her brother her new acquisition and convince him she'd made the right decision. Unfortunately, on the third serve of their first set, the stringing on Kelly's beautiful new Pro let go, utterly loose. Kelly began to feel doubtful about her purchase. Standing there in front of her brother holding her brand-new – but unstrung – racquet, she would have liked to tell "AllSports Direct" what to do with their racquet – keep it!

_____ 5. Kelly was mainly concerned with her ideal self.

_____ 6. Need arousal occurred in Kelly because of dissatisfaction with the racquet she already owned.

_____ 7. Kelly bought her new racquet because of subliminal perception.

_____ 8. Kelly is probably a member of the lower class.

_____ 9. Kelly's search for alternatives was affected by both personal and interpersonal factors.

10. Kelly's decision to buy the Prince racquet because of her friends' influence helped satisfy which of the following level of needs?
    a. physiological
    b. safety
    c. social
    d. esteem
    e. self-actualization

11. If Maslow's theory of needs is true for Kelly, she has at least partially satisfied which of the following levels of needs.
    a. physiological
    b. safety
    c. social
    d. all of the above.
    e. none of the above.

12. For this purchase, the most important influence on Kelly was
    a. social class.
    b. reference group.
    c. culture.
    d. attitude.
    e. family.

13. Kelly's postpurchase doubt about her purchase is an example of
    a. cognitive dissonance.
    b. subliminal perception.
    c. psychotic imbalance.
    d. psychographic influence.
    e. status loss.

14. Kelly may have learned not to buy Prince racquets because
    a. reinforcement did not take place.
    b. no drive was present.
    c. her response was inconsistent with her drive.
    d. the cues were correct.

Name_____   Instructor_____

Section _____   Date_____

Surfing the Net

Keeping in mind that addresses change and what's on the Web now may have changed by the time you read this, let's take a look at some of the places on the Net that reflect aspects of consumer behavior. We are not endorsing or recommending any of these sources, merely making note of the information and services that people have elected to offer through the Internet.

Tired of letting someone else drive? Learn to fly using information you can get at **http://www.avhome.com/fschools.html**. This site features an extensive list of flight schools of all sorts, from colleges and universities with flight programs to independent local firms that will teach you how to soar in the cerulean blue. That one not good enough for your? Try **http://www.aopa.org/learntofly/startfly/,** a site maintained by the Aircraft Owners' and Pilots' Association. This site offers a lot of advice on the right way to go about learning how to fly. And when you decide you need your very own plane, then **http://www.aircraftdealer.com** is the place to go.

Been ripped off on the Web? There is a site devoted to complaints. It's at **http://www.abuse.net** and lets you complain about any Web site you feel has caused you a problem, whether by misrepresentation or fraud or even just plain bad taste. Need to vent your spleen about someone or something in cyberspace? That's the place to go.

Remember the The Muppet Show? Apparently lots of people do, and there's a Web site devoted to Kermit, Miss Piggy, and all the gang. It's **http://www.muppetcentral.com**, and they provide audio and video clips and even memorabilia of the show. My favorite was the Swedish chef, and he's alive and well on the Net at **http://www.twinpines.nl/chef/English**. Make sure of that last part, or you'll get the text in Dutch because the site's in the Netherlands. Of course, if you speak Dutch just substitute "Nederlandse" for "English." My favorite part is the translator that turns English into "Cheffish." If that weren't enough, you can even access "encheferizer" software that turns normal English into "chefspeak" by going to **http://www.rinkworks.com/dialect.** This site also features translators that will turn normal English into several other dialects, as well.

Love junk food? Get in touch with The Twinkies Project. This hilarious site deals with the results of scientific (?) testing of these little goo-filled cakes. Bring your own milk when you try **http://www.twinkiesproject.com**. It's been around for a while, but some of the stuff they talk about is still hilarious.

Need a car – or better yet, a price on one? There are several sites that offer all sorts of information, deals, financing, and other features related to buying a new car. Try **http://www.carbuyer.com** for all the basics. An alternative is **http://www.autotrader.com.** If that doesn't work for you, try **http://www.carsdirect.com**. If you're interested in buying a used car and want to know how to spot a bad deal, check out **http://www.defect.com**. Or if you want to find out about state laws about automotive "lemons," try **http://autopedia.com/lemon**. They'll even refer you to an attorney if you need one.

Sites verified August 15, 2004.

Chapter 6
Business-to-Business (B2B) Marketing

Chapter Outline

You may want to use the following outline as a guide in taking notes.

I. Chapter Overview

Business-to-Business (or B2B) Marketing deals with organizational purchases of goods and services to support production of other products, to facilitate daily company operations, or for resale.

II. The Nature of the Business market is such that vendors sell fewer standardized products to organizational buyers than to ultimate consumers, customer service is very important to buying organizations, and advertising is much less important than is the case in the consumer market. Personal selling plays a much bigger role in business markets than in consumer markets, distribution channels are shorter, customer relationships tend to last longer, and purchase decisions can involve multiple decision makers. Organizations buy products to fill the needs of their customers. Environmental, organizational, and interpersonal factors are among the influences in B2B markets, as are budgetary, cost, and profit considerations and complex interactions among many people.
Some firms focus entirely on business markets, others sell to both consumer and business markets. Marketing strategies developed in consumer marketing are often appropriate for business use. The B2B market is diverse.

A. Components of the business market: commerce, resellers, government, institutions
  1. The commercial market is the largest segment of the business market including all individuals and firms that acquire products to support, directly or indirectly, the production of other goods and services.
  2. The trade industries include wholesalers and retailers, known as resellers, who purchase finished or near-finished goods for resale either as-is or after minimal processing.
  3. Government organizations include domestic units of government – federal, state, and local – as well as foreign governments.
  4. Public and private institutions comprise the fourth component of the business market.

B. B2B Markets: the Internet Connection
  1. More than 90 percent of all Internet sales are B2B transactions.
  2. The Internet has opened up foreign markets to sellers.

C. Differences in foreign business markets
  1. Differences in government regulations and cultural practices result in differences between the U.S. B2B markets and similar markets in other countries.
  2. Success in foreign markets requires adaptation to local customs and business practices.

III. Segmenting business-to-business markets is somewhat different than segmenting consumer markets because the underlying criteria are different, but the basic principles are the same.

A. Segmenting by demographic characteristics usually means customers are grouped by size, sales revenue, or number of employees

B. Segmentation by customer type can be applied in several ways, using broad categories such as manufacturer, service provider, government agency, not-for-profit organization, or by industry. Customer-based segmentation looks at firms based on the kinds of customers they serve.
   1. The Standard Industry Classification system for almost seventy years defined the industry in which each firm in the United States participated.
   2. The North American Industrial Classification System replaces the SIC system as a result of the implementation of the North American Free Trade Agreement, reconciliating the systems used in Canada, the U.S., and Mexico into a single, somewhat more detailed system.

C. Segmentation by end-use application focuses on the precise way in which a business purchaser will use a product.
   1. Industrial gases provide an excellent example of how specific end-uses determine the nature of the product that will be used.

D. Segmentation by purchasing situation or purchase categories divides business markets centering on how they handle purchasing. Firms generally use more complex purchasing arrangements than do individuals, and are often organized differently. Whether the customer has bought previously or is buying for the first time has an effect on this aspect of segmentation. Firms that use a customer relationship management system can segment on the basis of the stage of the relationship that has been reached.

IV. Characteristics of the B2B Market

A. Geographic market concentration refers to the likelihood for manufacturers to converge in certain regions of the country, often near their sources of raw materials, making these areas excellent targets for business marketers.
   1. Certain industries locate in particular areas to be near their customers. (Traditionally, others have located near their sources of supply).
   2. In the automotive industry, suppliers of components and assemblies frequently build plants near those of their customers.
   3. As Internet-based technology continues to improve, business markets may become less geographically concentrated.

B. Sizes and numbers of buyers – the business market possesses a limited number of buyers.
   1. Many buyers in limited-buyer markets are large organizations.
   2. The federal government, trade associations and business publications provide information on the business market.

C. The business purchase decision process, especially among large corporations, may involve multiple buyers and decision makers at several levels, as well as a more formal and professional process than is the case in the consumer market. Decisions often take longer because of their complexity and competition. Negotiations often take more than one round to come to fruition.

D. Buyer-seller relationships in the business market are more intense and require better communication among the participants than is the case in the consumer market.
  1. A primary goal of B2B relationships is to provide advantages no other vendor can provide.
  2. Close cooperation enables companies to meet buyers' needs for quality products and customer service.

E. Evaluating international business markets poses a particular problem for B2B marketers.
  1. In addition to quantitative data such as the size of the potential market, companies must also weigh its qualitative features.
  2. American firms are finding that China is an excellent market for B2B products, but that the Chinese must see products demonstrated before they will buy.
  3. Global sourcing – contracting to purchase goods and services from suppliers world-wide – can result in substantial cost savings.
  4. Global sourcing requires companies to learn to think differently – some even reorganize their operations

V. Business Market Demand characteristics differ in the B2B markets from those in the consumer market.

A. Derived demand refers to the linkage between consumer demand for a company's output and its purchases of business products.
  1. The demand for microprocessor chips is derived from the consumer demand for the products in which they are used.
  2. Organizational buyers purchase two categories of business products: capital items and expense items.
    a. Capital items are long-lived business assets that must be depreciated over time.
    b. Expense items are items consumed within short periods of time.

B. Volatile demand arises out of derived demand, since the need for assets by businesses grows out of their production for the consumer market. Thus, a small change in consumer demand results in a much larger change in demand for business assets related to the change.

C. Joint demand occurs when the demand for one business product is related to the demand for another business product used in combination with the first item, such as coke and iron ore in the production of steel or power plant structures and turbogenerators in electricity production.

D. Inelastic demand means that demand throughout an industry will not change significantly due to a price change.

E. Inventory adjustments and inventory policies affect business demand. Businesses keep inventories measured in months of raw materials and components. If consumer demand changes, inventories will be corrected to reflect the change.
  1. Implementation of "just-in-time" inventory programs requires suppliers to deliver inputs as the production process needs them and may result in sole sourcing, that is, buying a firm's entire stock of product from only one supplier.

2. The newest trend, "just-in-time II," leads suppliers to place representatives at the customer's facility to work as part of an on-site customer-supplier team

3. Inventory adjustments are as vital to wholesalers and retailers as well as to manufacturers.

VI. The Make, Buy, or Lease Decision deals with the choice among three possibilities for acquiring finished goods, component parts, or services. If the company has the capability to do so, making the product itself may be the best choice. On the other hand, most firms can't make all the things they need. They may choose to let others produce them or they may lease these inputs. Leasing spreads out costs compared with lump-sum payment for up-front purchases. Leasing may also be an option for sophisticated computers and heavy equipment.

A. The rise of outsourcing of such functions as finance and accounting operations, human resources, and information technology allows firms to concentrate on what they do best.
   1. The interest in improving efficiency causes firms to look outside their walls for practically every service imaginable, including, in addition to the above, mailroom management, customer service, manufacturing, and even distribution.
   2. Outsourcing allows firms to concentrate their resources on their core businesses.
   3. About 60 percent of all outsourcing is done by North American-based companies.
   4. In the aftermath of September 11, 2001, companies began to consider outsourcing their computer networks for firewall protection as well as reliability and flexibility.
   5. Outsourcing allows firms to reduce costs to remain competitive, improve the quality and speed of software maintenance and development, and receive greater value for their money.

B. Problems with outsourcing include the failure of promised cost savings to materialize, cost increases during the later years of multi-year contracts, and the risk of losing proprietary technology through   security leaks.
   1. Outsourcing can reduce a company's ability to respond quickly to the marketplace or slow efforts to bring new products to market.
   2. Another major danger of outsourcing is the risk of losing touch with customers.
   3. A firm may inherit an outsourcing contract when it acquires another firm and find that the terms don't suit its needs.
   4. Outsourcing is a controversial topic with unions, especially as the percentage of components made in-house has steadily dropped.

VII. The Business Buying Process is quite complex, involving analysis of needs, determination of goals that the project should accomplish, developing technical specifications for the equipment, and setting a budget.

A. Influences on purchase decisions include environmental, organizational, and interpersonal factors
   1. Environmental conditions such as economic, political, regulatory, competitive, and technological considerations influence business buying decisions.
   2. Successful business-to-business marketers understand their customers' organizational structures, policies, and purchasing systems.
      a. Because purchasing operations spend half of each dollar companies earn, consolidating vendor relationships can lead to large cost savings.

    b. On the other hand, many buyers practice multiple sourcing – purchasing from multiple vendors to ensure against shortages if one supplier cannot fulfill all the buyer's needs.

3. Many people influence B2B purchases, and considerable time may be spent obtaining the input and consent of members of the organization.

    a. Business marketers should know who influences buying decisions in an organization that buys their products and should know each of their priorities.

    b. Specific users of a company's products may differ widely in their conception of what is important in its acquisition and use.

    c. To effectively address the concerns of the people involved in the buying decision, sales representatives must know the technical features of their products well.

4. The role of the professional buyer is to make purchases for his or her employer using systematic procedures.

    a. In the trade industries, professional buyers are often known as merchandisers and seek the best possible products at the lowest prices.

    b. Firms often seek to streamline the buying process through systems integration, or centralization of the procurement function, which may be done in-house or by designating a major supplier called a category captain – to do the job.

    c. A sales organization may be set up to serve national accounts.

    d. The Internet has changed the nature of B2B selling and will continue to do so into the future.

B. The eight-stage model of the organizational buying process grows out of the complexity of the business buying process, which exceeds that of the consumer buying process.

1. Stage 1: Anticipate or Recognize a Problem or Opportunity and a General Solution – a coordinated, team-based approach involving a number of people is typical of this stage.

2. Stage 2: Determine the Characteristics and Quantity of a Needed Good or Service – the market conditions that relate to what needs to be done are outlined.

3. Stage 3: Describe Characteristics and the Quantity of a Needed Good or Service – it is at this stage that specifications for the needed product are worked out in detail.

4. Stage 4: Search for and Qualify Potential Sources – available suppliers are identified and their abilities determined.

5. Stage 5: Acquire and Analyze Proposals – the formal nature of the business buying process often requires that suppliers provide written offers outlining their proposed means of providing the desired product. Competitive bidding may be required for government entities and some nonbusiness customers.

6. Stage 6: Evaluate Proposals and Select Suppliers – The ball is now in the buyer's court and vendors' proposals must be compared and the best chosen. Price is not the only basis for choice; other factors such as reliability, delivery record, time from order to delivery, product quality, and order-filling accuracy also count.

7. Stage 7: Select an Order Routine – Once a supplier has been selected, vendor and buyer must work out the best way to process future purchases.

8. Stage 8: Obtain Feedback and Evaluate Performance – Once a purchase has been made, the supplier will be evaluated for performance, large firms being more likely to do this formally than smaller firms.

C. Classifying business buying situations: straight rebuy, modified rebuy, new-task buying, and the role of reciprocity
1. The simplest buying situation is the straight rebuy, a recurring purchase decision in which an existing customer places a new order for a familiar product that has performed satisfactorily in the past.
   a. Examples of straight rebuys include items such as paper clips and pencils for the office.
   b. The marketer that wants to ensure customers think of them for straight rebuys should develop good relationships with customers by providing excellent service and delivery.
2. In the modified rebuy, a purchaser is willing to reevaluate available options. (Modifed rebuys resemble limited problem solving by consumers.)
   a. The modified rebuy is most common in situations where there is active competition for the customer's business.
3. New-task buying is a first-time or unique purchase situation that requires considerable effort by decision makers.
   a. The purchaser in a new-task buying situation may engage in extensive analysis of competing vendors and products before deciding exactly what to do.
4. Reciprocity is the practice of buying from suppliers who are also customers and is controversial in a number of organizational buying situations.
   a. Reciprocity suggests close links among participants in the organizational marketplace, links that may violate anti-trust legislation in the United States.
   b. Outside the U.S., reciprocity may be treated more favorably by governments.

D. Analysis tools: Value and vendor analysis
1. Vendor analysis examines each component of a purchase in an attempt to either delete an item or replace it with a more cost-effective substitute.
2. Vendor analysis carries out an ongoing evaluation of a supplier's performance in categories such as price, EDI capability, back orders, delivery times, liability insurance, and attention to special requests.

VIII. The Buying Center Concept provides a vital model for understanding organizational buying behavior. The buying center is everyone who is involved in any aspect of a firm's buying action. It is not part of a firm's formal organizational structure, but is an informal group of varying size and composition.

A. Buying center roles are numerous and informal, so identifying the people who occupy them is extremely important to vendors.
1. Users are the people who will actually use the good or service.
2. Gatekeepers control the information that all buying center members will review.
3. Influencers affect the buying situation by supplying information to guide evaluation of alternatives or by setting buying specifications.
4. Deciders actually choose a good or service, even though someone else may have the formal authority to do so.
5. The buyer has the formal authority to select a supplier and to implement the procedures for securing the good or service.
6. B2B marketers must determine the specific role and relative decision-making influence of each buying-center participant and target appropriate personnel at each stage of the buying process.

B. International buying centers provide different challenges than do those in the domestic market.
   1. It is difficult to identify members of the foreign buying center because of cultural and organizational differences.
   2. Buying centers in foreign companies often include more participants than is the case in the U.S.

C. Team selling combines several sales associates or other members of the organization to assist the lead sales representative in reaching everyone who will influence the purchase decision. It may be extended to include members of the seller firm's supply network.

IX. Developing Effective Business-to-Business Marketing Strategies

A. Challenges of government markets – governments constitute the largest single customer in the United States. Government purchases typically involve dozens of interested parties who evaluate, specify, or use the purchased goods or services. Government purchases often are influenced by social goals, such as minority subcontracting programs. Contractual guidelines are another important influence in selling to government markets. Fixed-price contracts specify the cost of the products before the contract is finalized. Cost-reimbursement contracts allow the supplier to recover allowable costs, including profits incurred during the performance of the contract.
   1. Federal government purchasing procedures are often handled by the General Services Administration, an agency involved in procurement, property management, and information resources management.
      a. By law, most federal purchases must be awarded on the basis of bids from vendors.
      b. The government has succeeded in making its acquisition system more responsive and effective in recent years.
      c. State and local government purchasing procedures resemble federal procedures.
      d. Government spending patterns may differ from those of private industry, in part because of the government's use of a fiscal year that differs from the calendar year.
   2. Online with the federal government has become "the way to go" with the streamlined new procedures brought about by technology.
      a. Vendors have three electronic options in selling to the federal government.
         i.   Web sites featuring interactive convenience for both parties, the government making purchases by credit card much like a consumer.
         ii. Government-sponsored electronic ordering systems help standardize the buying process.
         iii. The Electronic Posting System sends automatic notices of opportunities to sell to the government to more than 29,000 sponsored vendors.
   3. Many government agencies remain less sophisticated than private-sector businesses.

B. Challenges of institutional markets that include a wide variety of organizations such as schools, hospitals, libraries, foundations, clinics, churches, and not-for-profit agencies.
    1. Institutional markets are characterized by widely diverse buying practices.
    2. Buying practices can differ even between institutions of the same type.
    3. Within a single institution, multiple-buying influences may affect decisions.
    4. Group purchasing is an important factor in institutional markets since many institutions join cooperative associations to pool purchases for quantity discounts.
    5. The diverse practices in institutional markets pose special problems for B2B marketers.

C. Challenges of international markets include buyers' attitudes and cultural patterns in the areas in which they operate.
    1. Cultural values may shift, resulting in changes in how marketers may approach a market.
    2. Local industries, economic conditions, geographic characteristics, and legal restrictions must be considered in international marketing.
    3. Remanufacturing – production to restore worn-out products to like-new condition – can be an important marketing strategy in a country that can't afford to buy new products.
    4. Foreign governments represent an important business market.

Name_____   Instructor_____

Section_____   Date_____

Key Concepts

The purpose of this section is to allow you to determine if you can match key concepts with the definitions of the concepts. It is essential that you know the definitions of the concepts prior to applying the concepts in later exercises in this chapter.

From the list of lettered items, select the one that best fits each of the numbered statements below. Write the letter of that choice in the space provided.

Key Terms

a. business-to-business (B2B) marketing
b. commercial market
c. trade industries
d. resellers
e. customer-based segmentation
f. North American Industrial Classification System
g. end-use application segmentation
h. global sourcing
i. derived demand
j. joint demand
k. inelastic demand
l. outsourcing
m. value analysis
n. vendor analysis
o. buying center

_____ 1. Wholesalers or retailers that purchase products for resale to others.

_____ 2. Demand for one business product that depends on the demand for a second business product that is required to use the first.

_____ 3. Dividing a business-to-business market into homogeneous groups based on buyers' product requirements.

_____ 4. Contracting to purchase goods and services from suppliers worldwide.

_____ 5. Using outside vendors to produce goods and services formerly produced in-house

_____ 6. Segmentation of a B2B market based on how industrial purchasers will use the product.

_____ 7. Replacement for the Standard Industrial Classification (SIC) now used by NAFTA countries to categorize the business market into detailed segments.

_____ 8. Individuals and firms that acquire products (goods and services) to support production of other products whether directly or indirectly.

_____ 9. Demand for a resource that depends on the demand for goods and services that are produced by that resource.

_____ 10.   Assessment of supplier performance in areas such as price, back orders, timeliness of deliveries, and attention to special requests.

_____ 11.   Organizational purchases of goods and services to support production of other goods and services, for use in daily company operations, or for resale.

_____ 12.   Systematic study of the components of a purchase to determine the most cost-effective way to acquire the needed goods or services.

_____ 13.   Anyone who is involved in any way in any aspect of a company's buying activity.

_____ 14.   Marketing intermediaries that operate in the trade sector.

_____ 15.   Condition that exists when demand throughout an industry will not change significantly due to a price change.

Name_____   Instructor_____

Section_____   Date_____

Self-Quiz

You should use these objective questions to test your understanding of the chapter material. You can check your answers with those provided at the end of the chapter.

While these questions cover most of the chapter topics, they are not intended to be the same as the test questions your instructor may use in an examination. A good understanding of all aspects of the course material is essential to good performance on any examination.

True/False

Write "T" for True or "F" for False for each of the following statements.

_____ 1. The trade industries are the largest segment of the business market.

_____ 2. The highest level of industrial concentration in the United States is in the states of the East North Central region – Ohio, Indiana, Michigan, Illinois, and Wisconsin.

_____ 3. Because of the professionalism and expertise of business buyers, the typical business purchase requires less time than is the case with consumer purchasing.

_____ 4. Buying center participants in any purchase seek to satisfy personal needs such as participation or status as well as organizational needs.

_____ 5. In the buying center, "gatekeepers" control the information that all buying center members will review.

_____ 6. The government market includes federal, state, and local organizations, but foreign governments are not considered part of the market.

_____ 7. Because the federal government's fiscal year runs from October 1 through September 30, many agencies hoard their funds to cover unexpected expenses and when the need for the funds doesn't arise find themselves with money to spend in late summer.

_____ 8. The NAICS improved on the SICC by creating new service sector classifications to better reflect the economy of the year 2000 and beyond.

_____ 9. Capital items purchased by organizational buyers typically include things such as paper clips, pencils, and related business supplies.

_____ 10. Under a government cost-reimbursement contract, the government pays the vendor for allowable costs, including profits, incurred during the performance of the contract.

_____ 11. As the price for lumber drops, construction firms will buy more lumber from their suppliers because of the inelasticity of business demand.

_____ 12. The business buying process is more complex than the consumer decision process because, among other considerations, it involves many people with complex interactions between them and the organization's goals.

_____ 13. Vendor analysis supports use of the material Kevlar for aircraft components because it weighs less than the metals it can replace, creating significant fuel savings.

_____ 14. The activity of team selling combines several sales associates or other members of the organization to assist the lead sales representative in reaching all those who influence the purchase decision.

_____ 15. The North American Industrial Classification System, because it lacks detail, is of little use for segmenting markets and identifying new customers.

_____ 16. Describing the characteristics and the quantity of a needed good or service is the fifth stage of the organizational buying process.

_____ 17. Just-in-time II (JIT II) inventory policies involve suppliers placing representatives at the customer's facility to work as part of an integrated, on-site customer-supplier team.

_____ 18. Businesses that have developed customer relationship management systems are able to segment customers in terms of the stage of the relationship between the business and the customer.

_____ 19. Reciprocal arrangements traditionally have been common in industries featuring heterogeneous products with widely differing products.

_____ 20. Selecting an order routine, the activity in which buyer and vendor work out the best way to process future purchases, is the last stage of the organizational buying process.

_____ 21. Marketers who want to ensure continuing straight rebuys should concentrate on maintaining good relationships with buyers by providing high-quality products, excellent service and prompt delivery.

_____ 22. The commercial market includes manufacturing firms, farmers and members of other resource producing industries, construction contractors, and providers of such services as transportation, public utilities, finance, insurance, and real estate brokerage.

_____ 23. Remanufacturing can be an important strategy in a nation that can't afford to buy new products.

_____ 24. In a buying center situation, people in the decider's role supply information for the evaluation of alternatives or set buying specifications.

_____ 25. Outsourcing always increases a company's ability to respond quickly to the marketplace and speed efforts to bring new products to market.

Multiple Choice

Circle the letter of the word or phrase that best completes the sentence or answers the question.

26. The business-to-business market is also known as
    a. trade or reseller industries.
    b. the organizational market.
    c. the government market.
    d. the institutional market
    e. the commercial market

27. Which of the following is NOT a component of the business market?
    a. the commercial market
    b. trade industries
    c. government organizations
    d. consumer services
    e. institutions

28. The truck has become the vehicle of choice for the consumer, largely because of the popularity of sport utility vehicles. As a result, sales of the larger tires required for these vehicles have increased significantly. This is an example of what phenomenon?
    a. derived demand
    b. joint demand
    c. demand variability
    d. inventory adjustments
    e. specific demand

29. Because business buyers are geographically concentrated, relatively few in number, and the purchase decision process they use is so complex,
    a. the marketing channel for industrial goods is typically much longer than for consumer goods.
    b. retailers are more frequently used to handle their business than they are in the consumer goods field.
    c. the relationship between buyers and sellers is more complex than consumer relationships and better communications among the organizations' personnel is necessary.
    d. advertising plays a much larger role in the industrial market than it does in the consumer market.
    e. personal selling is seldom used as the promotional tool of choice by vendors to this market.

30. In addition to the federal government, a source of additional information on the business market is
    a. advertising agents and other public relations sources.
    b. trade price listings.
    c. trade associations and business publications.
    d. a buying center organization.
    e. distributors' guides.

31. Which of the following properly defines the NAICS Code for firms located in the United States engaged in wholesaling motor vehicles?
    a. 421110
    b. 421
    c. 4211
    d. 42111
    e. 42

32. Angiovia, Inc., a manufacturer of hand-held electronic testing equipment, has based the readouts of its meters on analog technology for the last twenty years. If it were suddenly to decide to change over to digital technology, its instruments would have to be massively re-designed for the new technology. The buying situation for most components would then probably change from
    a. modified rebuy or new-task rebuy to straight rebuy conditions.
    b. straight rebuy or new-task rebuy to modified rebuy conditions.
    c. forward rebuy to new-task buying conditions.
    d. straight or occasional modified rebuy to new-task buying conditions.
    e. new-task buying to modified rebuy conditions.

33. Which of the following would you expect to have no effect on an organizational buyer's purchase process?
    a. the complexity of the decisions which must be made
    b. the existence of competing proposals
    c. the formality and professionalism of the purchasing process
    d. the necessity to meet technical requirements and specifications
    e. All of the above would have some effect on the purchase process.

34. Value analysis may be defined as
    a. securing needed products at the best possible price.
    b. using a professional buyer to systematize purchasing.
    c. examining each component of a purchase in an attempt either to delete the item or replace it with a more cost-effective substitute.
    d. convening a committee which will be charged with all the buying responsibility for the firm.
    e. evaluating suppliers' performance in categories such as price, back orders, delivery time, and attention to special requests.

35. A competitor seeking to win over another vendor's straight rebuy customers by converting the straight rebuy situation to a modified rebuy should
    a. raise issues that will make customers reconsider their purchasing decisions.
    b. work to sell other accounts; these accounts are in the other vendor's bag.
    c. hope that the other vendor will maintain a high standard of delivery and service; this bores customers and makes them more likely to listen to other vendors.
    d. try and convince the customers that the buying situation is entirely new or completely unique.
    e. recognize that a paper clip is a paper clip and try to sell the customers other products.

36. In the buying center, the role filled by the individual who has the formal authority to select a supplier or implement procedures to secure a good or service is the
    a. user.
    b. gatekeeper.
    c. decider.
    d. influencer.
    e. buyer.

37. Most federal government purchases, by law, must be made on the basis of
    a. the availability of the most graft to the greatest number.
    b. book value of the item needed.
    c. estimates prepared by government personnel.
    d. cost/benefit studies of the goods required.
    e. bids – written sales proposals from vendors.

38. In the trade industries, merchandisers
    a. are responsible for procuring needed products at the best possible prices..
    b. incorporate periodic buying decisions with other activities.
    c. devote a small part of their time and effort to determining needs and evaluating supplies.
    d. treat purchase decisions for capital items exactly as they treat those for expense items.
    e. avoid using systematic procedures; keep suppliers confused about what's going to happen next.

39. Which of the following is typically a part of the fifth stage of the organizational buying process?
    a. recognition of a problem, need, or opportunity
    b. acquisition and analysis of supplier proposals
    c. determination of characteristics of and quantity of a needed good or service
    d. selecting an order routine
    e. acquisition and analysis of proposals

40. Which of the following characteristics is MOST typical of the business-to-business market?
    a. a formal, professional, and complex decision process
    b. geographic dispersion of members of the market
    c. large number of buyers of a given class of goods
    d. purchases are never made for resale, only for use in production
    e. public benefit is primary motivation of the market

41. As a general rule, a significant difference between domestic buying centers and the buying centers of foreign companies is that the foreign buying center
    a. tends to have members who are easier to identify than is the case in the U.S.
    b. will usually be operated by staff, rather than line, personnel.
    c. is often much larger than is usually the case in the U.S.
    d. is seldom affected by cultural differences in decision making.
    e. is usually unresponsive to political and economic trends.

42. Which of the following organizations would be considered member of the institutional sector of the business market?
    a. Metropolitan Life and Casualty Insurance Company of New York
    b. Fifth Third Bank and Trust Company of Cincinnati
    c. National Stock and Bond Trading Corporation of St. Louis
    d. The American Red Cross, Hattiesburg/Southern Mississippi Chapter
    e. Rubenstein Brothers Men's Clothing Store, New Orleans

43. Which of the following is typical of the buying practices which have been evident in the federal government market during the last several years?
    a. Extensive corruption because each agency maintains its own procurement department
    b. Greater difficulty in meeting specifications because of the executive order which requires that all vehicles owned by the federal government have some military usefulness in the event of war
    c. Allocation of resources to departments which have shown the greatest ability to spend their budget allotment early in the fiscal year
    d. Development of unit-system costing techniques to reduce the cost of particular government operations
    e. The influence of social goals such as minority subcontracting programs

44. As evidence of the importance of the Internet in business-to-business marketing, it should be realized that
    a. though the bulk of e-Commerce is consumer-based, almost 15 percent of business-to-business sales occur on the Internet.
    b. a far larger number of e-Commerce vendors are targeted to consumers than to the market, and consumers spend 80 percent of all the money earned by Internet vendors.
    c. more than 90 percent of all Internet sales are business-to-business transactions.
    d. were it not for government interference, the Internet would account for at least 50 percent of B2B sales.
    e. some firms do all their purchasing on the Internet.

45. The most complex category of business buying is
    a. reciprocal arrangements with other firms.
    b. new-task buying.
    c. straight rebuys
    d. modified rebuys.
    e. value analysis

46. A good definition of the business-to-business market should include
    a. recognition that nonprofit organizations are not and cannot be members.
    b. a managerial philosophy oriented toward heavy industry.
    c. the condition that its primary need is meeting the internal demand of the firm.
    d. recognition of the informal nature of its structure and context.
    e. mention of retailers and wholesalers as an integral part of the market.

47. Heldamen Engineering Corporation designs and builds railroad bridges. It has developed a close working relationship with Tennessee Coal and Iron Corporation, one of its suppliers, because T C & I has developed an assortment of steel shapes specifically designed for railroad bridge construction. From this evidence, it can be concluded that T C & I probably segments its market by
    a. using demographics or the type of purchasing situation encountered.
    b. breaking it down into foreign and domestic segments.
    c. analyzing the customer type or purchasing situation encountered.
    d. customer-based or end-use application methods.
    e. analysis of sales made through the Internet.

48. Which of the following would be an example of a member of the commercial market?
    a. The Texas Highway Patrol (State law enforcement agency)
    b. National Metal Stamping Co. (produces steel parts for automobiles)
    c. The Missouri School of Mines (an engineering school)
    d. Ernest F. Ladd/ E. B. Peebles Memorial Stadium (a city-owned football stadium)
    e. Lumber Products Company (wood products wholesale and retail)

49. A large change in the demand for a business good (like gasoline pumps) that results from a relatively small change in demand for a consumer good (like gasoline)
    a. is an example of the volatile nature of business demand growing out of derived demand.
    b. is very unusual and is symptomatic of supply-chain breakdown. Such conditions seldom exist.
    c. occurs because many business products are subject to conditions of joint demand.
    d. reflects the demands being made on producers by JIT inventory policies.
    e. is called reciprocal reaction to market fluctuations.

50. The practice of extending purchasing preference to firms that are also customers is called
    a. value analysis.
    b. reverse reciprocity.
    c. professional purchasing behavior.
    d. reciprocity.
    e. international trade.

Name_____   Instructor_____

Section_____   Date_____

Applying Marketing Concepts

Joe House, director of marketing for Alphagen Desmoulin, Inc. (ADI), a producer of animal feeds, was pondering two reports which had just arrived in his office. Both were somewhat disturbing because they told him that his firm had lost two major sales to competition that he thought was at least a little bit less than fair. In the first instance, ADI had lost out on a contract to supply special feeds to American Beef Growers (ABG) because ABG had decided to buy from Chessboard Feeds. Mr. House felt that the decision had been based, not on the quality of Chessboard's product, but on the fact that Chessboard had a substantial interest in North Central Supers, a firm which bought ABG products extensively for sale in its supermarkets. In the second case, it appeared that ADI had lost out to a Canadian firm on a U.S. Army contract to supply feed rations for Army's extensive herds of mules* because the Canadians could supply the needed feed at a lower price. The Army ignored ADI's arguments that the Canadian product would cost substantially more in the long run because of losses in storage because it had a shorter shelf-life than that of ADI's product and would become unusable sooner.

_____ 1.   In all likelihood, ADI had to supply a written sales proposal or bid for the
            Army contract.

_____ 2.   The two episodes outlined involved purchases by members of the commercial and
            government segments of the organizational market.

3.   The case of ABG favoring Chessboard Feeds over ADI was most probably caused by
     a.   bribery.
     b.   reciprocity.
     c.   derived demand.
     d.   threats of force or violence.

4.   The NAICS general code for North Central Supers would probably be
     a.   11; agriculture, forestry, hunting, and fishing.
     b.   42; wholesale trade.
     c.   44-45; retail trade
     d.   48-49; transportation and warehousing.
     e.   72; accommodation and food services.

5.   The main reason ADI lost the Army contract was because
     a.   their bid price was too high.
     b.   their product was of inferior quality.
     c.   the Army thought they might be an uncertain source of supply.
     d.   they were unable to provide the needed service.
     e.   somebody got bribed.

*Yes, the Army still maintains a large number of mules for use where terrain prevents or deters the use of alternative means of cargo transportation. It also keeps over 10,000 dogs for various military purposes, the most significant of which are as guards and drug sniffers.

6. ADI might have gotten the Army contract if
    a. international politics hadn't tainted the decision.
    b. it had pressed the issue of foreign ownership of the Canadian firm
    c. the Canadian product hadn't been vastly superior in quality.
    d. American Beef Growers hadn't interfered with the sale.
    e. The Army hadn't heard about the Middledale incident.

Ford, like most American automobile manufacturers, makes extensive use of components made by other firms: electrical equipment from Autolite and National Switch; cooling system and air conditioning components from McCord Radiator and Aircool companies; brake parts from Bendix and Lockheed; tires from General Tire Company and Goodyear; and turbosuperchargers from both Garret and Airboost. They have even been known to buy whole vehicles from other manufacturers, such as Mazda. A given Ford, Mercury, or Lincoln may contain parts from as many as fifty different manufacturers.

7. If consumer demand for Ford products declined, demand for Goodyear tires would also decline. This is a case of
    a. reciprocity.
    b. joint demand.
    c. derived demand.
    d. variable supply.
    e. inventory failure.

8. In deciding to buy components from outside suppliers rather than make them themselves, and in choosing the sources from which those parts would be bought, Ford probably bases their decision on
    a. value analysis.
    b. vendor analysis.
    c. a combination of value analysis and vendor analysis.
    d. their desire to be innovative and to be leaders in automotive engineering technology.
    e. their need to keep the price of their cars down.

9. Suppose that Ford management had decided that a two-month inventory of parts was not enough to have on hand to assure that production would continue if the availability of air conditioner compressors was curtailed and increased its stock-on-hand to four months' worth. This would be an example of
    a. an inventory adjustment.
    b. conservative thinking.
    c. demand variability.
    d. derived demand.
    e. usual demand.

10. The basic NAICS for Ford Motor Company would have been
    a. 11-12; agriculture, forestry, fisheries, hunting.
    b. 21-24; mining.
    c. 31-33; manufacturing.
    d. 48-49; transportation and warehousing.
    e. 81-85; services except public or as otherwise noted.

Lavoratorios Orione, Sp.A., of Lago Pesca, Campania, is a maker of industrial alcohol. The alcohol, made from grapes rejected for use in the making of wine, is because of the high sugar content of the original mash and the extreme care taken by the Lab, is extremely high-proof and remarkably free of congeners (impurities). It is also drinkable.

After being denatured (rendered undrinkable) by Orione, the alcohol is sold domestically to a number of makers of shellac. Sales are usually accomplished in 60,000 litre (approx. 15,850 gallon) containers. The shellac makers use the alcohol as a solvent in the making of their product. The resulting product is then sold, usually in 5 litre cans, to paint distributors who then sell it to paint retailers who sell it to the public.

There is also substantial demand for the Orione product from brewers and vintners all over Europe for use as a fortifier in their Sherries and Ports and also in the fortified beers of Bavaria – the beers whose names end in "ator," such as Salvator, Triumphator, and Vindicator, and whose alcohol content can reach fifteen percent. The vintners add the alcohol to the wine after aging, while the brewers add it during the bottling process. The wine and beer are both sold by liquor wholesalers and retailers to the consuming public.

_____ 11. Lavorotorios Orione is a member of the commercial market.

_____ 12. The makers of shellac that use the Orione product are members of the trade industries.

_____ 13. The liquor wholesalers and retailers that sell the product to the public are members of the trade industries.

_____ 14. The brewers, because they make no changes in the alcohol, are members of the trade industries.

Name_____   Instructor_____

Section_____   Date_____

Surfing the Net

Keeping in mind that addresses change and what's on the Web now may have changed by the time you read this, let's take a look at some of the places on the Net that reflect aspects of business-to-business marketing. We are not endorsing or recommending any of these sources, merely making note of the information and services that people have elected to offer through the Internet.

Interested in risk on a global level? You can get into investigating international trade at the Global Trade Center at **http://www.tradezone.com/.** Find out what's involved in dealing in everything from falafel to spaghetti in the world market.

Government Business? Browse the *F B O Daily* (the F B O stands for Federal Business Opportunities) and see what it's like to consider becoming a supplier of government. The Web site's at **http://www.fbodaily.com/.** (Leave the last period off. It's not part of the address.)

How's Asian business doing? Try the Web site of Nihon Keizai Shimbun (Japan Business News). The English language version of this major firm's news service – they're the people who do the Nikkei Index, Japan's equivalent of the Dow-Jones – is on the Web as Nikkei Net Interactive at **http://www.nni.nikkei.co.jp/.** If you prefer a domestic source, try the business section of the *New York Times* at **http://www.nytimes.com/.** Alternatively, you can check practically any business situation at *The Wall Street Journal,* **http://www.wsj.com/public/us.**

A general overview? We can't leave out the U.S. Commerce Department's Web Site at **http://www.commerce.gov.** Numerous subagencies are available at this address that do all sorts of things having to do with business. This is the Department's main Internet Site with links to numerous other sites.

Sites verified August 17, 2004.

Chapter 7
Serving Global Markets

Chapter Outline

You may wish to use the outline that follows as a guide in note taking.

I. Chapter Overview

International trade now accounts for 25 percent of the U.S. gross domestic product compared with 5 percent thirty years ago. The top ten trading partners of the U.S. account for nearly 70 percent of U.S. imports and two-thirds of U.S. exports. International trade involving exporting and importing is vital to a nation because it expands markets, makes production and distribution economies possible, allows companies to explore growth opportunities in other nations, and makes firms less dependent on economic conditions in the home countries. The U.S. and Canadian markets are mature, but the economies of many other parts of the world are growing rapidly. This growth opens new markets. The marketing concept basically applies internationally as it applies domestically, but the question of how products may fit in a foreign environment must be addressed.

II. The Importance of Global Marketing – half of the world's ten largest corporations are headquartered in the United States. Global marketing is becoming a necessity for most American firms. American exports have grown at an average rate of ten percent per year for the last twenty years. Agricultural products, electrical machinery, computers and office equipment, industrial machinery, and motor vehicle parts are the nation's leading exports. WalMart is the world's largest retailer and private employer, and aims for global dominance. The Internet has made the world market accessible to even very small firms. Finally, it should be remembered that some firms rely on purchase of raw materials and finished goods from abroad for their success domestically.

   A. Service and retail exports – the U.S. is a world leader.
      1. Travel and tourism is the third largest industry in the U.S. and accounts for more than half of the nation's service exports. Only China hosts more tourists in a given year.
      2. The most profitable U.S. service exports are business and technical services, including engineering, financial, computing, legal services, and entertainment.
      3. Many American service exporters such as American Express, AT&T, Citicorp, Disney, and Allstate Insurance earn a substantial portion of their revenues from international sales.
      4. The entertainment industry is another major exporter – of movies, TV shows, and music.
      5. American retailers have found success in the global arena, with firms such as Victoria's Secret, the Gap, and even Office Depot and Costco opening stores worldwide at a rapid pace.
      6. The world is not immune to U.S. fast food franchises. McDonald's, Burger King, Krispy Kreme, and Starbucks all operate in the global market.

   B. Benefits of going global – it's not only about money.
      1. Going global makes money, but it also gives firms new insights into consumer behavior, alternative distribution strategies, and advance notice of new products;

they may also gain invaluable experience with new products, new approaches to distribution, or new promotions.

2. Global firms usually find themselves well-positioned to compete effectively with foreign firms.
3. The successful firm learns to adapt its products to local preferences wherever they operate.
4. Since the marketing functions must be performed, it might seem there is little difference between the home market and a foreign one, but there are similarities and differences between strategies appropriate to each location.

III. The International Marketplace – huge, diverse, and different. It is rare to find a U.S. firm not involved in some foreign marketing; firms with Web sites may be solicited for business from anywhere in the world.

   A. Market size – By 2025, world population is expected to reach 8 billion people
     1. Africa, Asia, and Latin America lead in population growth.
     2. The world is becoming increasingly urban, with 50 percent of the population now resident in large cities.
     3. The rate of population growth does not necessarily relate to a nation's level of economic development; subsistence economies don't make very good markets for international trade; newly industrialized countries offer more opportunity, and industrial nations have the greatest potential both as importers and exporters.
     4. The infrastructure – the underlying capacity of the area to support modern life – including transportation and communications, banking, utilities, and public services defines the capacity of a culture to generate international trade.
     5. The growth of the middle class in East Asia as well as in Mexico, South America, and sub-Saharan Africa will create new demand for consumer goods.

   B. Buyer behavior – consumption rates, individual tastes, and local preferences.
     1. Soft drink consumption in other countries is much lower than in the U.S., but the Coca-Cola Company still does well overseas by tailoring its product offerings to local tastes. Blockbuster Video shut down its Hong Kong operation because of rampant piracy of pre-recorded movies.
     2. Differences in buying patterns often require considerable research before a firm enters a foreign market. Among the factors that should be considered are
       a. demand.
       b. the competitive environment.
       c. the economic environment.
       d. the social-cultural environment.
       e. the political-legal environment.
       f. the technological environment.

IV. The International Marketing Environment – the basis for international business expansion.

   A. International economic environment
     1. Size, per capita income, and stage of economic development all affect a nation's prospects.
     2. Poor countries may not buy high-tech industrial equipment but may be a good market for agricultural hand tools. Indians are frugal because their country is poor, but both Indian and Chinese economies are growing rapidly.

3. A nation's infrastructure reflects its economic well-being. An inadequate infrastructure affects production, promotion, and distribution of products.
4. China had to develop its infrastructure in very short order, so skipped the entire era of the wired telephone and went straight to cellular service. Similarly, some underdeveloped countries may have to create a healthcare infrastructure of much better quality if they are to secure international business.
5. Monetary rates of exchange have an effect on the well-being of a country. An unfavorable exchange rate and a "soft" currency such as the Russian ruble make it difficult for the countries possessing them to do business internationally.
6. International currencies such as the Euro represent an effort to counteract unfavorable rates of exchange by stabilizing a region's price structure.

B. International social-cultural environment
1. Before entering a market, marketers should study its culture: its language, educational institutions, religious attitudes, and social values.
2. Language is perhaps the most easily confused and confusing aspect of culture. Misunderstandings can be hilarious – or disastrous.

C. International technological environment
1. Internet technology has made it possible for both large and small firms to connect to the entire world.
2. A global medium, the Internet provides a means of communication that is reshaping social and cultural values.
3. Technology's innovations, such as genetic engineering of food products, have different effects in different places.

D. International political-legal environment
1. Each country possesses its own laws and trade regulations that affect marketing.
2. Political conditions often affect international marketing through unrest.
    a. Political risk assessment may be necessary to evaluate the desirability of a new market.
3. Politics and labor conditions tend to affect each other. Labor may be a force in the government or it may be the sworn enemy of the establishment.
4. U.S. firms are affected by three forces in the legal environment
    a. International law, including such issues as ISO 9002 certification.
    b. U.S. laws, including treaties with other nations, trade regulations, tax laws, and import/export requirements.
    c. Legal requirements of host nations, which may be quite complex and very different from those of the United States.

E. Trade barriers affect global marketing. These include two classes or categories: tariffs and non-tariff or administrative barriers.
1. Tariffs
    a. Protective tariffs are designed to keep the prices of domestic products at the same level as those of imports. This protects domestic industry but penalizes domestic consumers by raising prices.
    b. Revenue tariffs raise money for the government, and were once the major source of government income.
    c. Under U.S. law, countries that unfairly impede trade with the U.S. can be penalized with tariffs or quotas on the import of their products into the U.S.

   2. Administrative barriers
      a. Import quotas limit the amount of certain products that can be imported in the host country.
      b. Embargoes prohibit the importation of a product from a specified country. Cuban cigars are under an embargo in the U.S.
      c. Some countries subsidize certain industries, that is, pay the industry to stay in business. The effect is to give the industry an advantage over foreign competitors.
      d. Exchange control is an administrative barrier to trade that requires that all monetary transactions go through the nation's central bank that then adjusts the price of the currency being bought and sold to facilitate the government's objectives.
   3. Dumping is the practice of selling a product in a foreign market for less than it sells for in the home market.

V. Multinational Economic Integration – since the end of World War II, there has been a tendency for nations to integrate their economies for mutual benefit. Three levels of integration have been typical: the *free trade area* in which participating nations open their borders to each other, abolishing tariffs and trade restrictions among themselves; the *customs union*, which adds a common tariff structure with respect to nations outside the organization in addition to abolishing tariffs and trade restrictions among the members states; and the *common market*, which seeks to reconcile all government regulations of the members that affect trade.

   A. General Agreement on Tariffs and Trade and the World Trade Organization – Fifty years of tariff reduction.
      1. The GATT was a 117 nation organization that sponsors rounds of tariff negotiation.
      2. The Uruguay Round, that ended in 1994, resulted in many tariff reductions.
      3. Also growing out of the Uruguay Round was the foundation of the World Trade Organization to succeed GATT.
      4. The WTO's major policy initiatives – liberalizing world financial service, telecommunications, and maritime markets – have not yet been realized.
      5. Major conflicts between developed and developing countries have hampered the WTO's efforts.

   B. The NAFTA Accord – still subject to intense controversy, this treaty among the U.S., Mexico, and Canada removing trade barriers among them over a 14-year period has its adherents and its opponents
      1. The doubters originally thought that cheaper Mexican labor would cause the loss of jobs in the U.S. and Canada.
      2. To date, the effect of the pact seems to have been beneficial to both the U.S. and Mexico, increasing jobs in Mexico without causing inflation.
      3. During the U.S.' recent recession, however, Mexico suffered a downturn in production because Chinese products became cheaper and U.S. firms switched suppliers to save money.

   C. The Free Trade Area of the Americas – the next step in American economic integration.
      1. If and when it is effected, this organization would stretch from Cape Horn to the Bering Strait and include most of the nations of both North and South America and a gross domestic product of more than $11 trillion.

    D. The European Union – composed of 25 countries, this has been the most successful common market yet.
      1. Its objective is to eventually remove all barriers to free trade among its members and definite progress has been made in that direction.
      2. At present, customs rates among the EU nations still differ and there is no uniform postal system.
        a. The euro, the uniform currency of the European Union, has not been universally adopted.

VI. Going Global – while most large firms have become involved in global commerce, their motives and approaches differ.

    A. First steps in deciding to market globally
      1. The first step toward global marketing is that top management must support the activity.
      2. The next step is to research the export process and potential markets.

    B. Strategies for entering international markets – three basic approaches
      1. Importing and exporting, as a strategy, requires the lowest level of resource commitment
        a. Importing requires knowledge of the domestic market and access to it.
        b. Exporting involves attempting to market the firm's products to customers in other countries.
          i. Export-trading companies act as merchant intermediaries, buying products domestically and selling them in foreign countries.
          ii. Export-management companies can handle the paperwork and work with foreign firms to smoothly complete transactions
          iii. Offset agreements team small domestic firms with large foreign companies to facilitate the entry of the small firms into the foreign country.
      2. Contractual agreements involve creating an abiding legal relationship between a domestic firm and a foreign company.
        a. In franchising, the franchisee – a wholesaler or retailer – agrees to meet the operating requirements of a manufacturer or other franchiser. The franchisee receives the right to sell the products of and use the franchiser's name and marketing, management, and other services.
        b. Foreign licensing authorizes the licensee, a foreign firm, to distribute the licenser's merchandise or use its trademark, patent, or process in a defined geographic area.
        c. Subcontracting, as the name implies, occurs when production of goods and services is assigned to firms in the foreign market.
      3. International direct investment
        a. At present, U.S. direct investment abroad amounts $2.2 trillion, while foreign direct investment in the U.S. is $2.1 trillion.
        b. Direct investment involves high levels of involvement and potentially high risk.
        c. Foreign sales offices, overseas marketing subsidiaries, and foreign offices and manufacturing facilities all represent direct investment.
        d. An alternative to other direct investments is the joint venture, a combination of a domestic and foreign firm in a separate, third entity, operated by both.

E.   From multinational corporation to global marketer
1.   A multinational corporation is a firm with significant operations and marketing activities outside its home country.
2.   Though most were originally of U.S. origin, multinationals may now have their origins in any country.
3.   The multinational orientation has become much more interactive than was originally the case, now involving interchange of ideas, capital, and technology between international partners.
4.   Many multinationals are now truly global with independent operations in many countries.
5.   Many U.S. firms are now targets for takeover by other multinationals – British Petroleum's acquisition of Amoco is a prime example.

VII.   Developing an International Marketing Strategy – two alternative approaches are available: a global strategy or a multidomestic strategy. The first of these takes a standard marketing mix and applies it with minimal modifications in all foreign markets, yielding economies of scale in production and marketing. The second assumes that differences between market characteristics and competitive situations in different countries require customization of marketing decisions to reach individual marketplaces. Many marketers favor the latter strategy because differences between markets can be quite significant in the global context.

A.   International product and promotion strategies – five choices are available for each foreign market.
1.   Straight extension – using the same product with the same promotional appeal in each market in which the product is sold.
2.   Product adaptation – altering the product to local expectations, requirements, and tastes while keeping the promotional appeal essentially the same.
3.   Promotional adaptation – the product remains the same, but the promotional appeal is changed to reflect different users or uses to which the product is targeted.
4.   Dual adaptation – both product and promotional program are altered to better suit the foreign market.
5.   Product invention – the most radical of the available strategies, this involves creating an entirely new product, hence a new marketing mix, to suit a particular foreign market (or markets).

B.   International distribution strategy – both channels and physical distribution methods may need adaptation
1.   While channels are relatively easy to create, an inadequate physical distribution system is not at all unusual and creates extensive problems.
2.   Distribution requires, first, that a method of entering the foreign market be determined and, second, that a method of how to distribute the product through that entry channel be developed.
3.   The nature of the firm's product, consumer tastes and buying habits, competition, and transportation options must be balanced for the market.

C.   Pricing strategy – competitive, economic, political, and legal constraints must be dealt with.
1.   Until recently, the delivery of goods to foreign destinations, one of the major costs of accessing those markets, was unreliable at best.
2.   Price may be controlled or influenced by a commodity marketing organization such as OPEC.

D. Countertrades – a form of exporting in which a firm barters products rather than selling them for cash may be required to do business with certain less-wealthy countries.

    1. Developed during the period when eastern European countries' currencies could not be bought or sold, the countertrade involves a goods-for-goods transfer of owner-ship.

    2. Countertrades may account for as much as twenty-five percent of all world trade.

VIII. The U.S. as a Target for International Marketers – it has a large population, high levels of discretionary income, political stability, a favorable attitude toward foreign investment, and a well-controlled economy. Foreign investment in the U.S. reflects the globalization of non-U.S. firms. Automotive manufacturers, entertainment firms, consumer products companies, cosmetics firms, and oil products companies from foreign countries have all staked their claim to a share of the U.S. market.

Name_____   Instructor_____

Section_____   Date_____

Key Concepts

The purpose of this section is to allow you to determine if you can match key concepts with the definitions of the concepts. It is essential that you know the definitions of the concepts prior to applying the concepts in later exercises in this chapter.

From the list of lettered terms, select the one that best fits each of the numbered statements below. Write the letter of that choice in the space provided.

Key Terms

a. exporting
b. importing
c. infrastructure
d. exchange rate
e. tariff
f. import quota
g. free-trade area
h. General Agreement on Tariffs and Trade (GATT)
i. World Trade Organization

j. North American Free Trade Agreement (NAFTA)
k. Free Trade Area of the Americas
l. European Union
m. franchise
n. foreign licensing
o. multinational corporation
p. global marketing strategy
q. multidomestic marketing strategy
r. countertrade

_____ 1. International trade agreement that has helped reduce world tariffs.

_____ 2. A nation's basic system of communications networks, transportation networks, and energy facilities.

_____ 3. Organization that replaces GATT and oversees trade agreements, makes binding decisions in mediating disputes, and strives to reduce trade barriers.

_____ 4. Domestic purchasing of foreign-produced goods, services, and raw materials.

_____ 5. Marketing domestically produced goods and services in foreign countries.

_____ 6. Tax levied on imported products.

_____ 7. Program of market segmentation that identifies specific foreign markets and tailors the marketing mix to match specific traits in each nation.

_____ 8. Agreement by which a firm permits a foreign company to produce or distribute goods in a foreign country or gives it the right to use the firm's trademark, patent, or processes in a specified geographical area.

_____ 9. Contractual arrangement in which a wholesaler or retailer agrees to make some payment and to meet the operating requirements of a manufacturer or other business in return for the right to market the manufacturer's or other business's goods or services under its brand name.

_____ 10. Price of one nation's currency in terms of other countries' currencies.

_____ 11. Firm with significant operations and marketing activities outside its home country.

_____ 12. Accord that removes trade barriers among the United States, Canada, and Mexico

_____ 13. Form of exporting whereby products and services are bartered rather than sold for cash.

_____ 14. Trade restriction that limits the number of units of certain goods that can enter a country for resale.

_____ 15. Customs union moving in the direction of economic union by adopting a common currency, removing trade restrictions, and allowing free flow of goods and labor throughout its membership.

_____ 16. Standardized marketing mix with minimal modifications that a firm uses in all of its domestic and foreign markets.

_____ 17. Region in which participating nations agree to the free trade of goods among themselves, abolishing tariffs and trade restrictions.

_____ 18. Proposed free trade area stretching the length of the entire Western Hemisphere and designed to extend free trade benefits to additional nations in North, Central, and South America.

Name_____   Instructor_____

Section_____   Date_____

Self-Quiz

You should use these questions to test your understanding of the chapter material. Check your answers against those provided at the end of the chapter.

While these questions cover most of the chapter topics, they are not intended to be the same as the test questions your instructor may use in an examination. A good understanding of all aspects of the course material is essential to good performance on any examination.

True/False

Write "T" for True and "F" for False for each of the following statements.

_____ 1.   Annual U.S. exports have increased to 25 percent of the nation's gross domestic product from 5 percent thirty years ago.

_____ 2.   The United States' leading export to the rest of the world over the last 15 years has been computers and office machinery.

_____ 3.   The top ten trading partners of the United States include mainland China, Canada, and Japan.

_____ 4.   Though many U.S. manufacturers are heavily involved in the international market, American service firms have not found the international market attractive enough to induce their entry.

_____ 5.   Among the good reasons to become a global marketer are that a firm may gain advance notice of new products and acquire new insights into consumer behavior.

_____ 6.   In newly industrialized countries like Korea and Brazil, where most people still engage in agriculture and per capita income is very low, few opportunities for international trade exist.

_____ 7.   The population growth rate in affluent countries is approximately five times as great as the population growth rate in less-developed countries.

_____ 8.   The world's largest city in terms of population is now Mexico City, the population of which is expected to grow to 31 million by the year 2010.

_____ 9.   India's middle class now amounts to nearly 300 million people, a number greater than the entire population of the United States.

_____ 10. Nations with low per-capita incomes may be poor markets for the technical equipment typical of an industrialized society but good markets for expensive industrial machinery.

____ 11. China now possesses the largest cellular telephone market in the world, with the number of subscribers expected to grow to 500 million by the year 2007.

____ 12. The U.S. *Foreign Corrupt Practices Act* exempts companies from antitrust regulations so they can form export groups to serve foreign buyers.

____ 13. Protective tariffs, when applied by the U.S. government, are generally higher than revenue tariffs.

____ 14. Under the terms of the *Omnibus Trade and Competitiveness Act of 1988*, the United States can now single out countries that unfairly impede trade with U.S. domestic companies and penalize them by placing tariffs or quotas on the offenders' goods imported into the U.S.

____ 15. The practice of selling a product in the domestic market at a lower price than what it commands in foreign markets is called "dumping."

____ 16. The standardized operations offered the marketer by a franchise in the international market typically reduce costs, increase operating efficiencies, and provide greater international recognizability.

____ 17. The North American Free Trade Agreement strengthens trade restrictions among Canada, the United States, and Mexico, and is the western hemisphere's only functioning trade bloc.

____ 18. Companies using a global marketing strategy change their approach to the market in each foreign market in which they become involved.

____ 19. One approach to a strategy for a foreign market involves straight extension of a one-product, one-message approach like Pepsi-Cola's as part of a global marketing strategy.

____ 20. The marketing of different blends and roasts of coffee combined with different promotional programs in the various markets where those products are sold would be an example of a dual adaptation strategy.

____ 21. Foreign markets may offer poor transportation systems and warehousing facilities – or none at all – thus creating extensive physical distribution problems.

____ 22. The tried and true pricing strategies which have stood the test of time here in the United States require little adaptation for foreign markets and are seldom changed as conditions change.

____ 23. The Organization of Petroleum Exporting Countries is an example of a commodity marketing organization that tries to control prices through collective action.

____ 24. Countertrading is a form of exporting where goods are sold "counter to the interests" of one or both of the nations involved in the transaction; in other words, countertrading involves dealing in contraband.

____ 25. Major U.S. companies owned by foreign firms include Random House Publishing Company, *Family Circle* and *Inc.* magazines, and Arista Records, all owned by German firm Bertelsmann AG.

Multiple Choice

Circle the letter of the phrase or sentence that best completes the sentence or answers the question.

26. When Mississippi's Howard Furniture Company, a manufacturer of wood furniture, purchases kiln-dried spruce or ash lumber from a Canadian supplier, it is
    a. importing goods to complement its main product line.
    b. taking advantage of foreign innovation to improve quality of its own products.
    c. forestalling foreign competition by getting involved by direct investment in a market abroad.
    d. importing necessary raw materials abroad to use in its domestic manufacturing operations.
    e. speculating on scarcity of spruce and ash by laying in a supply to beat market fluctuations in the price.

27. Many eastern European currencies such as the Russian ruble are "soft." This means that
    a. they cannot readily be converted into hard currencies such as the dollar, the yen, or the euro.
    b. they trade in the open money market and their value fluctuates widely from day to day.
    c. their value depends on the nature of the transaction; they may be more or less valuable depending on what's being bought or sold.
    d. they have unusual names that frequently change, along with their exchange value, with changes in the government of the country issuing them.
    e. currency dealers are reluctant to trade in them until more is known about the political stability of the countries issuing them.

28. Reflecting its "newly industrialized" status, imports to Brazil tend to be
    a. comprised mainly of pizzas bought from Domino's.
    b. few and far between; the economy can't yet support them.
    c. primarily agricultural products needed to feed the population.
    d. largely dominated by services bought from the United States.
    e. industrial goods such as high-tech equipment and consumer goods.

29. Coca-Cola Company's decision to promote Leaf, its new canned tea product, heavily in Japan in preference to its main-line product, Coke, was done in recognition of the fact that
    a. new middle-class consumers often seek strange products to express their success.
    b. marketing strategies must be matched to local customs, tastes, and living conditions.
    c. the shortage of onions had to be met some way.
    d. color is an important component of product appeal. Purple goes well with beef.
    e. people can sometimes be convinced to buy almost anything.

30. The introduction of the euro as a unit of currency
    a. destabilized the economies of western Europe and the euro had to be withdrawn.
    b. serves only as an accounting convenience, all the EC domestic currencies remaining unchanged.
    c. reduced variations in prices charged for the same goods and services among European countries.
    d. is not expected to have any long-term consequences for European prices or national growth.
    e. is designed to strengthen Europe's competitiveness in the global marketplace.

31. The U.S. Export Trading Company Act of 1982
    a. exempts from antitrust regulations companies forming export groups to offer products to foreign buyers.
    b. prohibits U.S. businesspeople from bribing foreign officials in soliciting new or repeat sales abroad.
    c. seeks to impose trade sanctions against Cuba by allowing U.S. interests to sue foreign firms for using expropriated U.S. assets to do business in Cuba.
    d. places high tariffs on goods coming from countries known to be "tainted" by internal corruption.
    e. denies U.S. visas to corporate executives of firms accused of violating the act.

32. A nation's language, education, religious attitudes, and social values are characteristics of its
    a. social-cultural environment.
    b. technological environment.
    c. political-legal environment.
    d. competitive environment.
    e. economic environment.

33. When one examines the level of development of a nation's highway and railroad system, the availability and coverage of its radio, TV, and newspaper network, and how much energy is available from its generators, gas pipelines, and other utilities, one is scrutinizing
    a. the social environment of the country from an industrial point of view.
    b. the government's ability to deliver social services to its people.
    c. the likelihood of the country to experience a revolutionary takeover.
    d. the adequacy of the infrastructure provided by that nation's economy.
    e. the possibility of getting caught should the necessity for a fast getaway arise.

34. Which of the following is NOT an administrative barrier to trade?
    a. import quotas.
    b. protective tariffs.
    c. embargos
    d. subsidies.
    e. exchange controls.

35. The degree of a nation's multinational economic integration is reflected in its
    a. size, per capita income, and stage of economic development.
    b. laws, trade regulations, and political stability.
    c. membership in a customs union, common market, or free-trade area.
    d. participation in such activities as dumping, protective tariffs, and exchange control.
    e. language, educational system, religious attitudes, and social values.

36. ISO 9000-series certification
    a. is of no significance to most U.S. firms.
    b. was developed in the United States to assure internationally common goods.
    c. is unavailable to small businesses – only firms above a certain size may apply.
    d. does not usually lead to increased prestige or access to more markets.
    e. ensures that a company's products and services meet established quality levels.

37. The body of international law emerges from the
    a. United States Statutes and Code of Federal Regulations for citizens of the United States.
    b. statutes, laws, and regulations of the appropriate country of jurisdiction.
    c. treaties, conventions, and agreements that exist among nations.
    d. Codes and Resolutions of the United Nations.
    e. Laws and Regulations of the Admiralty.

38. The function of the U.S. Foreign Corrupt Practices Act is to
    a. empower the United States Coast Guard to search and seize vessels found to have contraband aboard regardless of whether they are inbound or outbound.
    b. control the shipment of U.S. goods to foreign countries in ships of other than U.S. registry.
    c. make it illegal to bribe a foreign official in an attempt to solicit new or repeat sales abroad.
    d. encourage export of U.S. products by subsidizing American firms which actively participate in foreign trade.
    e. establish a U.S. foreign trade commission which negotiates with nations abroad for special privileges for U.S. firms.

39. Taxes levied against imported products for the purpose of raising funds for the importing government are called
    a. exchange taxes.
    b. import quotas.
    c. protective tariffs.
    d. antidumping penalties.
    e. revenue tariffs.

40. Which of the following would be the best example of a countertrade?
    a. Cincinnati-Milacron sells computer controlled milling machines to a German Company and the Germans pay in U.S. dollars.
    b. General Motors sells jet engines to a British firm. The British pay in Pounds Sterling.
    c. Turnbull Cone Baking Company sells a shipload of ice cream cones to a firm in Bolivia. The Bolivians pay by shipping tin ingots to the Turnbull people.
    d. Peerless Valve Company sells water valves to the City of Milan, Italy. The city pays in a combination of U.S. dollars, Italian Lire, and West German bearer bonds.
    e. Rolls-Royce ships nine Silver Cloud convertibles to the Pasha of Ranjipur. The Pasha pays in gold.

41. Dumping is the practice of
    a. selling defective or contaminated goods in the international market rather than in the home market.
    b. escaping undesirable foreign contracts simply by dumping on the foreign party to the contract and abandoning the agreement.
    c. selling a product in a foreign market for a price lower than that which it brings in the home market
    d. taking materials which have been seized by the government under the Contraband Products Act out to sea and throwing them overboard.
    e. selling merchandise overseas before it has been introduced in the home market to prevent foreign competitors from entering the home market.

42. The European Union (EU), as its members now prefer to have it called, is the world's best-known
    a.   mutual defense organization like NATO or the former Warsaw Pact countries.
    b.   an internally self-competitive organization of national powers.
    c.   example of how fragile any treaty-based organization must be, as its recent collapse will attest.
    d.   multinational economic community forming a huge common market.
    e.   free trade area moving in the direction of customs union.

43. The least risky way of entering the international market is by
    a.   franchising or subcontracting.
    b.   exporting or importing.
    c.   joint ventures.
    d.   dealing in contraband.
    e.   acquisition of a foreign firm.

44. When a domestic firm enters into an arrangement under which it agrees to share the risks, costs, and management of a foreign operation with one or more foreign companies, it has
    a.   issued a license to the foreign firms.
    b.   formed a joint venture with the foreign companies.
    c.   engaged in foreign marketing of its products and services.
    d.   laid the groundwork for foreign production and marketing by its own people.
    e.   forever lost its rights to those assets which it has allowed the foreign companies to use.

45 A firm that chooses to use a "global marketing strategy" will
    a.   use a standardized marketing mix in every market in which it becomes involved, making minimal modifications as required.
    b.   alter its products but not its promotional mix as necessary to appeal to the tastes and preferences of its various markets.
    c.   alter its promotional mix but not its products as it enters various foreign markets.
    d.   modify both its products and its promotional mix for each of the different markets it enters.
    e.   be prepared to take whatever actions are necessary to assure itself of success in each of its different markets.

46. A firm that approaches the international market with a product unlike anything it has ever sold in the domestic market is probably applying a
    a.   straight extension strategy for entering the international market.
    b.   promotion adaptation strategy for entering that market.
    c.   dual adaptation strategy for market entry into a foreign market.
    d.   product invention strategy, recognizing unique opportunities in the foreign market.
    e.   product adaptation strategy for entry into foreign markets.

47. The first decision that must be made concerning distribution strategy for a foreign market is
    a.   how the product will be distributed within the foreign market.
    b.   the method that will be used to enter the foreign market.
    c.   who is going to exercise control over distribution in the foreign market.
    d.   what devices will be used to maintain product quality during the distribution process.
    e.   whether the product will be packaged differently in the foreign market than at home.

48. A tax levied against imported goods whose purpose is to protect domestic industry is a
    a. protective tariff.
    b. revenue quota.
    c. control for monetary exchange.
    d. general agreement tariff.
    e. revenue tariff.

49. Pricing decisions in the foreign market
    a. can always be approached the same way they are in the United States; this aspect of marketing never varies.
    b. are seldom subject to political constraints; politicians recognize that without profits, products aren't produced or sold.
    c. are relatively free of competitive implications; most foreign economies are much more highly controlled than is that of the U.S., and competition much less active.
    d. may require modifications to recognize competitive, economic, political, and legal constraints on decisions about foreign pricing.
    e. are little affected by the actions of groups like the Organization of Petroleum Exporting Countries.

50. The dominant theme of foreign investment in America continues to be
    a. franchising outlets in the United States.
    b. foreign licensing to U.S. businesses.
    c. joint ventures between foreign and American firms.
    d. subcontracting for American manufacturers.
    e. acquisition of domestic firms by foreign interests.

Name_____   Instructor_____

Section_____   Date_____

Applying Marketing Concepts

Food Processing Supply Company, Ltd. (FPSC), of Manchester, England is a well-established manufacturer of specialty equipment for the processing of unusual foodstuffs. Founded in 1958, the firm made its name in Britain by producing and marketing a range of processing and canning machines designed to serve the needs of the sardine industry. These machines, known as "FPSC Smallfish" are heavy duty devices that seldom need service or repairs and have a built-in diagnostic system that senses and reports impending failures before they happen. Many of the features of the equipment are covered by an array of patents. Recently, FPSC was approached by NovaProd A.S., a Finnish manufacturer, who asked to enter into an arrangement to incorporate some of FPSC's patented technical features in equipment of their manufacture, selling the resulting machines as "NovaProd Autopacks." NovaProd would provide the manufacturing facilities and FPSC the patents, quality control, some components, and marketing expertise. Profits would be shared between the two firms.

FPSC has told NovaProd it will consider the arrangement, but in the meantime it is exploring other possibilities. It recognizes that, should it decide to enter the Finnish market on its own, its machines would at least have to be modified to use the Finnish electrical supply of 145 Volts at 25 Hertz rather than the British 220 Volt, 50 Hertz supply. There is considerable concern, as well, over whether the Finnish market can be approached the same way as the British market. Data indicate that the present Finnish market for equipment such as this lies with packers of the Arctic smelt, a fish calling for somewhat different handling than the open water sardine. One officer of FPSC has even suggested that the company develop a machine of a totally different design to satisfy this unique demand.

1. If FPSC enters into the arrangement suggested by NovaProd, it will have created a(n)
   a. export contract.
   b. licensing agreement.
   c. joint venture contract.
   d. shared-rights consortium.
   e. export trade law standard relationship.

2. If FPCS makes only the modifications required by the Finnish electrical supply and exports machines to that country, promoting them the same way it promotes them in Britain, its strategy will be
   a. straight extension.
   b. dual adaptation.
   c. triple adaptation.
   d. product adaptation.
   e. promotion adaptation.

3. If FPSC accepts the theory that smelt-canning companies are the target market for its products in Finland, modifying its promotional program as well as some of the features of its equipment to better suit that market, it will be adopting a
   a. dual adaptation strategy.
   b. marginal entry strategy.
   c. promotion adaptation strategy.
   d. product invention strategy.
   e. product adaptation strategy.

4. Heeding the advice of the executive who proposes the development of entirely different machines for the different requirements of the Finnish market would result in the adoption of a
   a. dual adaptation strategy.
   b. straight extension strategy.
   c. product invention strategy.
   d. product adaptation strategy.
   e. market development strategy.

Acadian Entertainment Corporation of Opelousas, Louisiana, has been making and selling for over 50 years its repertoire of recordings of famous and would-be-famous Cajun and Creole musical artists from the Lafayette/Opelousas area of the state. In connection with this activity, the company is the exclusive booking agent for more than 30 dancehalls all over rural Louisiana.

Acadian recently received an inquiry from a Swedish geologist working in nearby Alexandria. The geologist, Luke Hankammer, has apparently become quite fond of the music of the area and believes that it would be quite a success back home in Stockholm, where the inhabitants have historically been fond of all varieties of American music – even when it really wasn't. Cajun music is really French country music played the same way it was 200 years ago. Creole music is similar, though a bit more sophisticated and sung in a more understandable dialect of French. The best really domestic comparison is between Blue Grass and Western swing. Hankammer has asked Acadian for the exclusive rights to produce and distribute their recordings in his homeland.

The company, realizing that Sweden's population of some 4 million people is roughly the same size as the one it now serves, countered by offering to bring Lutke into the firm. After a brief training period, he would be sent to Sweden to introduce the Acadian record line to the market. He did not reject the offer outright, but did mention that he wanted a proprietary interest in any such venture.

Further investigation of the Swedish market by Acadian officials proved very interesting. While some Swedes, particularly in heavily populated Stockholm, are very cosmopolitan and sophisticated and not fond of anything "country" from anywhere, the rural folk have their own forms of country dancing and music that they dearly love. Cajun and Creole music are similar, with the use of similar instruments playing similar melodies and songs about love, both requited and unrequited, and the perils and pitfalls of rural life. Obviously, however, the Swedish songs were not in French and some of the song lines wouldn't make a whole lot of sense to a Swede. References to the heat of summer, crawfish pie, gator sauce piquant, and similar causes for joy or distress would probably be lost on the average Swede.

Armed with those observations, Acadian executives rethought their position. Why should they take a financial risk? Since Hankammer seemed to have financial backing, they decided to let him have rights to their recording library in the Swedish market for a number of years, provided he paid them a sizable royalty on sales.

5. The level of involvement of the Acadian firm under Lutke's proposal would be
   a. exporting.
   b. foreign licensing.
   c. overseas marketing.
   d. direct investment in foreign production and marketing.
   e. direct exporting.

6. The level of involvement of the firm under their original counterproposal to Lutke would be
   a. exporting.
   b. foreign licensing.
   c. overseas marketing.
   d. direct investment in foreign production and marketing..
   e. direct exporting.

7. The major barrier to the introduction of Cajun and Creole music into Sweden, as shown in the testimony of the Acadian executives, was
   a. cultural.
   b. economic.
   c. trade restrictions.
   d. political.
   e. exchange rate controls.

8. Which component of the marketing mix seems to present the greatest challenge for firms entering the Swedish recorded music market?
   a. distribution
   b. price
   c. product
   d. promotion
   e. none of them do

_____ 9. It is very likely that Acadian's recordings will have to be modified to be compatible with Swedish tastes.

_____ 10. It is likely that Mr. Hankammer and Acadian will be faced with Swedish tariffs and import restrictions.

_____ 11. Wealthier countries such as Sweden may prove to be prime markets for U.S. products, particularly consumer goods.

_____ 12. If Acadian and Mr. Hankammer come to terms, there is a real danger that Acadian will be guilty of dumping.

_____ 13. Acadian is following a global marketing strategy.

_____ 14. Mr. Hankammer's original proposal was in the nature of a request for a joint venture arrangement.

Name _____   Instructor_____

Section_____   Date_____

Surfing the Net

Keeping in mind that addresses change and what's on the Web now may have changed by the time you read this, let's take a look at some of the places on the Net that reflect aspects of global marketing. We are not endorsing or recommending any of these sources, merely making note of the information and services that people have elected to offer through the Internet.

I don't know what they are, but you can get arabidopsis seed in an utterly astonishing array of genetic pedigrees from the Arabidopsis Stock Centre at the University of Nottingham, UK. Their address is **http://nasc.life.nott.ac.uk.** The seed will actually come from their North American branch, the Arabidopsis Information Resource at the Carnegie Institution in Stanford, California if you're in Canada or the United States. These folks have their own Website at **http://arabidopsis.org.**

Demographics and other data for Britain and much of the rest of Europe are available at the University of Bristol (U.K.) at their site **http://sosig. esrc.bris.ac.uk/.** This is the Social Science Information Gateway and has links to all sorts of sources of European Social Science (and Humanities) Sites. It's pretty neat.

On the other hand, you can visit Australia's Charles Sturt University (no, it's not misspelled) at **http://www.csu.edu.au/** and read all about Australian education and tourism. Brazil (if you speak Portugese) can be found at **http://www.brazil.gov.br,** or if you prefer your information about Brazil in English, try **http://www.idrc.ca,** a business-oriented site in Canada. Ireland may be visited at   **http://www.enterprise-ireland.com/english.isp** France has an interesting site at **http://www.urec.cnrs.fr/,** run by the Centre National de Recherche Scientifique. The Louvre Museum of Paris may be found at **http://www.louvre.fr/** in English, and the America-German Business Club, an organization with chapters all over Germany and here in the U.S. is at **http://www.agbc.de.** There are, of course, many other foreign travel and business destinations. As you browse, you'll surely discover them. Here are some colleges and universities you might find interesting. In Canada, there's HEC Montreal, the business-only school open to people speaking French, English, and Spanish who want to study business in French Canada at **http://www.hec.ca.** In Australia, we have the University of New South Wales at **http://www.unsw.edu.au.** It's in Sydney, just in case you're not familiar with Aussie geography. In France, there's always the Sorbonne, which since the thirteenth century has been Paris' liberal arts university. They are at **http://www.sorbonne.fr.** And finally, just in case you're interested, there's always M. V. Lomonosov Moscow State University at **http://www.msu.ru/english.**

You might have noticed that foreign destinations have an additional "tag" at the ends of their addresses, such as .uk, .ca, .au, .ru, or .de. The tag is the first two letters of the country's name or its "initials" in its own language, so .de stands for Deutschland, or Germany, .uk for the United Kingdom (Britain), and so forth. Generally, these are the same initials you'll see on automobile national signs – little oval stickers on car trunks – seen in the rest of the world.

Sites verified August 18, 2004

Part 2
Creating a Marketing Plan: Getting Started

The information you will receive in this part will help you to complete Parts I.A. and I.B. of your marketing plan for Logeto Enterprises.

Episode Two

In episode one, we learned of the decision by Sandy, Suzette, and Mel to get together and start a company called Sumesa Enterprises. For reasons of simplicity, and because of their families, the three ultimately decided to return to their home, a city of some 1.3 million people located in the American Southwest. After careful consideration of their resources, they decided that they could not possibly afford to enter the highly competitive general service market for digital wireless, as there were already over 150 vendors operating locally. They also discovered that specialized custom encryption and security software was available from no fewer than 85 in-city sources. Having absorbed the marketing concept and wishing to match their abilities and resources with some untapped pool of demand, they cast about a little further and discovered that, at least as it looked on the surface, though 150 local firms sold digital wireless devices and related products, 85 developed specialized software for them, and 60 companies were equipped to repair them, only about 35 firms in the area were involved in the creation and maintenance of corporate digital wireless systems. A few hours in the library revealed that the market for firms that could provide and maintain a secure corporate digital wireless system was expected to reach $15 billion in potential for the current year, increasing at a rate of some 14 percent per year into the foreseeable future. Of the $15 billion current potential in the corporate digital wireless development and maintenance market, some $1.3 billion was expected to be derived from service to small firms requiring secure communications for up to 5 digital wireless send/receive units, with the remainder coming from larger firms with from 6 to several hundred units. It was further predicted that the market for site maintenance for large businesses actively using the digital wireless option for their communications needs would grow at a rate of 33% per year, leading all other communications service fields by a substantial margin.

Environmentally, analysis revealed that a corporate-oriented digital wireless development and maintenance company faced no special inhibitions in law; but that a business license would be needed and a sales tax account would have to be opened (sales taxes were collected on <u>any</u> physical goods sold, but not on pure services). There was, of course, competition in the local market, but it seemed to be divided along very specific lines: some firms worked only with very large companies and others did very little original work, simply adapting Acanned@ software and packaged send/receive equipment for their customers. The local economy was simply a miniature of the national economy. Projections made for the national scene could be scaled down to fit the local. The influence of the social environment on the firm would be minimal, except of course that people who use corporate digital wireless systems extensively and whose businesses have a presence there tend to be affluent and leaders of the community. Finally, the technological environment offers perhaps the greatest risk and complication to Sumesa Enterprises. Changes in technology could conceivably lead to something well beyond the current state-of-the-art as far as communications are concerned. In other words, the pace of change in this industry has been such that it may soon become possible to create an entirely secure corporate digital wireless communications system with out-of-the-box components. Mitigating this possibility is the idea that the communications system is interactive, so that some means of tailoring the process to the specific needs of particular firms and individuals must be maintained if the interaction is to occur.

A research project conducted by the partners acquired additional information about the local market. This information is summarized in Table P2-2.

Table P2-2: Characteristics of the Local Market

Total Population: 1,300,000
Proportion of National Population: 0.52%
Number of households: 335,000
Proportion of households owning cellphones (Est.): 52.5%
Proportion of households with commercial digital wireless service (Est.): 11.0%

Businesses in the Local Market:

		By Number of Employees				
	Total	1-5	6-9	10-19	20-49	50 up
Central Area	23,521	12,597	4,548	2,976	2,059	1,341
Suburbs	2,374	1,294	481	278	186	135
Total	25,895	13,891	5,029	3,254	2,245	1,476
% Using Cell Systems (Est.)	35	10	12	20	40	60

The partners, who, by the way, are going to incorporate their firm for reasons of taxation and personal liability, have on hand at present $240,000 in cash. $60,000 of this is their own, the remaining having been borrowed from various friends, relatives, and a local bank.

Guidelines:

a. In the context of part I.A. of the outline of the marketing plan, how would you characterize the likely nature of this firm?

a. On the basis of the information presented, complete part I.B. of the marketing plan. Basically, the points to be considered should relate, first, to the segments available for penetration, which segments may appear feasible for these people, and which you think they should choose.

Part 3
Target Market Selection

The purpose of marketing research is to provide useful information for marketing decision making. It has a fascinating history, but survives because of its usefulness. Many firms do their own marketing research, but additional marketing research suppliers include syndicated services, full-service research suppliers, and limited-service research suppliers. The marketing research process consists of defining the problem, conducting exploratory research, formulating an hypothesis, designing the research method, collecting data, and interpreting and presenting results.

Generally, secondary data – either externally or internally generated – are used first in marketing research because they are less expensive and easier to acquire than primary data. They may come from sources internal to the organization or exterior to it. Primary data collection must be based on a research design which assures that it is gathered without bias and is truly representative of the population from which it was taken. Hypotheses are tentative explanations of some specific event posed as concepts to be tested by research.

Research design involves decisions about how primary data are to be gathered (observation, experiment, or survey methods), and who is to collect them. Design decisions are usually based on the types of information needed and the resources and time available. Related to these decisions is the question of how to select the sample from the population. Probability sampling methods such as simple random sampling or nonprobability methods such as convenience sampling may be used. The methods of collecting data include observation, the survey method, and experimentation. The survey method is most commonly used, primarily because there are so many ways to conduct a survey. Presenting research information often requires a meeting of the minds between two very dissimilar people – the researcher and the executive who commissioned the research.

Marketing research generates some of the information needed by marketing managers, but a great deal of it should come from a marketing information system (MIS) appropriate to their needs. Marketing information systems are computer-accessible data bases that managers may use to access important company and industry information, while marketing decision support systems (MDSSs) are interactive processes somewhat like computer games that allow the manager to explore alternative scenarios related to decision making and its results. MDSSs also help handle the flow of information needed by every firm. Data mining is a process of data analysis used to detect patterns of behavior in customer files so those patterns can be used to discover potential basis for relationship development.

Forecasts of sales can be developed using quantitative or qualitative forecasting methods. A number of different techniques are available for either method. Companies using a top-down process develop their forecasts of company sales from forecasts of industry sales that are based on forecasts of Gross Domestic Product and economic indicators. Company and product sales forecasts are based on past performance and the marketing plan. Grass-roots forecasts, on the other hand, begin with sales estimates by each sales representative and are combined and aggregated till an overall projection can be made.

A market is people or institutions with purchasing power and the authority and willingness to buy. Segmentation is the process of dividing the aggregate market (the whole thing) into smaller, relatively homogeneous groups. Each segment must have measurable purchasing power and size, must be possible to promote to and serve effectively, must be sufficiently large to provide adequate profits, and must match the marketing capabilities of the firm. The two largest segments of the aggregate market are the consumer and the business markets. Segmenting the consumer market may be done geographically, demographically, psychographically, and/or based on people's relationships to products: by benefits sought, by usage rates, or on the basis of brand loyalty. Each of these methods can be applied using a number of different criteria.

Geographic segmentation is the least elegant of the segmentation methods for consumers, consisting essentially of grouping people according to where they are to be found. Demographic segmentation uses variables such as age, sex, income, occupation, education, household size, and stage of the family life cycle as bases for segmentation. This large number of possibilities provides for extensive segmentation possibilities. Psychographic segmentation is based on peoples' psychologies, values and lifestyles. Product-related segmentation uses consumers' relationships to the product, rather than any other factor or set of factors, as a segmentation base. It examines the benefits people seek in a product, the rates at which they use it, and their level of brand loyalty.

The market segmentation process involves five steps: identifying the process to be used; developing a relevant profile for each segment; forecasting market potential; forecasting probable market share; and selecting specific segments. Segments may be reached by using the strategies of undifferentiated marketing, differentiated marketing, concentrated marketing, and and/or micromarketing.

Relationship marketing is different in approach and objectives to the transactions-based marketing it replaces. It typically involves creating class ties between buyer and seller through the use of database technology to identify current and potential customers, modification of the marketing mix to target the individual customer, and monitoring of the relationship to measure the success of the resulting program. Software is used to orient the organization toward building a unique differentiation based on relationships with customers. The link between vendor and customer movies through three levels of intensity from the customer's point of view, beginning with the level of economic incentive (low price), progressing to the level of social benefit, and finally reaching the structural level of interdependent partnership. Customers who reach the third level can often be retained for very long periods. Consumer satisfaction can be enhanced by understanding consumer needs and obtaining consumer feedback concerning vendor performance.

Affinity and frequent buyer/user programs are common tools for developing a relationship with customers. These are facilitated by the use of databases to target appropriate types of customers. Customer relationship management uses software systems to make sense of the vast amount of data that technology allows firms to collect and using it to create a complete strategy in which people, processes, and technology are oriented to providing superior value to customers. Relationship marketing applies to business-to-business situations as it does to business-to-consumer interactions. The partnership level of relationship for businesses offers significant advantages to both partners. Businesses may form four types of partnership with other businesses: buyer partnerships, seller partnerships, internal partnerships, and lateral partnerships. Relationship marketing provides the basis for national account selling, use of business-to-business databases, electronic data interchange as a feasible strategy, and vendor-managed inventory. It also provides the basis for efficient management of the supply chain and well-designed business-to-business alliances.

A crucial measure of the value of customer relationship marketing programs is the "lifetime value of a customer," which is the revenue and intangible benefits each customer brings to the seller over a lifetime less the cost of acquiring, marketing to, and servicing that customer. The realization that has grown out of calculation of this datum is that it is far more profitable to keep an existing customer than it is to find a new one.

Chapter 8
Marketing Research, Decision Support
Systems, and Sales Forecasting

Chapter Outline

You may want to use the following outline as a guide in taking notes.

I. Chapter Overview

    Marketing research is the process of collecting and using information for marketing decision making. Data comes from studies, sales force reports, accounting records, and published reports. It may also come from controlled experiments and computer simulations. Its purpose is to aid decision makers in analyzing data and suggesting possible actions.

II. The Marketing Research Function – Marketing research has a history, involves people and organizations, and entails the performance of specific activities. It is central to effective customer satisfaction and relationship programs.

    A   Development of the marketing research function
        1. N. W. Ayer conducted the first organized marketing research in the U.S. in 1879.
        2. Charles C. Parlin, an ad salesman for Curtis Publishing Company, started the first commercial research department in the U.S. in 1911. Parlin gathered data by examining people's garbage, a technique that remains popular today.
        3. Until 1930, research tended to consist of testimonials from purchasers of firms' products.
        4. Beginning in the 1930s, the development of statistical techniques led to better sampling procedures and greater research accuracy.
        5. Recent advances in technology have accelerated the pace and scope of data collection and made analysis more complete and valuable.

    B. Who conducts marketing research? The size and organizational form of the marketing research function depends on the structure of the company. Some firms do their own research, perhaps basing their work on the basis of the lines they market, their brands, or geographic areas. Others set up on the basis of the kind of research they need done, such as sales analysis, new-product development, or sales forecasting. Other firms depend on independent research firms. Cost is the primary determining factor for whether research is done in-house or externally. A second factor is the reliability and accuracy of the information that outside organizations collect. Marketing research firms may consist of a single individual or be a very large, international organization.
        1. Syndicated services are organizations that provide a standardized set of data to all customers.
        2. Full-service research suppliers contract with clients to conduct complete marketing research projects.
        3. Limited-service research suppliers specialize in a limited number of activities such as conducting field interviews or performing data processing.

    C. Customer satisfaction measurement programs may examine the satisfaction levels of current customers but others track the dissatisfaction that leads customers to abandon or even partially abandon certain products for those of competitors.

III. The Marketing Research Process is a six-step process that improves the chances of making good decisions by providing the right information to decision makers at the right time.

   A. Defining the problem. A well-defined problem permits the researcher to focus on getting the exact information needed to solve the problem. Researchers must be careful not to confuse the symptoms of the problem with the problem itself. Good places to start are by evaluating the marketing mix and the target market. Ultimately, customer satisfaction is the objective of all marketing effort.

   B. Conducting exploratory research is designed to discover the cause of a problem by discussing the problem with informed sources within and outside the firm and by examining other sources of data.
      1. Using internal data involves examining the firm's own records for valuable information. Common sources are sales records, financial statements, and marketing cost analyses.
         a. Sales records typically provide sales forecasts by territory, product, customer, and salesperson, and allow actual performance to be compared with that expected. It is also possible to break down sales records by customer type, product, sales method, type of order, and order size.
         b. Accounting data, as reported in the financial statements or a firm, can also be used to identify financial problems that influence marketing.
         c. Marketing cost analysis evaluates the expenses incurred for such tasks as selling, warehousing, advertising, and delivery to determine the profitability of particular customers, territories, and product lines.
         d. Each of these techniques works best when it provides information linked to other forms of marketing research.

   C. Formulating an hypothesis consists of formulating a statement about the relationships among variables that carries clear implications for testing the relationship.

   D. Creating a research design is the activity of designing a master plan for conducting marketing research.
      1. Studies must measure what they set out to measure.
      2. Sampling processes, if used, must produce samples representative of the population they seek to measure.

   E. Collecting data involves acquiring either or both of two kinds of information.
      1. Secondary data is information from previously published or compiled sources.
      2. Primary data is information collected for the first time specifically for a marketing research study.
      3. Secondary data has the two advantages of being less expensive and quicker to gather than primary data.
      4. Among the limitations of secondary data are that published data quickly becomes obsolete and that data not collected for a specific purpose may not be completely relevant to the marketer's needs.
      5. Primary data may cost more and take longer to get than secondary data but it offers richer, more detailed information that secondary data does.

F. Interpreting and presenting research information requires that the researcher present findings to management so that the information can be used to make effective judgments.
   1. Cooperation between the researcher and management is essential at every stage of the research process

IV. Marketing Research Methods involve the most commonly used methods by which marketing researchers find both secondary and primary data.

   A. Secondary data collection consists of two types: internal and external. Internal data was discussed previously, external data includes the following categories.
      1. Government data
         a. The federal government is the nation's most important source of marketing data. The publications of the Bureau of the Census include censuses of housing, population, business, manufacturers, agriculture, minerals, and governments.
         b. The census of population contains a wealth of valuable information for marketers.
         c. The government's computerized mapping database – the TIGER system – combines topographic information with census data.
         d. The federal government also produces monthly (*Statistical Abstract of the United States*), yearly (*Survey of Current Business*), and less-than yearly publications (*County and City Data Book* – every three years) of significant value to marketers.
         e. State and city governments provide data on employment, production, and sales activities.
         f. University bureaus of business and economic research frequently collect and distribute information.
      2. Private data
         a. Trade associations provide information for marketing decision makers.
         b. Business, trade, and general business magazines publish a wide range of valuable data.
         c. A good way to access trade journals is directly through the publishers or online from periodical databases.
         d. A number of national firms offer information to businesses on a subscription basis.
         e. Data for inventory control, ordering, and delivery is provided from data gathered by scanner-based information services that record consumer purchases of UPC-coded products.
         f. A.C. Nielsen SalesNet uses the Internet as a quick delivery vehicle for scanner data.
      3. Online sources of secondary data
         a. Hundreds of databases and other information sources are available online.
         b. Internet research can be quicker and cost less than alternative research designs.
         c. At present, more than 70 percent of marketing research firms conduct some forms of Internet research.
         d. The Internet has helped create research aggregators – firms that acquire, catalog, reformat, segment, and sell premium research reports that have previously been published.
         e. Search engines such as Google and Yahoo! can find sites dealing with specific topics of interest to the researcher.
         f. Since the Internet is free for use by anyone, researchers must carefully evaluate the validity of information they find there.

B. Sampling techniques are the methods used by marketing researchers to select survey respondents or research participants.

   1. The total group of people that a researcher wants to study is called the *population* or *universe*.

   2. A probability sample is one that gives every member of the population a chance of being chosen.

      a. A *simple random sample* is one in which every member of the population has an equal likelihood of being selected.

      b. In a *stratified sample,* randomly selected samples of different groups are represented in the total sample.

      c. *Cluster sampling* is a sampling method in which areas (or clusters) are selected from the population from which sample members are chosen.

   3. Nonprobability sampling is a sampling method that creates arbitrary groups that do not permit the use of standard statistical tests.

      a. *Convenience samples* are nonprobability samples selected from among readily available respondents.

      b. *Quota samples* are nonprobability samples structured to maintain representation of different segments or groups.

C. Primary research methods include observation, surveys, and controlled experiments. Which to use depends on the issues under study as well as the decisions that marketers need to make.

   1. The observation method requires researchers to view the overt actions of their subjects. Researchers may observe directly or indirectly, such as by counting license plates in a parking lot.

      a. Technology has increased the sophistication of the observation technique through the use of devices such as people meters.

      b. A newer version of the people meter is carried by study participants and records their exposure to radio and television programs automatically. The most recent version also captures demographic data about TV viewers.

      c. Videotaping consumers in action is a developing research technique.

      d. TiVo, the digital recording device, has the capacity to gather data about its viewers and keep it anonymous.

      e. Researchers have also used beepers and disposable cameras to record people's behavior with respect to their tastes in music and the possessions they regard as their favorites.

      f. A firm called Look-Look uses instant messaging, digital cameras, and pagers to get information from the 14 to 30 age group.

      g *Ethnography* – or "going native," sometimes called interpretative research, is an old, still used technique of observational research, especially good for interpreting consumer behavior in a foreign culture.

   2. The survey method is used to get information on people's attitudes, motives, and opinions, as well as information on demographics. The methods used include interviews and questionnaires.

      a. Telephone interviews are quick and inexpensive to administer if the quantity of information needed is small but they do possess significant drawbacks.

         i. The refusal rate for telephone interviews is high, approximating 44 percent.

         ii. Many would-be respondents are reluctant to divulge personal characteristics to interviewers over the telephone.

        iii. Caller ID systems create additional obstacles to getting in touch with respondents.

        iv. Internationally, the lack of telephone subscribers and telephone directories create additional problems.

  b. Personal interviews are usually the best method for obtaining detailed information about consumers, though they are slow and expensive to conduct.

  c. Focus groups bring together 8 to 12 individuals in one location to discuss a subject of interest.

        i. The focus group moderator explains the purpose of the meeting and suggests an opening topic with objective of stimulating discussion among the participants.

        ii. Focus group sessions last one or two hours and are recorded for later transcription.

        iii. Marketers use focus groups for a number of purposes usually related to people's views of products or aspects of their lives.

        iv. Focus groups are usually used for exploratory research.

        v. Among the drawbacks of focus groups are their unnatural and sterile settings, according to some critics, as well as the small sizes of the groups involved.

        vi. Some researchers have created focus-group-like situations over the Internet. This new methodology shows promise as a device to expand the applicability of the technique world-wide. Greenfield Online's Captain Morgan Spiced Rum research and Groupspark are two examples

  d. Mail surveys are cost-effective and provide anonymity to respondents, a feature that may encourage truthful answers.

        i. Mail surveys allow tracking of respondents over a period of time through ongoing research

        ii. Among the drawbacks of mail surveys are their low response rate, the time it takes to conduct them, and the inability for the researcher to react to unanticipated questions from respondents. Complex questions do not work well, and there may be bias because respondents are not necessarily like nonrespondents.

        iii. Administering mail surveys calls for special care in developing and administering questionnaires.

  e. Fax surveys are an alternative to and often supplement mail surveys.

  f. Online surveys offer the advantage of being very fast to administer, less intrusive than telephone surveys, and relatively inexpensive. Moreover, more complex questions can be asked and the novelty of the means of administration helps increase response rates.

        i. Questionnaires are becoming part of many Websites to solicit demographics, attitudes, and comments and suggestions to the firm.

        ii. In addition to traditional questionnaires, the Web is becoming home to electronic bulletin boards designed to extract information from their users.

        iii. As the Internet continues to grow, new research techniques to capture information about Web site visitors will continue to develop.

        iv. New software can monitor the sites that Web users visit and display advertising designed to be of interest to the individual.

3. The experimental method features the use of scientific investigations in which a researcher controls or manipulates a test group and compares the results with those of a control group that did not receive the experimental controls of manipulations.

  a. The least used method for collecting primary data is the *controlled experiment.*

    b. The most common use of the experimental method by marketers is in *test marketing,* in which a new product accompanied by a complete marketing campaign is introduced into a city or a TV market.

    c. Three problems with test marketing are that it is expensive, competitors quickly learn of the new product, and some products are not well-suited to test marketing

D. Conducting international marketing research has become necessary as corporations expand globally. Many secondary sources are available to support research in global markets, and the U.S. Commerce Department is an excellent source.

    1. Language and cultural issues must always be prepared for in global marketing research.

    2. Data collection methods may require adjustment if primary research is to be conducted in foreign countries because some methods do not transfer well from one environment to another.

    3. Mail surveys cannot successfully be used in some nations because literacy is low, mail service unreliable, and address lists unavailable.

    4. Use of marketing research firms located in the country one wishes to research is often a very good idea.

V. Interpretative Research is a method of observing a customer or group of customers in their natural settings and then interprets their behavior based on an understanding of relevant social and cultural characteristics of the setting. Originally developed by social anthropologists, the method is also known as *ethnography.* Widely used to examine foreign cultures, the method is also applicable domestically. The interpretative technique focuses on understanding the meaning of a product or the consumption experience in a consumer's life. The method is increasing in popularity, but it is expensive and takes quite a bit of time to do.

VI. Computer Technology in Marketing Research provides databases containing a wealth of information for marketing research; the ability to gather and analyze business intelligence quickly creates a substantial strategic advantage.

A. The Marketing information system is a planned, computer-based system designed to provide decision makers with a continuous flow of information relevant to their areas of responsibility.

    1. A well designed and constructed MIS serves as a firm's nerve center, continually monitoring the marketing environment.

B. The Marketing decision support system (MDSS) consists of software that helps quickly obtain and apply information in a way that supports marketing decisions.

    1. While the MIS provides raw data, the MDSS develops this idea into business intelligence – information useful for decision making.

C. Data mining is the process of searching through customer files to detect patterns.

    1. Data mining is an efficient way to sort through huge amounts of data and make sense of that data.

    2. Advances in data mining applications allow for real-time analysis of data flows that facilitate discovery of non-obvious relationships.

    3. Associations revealed by data mining can be unexpected as well as enlightening. Purchasers over the age of 65 buying rap and alternative music selections at Camelot Music surprised that firm until it was discovered that they were purchasing the selections for their grandchildren.

D. Business intelligence consists of gathering information and analyzing it to improve business strategies, tactics, and daily operations. Using sophisticated software, sources from both within and without the organization can be tapped. The key is not merely getting the information but getting it into forms that employees can understand and use for decision making and planning.

E. Competitive intelligence is a form of business intelligence that focuses on finding information about competitors using published sources, interviews, observations by salespeople and suppliers to the industry, and a legion of other places. The idea is to document the competitors' advantages and change plans to overwhelm them.

VII. Sales forecasting estimates a firm's revenue for a specified future period. Marketing research techniques are used to deliver accurate sales forecasts, thus aiding correct decision-making by marketers. Sales forecasts are created for the short-, intermediate-, and long-run. Two kinds of sales forecasting techniques – qualitative and quantitative – are typically applied.

A. Qualitative forecasting techniques apply judgmental or subjective methods to derive the information they produce.
  1. The *jury of executive opinion* combines and averages the outlooks of top executives from such areas as finance, production, marketing, and purchasing.
  2. The *Delphi Technique* solicits opinions from several people but also gathers input from experts outside the firm rather than relying completely on company executives.
    a. The Delphi Technique uses repeated solicitations of its panel members to refine an initial estimate until a consensus is developed.
  3. The *sales force composite* develops forecasts based on the idea that organization members closest to the marketplace offer the best insights concerning short-term future sales.
    a. A word of caution about the sales force composite: since sales representatives recognize the role of their sales forecasts in setting sales quotas for their territories, they a re likely to make conservative estimates; thus it is best to use this technique in combination with other techniques.
  4. A *survey of buyer intentions* gathers input through mail-in questionnaires, online feedback, telephone polls, and personal interviews to determine the purchasing intentions of a representative group of present and potential customers.

B. Quantitative forecasting techniques attempt to eliminate the subjectivity of the qualitative methods.
  1. In a *test market*, experimenters establish a small number of test locations to gauge consumer reaction to a new product under real-world conditions; variables may then be manipulated among the test markets to determine their effects.
  2. *Trend analysis* develops forecasts for future sales by analyzing the historical relationship between sales and time.
    a. Data from the past must be available in order for trend analysis to be completed.
    b. Trend analysis also makes the dangerous assumption that the future will develop as has the past.
  3. *Exponential smoothing* is a mathematical technique that uses weighted trend analysis to give greater weight to more recent occurrences
    a. This is the most commonly used method of quantitative forecasting.

Name_____   Instructor_____

Section_____   Date_____

Key Concepts

The purpose of this section is to allow you to determine if you can match key concepts with the definitions of the concepts. It is essential that you know the definitions of the concepts prior to applying them in later exercises in this chapter.

From the list of lettered terms, select the one that best fits each of the numbered statements below. Write the letter of that choice in the space provided.

Key Terms

a. marketing research
b. exploratory research
c. secondary data
d. primary data
e. sampling
f. probability sample
g. nonprobability sample
h. interpretative research

i. focus group
j. marketing decision support system.
k. sales forecast
l. jury of executive opinion
m. Delphi technique
n. sales force composite
o. trend analysis
p. exponential smoothing

_____ 1. Previously published data.

_____ 2. Arbitrary grouping that produces data unsuited for most standard statistical tests.

_____ 3. Information collected for the first time.

_____ 4. Information-gathering procedure in marketing research that typically brings 8 to 12 people together to discuss a given subject.

_____ 5. Sample that gives every element of the population a chance of being selected.

_____ 6. Estimate of company revenue for a specified future period.

_____ 7. Sales forecast based on the combined sales estimates of the firm's salespeople.

_____ 8. Process of collection and use of information for marketing decision making.

_____ 9. Process of selecting survey respondents or other research participants.

_____ 10. Sales forecasting method that gathers and redistributes several rounds of anonymous forecasts until the participants reach a consensus.

_____ 11. Discussing a marketing problem with informed sources within the firm as well as outside it and examining information from secondary sources.

_____ 12. Sales forecasting method that estimates future sales through statistical analyses of historical sales patterns.

_____ 13.   Sales forecasting method that considers the sales expectations of various executives.

_____ 14.   Forecasting technique that assigns weights to historical sales data, giving the greatest weight to the most recent data.

_____ 15.   Research method that observes a customer or group of customers in their natural settings and then interprets their behavior based on an understanding of relevant social and cultural characteristics.

_____ 16.   Software that helps users quickly obtain and apply information in a way that supports marketing decisions.

Name_____   Instructor_____

Section_____   Date_____

Self-Quiz

You should use these questions to test your understanding of the chapter material. You can check your answers with those provided at the end of the chapter.

While these questions cover most of the chapter topics, they are not intended to be the same as the test questions your instructor may use in an examination. A good understanding of all aspects of course material is essential to good performance on an examination.

True/False

Write "T" for True and "F" for False for each of the following statements.

_____ 1.   The first organized marketing research project was conducted by N.W. Ayer in 1779.

_____ 2.   Charles C. Parlin, who got his start as a marketing researcher by counting soup cans in Philadelphia's garbage, became the manager of the nation's first commercial research department in 1911.

_____ 3.   The size and organizational form of the marketing research function is independent of the structure of the company doing the research.

_____ 4.   One of the drawbacks to using secondary data is that the information may be obsolete by the time the researcher gets it.

_____ 5.   The National Research Group (NRG) is a full-service research supplier that specializes in rating the motion picture industry.

_____ 6.   Counting the cars passing by a potential site for a new drive-in bank branch would be secondary data for the firm that did the study.

_____ 7.   An organization that regularly provides a standardized set of research data to all its customers is called a syndicated service.

_____ 8.   The least commonly used version of the least-used of the primary data gathering methods is test-marketing.

_____ 9.   In their marketing research, firms implement customer satisfaction measurement programs that examine the satisfaction levels of current customers; they may also track the dissatisfaction that leads customers to abandon certain products for those of competitors.

_____ 10.   In using sales analysis as an exploratory research tool, once the sales quota has been established it is a simple process to compare actual results with expected performance.

_____ 11. Secondary data collected for an unrelated purpose is usually completely relevant to the marketer's specific needs.

_____ 12. Simple random sampling and cluster sampling are two types of nonprobability samples.

_____ 13. Unlike other interview techniques, focus groups usually discourage a general discussion of a predetermined topic.

_____ 14. While a standard marketing research project can take up to eight weeks to complete, a thorough online project may take two weeks or less.

_____ 15. Marketing Decision Support Systems have four main characteristics – interactive, investigative, inflexible, and inaccessible.

_____ 16. The huge databases that form the foundation for data mining are called "data warehouses."

_____ 17. The Delphi technique of sales forecasting combines and averages the outlooks of top executives within the firm in areas such as finance, production, marketing, and purchasing.

_____ 18. Test-marketing typically begins when the firm introduces a new product in a specific area and then observes its degree of success.

_____ 19. The most important source of secondary marketing data in the United States is the trade magazines.

_____ 20. NORA software was devised to help casinos identify obvious relationships between data from multiple sources.

_____ 21. Technological advances have provided increasingly sophisticated ways for marketing researchers to observe consumer behavior.

_____ 22. Telephone surveys suffer from lowered response rates because, among other reasons, people are data privacy and associate phone surveys with telemarketing.

_____ 23. Some researchers believe that focus groups produce honest responses to questions because the members of the group feel a need to identify with the other members of the group.

_____ 24. Interviews conducted in shopping centers are typically called *mall calls.*

_____ 25. Mail surveys have the drawback, by comparison with personal interviews, of taking much longer to conduct because researchers must wait for questionnaire recipients to complete and return them.

Multiple Choice

Circle the letter of the word or phrase that best completes the sentence or best answers the question.

26. Marketing research is best described as the process of collecting and using information to
    a. most efficiently apply new technologies in business.
    b.   make marketing decisions.
    c. acquire testimonials from famous criminals.
    d. decrease the cost of products.
    e. analyze sales information.

27. The decision of whether to conduct a marketing research study internally to the firm or externally generally comes down to
    a. deciding who is best able to do the work.
    b. solving problems related to what precisely the research user needs to know.
    c. the cost of doing the job; the cheaper provider will usually get the work.
    d. finding information that is already available and using that as a basis for the decision.
    e. flipping a coin and letting the gods of chance make the decision.

28. The type of marketing research organization that specializes in a limited number of activities such as conducting field interviews or data processing is called a
    a. full-service research supplier.
    b. industrial research supplier.
    c. contract research firm.
    d. syndicated service.
    e. limited-service research supplier.

29. The first task of the marketing researcher when embarking on a new project is to
    a. conduct exploratory research – talk to everyone who might have some knowledge of the situation.
    b. go to the library or some convenient bar for reflection on the matter.
    c. create an accurate definition of the problem.
    d. do a sales and cost analysis of the project as proposed.
    e. plan a research design.

30. The marketing research process ordinarily follows the sequence of
    a. interpretation and presentation, problem definition, exploratory research, research design, data collection, hypothesis.
    b. problem definition, interpretation and presentation, data collection, research design, hypothesis, exploratory research.
    c. problem definition, research design, hypothesis, exploratory research, data collection, interpretation and presentation.
    d. problem definition, exploratory research, hypothesis, research design, data collection, interpretation and presentation.
    e. interpretation and presentation, problem definition, exploratory research, research design, data collection.

31. Which of the following can be sources of secondary data?
    a. in-house product performance reviews.
    b. online databases available on the Internet
    c. industry sales figures published by a trade organization
    d. government publications such as the *Survey of Current Business*
    e. all of the above are sources of secondary data

32. Compared to secondary data, primary data has the advantage of
    a. providing richer, more detailed information.
    b. usually being less expensive to collect.
    c. taking less time to acquire and process.
    d. being readily available from the U. S. government and other sources.
    e. possessing all of the above characteristics.

33. The purpose of an analysis of sales performance records is to
    a. eliminate accountants' jobs by demonstrating how inefficient they are..
    b. gain an overall view of company efficiency and find clues to potential problems.
    c. evaluate such items as selling costs, warehousing, advertising, and delivery expenses.
    d. use ratio analysis to compare performance in current and previous years with industry benchmarks.
    e. acquire external secondary data to make decision-making more successful.

34. One of the most basic criteria for designing a research project is the assurance that
    a. the study will measure what it's intended to measure.
    b. the results are what the president of the company wants to see.
    c. budgetary constraints can be met even at the cost of accuracy.
    d. no one's job will be put at risk because of the study results.
    e. the measures used will be acceptable to the users.

35 Which of the following correctly matches the type of survey to the reason for choosing it?
    a. focus group B need to interview many people, perhaps even in groups, at low cost.
    b. mall intercept B required to contact people where they live.
    c. mail survey B necessary to take advantage of very high response rates to efficiently gather data.
    d. personal interview - desire to contact people living all over the world at the lowest possible cost.
    e. telephone interview B desire to gather small amounts of relatively impersonal information cheaply and quickly.

36. Which of the following correctly matches the type of sample with an appropriate example?
    a. cluster sample – researchers choose six city blocks from within Toulminville, Alabama, and attempt to interview every resident of the six areas
    b. stratified sample – people are solicited for interviews as they pass on the street based on how they look.
    c. simple random sample – after randomly choosing the first name, call every tenth name in the telephone directory.
    d. convenience sample – you interview anyone who will talk to you as you stand in front of Melvin's Men's Store in the downtown area.
    e. quota sample – interview 100 students selected by a random process from a list of all students.

37. The focus group is an example of
    a. an experimental research technique involving physical measurements of each subject.
    b. a type of interview research technique that doesn't ask questions but encourages discussion.
    c. an observational research technique using high-tech equipment to gather data.
    d. a method of collecting secondary personal data by reading people's mail.
    e. a method of assuring the accuracy of nonprobabilistic samples by forcing participation.

38. Marketing information systems
    a. gather information only from within the organization using them.
    b. periodically monitor the marketplace and provide occasional, sometimes inaccurate, information about it.
    c. store data for later use, though retrieving it may not be so easy because of the complexity of storage structure.
    d. are components of the organization's overall management information system that deal specifically with marketing data and problems.
    e. rely on information stored in hard-copy form kept in filing cabinets to generate the usual paperwork of the business.

39. Data mining
    a. is an efficient way to sort through huge amounts of data and to make sense of that data.
    b. relies on the existence of a "data repository," a giant database in which customer records are stored.
    c. works if and only if the data presents obvious relationships among variables.
    d. is not yet capable of relating one component of a data stream to other components.
    e. requires the use of a hard hat, safety glasses, and miner's lamp.

40. A simple random sample is
    a. a probability sample in which every item in the population has an equal chance of being selected.
    b. a probability sample arranged so that randomly selected subsamples of different groups within the population are represented in the sample.
    c. a probability sample in which areas are selected from which respondents are drawn in groups.
    d. a nonprobability sample based on the selection of readily available respondents.
    e. a nonprobability sample designed so that each subgroup in the population will be represented in the sample in proportion to its representation in the population.

41. Among the challenges faced by marketing researchers in global markets are
    a. language issues involving the most effective means of communication.
    b. cultural issues related to capturing local citizens' interest without offending them.
    c. the possibility that data gathering methods used at home may not be successful elsewhere.
    d. conditions in the business environment such as political and economic conditions.
    e. all of the above may be challenges the global researcher may have to meet.

42. This sales forecasting technique typically works from the "bottom up," that is, data is generated first at the district level, then refined at the regional, and finally consolidated nationally to create a tri-level estimate. It is
    a.   the survey of buyer intentions.
    b.   the Delphi technique.
    c.   a sales force composite.
    d.   trend analysis.
    e.   exponential smoothing.

43. The most commonly used quantitative forecasting technique, one that is a more sophisticated version of another forecasting technique, is
    a.   exponential smoothing, the scheme that weights each year's sales data.
    b.   the jury of executive opinion, basically a survey of local executives about the research topic.
    c.   Selmonev counting, a technique that allows various types of data to be counted the same way.
    d.   historical analysis that examines consumer behavior over many hundreds of years.
    e.   the Delphi technique, a system of repetitive analysis that uses computers to evaluate the worth of data.

44. Elmon Arriaga LLC is an organization that contracts with clients to conduct complete marketing research projects having to do with a broad array of consumer goods distribution issues in the Southeast. Elmon Arriaga is
    a.   a syndicated service company.
    b.   a captive research source.
    c.   a full-service research supplier.
    d.   a limited-service research supplier.
    e.   an audience measurement firm.

45. The cardinal rule of presenting marketing research requires
    a.   that it involve a complete discussion of its limitations as well as its strengths.
    b.   that it be presented in a format that allows management to make effective judgments.
    c.   direction of the presentation toward other researchers to avoid embarrassment.
    d.   discussion of the technical details as a central part of the presentation.
    e.   creation of a report that will impress management with the researchers, skill.

46. Using data obtained from the Internet
    a.   is completely safe because of the protections provided by the operators of news groups and bulletin boards that keep erroneous or dangerous information from appearing.
    b.   is the same as using well-researched data from a reputable trade or government publication.
    c.   calls for careful evaluation because people without in-depth knowledge of the topic may post information to the Net.
    d.   is safe because it is obvious whether acceptable research methods were used or not.
    e.   is seldom wise because the better class of researchers and publishers do not allow their work on the Net.

47. Sales analysis
    a. involves a spot examination of specific sales.
    b. requires that sales representatives provide detailed summaries of their work activities.
    c. consists of whatever the sales manager thinks it should be
    d. is one of the least expensive and most important sources of marketing information.
    e. is basically wishful thinking.

48. Which of the following is an example of an hypothesis?
    a. We sell 53 percent of the total quantity of this product sold in the world.
    b. Our sales force consists of 57 people, 14 of whom work in the field; the rest are support staff.
    c. Our president is an engineer; his brother, who serves as vice-president of finance, is an accountant.
    d. When buying a car, people first investigate to determine which cars are in their price range; then they look for a car in the preferred range.
    e. Gianetti jeans are designed with the active woman in mind.

49. Of all of the sources of primary research data, the one which is the best means of obtaining detailed information about consumers is
    a. observation.
    b. the mail survey.
    c. experimentation.
    d. the telephone interview .
    e. the personal interview.

50. If your supervisor in the marketing research department of the Southern States Life, Health, and Accident Insurance Company told you that she wanted you to take a probabilistic sample such that the members of the sample were broken down into the age groups 18-35, 36-49, and over 49 in the same proportion that those ages were distributed in the population, you would take a
    a. simple random sample.
    b. stratified sample.
    c. systematic sample.
    d. convenience sample.
    e. quota sample.

Name_____ Instructor_____

Section_____ Date_____

Applying Marketing Concepts

Aaron Silverman, marketing research analyst for Elgae Manufacturing Company (that,s Eagle spelled backwards), a national supplier of commercial food coolers, was told to find out why the model H18AR, the company's new twin-side high-speed cooler (a model designed to cool hot foods from 200 to 250 degrees Fahrenheit to 40 degrees in approximately 90 seconds) wasn't doing as well as it they thought it should in the marketplace and to report back to the executive committee in two weeks. Each unit sold for an average of $2400 each, depending on accessories ordered by the customer.

He decided that the first thing to do was to gather primary data from all the customers who'd bought the 750 H18ARs that were sold during the past year. His main concern was to find out why the customers weren't making repeat purchases of the product. After reviewing bids from three outside marketing research suppliers, Aaron chose the Mendarius Company because its bid was the lowest. Mr. Silverman directed Mendarius to design and conduct the study of all H18AR customers without talking to any Elgae management personnel.

After the primary research study was commissioned, Mr. Silverman talked with Elgae's sales force and wholesalers to attempt to determine the cause of the H18AR's lackluster sales performance. Finally, he reviewed the records available in the company's marketing information system. These records included breakdowns of sales and marketing costs for the H18AR in each territory. This data is reproduced below

TERRITORY

	Eastern Actual*	Eastern Quota*	Western Actual*	Western Quota*	Northern Actual*	Northern Quota*	Southern Actual*	Southern Quota*
Sales	$500	$400	$300	$200	$400	$300	$600	$500
Cost of Sales	300		180		120		180	
Gross Margin	200		120		280		420	
Marktg.Expenses	400	120	90	60	240	90	500	150
Contribution	(200)		30		40		(80)	

*thousands of dollars

_____ 1. Mr. Silverman was collecting primary data before examining the secondary data.

_____ 2. A census of Elgae's customers was the objective of the primary research.

_____ 3. Outside marketing research organizations should conduct research projects without ever talking to the users of the research information.

_____ 4. Very few organizations purchase outside marketing research services.

_____ 5. Elgae should not need marketing research if its marketing information system is effective.

6. The best way to gather the information Mr. Silverman wanted from customers in two weeks would be by means of
   a. observation.
   b. telephone interviews.
   c. personal interviews.
   d. focus group interviews.
   e. a mail survey.

7. The sales and expense analysis suggests that
   a. sales in all territories were below expectations.
   b. the East territory was the only problem market.
   c. marketing expenses were above expected levels in all territories.
   d. the sales force is incurring excessive travel and entertainment expenses.
   e. customers do not like the products.

8. Mr. Silverman's decision to do primary research before sales and expense analysis was based on the conclusion that answers about the causes of the H18AR's problems could be obtained from
   a. Elgae's customers
   b. ultimate consumers of products processed using Elgae equipment.
   c. the Elgae sales force.
   d. government publications.
   e. company management.

9. The results of her investigation should be
   a. discarded immediately never to be seen again.
   b. reviewed by management and then discarded.
   c. stored in Elgae's marketing information system for future use.
   d. acted upon immediately.

10. The major reason why Mr. Silverman chose the Mendarius Company is that
    a. it was the cheapest.
    b. it had the desired expertise.
    c. it was intellectually detached.
    d. it was a subsidiary of Elgae.
    e. the Mendarius Company had done many similar projects for other companies.

Mary Theresa Elizabeth, services director for the St. Dismas General Hospital system, was perturbed. She knew that the government charter under which her company provided broad-spectrum medical services to Elbow Bend required it to provide a free clinic to the community. Though the charter said that access to the treatment facilities and laboratories of St. Dismas' free clinic should be without charge for diagnosis and treatment of the indigent, and the hospital's managers, the Medical Order of St. Polycarp, viewed this as part of their duty, there was nothing in the charter which said that the hospital could not solicit and accept contributions from the general public to help them defray the expense of running the free clinic. Ms. Elizabeth wondered if making such a solicitation would be worthwhile. She also felt that she should get the information as soon as possible, for she knew that St. Dismas was soon scheduled to go before the city council to plead for a renewal of its charter to provide service, and even if it didn't prove possible to launch a solicitation at the present, it would be good to have the information about potential donors for the council hearings on renewal. They might realize that such a course could be "a tax on people who want to pay" and approve the idea for future use without additional hearings. The general rule of such fund raisers is that the cost of solicitation should not exceed 30 percent of the expected revenue the solicitation will realize

_____ 11.   Ms. Elizabeth's project is in the nature of an exploratory study.

_____ 12.   Most of the data for this project must be gathered from primary sources.

_____ 13.   A major source of secondary information for this study would be St. Dismas' logs of patients treated in its free clinic.

14. The most appropriate definition of Ms Elizabeth's problem is
    a.   She does not know how many patients are served by the free clinic.
    b.   She does not know the size and characteristics of the pool of people who would be willing to donate.
    c.   She does not know who the patients of the free clinic are.
    d.   She is unaware of the legal implications of the charter's "free clinic" provision.

15. Since Ms. Elizabeth needs her information in a short period of time, the best way to get it would be
    a.   by use of the experimental method.
    b.   through use of a mail survey.
    c.   over the telephone; use telephone interviews.
    d.   by stopping people on the street and asking them questions about St. Dismas' free clinic.

16. Which of the following might be an acceptable hypothesis upon which Ms. Elizabeth might develop her research?
    a.   The public wants to see more sophisticated treatment and less charitable work at their local hospital.
    b.   The quality of treatment at the free clinic is inferior to the quality of treatment in the hospital in general.
    c.   Free clinics are a waste of time and should be disallowed as a disservice to the community.
    d.   St. Dismas has a sufficiently good reputation that donors would be willing to give enough to support the free clinic to defray a substantial portion of the cost of operating it..

17. If Ms. Elizabeth does decide to use primary research and to design a sample-based method, which of the following would you suggest to her is most appropriate?
    a.   She should carefully analyze the location characteristics of Elbow Bend's more affluent residents and probabilistically sample them to determine their likelihood of giving and what the amount of the average gift might be.
    b.   She should conduct depth interviews with highly-placed executives at St. Dismas to get the benefit of their expertise and knowledge about how people support hospitals by donations.
    c.   She should draw a sample using a nonprobabilistic method so that she can avoid statistical analysis of her data.
    d.   She should randomly sample people from St. Dismas' list of free clinic patients who have been treated within a year

Name_____   Instructor_____

Section_____   Date_____

Surfing the Net

Keeping in mind that addresses change and what's on the Web now may have changed by the time you read this, let's take a look at some of the places on the Net that reflect aspects of marketing research. We are not endorsing or recommending any of these sources, merely making note of the information and services that people have elected to offer through the Internet.

Secondary data on the Web.   One way of finding information is by using a **search engine.** A search engine provides access to a database of many million Web sites. Some examples of search engines are *Excite,* at **http://www.excite.com.** Excite indexes over fifty million Web sites. These are made accessible by key word searches. Other search engines include *Alta Vista* at **http://www.altavista.com,** *HotBot* at **http://hotbot.com**, and *Infoseek* at **http://infoseek.go.com**. Also long to the Internet are **http://www.yahoo.com** or alternatively **http://www.ask.com** (also known as AskJeeves). Your Web Browser probably gives you a choice of several search engines to use. It is often interesting to conduct the same search on several of these just to see how their databases contain often quite different entries keyed to the same search string (that's the several words you enter to trigger the search.) You may have already developed a preference for a particular search engine.

You should also consider the metasearch engines, search engines that scan the databases of several other search engines and report their findings. The two most popular of these are **http://www.google.com** and **http://www.dogpile.com.** The major difference between the first two is that **dogpile** reports the databases it has searched, while **google** does not. Both are excellent tools.   Two other good choices are **http://www.ithaki.net** and **http;//www.ixquick.com.** A new metasearch engine is **http://www.vivisimo.com.**

Dun and Bradstreet's Web Site is at **http://www.dnb.com.**   This firm compiles data on firms all over the United States. Searches and registration are free, but should you want a Dun and Bradstreet report, the charge is $20.

Most major newspapers are on the Net. For the *Houston Chronicle,* try **http://www.chron.com/.** The *London Times* is at **http://www.the-times.co.uk.**   If for some reason you should develop an interest in the New Orleans Times-Picayune, their sponsored site is at **http://www.nola.com.** This site has a number of other sponsors, which makes it at tad more interesting than it otherwise would be. And the "things to do" section is impressive.

A number of professional research services may be accessed through the Web. Burke, Incorporated, parent company of Burke Marketing Research, has its site at **http://www.burke.com** and A. C. Nielsen Company, the giant of the industry, is located at **http://www.acnielsen.com.** You might be interested to see how these firms of varying background, specialties, and style write their Web sites. Ipsos-ASI Marketing Research, a firm that specializes in copy testing, sponsors the Marketing Research Center at **http://www.ipsos-asi.com**. They offer links to the market research industry and an e-mail directory of research professionals.

Need secondary data? American Demographics, Inc., can be reached at
http://www.demographics.com, at which site you can search the archives of their two magazines, *American Demographics* and *Marketing Tools.*

<u>Sites verified August 21, 2004</u>

Chapter 9
Market Segmentation, Targeting, and Positioning

Chapter Outline

You may want to use the following outline as a guide in taking notes.

I. Chapter Overview

A market is composed of people or institutions with sufficient purchasing power, authority, and willingness to buy. It is unusual for a single marketing mix strategy to attract all sectors of a market. The target market for a product is the specific segment of consumers most likely to purchase a particular product. To identify target markets, marketers must determine useful ways for segmenting different populations and communicating with them successfully.

II. Types of Markets include business products and consumer products. Consumer products are those bought by ultimate consumers for personal use. Business products are goods and services purchased for use either directly or indirectly in the production of other goods and services for resale.

   A. Sometimes a single product can serve different uses and be at times a consumer product and at times a business product. Some authors add another category, commercial products, non-consumer products that do not contribute directly to the production of other goods.

III. The Role of Market Segmentation is to identify the factors that affect purchase decisions and then group consumers according to the presence or absence of these factors. Marketing strategies are then adjusted to meet the needs of each group. The division of the total market into smaller, relatively homogeneous groups is market segmentation. Segmentation is practiced by both for-profit and not-for-profit organizations.

   A. Criteria for effective segmentation include four basic requirements.
      1. The market segment must possess measurable purchasing power and size.
      2. There must be a way to promote effectively to and to serve the market segment.
      3. Marketers must be able to identify which segments are sufficiently large to give them good profit potential.
      4. The firm must aim for segments that match its marketing capabilities.

IV. Segmenting Consumer Markets attempts to isolate the traits that distinguish a certain group of customers from the overall market. Each group's characteristics play a role in the development of a successful marketing strategy. The four most common bases for segmenting consumer markets are geography, demography, psychography, and product-related characteristics.

   A. Geographic segmentation, which consists of dividing an overall market into homogeneous groups on the basis of their locations, has been in use for literally hundreds of years. Geographical segmentation does not guarantee that all consumers in an area will make the same buying decisions, but it does help to identify some general patterns. Population size alone is not reason enough for a business to expand into a specific region or country. Economic factors may argue for a grouping of countries rather than treating each uniquely. Other geographic indicators such as population growth may influence and guide marketers depending on the types of products they sell. Population migration patterns may differ from place to place as well. In the U.S., population is shifting toward the Southeast and Southwest and the West. In recognition of the change from an urban to suburban economy, the government now classified urban areas into five categories:

1. the Core-Based Statistical Area (CBSA), a micropolitan or metropolitan statistical area containing at least one urban area with a population of 10,000 or more.
    a. Metropolitan Statistical Areas (MSA) are freestanding urban centers with a population in the urban center of at least 50,000 and a total population of 100,000 or more;
    b. Micropolitan Statistical Areas, areas that contain at least one town of 10,000 to 49,999 people with relatively few of its residents commuting outside the area.
2. the Primary Metropolitan Statistical Area (PMSA), including a county or a set of counties with close ties and a population of a million or more; and
3. finally, the Consolidated Metropolitan Statistical Area (CMSA), which defines the nation's 25 or so urban giants and must contain at least two PMSAs.
4. Using geographic segmentation requires that marketers examine several factors that affect sales.
    a. Demand for some goods and services is concentrated in "core regions" where 40 to 80 percent of their sales originate.
    b. Residence location within a geographic area is an important segmentation variable.
    c. Climate is an important geographic segmentation factor.
    d. Geographic segmentation is useful when regional needs or preferences exist. No one wants to own a snowblower, but some people must.

B. Demand for some categories of goods and services can vary according to geographic region, and marketers need to understand how these regions differ. Major brand marketers are particularly interested in defining their core regions, the places where they get 40 to 80 percent of their sales. Residence location within a geographic area is an important segmentation variable, as is climate. When regional preferences or needs exist, geographic segmentation produces useful distinctions.

C. Geographic Information Systems (GIS) simplify the job of analyzing marketing information by placing data in a special format. The result is a geographical map overlaid digital data about consumers in a particular area. The earliest GIS systems were prohibitively expensive for all except the largest firms. They are now much more reasonably priced, allowing small firms to use them.

D. Demographic segmentation – the most common approach to consumer segmentation – defines consumer groups according to variables such as age, sex, income, occupation, education, household size, and stage in the family life cycle.
1. Segmenting by gender is an obvious choice that helps define markets for certain products.
    a. Occasionally, even though marketers think they have targeted a gender market correctly, a product may miss its audience.
    b. Some firms market the same product successfully to people of both sexes.
    c. Other firms start by targeting one sex and later switch to both.
2. Segmenting by age is appropriate for some products that specifically meet the needs of certain groups.
    a. Baby food meets the needs of infants, while retirement communities serve the elderly.

    b. Tweens (preteens) and teens together constitute a $150 billion per year market who like being advertised to.

    c. The *cohort effect* refers to the tendency of members of a generation to be influenced and bound together by significant events occurring during their formative years – roughly 17 to 22 years of age.

    d. Baby boomers were born between 1946 and 1965 and represent 42 percent of U.S. adults. Their values were formed by the Vietnam War and the career orientation of the following years.

        i.   Boomers are now between 39 and 59 years of age and represent a lucrative market with high disposable incomes, but are not a homogeneous group.

        ii. There are many subgroups among the boomers because of their age dispersion.

        iii. Boomers have an interest in nostalgic items that remind them of their own childhoods and adolescence.

    e. Seniors are the people above the age of 65 who will, by the year 2025, represent nearly 20 percent of the population.

        i.   Seniors are expected to live much longer than was the case in even the recent past, those currently in the group to well in their 80s.

        ii. A powerful economic force, seniors control about three-quarters of the country's wealth, and those most affluent are known as WOOFs – well-off older folks.

        iii. Since the 1950s, many firms have given seniors discounts on their purchases; many of these discounts are being discontinued as the economy slows.

3. Segmenting by Ethnic Group is becoming more important because the diversity of the U.S. population is increasing.

    a. By 2050, it is estimated that nearly half the U.S. population will belong to non-white minority groups.

    b. The three largest and fastest-growing ethnic groups in the U.S. are Hispanics, African-Americans, and Asian Americans.

        i.   Hispanics and African-Americans are the largest ethnic minority groups in the United States, each accounting for around 13 percent of the population.

        ii. The Hispanic market has been a serious target for many firms during the last few years.

    c. Asian-Americans and Pacific Islanders are the second fastest-growing segment of the U.S. population.

        i.   The Asian-American population is concentrated in fewer geographic areas than are other ethnic markets.

    d. Native Americans, although only 2 million strong, have begun to establish economic and political clout by developing various entertainment centers and other attractions throughout the United States.

    e. Different ethnic and racial segments of the population exhibit different consumer preferences, motivations, and buying habits.

4. Segmenting by the stage of the family life cycle – the particular section of the process of family formation and dissolution in which one finds oneself – is based on the idea that it is not age, but this phenomenon that affects much buyer behavior.

    a. An unmarried person setting up an apartment for the first time is likely to be a good prospect for inexpensive furniture and small home appliances.

    b. The birth of a first child changes any couple's consumer profile considerably, cribs, changing tables, and baby clothes becoming likely products of choice.

    c. Financial expenditures are typically greatest during the children's growth years.

      d. Married couples whose children have left home – "empty nesters" – are an attractive life-cycle segment for marketers because their lifestyles begin to change as a result of their children's departure.

      e. Adult children who return home, often bringing their children with them, are a new phenomenon in the family life cycle – the boomerangs.

  5. Segmenting by household type deals with issues related to number of people in a household, changes in family structure, and differences in family members' roles.

      a. The size of the American household is declining due to lower fertility rates, the tendency to postpone marriage, people's desire to have no children or few children, the ease and frequency of divorce, and the tendency to live alone.

      b. The traditional family is becoming less common than was the case prior to the past decade. Diversity is much more common than was the case earlier.

      c. Same-sex couples who share households are on the rise. Many are raising children, and companies have begun to provide benefits for them.

      d. People living alone constitute a household type now present in sufficient numbers to provide a worthwhile set of market segments.

  6. Segmenting by income and expenditure patterns is a common basis for consumer market segmentation.

      a. Engel's laws, now over a century old, supposedly describe the impact of household income changes on consumer spending behavior. There are three of these laws, all of which relate to what happens when household income increases. In other words, as family income increases, according to Engel

         i. a smaller percentage of expenditures go for food.

        ii. the percentage spent on housing and household operations and clothing remains constant.

       iii. the percentage spent on other items such as recreation and education increases.

      b. Newer studies say that, despite the passage of time, Engel's laws are still largely true, the differences growing out of the higher absolute levels of income prevailing in the early twenty-first century.

  7. Demographic segmentation abroad is more difficult than is the case in the United States because of the lack of data from a number of foreign markets

      a. Many foreign countries do not or seldom conduct censuses of their population, or they may conduct them at intervals greater or less than those used in the U.S.

      b. Some foreign demographic data includes categories, such as religion, not collected in the U.S.

      c. The International Programs Center of the U.S. Bureau of the Census is a good source of global demographic data.

C. Psychographic segmentation is a more recently developed segmentation tool than the previous examples.

  1. What is psychographic segmentation? It is a process that divides a population into groups that have similar psychological characteristics, values, and lifestyles (which are people's modes of living).

      a. The most common way to develop the psychological profile of a population is to conduct a large-scale survey that measures people's activities, interests, and opinions.

      b. Marketing researchers have conducted studies on hundreds of goods and services, from beer to air travel.

2. VALS 2 is the second generation of a psychographic segmentation system based on the analysis of values and lifestyles pioneered by consulting firm SRI International a quarter century ago.
   a. The VALS2 scheme divides consumers into eight psychographic categories based on resources and self-orientation.
   b. SRI supplies several specialized segmentation systems based on the VALS2 approach.
   c. VALS2 is available to marketers on a subscriber/client basis
   d. There are services other than VALS2 available to marketers, such as LifeMatrix from RoperASW and Mediamark Research.
3. Psychographic segmentation of global markets include such efforts as JapanVALS and a recent study by Roper Starch Worldwide that identified six psychographic consumer segments that exist in 35 nations.
   a. The six RoperStarch categories include Strivers, Devouts, Altruists, Intimates, Fun Seekers, and Creatives, all of whom are present in varying numbers in many cultures.
4. Using psychographic segmentation involves applying tools such as VALS2 and the Roper categories to describe target markets much more richly than other techniques allow.
   a. Identifying the psychographic segments that prevail in certain markets allows for better planning and promotion.
   b. Psychographic segmentation is a good supplement to demographic and geographic segmentation.

D. Product-Related Segmentation involves dividing a consumer population into homogeneous groups based on characteristics of their relationships to the product – the benefits they seek when they buy it, the rate at which they use it, or their brand loyalty to it.
   1. Segmenting by benefits sought focuses on the attributes that people seek in a good or service and the benefits they expect to receive from the good or service.
      a. Starbucks customers, for example, aren't just buying caffeine; they're seeking a pleasant experience and the sense of being pampered.
      b. Even a one-product-line business must remember to consider product benefits because people buy the same products for different reasons.
   2. Segmenting by usage rates involves grouping people on the basis of the quantity of a product they buy and use.
      a. The 80/20 principle (also known as Praedo's Law) says that approximately 80 percent of a product's revenues come from approximately 20 percent of the product's buyers – the loyal ones.
      b. Marketers may choose to target heavy, moderate, or light users or even nonusers.
   3. Segmenting by brand loyalty groups customers according to the strength of their attachment to the product.
      a. Airline frequent-flyer programs are classic examples of brand loyalty segmentation.

V. The Market Segmentation Process – here's the do-it-yourself guide to segmentation

   A. Stage I: Identify market segmentation processes.
      1. Segmentation begins when marketers determine the bases on which to identify markets, whether they use a management-driven method or a market-driven method.
      2. Sometimes there is difficulty isolating a preferred segment or may decide to serve a variety of segments.

B. Stage II: Develop a relevant profile for each segment
1. After identifying promising segments, marketers seek to understand the customers in each one.
2. The task at this stage is to develop a profile of the typical customer in each segment.

C. Stage III: Forecast market potential
1. At this stage, market segmentation and market opportunity analysis combine to produce a forecast of market potential within each segment.
2. A segment that shows tremendous market potential is U.S. children ages 4 to 12.

D. Stage IV: Forecast probable market share
1. Once market potential has been estimated, a firm must forecast its probable market share.
2. Competitors' positions in the selected market share must also be evaluated because they will have some effect on the firm's profit potential.

E. Stage V: Select specific market segments
1. The information acquired in stages I through IV is used to assess the likelihood of achieving company goals and justifying committing resources to one or more market segments.
2. Monetary, organizational, and environmental factors must all be considered and weighed but some sort of decision ultimately is taken.

VI. Strategies for Reaching Target Markets

A. Undifferentiated marketing
1. A firm that produces only a single product line and promotes it to all customers with a single marketing mix is said to practice undifferentiated marketing.
2. This strategy is efficient from a production point of view, but it opens the competitive door to firms that may choose to offer specialized products to smaller segments of the aggregate market.

B. Differentiated marketing
1. Firms that promote numerous products with different marketing mixes designed to satisfy smaller segments are said to engage in differentiated marketing.
2. Even though it is more expensive than undifferentiated marketing, an organization may be forced to practice differentiated marketing to remain competitive.

C. Concentrated marketing
1. The firm that chooses to implement concentrated marketing (also known as niche marketing) focuses its efforts on profitably satisfying only one market segment.
2. Magazine publishers are among the firms currently using niche marketing strategies to access desirable market segments.
3. Concentrated marketing possesses the danger of creating a difficulty for the using firm if new competitors appeal successfully to the same target market.

D. Micromarketing
1. Micromarketing is a strategy even more narrowly focused than concentrated marketing, targeting potential customers on a very basic level such as by zip code, specific occupation, or lifestyle.

    2. Micromarketing, like niche marketing, runs the risk of being subject to losses if firms spend too much time, effort, and money on a target market that is too small and specialized to be profitable.

E. Selecting and executing a strategy
1. Though most firms choose some type of differentiated strategy, no single best choice suits all firms.
2. A firm with limited resources may have to choose a concentrated marketing strategy because of financial, sales force, and promotional budget limitations.
3. The firm's strategy may change as the product moves through the stages of the product life cycle.
4. The strategies of competitors may affect the choice of segmentation strategy made by a firm.
5. Once a strategy has been chosen, the issue of positioning the product is then raised, and a firm may choose a number of positioning strategies, such as positioning by attributes, price/quality, competitors, application, product user, or product class.
6. Regardless of strategy, marketers want to emphasize a product's unique advantages and differentiate it from the competition. A positioning map often facilitates this process.
7. Sometimes, changes in the competitive advantage may force marketers to reposition a product.

Name_____   Instructor_____

Section_____   Date_____

Key Concepts

The purpose of this section is to allow you to determine if you can match key concepts with the definitions of the concepts. It is essential that you know the definitions of the concepts prior to applying them in later exercises in this chapter.

From the list of lettered terms, select the one that best fits each of the numbered statements below. Write the letter of that choice in the space provided.

Key Terms

a. market
b. target market
c. consumer products
d. business products
e. market segmentation
f. geographic segmentation
g. geographic information system (GIS)
h. demographic segmentation

i. psychographic segmentation
j. product-related segmentation
k. undifferentiated marketing
l. differentiated marketing
m. concentrated marketing
n. micromarketing
o. positioning

_____ 1. Marketing strategy that commits all of a firm's marketing resources to serve a single market segment.

_____ 2. Goods or services purchased for use either directly or indirectly in the production of other goods and services for resale.

_____ 3. Specific segment of consumers most likely to purchase a particular product.

_____ 4. A group of people or institutions who possess sufficient purchasing power and the authority and willingness to buy.

_____ 5. Dividing an overall market into homogeneous groups on the basis of population location.

_____ 6. Dividing a consumer population into homogeneous groups based on the benefits they seek when buying, their usage rates of, or their brand loyalty to a product.

_____ 7. Marketing strategy used by firms that produce only one product and market it to all customers using a single marketing mix.

_____ 8. Marketing strategy to target potential customers at basic levels such as by ZIP code, occupation, or lifestyle.

_____ 9. Dividing consumer groups into homogeneous segments on the basis of characteristics such as age, sex, income level, and stage in the family life cycle.

_____ 10. Division of the total market into smaller, relatively homogeneous groups.

_____ 11. Goods or services purchased by the ultimate consumer for personal use.

_____ 12. Dividing a consumer population into homogeneous groups based on their psychological and lifestyle profiles.

_____ 13. Computer technology that records several layers of digital data on a single map.

_____ 14. Marketing strategy that emphasizes serving a specific market segment by achieving a certain position in buyers' minds.

_____ 15. Strategy used by organizations that produce numerous products and use different marketing mixes to satisfy smaller market segments.

Name_____   Instructor_____

Section_____   Date_____

Self-Quiz

You should use these objective questions to test your understanding of the chapter material. You can check your answers with those provided at the end of the chapter.

While these questions cover most of the chapter topics, they are not intended to be the same as the test questions your instructor may use in an examination. A good understanding of all aspects of course material is essential to good performance on any examination.

_____ 1. The key to proper classification of goods and services is determining the identity of the purchaser and how and why the product will be used.

_____ 2. Henry Ford, because of his willingness to adapt to customer needs, was one of the pioneers in the segmentation of the U.S. automobile industry.

_____ 3. A market requires that there be people or institutions with sufficient purchasing power, authority, and the willingness to buy.

_____ 4. Light bulbs sold to lamp manufacturers to be sold with their lamps are business products. Light bulbs sold to consumers to replace light bulbs in their home fixtures are consumer products.

_____ 5. To segment a market effectively, the only requirements are that the segment must present measurable purchasing power and size and that it be possible to promote effectively to and serve the market segment.

_____ 6. Demographic segmentation is based on the concept that it is life stage, not age per se, that is the primary determinant of many consumer purchases.

_____ 7. Texas, with its population of 21 million people, is the United States' most heavily populated state.

_____ 8. According to the Census, the Western United States have experienced the fastest growth in recent years at 19.7 percent, with the South close behind at 17.3 percent.

_____ 9. East Baton Rouge, Louisiana, with its population of 225,000, qualifies as a Consolidated Metropolitan Statistical Area.

_____ 10. Market segmentation is the process of dividing the total market into smaller, relatively homogeneous groups.

_____ 11. Geographic market segmentation of consumers is useful when specific regional preferences for products and services exist.

_____ 12. Geographic Information Systems software is still prohibitively expensive for all but the largest firms and organizations.

_____ 13. One of the reasons demographic market segmentation is the most common method of market segmentation is because vast quantities of demographic data are available to use in planning.

_____ 14. The median age of the American population has increased from 32.8 years of age to 39.2 years of age in the last ten years.

_____ 15. The fastest-growing of the ethnic minorities in the United States are Hispanics.

_____ 16. The significant events that a person experiences between the ages of about 23 to 29 tend to bind him or her to others of his or her generation. This is called the cohort effect.

_____ 17. Despite the fact that its marketing costs will be higher, a firm may be forced to resort of differentiated marketing to remain competitive.

_____ 18. Micromarketing – in which a firm devotes its efforts to profitably satisfying only one market segment – is also known as "niche marketing."

_____ 19. In terms of the family life cycle, couples without children are frequent buyers of personalized gifts, power tools, furniture, and homes.

_____ 20. The two key concepts underlying the VALS2 typology are occupation and income.

_____ 21. Product-related segmentation of the toothpaste market by brand loyalty might produce segments concerned with reducing tooth decay, enjoying the taste while brushing, or brightening the teeth.

_____ 22. According to the Census, some older couples are choosing to live together rather than get married because they prefer to keep their finances separate and because they could lose valuable health or pension benefits if they married.

_____ 23. One's demographic characteristics are the composite of his or her individual physical profile, including needs, motives, perceptions, and attitudes.

_____ 24. One of the problems encountered in using demographic segmentation abroad is that some countries do not have scheduled census programs, while others do not collect some of the demographic data commonly used as bases for segmentation in the United States and others collect data not collected in the United States.

_____ 25. Segments which have been identified by psychographic analysis as having different lifestyles cannot be expected to behave differently from each other.

Multiple Choice

Circle the letter of the word or phrase that best completes the sentence or best answers the question.

26. Markets require people, purchasing power, authority to buy, and
    a. engineering personnel.
    b. willingness to buy.
    c. a bargaining committee.
    d. descriptions of products.
    e. purchasing agents.

27. Analyzing competitors' positions in targeted segments and designing a marketing strategy to reach these segments is an intrinsic part of which phase of the market segmentation process?
    a. Stage II – forecasting market potential
    b. Stage III – forecasting probable market share
    c. Stage IV – selecting specific market segments
    d. Stage V – re-evaluation of current market positions
    e. Stage VI – exploring new opportunities

28. A basic reason why marketers elect to segment markets is because
    a. products always succeed by appealing to single, homogeneous markets.
    b. they need some means of solving the complex problem of finding buyers for their products.
    c. in today's business world, there are too many variables in consumer needs, preferences, and purchasing power to attract all consumers with a single marketing mix.
    d. when the production line goes into operation, it must turn out the millions of items necessary to secure economies of scale.
    e. competition will find it difficult to determine what is going to happen next.

29. Under which of the following conditions may segmentation not promote marketing success?
    a. When the market segment can be accurately measured in terms of both purchasing power and size.
    b. When it is feasible to promote effectively to the market segment.
    c. When the segment or segments of the market under consideration are large enough to be adequately profitable.
    d. When there are no apparent problems in providing the chosen segment or segments of the market with adequate service.
    e. When the firm cannot find a segment or segments that match its marketing capabilities.

30. A Primary Metropolitan Statistical Area (CMSA)
    a. must include two or more Consolidated Metropolitan Statistical Areas.
    b. is an urbanized county or counties with a population in excess of 1,000,000.
    c. usually borders on nonurbanized counties.
    d. must be a freestanding urban area with a population of at least 50,000.
    e. cannot include more than 6 counties or 3 incorporated municipalities.

31. In the context of gender segmentation, when it comes to home improvement products,
    a. women tend to understand the technology and function of products better than men.
    b. color makes all the difference between what men and women buy.
    c. men and women now tend to share the purchasing responsibility.
    d. you can't appeal to men and women with the same products.
    e. sinks and faucets are "man things" but dishwashers are "woman things."

32. A freestanding urban area with an urban center population of 50,000 and which has a total population of 100,000 or more within it would be defined by the U.S. government as a(n)
    a. undefined statistical area.
    b. metropolitan statistical area.
    c. micropolitan statistical area.
    d. primary metropolitan statistical area.
    e. consolidated metropolitan statistical area.

33. Which of the following is a psychographic variable?
    a. your opinion about conservative government
    b. the State in which you reside
    c. the rate at which you use a particular product
    d. your occupation, craft, or trade
    e. the number, ages, and genders of your children

34. The fastest-growing racial/ethnic minority group in the United States at present is
    a. Hispanics.
    b. Native Americans and Inuits.
    c. African-Americans.
    d. Asian-Americans and Pacific Islanders.
    e. Acadian-Americans.

35. A market segment based on the family life cycle concept is
    a. the high-income segment.
    b. people who buy new automobiles frequently.
    c. couples who have recently had their first child.
    d. residents of large eastern metropolitan areas.
    e. Polish-Americans.

36. Geographic Information Systems
    a. simplify the job of analyzing marketing information by relating data to their locations.
    b. present data in the form of a geographic map overlaid with digital data.
    c. can be used to identify favorable sites for new store locations.
    d. have not yet realized their full potential, though their use is increasing.
    e. All of the above statements are true.

37. According the Engel's laws, an increase in family income should bring
    a. a greater percentage of income expended for food.
    b. fewer dollars expended for housing.
    c. fewer dollars expended for education and recreation.
    d. an increase in the percentage of income spent on recreation and education.
    e. a higher percentage of income spent for more and better housing.

38. The group of people born between 1946 and 1965 and who now account for nearly 42 percent of the U.S. population are the
    a. seniors who control about three-quarters of the nation's total financial assets.
    b. members of generation R who are more generally liberal politically than the general population.
    c. "new" generation, more into alternative and new wave music and more computer literate.
    d. baby boomers, many of whose behavior is not as expected by forecasters.
    e. cohorts, those who do as their fellow members of this generation do with little variation.

39. According to the VALS2 typology, the image-conscious, relatively affluent people who are attracted to premium products and watch an average amount of television are the
    a. fulfilleds.
    b. believers.
    c. makers.
    d. actualizers.
    e. achievers.

40. Since the first census was taken in 1790, the size of the average American household has
    a. remained stable at about 3.7 persons per household.
    b. increased due to better diet and medicine from 3.7 persons to 5.6.
    c. decreased from 5.8 persons to 3.
    d. become impossible to measure because the definition of household has changed.
    e. been broadened to include pets as parts of the household (except guppies).

41. A firm that targets as potential customers only stockbrokers in the Dubuque, Iowa, area who place twenty or more of a specific type of limited partnership per year is using
    a. undifferentiated marketing.
    b. differentiated marketing.
    c. concentrated marketing.
    d. arbitrary segmentation.
    e. micromarketing.

42. Melrose Specialty Company has designed and markets a special package of computer software to people who value knowledge, like education and public affairs, and read widely and often, specifically designed to help them shop on the Internet. To determine to whom to target this product, Melrose used
    a. geographic segmentation.
    b. psychographic segmentation.
    c. demographic segmentation.
    d. marginal segmentation.
    e. undifferentiated segmentation.

43. The stage of the market segmentation process that involves examining, in addition to monetary costs and benefits, critical and often difficult-to-measure organizational factors that affect the choice of segments is
    a. developing a relevant profile for each segment.
    b. forecasting market potential.
    c. selecting specific market segments.
    d. forecasting probable market share.
    e. selecting market segmentation bases.

44. A firm which produces numerous products with different marketing mixes, each of which is designed to satisfy a specific segment of the market, is said to be practicing
    a. undifferentiated marketing.
    b. mass marketing.
    c. differentiated marketing.
    d. consolidated marketing.
    e. concentrated marketing.

45. Which of the following is an appropriate example of the indicated type of market segment?
    a. geographic – people living within 1.5 miles of a particular shopping center
    b. psychographic – young married couples with children
    c. demographic – people looking for the lowest cost watch
    d. benefits sought – people who attend sports events
    e. demographic – people with a positive attitude toward education

46. Retailer *Hot Topic* and General Motors' new vehicles, the Pontiac Solstice, Chevrolet HHR, and Chevy Nomad station wagon are examples of which type of marketing segmentation
    a. differentiated marketing.
    b. concentrated marketing.
    c. undifferentiated marketing
    d. micromarketing.
    e. melodramatic marketing.

47. At this stage in the market segmentation process, the marketer conducts an in-depth analysis of customers to match their needs with the firm's marketing offers. The stage in question is the one designed to
    a. develop a relevant profile for each segment.
    b. forecast market potential.
    c. select specific market segments.
    d. forecast probable market share.
    e. determine the bases on which to identify markets.

48. The world's two largest cities in terms of population are
    a. New York City, New York and Chicago, Illinois.
    b. Tokyo, Japan and Mexico City, Mexico.
    c. Beijing, China and Bangkok, Thailand.
    d. Rio de Janeiro, Brazil and Paris, France.
    e. New Delhi, India, and New Braunfels, Texas.

49. When a manufacturer creates a product such as a pickup truck called the "Texas Tornado" for sale in that state, selling the same model in adjoining Louisiana as the "Swamp Runner Special," it is using
    a. benefits-sought segmentation.
    b. geographic segmentation.
    c. end-use application segmentation
    d. psychographic segmentation.
    e. arbitrary segmentation.

50. Within the broader classification of product-related segmentation, the classic example of this segmentation technique is airline frequent flyer programs. The technique has evolved into
    a. segmenting by benefits sought.
    b. segmenting by usage rates.
    c. segmenting by demographic characteristics.
    d. segmenting by psychographics.
    e. segmenting by brand loyalty.

Name_____   Instructor_____

Section_____   Date_____

Applying Marketing Concepts

The Vaikkonen Products Company of Tikkakoski, Finland, has developed a line of disposable footware. The footware can be sold profitably for about half the price of conventional shoes. The items are durable enough to withstand wear for several weeks if desired, but can be easily disposed of simply by treating them with a special chemical solution in which they dissolve. Due to the manufacturing processes involved, the materials of which the shoes are made can only be made in solid colors. Children are expected to be major users of these shoes, so their parents will be the people with the authority, willingness, and purchasing power to buy. The company expects the most interest in its products to come from parents of younger children whose rough play and rapid growth require they get new shoes frequently. Executives at Vaikkonen also foresee a market for their product among individuals in hospitals and other locations where shoes can be contaminated by toxic or biohazardous materials. The solvent used to dissolve the Vaikkonen product kills every known bacterium and virus, and neutralizes chemical toxins.

_____ 1. By definition, the real market for Vaikkonen's disposable shoes is younger children.

_____ 2. According to Engel's laws, the percent of income spent on clothing stays the same over all levels of consumer income.

_____ 3. The disposable shoes sold to people who want to use them for their medical duties would be classed as commercial products.

4. The Vaikkonen Products Company is selling disposable footware as
   a. business products.
   b. consumer products.
   c. both business and consumer products.
   d. military hardware.
   e. fashion statements.

5. The segmentation method most appropriate to Vaikkonen's attempt to reach its target of the parents of small children is probably
   a. geographical, concentrating on the West where all the small children are.
   b. product-based, orienting toward brand loyalty.
   c. demographic, using the family life cycle as a basis.
   d. psychographic, targeting the strivers.

6. If benefits-sought segmentation is used by Vaikkonen, it should direct its efforts toward people who want
   a. long-lasting durability.
   b. high fashion, stylish shoes.
   c. convenience in use at reasonable cost.
   d. lowest overall cost shoes.

You have recently concluded a month-long visit to your company's main branch office in the Eastern European nation of Spolkvnece, which shares many cultural values with nearby Krasny Brod. You were impressed with the differences among the various groups of people you met there. Many of your contemporaries (you're in your early thirties) seemed really into education and knowledge, taking self-improvement courses at every opportunity. Others were working on science and engineering degrees or certificates.   Another group, about the same age, were more mellow, enjoying many parties and other social activities. Most of them were established professionals with some measure of success, and their homes and activities reflected their success, being well-appointed and very comfortable.

You did notice, though, that many of the people you met, whatever their status in life, seemed very home oriented. These, too, were generally well-educated and professionally active, often very well-respected, but liked to go home and be with their families rather than partying to all hours. Others of the citizens of Spolkvnece, who leaned toward the female side in numbers, seemed to be steeped in tradition and spent much of their time at the office, often going back in at night to "do their duty" and complete a task if they felt they had left something undone at quitting time.

Using the results reported in the Roper Starch Worldwide study reported in your text, how would you characterize each of the groups discussed above?

7. Your contemporaries who were heavily into education and technology would probably be classed by Roper-Starch as
   a. Devouts.
   b. Altruists.
   c. Apparatchiks.
   d. High pragmatics.
   e. Creatives.

8. Your mellower contemporaries are probably
   a. Devouts.
   b. Fun seekers.
   c. Strivers.
   d. High pragmatics.
   e. Altruists.

9. The group of people who were active professionally but home-oriented were probably
   a. Strivers.
   b. Altruists.
   c. Creatives.
   d. Intimates.
   e. Sustainers.

10. The people who seemed to be duty-oriented and more traditional would be classed as
   a. Strivers.
   b. Integrators.
   c. Devouts.
   d. Intimates.
   e. Sustainers.

Name_____   Instructor_____

Section_____   Date_____

Surfing the Net

Keeping in mind that addresses change and what's on the Web now may have changed by the time you read this, let's take a look at some of the places on the Net that reflect aspects of segmentation, targeting, and positioning. We are not endorsing or recommending any of these sources, merely making note of the information and services that people have elected to offer through the Internet.

How targeted can you get? The restaurant industry is an excellent example. There are Web sites for a number of fairly specialized restaurant chains on the Web. Consider Bagel Oasis at **http://www.bageloasis. com** or a California chain, The Fish Market, which can be reached at **http://www.thefishmarket. com.** If you like pretzels, try Keystone Pretzels at **http://www.keystonepretzels.com.** They're in Lititz, Pennsylvania and offer a specialty, Oatzels, that might strike your fancy.

Among soft-goods retailers (that's firms that sell clothes), the Net offers a number of interesting possibilities. One site is operated by Casual Male, a big and tall men's chain. They're at **http://www.thinkbig.com.** Looking for women's clothing? No problem. Active Body, in Scottsdale, Arizona, offers wardrobe consultations for the active woman; Casual Clothing Discounters, on the other hand, claims to offer comfortable, stylish clothing designed to mix and match, and at reasonable prices, on their Web Site. Try **http://www.activebody.com** for Active Body and **http://www.evertize.com** for Casual Clothing Discounters.

Here's another classic example of a well-segmented market – the retail record industry. Naxos, a vendor specializing in classical music, is on the net at **http://www.naxos.com.**   You don't groove on the classics? If Reggae and Ska are your kettle of fish, why not try **www.musicmania.com** for an extensive selection of reggae, ska, and related musical styles.

And just for fun, you can examine another highly targeted market on your own. The radio industry wouldn't have nearly as many stations if they weren't targeted to the many segments the industry has discovered, from classic through easy listening to Gospel, rap, and heavy metal. Most stations have Web sites, and those Web sites, as you might imagine, are keyed to the call letters of the stations. Try a few and see what your get. We connected to **wwno.org** (the University of New Orleans main transmitter), **wkbw.com** in Buffalo, New York (and got their TV site), **woai.com** in San Antonio, Texas, one of the very few "w" stations west of the Mississippi, **wowo.com** in Fort Wayne, Indiana, **kprc.com,** Houston, Texas, **kdka.com**, Pittsburgh, Pennsylvania, one of the few "k" stations east of the Mississippi, **wbrc.com**, Birmingham, Alabama, and finally, **kuam.com** on the furthest west place in the United States, Guam, where a typhoon was whipping the island with 80 mile-and-hour winds when we hooked up. If you know their station calls, you can access stations all over the world using the Internet.

Sites verified August 22, 2004.

Chapter 10
Relationship Marketing, Customer Relationship Management (CRM), and One-to-One Marketing

Chapter Outline

You may want to use the following as a guide in taking notes.

I. Chapter Overview

The shift away from transaction-based to relationship-based marketing is one of the most important trends in marketing today. Transaction-based marketing focuses on short-term, single exchanges, while relationship marketing is the development, growth, and mainte-nance of cost-effective, high-value relationships with individual customers, suppliers, retailers, and other partners for mutual value over time.

II. The Shift from Transaction-Based Marketing to Relationship Marketing – since earliest days, manufacturers have tended to be production-oriented, a philosophy that resulted in a trans-action-based approach to marketing. Buyer and seller exchanges are characterized by limited communications and little or no ongoing relationships. Some marketing exchanges, especially where the likelihood of future transactions is limited, continue to be transactions based. Many firms have begun to take a different approach, redefining the nature of the in-teractions between customers and sellers. Conflict changes to cooperation and infrequent contacts between buyers and sellers become ongoing exchanges. Superior service by sell-ers providing customers with added value from their relationship becomes a central component of the marketing program.

A. Elements of relationship marketing are four in number.
1. Database technology helps the company identify current and potential customers who possess selected demographic, purchase, and lifestyle characteristics.
2. Data is analyzed and used to modify the marketing mix to deliver differentiated mes-sages and
customized marketing programs to individual customers.
3. Using relationship marketing, interactions with customers are monitored to assess satisfaction or dissatisfaction with the service being provided and other useful information.
4. Using CRM software, marketers use intimate knowledge of customers and customer preferences to orient every part of the organization toward building a unique com-pany differentiation based on bonds with customers

B. People or organizations that buy or use a firm's services are its external customers. Employees and departments within the organization whose success depends on the work of other departments or employees are internal customers.
1. Internal Marketing involves managerial actions that enable all members of an organi-zation to understand, accept, and fulfill their roles in implementing a marketing strategy.
2. Employee knowledge and involvement are important goals of internal marketing. Knowledgeable employees find it easier to satisfy customers.

3. Satisfied employees are another major objective of internal marketing. Happy employees are more likely to satisfy customers than are disgruntled ones.

III. The Relationship Marketing Continuum – buyer-seller relationships function at a variety of levels. As the strength of the commitment between the parties increases, the likelihood of a continuing long-term relationship also grows.

A. First Level – Focus on Price
   1. Interactions at the first level of relationship marketing are the most superficial and the least likely to lead to a long-term relationship, relying as they do on pricing and other financial incentives to motivate customers.
   2. Such programs, though attractive, are not customized to the needs of individual buyers, so are easily duplicated by competitors.

B. Second Level – Social Interactions
   1. Second-level relationship marketing interactions go deeper and are less superficial than those at the first level.
   2. Customer service and communication are the key factors in developing the social relationship characteristic of this stage.

C. Third Level – Interdependent Partnership
   1. Relationships are transformed into structural changes that ensure buyer and seller are true business partners.
   2. Automobile manufacturers facilitate purchase of their products by using their Web sites to let prospective customers create the exact car they want and then placing them in touch with convenient dealers.

IV. Enhancing Customer Satisfaction – In order to measure and improve how well they meet customer needs, marketers follow a three-step process.

A. Understanding Customer Need
   1. Knowledge of what customers need, want, and expect is a central concern of companies focused on building long-term relationships.
   2. Satisfaction can be measured in terms of the gaps between what customers expected of a relationship and what they perceive they have received.

B. Obtaining Customer Feedback and Ensuring Customer Satisfaction
   1. In order to measure customer satisfaction, feedback from customers regarding present performance must be compiled.
      a. Reactive methods are usually used, including
         i. 800 telephone numbers
         ii. Monitoring online discussion groups
         iii. Hiring mystery shoppers
   2. UK-based Virgin Radio uses its Web site to obtain feedback, just as it uses its VIP club to target its customers. Listeners can rate programs and tell DJs the music they want to hear.
   3. Any method that makes it easy for customers to complain benefits a firm and may be considered a blessing in disguise.

4. Proactive methods can also be used to assess customer satisfaction, including visiting, calling, or mailing out written surveys to clients to measure their level of satisfaction.

V. Building Buyer-Seller Relationships – it is not enough to just simply create products and then sell them. Consumers form continuing relationships in part because of their desire to reduce choices. Through relationships, they can simplify their buying process and reduce the risk of dissatisfactions. A key benefit to consumers in long-term buyer-seller relationships is the perceived positive value they receive. Consumers end relationships for a number of reasons, perhaps to obtain better prices, better customer services, or superior products. They may also seek to escape a relationship they find confining.

A. How Marketers Keep Customers
   1. Marketers have realized that retaining customers is far more profitable than losing them.
   2. Marriott Rewards is a frequency marketing program that rewards top customers with cash, rebates, merchandise, or other premiums.
   3. Frequency marketing programs are used by all kinds of firms including fast-food restaurants, retail stores, telecommunications companies, and travel firms.
   4. The Internet is a fertile medium for frequency-marketing programs.
   5. Some firms use affinity marketing programs – based on such things as school loyalty – to retain customers.
   6. Affinity credit cards are a popular form of this marketing technique. Practically every major university offers its alumni(ae) the option of acquiring a school sponsored credit card.

B. Database Marketing – the use of information technology to analyze data about customers
   1. Credit card applications, software registration, and product warranties all provide vital statistics of individual customers, as do cash register scanners, customer opinion surveys, and sweepstakes entry forms.
   2. Good database management makes the customer feel that they are being well-treated and that someone cares about them – and they're usually right.
   3. Interactive television promises to offer even more valuable data as its popularity increases.
   4. As database marketing becomes more complex, new software will enable marketers to target consumers more and more narrowly while enriching their communications with selected groups.
   5. Applications service providers provide software to capture, manipulate, and analyze masses of consumer data.
   6. Database marketing can also be used to rebuild customer relationships that may have lapsed.

C. One-to-one Marketing – a marketing program that is customized to build long-term relationships with customers – one at a time.
   1. Marketers us a variety of tools to identify their company's best customers, communicate with them, and increase their loyalty.
   2. Sony music builds custom CDs for their business customers that can be sold through the customers' own catalogs or retail stores.

    3. So-called "grassroots marketing" involves connecting directly with existing and potential customers through nonmainstream channels.

    4. Viral marketing, traditionally known as "word of mouth," occurs when firms let satisfied customers get the word about products out to other consumers – like spreading a virus.

VI. Customer Relationship Management – combines strategies and technologies that empower relationship programs, reorienting the entire organization in a concentrated focus on satisfying customers. This represents a change in thinking for everyone related to a firm.

  A. CRM software programs are capable of making sense of the enormous amount of customer data that technology allows firms to collect. CRM systems are able to simplify complex business processes while keeping the best interests of customers at heart. The right CRM software can be critical to the success of a firm's entire CRM program.

  B. Software solutions, however, are not the only component of a successful CRM initiative. Successful CRM systems share the following qualities:
    1. They are results driven.
    2. They are implemented from the top down.
    3. They require investment in training.
    4. They communicate effectively across functions.
    5. They are streamlined.
    6. They involve end users in the creation of software solutions
    7. They constantly seek improvement.

  C. CRM is not without its problems. The strategy needs to be thought out in advance, everyone in the firm must be committed to it, and everyone must know how to use it or it is a waste of time and money. CRM failures often occur when companies approach it as a software project rather than a business strategy.

  D. Managing virtual relationships is becoming a more and more common problem. Because the participants seldom if ever see each other, some creativity is needed in making the relationships self-sustaining. Some   firms use the Internet as their relationship-building vehicle, while others use the telephone, e-mails, or even snail mail to show their interest in their customers.

  E. An important part of a CRM strategy is "customer winback," the process of rejuvenating lost relationships with customers. In many cases, a relationship gone bad can be made good again using the right approach.

VII. Buyer-Seller Relationships in Business-to-Business Markets – Business-to-business marketing involves an organization's purchase of goods and services to support company operations or the production of other products. A partnership is an affiliation of two or more companies that assist each other in the achievement of common goals. A variety of common goals motivate firms to form partnerships.

  A. Choosing Business Partners – involves locating firms that can add value to a relationship through financial resources, contacts, extra manufacturing capacity, technical know-how, or distribution capabilities and that share similar values and goals with the seeking firm to give the best chance of long-run success.

B. Types of Partnerships
   1. Buyer partnerships in which a firm purchases goods or services from one or more providers. The buyer's needs and how they are satisfied drive this relationship.
   2. Seller partnerships set up long-term exchanges in return for cash or other valuable consideration. In this case, the seller's needs drive the relationship.
   3. Internal partnerships result from the use of products of a company by other parts of the same company. The producing division becomes a selling partner, the using division a buying partner.
   4. Lateral partnerships include strategic alliances with other companies or not-for-profit organizations and research alliances with universities and colleges. The partners focus their attentions on external entities and no buyer-seller interactions between the partners occur.

C. Cobranding and Comarketing as business relationships
   1. Cobranding joins together two strong brand names, often owned by different companies, to sell a product. The relationship between L L. Bean and Subaru that makes Subaru the "official car" of L. L. Bean is an example of cobranding.
   2. In comarketing, two organizations join together to sell both their products in an allied marketing campaign. Over the years, many movies have comarketed themselves with everything from automobile brands to candy bars. The recent *Spongebob Squarepants* movie comarketed the sponge with products from Mattel, Mitsubishi, Burger King, Kellogg, and even the Cayman Islands.

VIII. Improving Buyer-Seller Relationships in Business-to-Business Markets – successful partnering often leads to lower prices, better products, improved distribution, higher revenues, and increased profits. High technology facilitates relationships because firms can communicate anytime and anyplace.

A. National Account Selling – takes place when manufacturers serve their largest, most profitable customers with teams dedicated to each account. The activity possesses many advantages from both participants' points of view.

B. Business-to-Business Databases – using information gleaned from sales reports, checkout counter scanners, and other sources, sellers can create databases to guide themselves and their customers who sell products to final users.

C. Electronic Data Interchange – involves computer-to-computer exchanges of invoices, orders, and other business documents, lowering costs and improving efficiency and competitiveness.

D. Vendor-Managed Inventory – is a system in which the seller determines how much of a product a buyer needs and automatically – subject to terms of a mutual agreement – ships new supplies to the buyer. Some firms have modified the basic model involving collaborative planning, forecasting, and replenishment.

E. Managing the Supply Chain – affects both upstream relationships with suppliers and downstream relationships with end users in the channel of distribution. It can provide a significant competitive advantage for the firm that does it well.

   F. Business-to-Business Alliances – may be structured using a new business unit in which each partner takes an ownership position or can operate more flexibly and change as market forces and other conditions dictate.

IX. Evaluating Customer Relationship Programs – may involve computing the lifetime value of a customer or, alternatively, the payback from a from a customer relationship. The first of these uses an estimated "customer life" and determines how much of the quantity "revenue less cost" a customer can expect to produce over that customer life. The second tracks customer purchases to determine how long it takes to recover the cost of acquiring a new customer from that customer's purchases. There are alternative methods to evaluate relationship programs, such as tracking rebate requests, coupon redemption, credit-card purchases, and product registrations; monitoring complaints and returned merchandise and analyzing why customers leave; reviewing reply cards, comment forms, and surveys; and monitoring "click-through" behavior at Web sites.

Name_____   Instructor_____

Section_____   Date_____

Key Concepts

The purpose of this section is to allow you to determine if you can match key concepts with the definitions of the concepts. It is essential that you know the definitions of the concepts prior to applying the concepts in later exercises in this chapter.

From the list of lettered terms, select the one that best fits in the blank of the numbered statement below. Write the letter of that choice in the space provided.

Key Terms

a. transaction-based marketing
b. relationship marketing
c. internal marketing
d. frequency marketing
e. affinity marketing
f. database marketing
g. one-to-one marketing
h. customer relationship management (CRM)

i. partnership
j. cobranding
k. comarketing
l. electronic data interchange
m. vendor-managed inventory
n. supply chain   .
o. lifetime value of a customer

_____ 1. Marketing effort sponsored by an organization such as an alumni association that solicits responses from individuals who share common interests and activities.

_____ 2. Use of software to analyze marketing information, identifying and targeting messages toward specific groups of potential customers.

_____ 3. Computer-to-computer exchanges of invoices, orders, and other business documents.

_____ 4. Buyer and seller exchanges characterized by limited communications and little or no ongoing relationship between the parties

_____ 5. Cooperative arrangement in which two or more businesses team up to closely link their names on a single product.

_____ 6. Combination of strategies and tools that empower relationship programs, reorienting the entire organization to a concentrated focus on satisfying customers.

_____ 7. The revenues and intangible benefits that a customer brings to the seller over an average lifetime less the amount the company must spend to acquire, market to, and service the customer.

_____   8.   Frequent buyer (or user) marketing program that rewards top-spending customers with rebates, cash, or other rewards.

_____   9.   The development and maintenance of long-term, cost-effective relationships with individual customers, suppliers, employees, and other partners for mutual benefit.

_____   10.   Sequence of suppliers that contribute to the creation and delivery of a good or service.

_____   11.   Inventory-management system in which the seller determines – based on an agreement with the buyer – how much product the buyer needs.

_____   12.   Managerial actions that help all members of the organization understand and accept their respective roles in implementing a marketing strategy.

_____   13.   Affiliation of two or more companies that assist each other in the achievement of common goals.

_____   14.   Program customized to build long-term relationships with customers one at a time.

_____   15.   Cooperative arrangement in which two businesses jointly market each other's products.

Name_____   Instructor_____

Section_____   Date_____

Self-Quiz

You should use these objective questions to test your understanding of the chapter material. You can check your answers with those provided at the end of the chapter.

While these questions cover most of the chapter topics, they are not intended to be the same as the test questions your instructor may use in an examination. A good understanding of all aspects of the course material is essential to good performance on any examination.

True/False

Write "T" for True or "F" for False for each of the following statements.

_____   1.   The financial incentive programs used at the first level of relationship marketing are attractive to users and tend to create long-term buyer-seller relationships because they are not easily duplicated by competitors.

_____   2.   Database marketing allows sellers to track customer buying patterns, develop relationship profiles, customize offerings and sales promotions, and personalize customer service to suit the needs of targeted customers.

_____   3.   When a company integrates customer service and quality with a traditional marketing mix, the result is a transaction-based marketing orientation.

_____   4.   Since the Industrial Revolution, most manufacturers have traditionally focused their energies on making products, promoting them, and then hoping enough people will buy them to cover costs and earn profits.

_____   5.   The auto dealership that calls its customers after they have had repairs done there to ask if they are satisfied with the repairs or have any questions is probably operating at the first level of the relationship marketing continuum.

_____   6.   One reason consumers form continuing relationships is their desire to increase the number of choices available to them.

_____   7.   Most companies obtain knowledge of what customers need, want, and expect through internal marketing.

_____   8.   Customer satisfaction can be measured in terms of the gaps between what customers expect and what they perceive they have received. Such gaps can produce only favorable impressions.

_____   9.   Twenty-first century marketers now understand that they must do more than simply create products and sell them.

_____ 10. Walt Disney Records' partnership with Kellogg's cereals is designed to generate excitement for two distinct products in the same promotion.

_____ 11. Customer Relationship Management represents a shift in thinking for everyone associated with a firm to recognize that solid customer relations are fostered by similarly strong relationships with other major stakeholders.

_____ 12. Purchasers at the second level of relationship marketing become involved in true partnerships with vendors, developing an interdependence that continues to grow over time.

_____ 13. Employee knowledge and involvement as well as employee satisfaction are all critical goals of the process of internal marketing.

_____ 14. Databases allow sellers to identify their most profitable customers, improve customer retention and referral rates, and reduce marketing and promotion costs, among other things.

_____ 15. Programs such as Virgin Radio's VIP club are good examples of third level relationship marketing programs.

_____ 16. Software solutions are the main component of a successful CRM initiative, independent of any strategic planning the firm may otherwise undertake.

_____ 17. The primary reasons why consumers switch their loyalties from one vendor to another are that they come to perceive that a competitor's products and customers service are better, they simply become bored with the present vendor, or that they dislike the feeling that they are locked into a relationship with one company.

_____ 18. The "average lifetime" of a customer relationship is independent of the industry involved or the characteristics of its products.

_____ 19. The problem with affinity programs is that they are limited only to the issuance of sponsored credit cards.

_____ 20. Frequency marketing programs are set up so that the more products or the more often one buys from a particular company the greater the rewards one earns.

_____ 21. Interactive television promises to deliver even more valuable data than is currently available – data on real consumer behavior and attitudes toward brands.

_____ 22. In a way, database marketing has created a situation such that the world of marketing is returning to the old days of mass marketing, where sellers offered a standardized product to several homogeneous segments of the market at once.

_____ 23. The first priority in choosing business partners is to locate firms that can add value to the relationship; the greater the value added, the greater the desirability of the partnership.

_____ 24. Lateral partnerships involve relationships between different parts of the same company, some of which act as suppliers and others of which are the customers.

_____ 25. Seller partnerships in the business-to-business market set up long-term exchanges of goods and services in return for cash or other valuable consideration.

Multiple Choice

Circle the letter of the word or phrase that best completes each sentence.

26. One of the compelling reasons which have induced marketers to pursue relationships is that
    a. they have realized that they can remain prosperous only by a continuous process of identifying and attracting new customers; old customers generate very few new sales.
    b. focusing on short-term, single exchanges implies a commitment to their customers.
    c. existing customers and suppliers can be counted on to remain loyal without efforts to retain them.
    d. they can develop a proper conflict resolution posture with customers in the event of trouble.
    e. retaining existing customers costs much less than acquiring new ones.

27. The individual who shops extensively each time he or she needs to buy a new automobile creates
    a   set of circumstances which usually put the buyer in a transaction-based situation with a vendor.
    b. an ideal environment to develop a marketing relationship with an automobile dealer.
    c. a cooperative environment involving ongoing interactions between buyer and seller.
    d. added value in their marketing experience through the shopping process.
    e. an array of complex, enduring economic relationships between the vendor and the buyer.

28. Every marketing transaction involves a relationship between buyer and seller. In a relationship-based situation, which of the following is NOT the case?
    a. extensive social relationships typically develop between buyer and seller.
    b. the relationship may be quite short in duration and narrow in scope.
    c. customer service and quality are usually integrated in the marketing effort.
    d. the effort to retain existing customers is well-developed.
    e. promises made and kept are the basis of the relationship.

29. Effective supply chain management may result in
    a. a decrease in innovation because solid relationships tend to stabilize the way products are made.
    b. increased costs because firms must make and deliver smaller lots of products to customers.
    c. problems with conflict resolution within the chain because of favoritism between chain members.
    d. improved communication and involvement among members of the chain.
    e. massive increases in the quantity of product demanded within the chain.

30. First level relationship marketing programs can be attractive to their users; they are also
    a. highly likely to lead to a long-term relationship.
    b. reliant upon creating a social bond between vendor and consumer.
    c. easily duplicated by competitors because they are not customized to the needs of individual buyers.
    d. the most likely type of program to result in a partnership relationship between buyer and seller.
    e. subject to the highest level of regulation of all such programs.

31. The fact that consumers form continuing relationships with vendors is evidence of the truth behind the idea that
    a. many consumers seek to increase the range of choices available to themselves by shopping.
    b. many consumers perceive long-term buyer-seller relationships to have positive value because of the increased ability to save money through discounts, rebates, and similar offers.
    c. consumers seek to lock themselves into relationships with convenient suppliers.
    d. the habitually chosen vendors are always the stores closest to the consumers' homes.
    e. consumers are insensitive to store choice – it's the product that matters.

32. The Van Helsing Company, a leading supplier of hotel and restaurant equipment, requires that its sales representatives become very familiar with the operations of each of their customers. They make every effort to find special needs that they are uniquely suited to satisfy. The Van Helsing Company is trying to develop
    a. a reciprocal relationship with each customer by becoming an exclusive supplier.
    b. an intelligence report on operations it can sell to its customers' competitors.
    c. a relationship based on mutual partnership between the firms based on what each can offer the other.
    d. a sense of identity between the sales representatives and their customers.
    e. dependency on the part of their customers so the Van Helsing company can take advantage of them.

33. One of the major forces driving the push from transaction-based marketing toward relationship marketing is the realization that
    a. consumers dislike the feeling that they are locked into a relationship.
    b. to succeed, companies must develop loyal, mutually beneficial relationships with existing customers, suppliers, and employees.
    c. new customers generate more business for a firm than do old ones, so identifying and attracting new customers is the key to success.
    d. unhappy customers don't usually tell anyone of their experiences but happy ones brag about how well they relate to their suppliers.
    e. customers always get bored with the firms that currently supply their needs and change them without reason.

34. As an alumnus of good old North Central Tennessee State, you find yourself bombarded with offers to join the Walrus Club (the school mascot is a Walrus), an alumni organization. With your membership, you get a subscription to *Tusks,* the school's alumni magazine; a bumper sticker with a Walrus on it; and your choice of a NCTSU VISA, MasterCard, or Discover Card. NCTSU is trying to get you to join
    a. the school's frequent user program – after all, it took you six years to finish.
    b. their database of alumni – they're not sure you actually graduated or when.
    c. the third level of relationship marketing – it's like a secret society and members are very special.
    d. an affinity program based on your alumni status – the credit card offer is the tipoff.
    e. a subversive anti-government organization – the walrus symbol is a dead giveaway.

35. The last time you got your car washed at Really Wet Car Wash, you were given a card with a hole punched in the edge and told that when you'd had your car washed there five more times and acquired the corresponding holes in your card, the sixth carwash would be free. This is typical of
    a. a frequent user program.
    b. an affinity program.
    c. database marketing.
    d. reciprocity.
    e. emphatic behavior.

36. Which of the following is a typical use of database systems in relationship marketing?
    a. developing customer relationship profiles
    b. tracking buying patterns
    c. customizing product offerings and sales promotions
    d. personalizing customer service
    e. all of the above are typical uses of database systems

37. The entire sequence of suppliers that contribute to the creation and delivery of a product is called the
    a. inventory-management system for the product.
    b. the supply chain (or value chain) along which the product passes.
    c. alliance partnership designed to retain customers for the product.
    d. integrative membership association for the product.
    e. coordinative linkage of association.

38. One of the characteristics of the second level of relationship marketing is that
    a. buyer and seller develop interactions on a social level through customer service and communication.
    b. structural changes occur that make buyer and seller into true business partners.
    c. marketing efforts rely on pricing and other financial incentives to motivate customers to buy.
    d. it is the most likely to result in very long-term buyer-seller relationships.
    e. as buyer and seller work closely together, they develop a dependence on each other.

39. One capability of databases as marketing tools is that their use allows a firm to
    a. more profitably target the mass market by producing a standardized product in huge volume.
    b. avoid the expense of providing a custom product even to a potentially valuable customer segment.
    c. sort through huge quantities of data from multiple sources on the buying habits and preferences of millions of customers.
    d. develop a product that disregards people's individual priorities about the features of a relationship.
    e. increase direct costs and marketing outlays.

40. An example of a lateral partnership in business-to-business marketing would be
    a. an arrangement for a long-term exchange of goods and services in return for value received.
    b. the relationship between the purchasing department of a firm and the manufacturing facility that assembles the parts it buys.
    c. a contractual relationship between a retail store and a law firm for the law firm to be the store's exclusive supplier of legal services.
    d. The use of Sylvania integrated circuit chips in RCA TV sets. .
    e. Ford Motor Company's agreement to produce an Eddie Bauer model of the Ford Bronco SUV

41. The first priority of a firm in choosing a business partner for a marketing relationship is
    a. to find a firm that really needs help; the more desperate it is, the better partner it will make.
    b. to prevent a competitor from establishing a partnership relationship with another firm, regardless of how beneficial a partnership with the other firm might be.
    c. to locate a firm that can add value to the relationship through resources of cash, contacts, extra manufacturing capacity, technical know-how, or distribution capabilities.
    d. finding a firm with different skills and resources; the idea is to complement each other, not duplicate expertise.
    e. to broaden the range of involvement of the two firms; no particular purpose for the partnership should be considered.

42. When a firm commits to be the exclusive provider of certain types of goods for another firm, it has entered into
    a. a seller partnership with the buying firm.
    b. an internal relationship with the other firm.
    c. a buyer partnership with that firm
    d. a lateral partnership with the buyer.
    e. a symbiotic partnership.

43. CRM software systems
    a. can make sense of the vast amounts of customer data that technology allows firms to collect.
    b. are developed from the bottom up; top management seldom knows about the system.
    c. often slow the delivery of customer service and put relationships in disarray.
    d. complicate business processes regardless of the interests of customers.
    e. need almost daily updating to remain current and useful.

44. Sony's offer made to retailers of the opportunity to create custom CDs to be sold to customers in their stores is an example of
   a. fine-tuned segmentation.
   b. high-order differentiation.
   c. the Ipswich conundrum.
   d. one-to-one marketing.
   e. an affinity program.

45. Which of the following is the best example of comarketing?
   a. company A buys components for its home entertainment centers from company B.
   b. company A sets up a long-term exchange of goods and services with as many of its customers as possible in return for cash.
   c. department K of company A orders most of its supplies through the purchasing department of company A.
   d. Selmer Brothers, perhaps the most famous brass musical instrument company on Earth, offers for sale a Wynton Marsalis model of its professional-grade trumpet.
   e. Eugene Applemann receives an offer of a job from Pascagoula Power and Light Company.

46. Electronic data interchange is most correctly described as
   a. the use of the telephone to place and confirm orders and invoices
   b. computer-to-computer exchanges of invoices, orders, and other business documents
   c. development of databases to allow members of the firm to check inventory levels.
   d. creation of an e-mail system to let employees exchange messages and letters.
   e. what happens when a bunch of hackers distribute a computer virus through the Internet.

47. In addition to lifetime value analysis, which of the following can be used to evaluate the success of relationship programs.
   a. the payback from the relationship (how long it takes to break even on customer acquisition cost)
   b. tracking rebate requests, coupon redemptions, credit-card purchases, and product registrations.
   c. monitoring complaints and returned products and analyzing why customers leave
   d. reviewing reply cards, comment forms, and surveys.
   e. all of these may be used to evaluate the success of relationship programs.

48. Partnerships between buyers and sellers in the business-to-business market
   a. may lead to lower prices between the two.
   b. often result in raising quality standards.
   c. may improve communications between partners.
   d. often lead to improved distribution.
   e. may result in all of the above happening.

49. Successful CRM systems possess which of the following qualities?
   a. They are input driven.
   b. They are implemented from the bottom up.
   c. They communicate effectively across functions.
   d. They constantly seek stability rather than improvement.
   e. They require no investment in training – they are intuitive.

50. The level of relationship marketing known as interdependent partnership (level 3) is best ex-emplified by
    a. Two Big Macs for the price of one at McDonald's.
    b. American Airlines AAdvantage frequent flyer program.
    c. Virgin Radio's VIP Club.
    d. an art gallery that throwa a cocktail party for its patrons.
    e. Saturn's Web site price and affordability calculators leading to information about the lo-cal dealer's location to an invitation to continue to carry out the sales process there.

Name_____   Instructor_____

Section_____   Date_____

Applying Marketing Concepts

"The time has come," thought Allard Morgenfeld, "to upgrade the old stereo yet again. Sometimes technology just moves too fast. I wish it would slow down just a little. This business of having to buy a new system every couple of years is a bit much." But reflecting on his experiences with home entertainment systems over the years, Allard ultimately decided things hadn't been all that bad. He felt that he had really been lucky back in 1994 when he decided to buy his first really good system by mail from Big Ear Entertainment – the people with the huge ears all over their shipping boxes.

They had been very easy to deal with from the very beginning. Of course, his first phone call to them had been sort of long, what with all the questions they'd asked about him – where he lived, what he did for a living, what he knew about stereos and why he felt he needed one, his tastes in recordings and movies and so forth. But now, all he had to do was pick up the phone and there was someone there to help him. The minute he mentioned his name, they were able to talk to him about his needs and his problems. And they fixed what was wrong, too. Allard even had his own advisor, Theresa, for whom he could leave messages and who would call him back if she couldn't take his call right away. Theresa seemed to know exactly what he needed before he mentioned it.

Allard even had his own Big Ear VISA card that he made a point of using on those occasions when he shopped at Cinder Block, the local electronics outlet, for the occasional CD, DVD, or other incidentals. Now that was NOT a fun place! All they seemed to want to do was to take your money and get you out the door. Service was not a part of their vocabulary, and the staff seemed all to have taken "surly lessons" at the same school for the unhelpful. Allard admitted he liked to use his Big Ear card there just because it seemed to irritate them so.

1. The people at Big Ear Entertainment had probably asked Allard a lot of questions during that first phone call
    a. just because they were curious.
    b. so that his profile would become part of a database to be used for marketing purposes.
    c. because it's a requirement of the law that a mail order vendor must qualify all customers to make sure they are legally able to buy the goods being offered.
    d. to kill time. They probably weren't getting a lot of calls just then and needed something to do.
    e. to decide whether Allard was a real customer or a competitor trying to gather information.

2. Theresa's ability to "know exactly what he needed before he mentioned it" is evidence that Big Ear's customer service department was
    a. using information from their database to determine the most likely reason for Allard's call given the nature and age of his equipment.
    b. psychic – how else would they have known ahead of time what Allard's problems were.
    c. in contact with Allard's family who were telling them what his stereo problems were.
    d. planning for product failures ahead of time and dealing with them as they were reported.
    e. always trying to sell existing customers new equipment whether they needed it or not.

3. The Big Ear VISA card of which Allard is so proud is part of
   a. the database that Big Ear has on him.
   b. a plan by the firm to make him totally dependent on them for credit.
   c. part of an electronic data interchange program.
   d. the business partnership between him and Big Ear.
   e. an affinity program created by Big Ear for its customers.

4. The fact that Allard thinks of Theresa as his very own advisor means that
   a. they have developed a social as well as a business relationship – as least as far as Allard is concerned.
   b. a co-dependent relationship has developed between Allard and Theresa.
   c. Big Ear uses an outside call-handling service to handle business like Allard's
   d. there exists a strategic alliance between Big Ear and Allard
   e. the relationship between them is reciprocal.

5. Allard's perception of the way they treat people at Cinder Block would lead one to believe that Cinder Block
   a. is still practicing transaction-based marketing.
   b. relies too much on its database and not enough on its people.
   c. makes and keeps promises.
   d. has an effective internal marketing program.
   e. trains its personnel well in the principles of effective service.

Harold Logan wondered what his customers would think if they ever saw the headquarters of National Specialty Fastener Corporation, his firm. The bare fifteen by thirty foot room was certainly anything but impressive, except for the row of computer terminals along both walls and the large mainframe at one end of the room. But Harold was very proud of that room. From his point of view, it represented the "state-of-the-art" in customer service. Stored in memory on that mainframe were the specifications for every type of heavy-duty and unusual – "specialty" – fastener commonly used on the North American continent. The specifications were cataloged for each type of industry that used them, and Harold could put product and user together in an instant.

When one of his customers needed a supply of fasteners, all they had to do was go online with him through his system of dedicated broadband cable lines (they never slept) and type an inquiry directly into the National terminal. A price and availability quote would immediately be flashed back, and often a purchase would be made "human-free" on the spot.

Harold worked closely with some of his biggest customers. Several of his personnel, in fact, were responsible for only one account. Jake Reese, for example, worked exclusively with the jet engine division of General Electric, living in Cincinnati so he could meet with their people every day if need be.

One of the side benefits of an efficient, customer-oriented operation, Harold knew, was improved efficiency all around. Today he was going to generate an order for the Torrington Mechanical Corporation. They hadn't ordered anything, but she knew their stock of HDS 18/08 (3343) 12 mm. threaded motor studs (an excellent design of which Harold was duly proud) was low and he was authorized to ship as needed. He had ordered the new supply from Southern Steel Studs in Birmingham (actually Red Level, Alabama) last week so they would be ready to ship today. Harold got a steady flow of business from the automated online system, he kept his inventory to a minimum, and his customers seldom got caught short when a new or replacement supply of specialty fasteners was needed.

6. Harold's ability to match customers with the products they need using his computer system indicates that
    a. his memory must be incredible; how many people do you suppose can do that?
    b. he is using database marketing; the information is stored in the computer.
    c. he has created an affinity program for her customers.
    d. her business is based on mutual trust and understanding.
    e. he must have a high level of intuitive understanding of his customers.

7. That Harold's customers can get price quotes and order online means that he
    a. has reduced the number of his employees to a minimum.
    b. has no idea what his customers really want.
    c. has a reciprocal arrangement with most customers.
    d. uses electronic data interchange as part of his marketing program.
    e. is operating at the first level of relationship marketing.

8. Jake Reese's role in Michelle's firm is as
    a. his brother-in-law.
    b. one of its laziest employees, servicing only one account.
    c. a national account representative.
    d. one of the VMI personnel.
    e. an out-of-the-way troublemaker.

9. This shipment to Torrington Mechanical indicates that, for some accounts at least, National Specialty Fastener
    a. operates a vendor-managed inventory program for that account.
    b. has some kind of scam going. Nobody accepts unordered goods.
    c. has a deep personal relationship with someone there and can do as they please.
    d. has formed a strategic alliance with the packaging department.
    e. is using an emphatic relationship to keep going.

10. Harold's obvious awareness of the needs and capabilities of his suppliers and customers indicates that
    a. he has done it all in this industry and should know how it works.
    b. he is skilled at managing the supply chain.
    c. he has an individual relationship with all of them.
    d. he probably should expand into other fields.
    e. his success is due to his incredible memory.

Name_____   Instructor_____

Section_____   Date_____

Surfing the Net

Keeping in mind that addresses change and what's on the Web now may have changed by the time you read this, let's take a look at some of the places on the Net that reflect aspects of relationship marketing. We are not endorsing or recommending any of these sources, merely making note of the information and services that people have elected to offer through the Internet.

You don't buy them very often, and the Toro Company knows that their snow blowers, lawn mowers, and garden tractors don't make very exciting copy, so their Website offers more in the way of guidance, fitting a customer to particular products on the basis of an online questionnaire. Give them a holler at **http://www. toro.com.**

Their repair parts and service database is reputed to be superb – the Frigidaire people will put you in touch with the nearest dealer that has the part you need. Just access **http://www.frigidaire.com.** OK, so you're not a Frigidaire fan! Try **http://www.whirlpool.com** or **http://www.subzero.com** or **http://www.maytag.com** or even **http://www.crosley.com** to see what wonders the major home appliance industry has for us these days. Note that Crosley, absent for many years, is back. Their site includes a very interesting corporate history. Also, by the way, so is RCA in electronics. Look at **http://www.rca.com** for some interesting new products.

A sleeper! Simmons Mattress Company will interpret your dreams, tell you about sleep disorders, and even analyze how much sleep you owe yourself due to bad sleeping habits. Try **http://www.simmonsco.com** or, as an alternative, their competitor, Sealy Mattress Company at **http://www.sealy.com**

Talk about relationships! Several sites offer credit analysis for businesses. As a condition for establishing a relationship in that market, knowing your possible partner's financial condition is a must. Take a look at the site of Corporate Performance Systems at **http://www.cpshome.com** Need help getting together your credit program? Try contacting Associated Credit Managers, Incorporated, at **http://www.ascmi.net.** You can also take a look at **http://www.nacm.org**, the National Association of Credit Management, for a bit more "professionally oriented" view of the credit process.

Buying lots of stuff that just HAS to be there tomorrow? Try one of these sites as a source. Need to make up with someone? In a BIG way. Try **http://www.flowerbud.com** for all your major floral needs overnight. Not your style? Ben and Jerry can handle it. They'll get that creamy treat to you overnight, no problem. Go to **http://www.benjerry.com** to order. Still not good enough? How about Broadway theatre tickets? The people at **http:// www.broadwaytickets.com** (which appears to be in the process of consolidation) can get those to you. If all else fails, how about a shrimp boil? You can have them overnight too, from **http://www.savannahshrimp.net**

Sites verified August 24, 2004.

Part 3
Creating a Marketing Plan

The information you will receive in this part will help you to complete Part I.C. of your marketing plan for Sumesa Enterprises, Incorporated.

Episode Three: Who's Out There?

Having performed the appropriate rituals and filled out the proper forms, Sumesa Enterprises was now duly and properly incorporated as a Subchapter S corporation under the laws of the state in which it was domiciled. The officers of the corporation were Suzette O'Malley, President; Mel Sandoval, Executive Vice President for operations; and Sandy St. Etienne, Executive Vice President for product development and security. Having gotten themselves organized, the three partners decided they needed more information about the nature of the competitive environment if they were to reduce the risk of business failure. They accordingly turned to that standard research volume which the telephone company thoughtfully provides to all of us – but which few of us use to its logical extent – the *Yellow Pages*. Searching through the current *Yellow Page* listings for New Blackpool, their home city, they discovered 34 firms listed under "Communications Service – Digital Wireless Commercial." A telephone survey of these 34 firms revealed that the telephones of 2 were no longer in service, 3 were actually located in cities well away from the New Blackpool metropolitan area, and 5 actually only serviced personal cellular equipment and didn't know anything about commercial digital wireless units – or event that they were listed under that heading in the *Yellow Pages*! That left 21 firms remaining active in the market as direct competitors of Sumesa.

The partners were aware, however, that a number of other types of firms, such as regular personal cellular service providers, might have some involvement in commercial digital wireless operations and maintenance. Accordingly, they checked their *Yellow Pages* once again, and determined that, of the 164 firms which survived the same sort of culling process as outlined above, 121 (75%) offered <u>some</u> commercial service, but only 102 (62%) claimed any competence in "always on" equipment operation and maintenance, and only 29 did either of these activities for people who were not what they called "regular customers."

Forty-one cellular service vendors (25%) indicated that they did not do commercial work of any kind, and 24 of these indicated that they did not make any recommendations to their customers about who they could get to provide such service for them. The 60 "service-and-repair" firms in the area were contacted, and none of them offered services to provide a commercial presence to customers. None of the 21 companies, which were known to be full service commercial communications firms, received more than one recommendation from a non-commercial wireless service vendor.

The partners, who conducted the two surveys themselves, remarked to each other on an aspect of their work which the raw statistics didn't reveal. As Mel put it, "These personal cellular telephone people don't seem to care about the commercial market at all. In fact, one guy I called said he knew his firm sold phones, but he wasn't sure about "that commercial thing." Suzette responded with, "You know, I noticed that even when I was talking to the places that didn't sell the phones themselves; you know, the "service and repair" companies. At 8 of the firms I talked to, and I did all the service and repair places, they put me on "hold" when I asked if they could fix digital commercial "always-on" equipment. It begins to look like we might have a fairly protected place in the equipment service market for commercial digital wireless hardware.

"You know something else," piped up Sandy, "there are over fifty display ads in the "Cellular Telephone – Dealers" section of the *Yellow Pages*, but only 2 displays in the "Digital Wireless Commercial Services" section. I wonder why that is?" (A display ad is an ad, usually in a box with pictures and copy text, unlike the usual plain listing in the *Yellow Pages,* and you have to pay extra for it.)

Guidelines:
There are both an objective and a subjective component to the analysis of competition. Apply both quantitative and qualitative analysis to the information presented above to complete part I. C. of your marketing plan.

Part 4
Product Decisions

The marketing mix of product, price, distribution, and promotion is designed to satisfy the target market. Products are bundles of physical, service, and symbolic attributes designed to satisfy wants. Some products are classed as goods and others as services. Services are intangible tasks that satisfy the needs of consumer and business users. Goods are tangible products that consumers can feel, taste, smell, touch, and/or hear. Goods may be distinguished from services by use of the goods-services continuum. In addition to being intangible, services are inseparable from the service provider, perishable, not easily standardized, often partly designed and distributed by their buyers, and of widely variable quality. Services have become crucial parts of everyday life. In the United States they comprise two-thirds of the economy.

Products may be classified as either business or consumer products and may be goods or services or a combination of the two. Consumer products are usually referred to as convenience, shopping, or specialty products. Business products are classified into the six categories of installations, accessory equipment, component parts and materials, raw materials, supplies, and business services. Quality has become a product strategy. The philosophy of total quality management (TQM) asks all employees of a firm to continually improve products and processes to improve customer satisfaction and world-class performance. Benchmarking is one of the tools used to set performance standards. Service quality is determined by five variables: tangibles, reliability, responsiveness, assurances, and empathy.

Product lines are series of related products. They serve to promote optimal use of resources and enhance a firm's market position. The firm's product mix is its assortment of product lines and individual products. Firms introducing new products must concern themselves with the stages through which the product will pass from the time it is introduced until it is removed from the market. The product life cycle, with its five stages of introduction, growth, maturity, decline, and death, is a major concept involved in the marketing process. It is important to understand techniques to extend a product's life by extending its product life cycle.

Very important to product strategy decisions are the availability and use of brands, brand names, symbols, trademarks, labeling, and packaging by companies to identify and differentiate their products. Brand loyalty begins with recognition, passes through the stage of preference, and, with skill, is ultimately turned into insistence. The growth of generic, captive, and private brands is a significant topic for today's marketer. Whether to family brand or, alternatively, brand products individually is another issue. Brand equity measures the value added to a product by its possession of a particular brand name. As product identification, brand names, brand marks, trademarks – especially in the global sphere – are crucial. Trademarks are brands for which their owners can claim exclusive legal protection.

Packaging adds value to products by providing protection for them, assisting in marketing them, and bearing labels for informative purposes. Brand extensions, co-branding, co-marketing, and brand licensing have assumed new importance in this field. Consumer knowledge and acceptance of brands also constitute major considerations in the formulation of strategy. The adoption process consumers follow in their acceptance of a new product and factors affecting its speed of acceptance must receive attention by marketers if new products are to be successful. Even labeling, because it provides so much information about the product to the potential user, has become an important part of the packaging process.

The consumer adoption process describes the series of stages consumers go through from first learning about new products to trying them to ultimately becoming regular users. The process starts with awareness of the product, develops into interest, passes through an evaluation period, moves into trial, and ultimately may result in adoption. Of course, the process may stop in any stage if the potential adopter decides the product is inappropriate to his or her use. All products do not get adopted at the same rate or for the same reasons. Five factors speed adoption; their absence retards it. They are: relative advantage; compatibility with current practice; lack of complexity; possibility of trial use; and observability of the results of use.

New product planning is an ongoing activity subject to a number of influences which affect the decision to develop a line of products rather than concentrate on a single product. The stages in the new product development process – idea generation, screening, development, test marketing, and commercialization – and methods of organizing for new product development using new product committees, new product departments, product managers, and venture teams – should be reviewed to ensure a thorough knowledge of this subject. Criteria for the deletion of existing products from the product line are also significant.

Chapter 11
Product and Service Strategies

Chapter Outline

You may want to use this outline as a guide in taking notes.

I. Chapter Overview

    The marketing mix of product, price, distribution, and promotion is designed to satisfy the target market. Planning begins with the choice of goods or services to offer. The other elements of the marketing mix must accommodate the product strategy selected. Marketers develop strategies to promote both goods and services, but the resulting marketing mixes may vary markedly. This chapter examines the differences and similarities between the marketing of goods and services.

II. What Is a Product? It is want satisfaction rather than objects. It is a bundle of physical, service, and symbolic attributes designed to satisfy a customer's wants and needs. It includes package design and labeling, brand name, warranty, and customer-service activities that add value for the customer.

III. What Are Goods and Services? Services are intangible tasks that satisfy the needs of consumer and business users, while goods are tangible products that people can see, hear, taste, smell, or touch. They can be distinguished from each other through the use of a goods-services continuum, a spectrum that helps people visualize the differences and similarities between the two.

    A. Services can be distinguished from goods in several ways.
        1. They are intangible, having no physical features that buyers can perceive.
        2. Services are inseparable from the people that provide them.
        3. They are perishable – if they are not used, they go to waste.
        4. Companies find it difficult to standardize services.
        5. Buyers often play important roles in the creation and distribution of services.
        6. Finally, the quality of services shows wide variations.

    B. Importance of the service sector – Modern life depends on the existence of a service sector of the economy. Services are a crucial part of everyday life.
        1. Two of the *Fortune* top 10 most admired companies are pure service firms – Southwest Airlines and Federal Express.
        2. Services account for two thirds of the U.S. economy, with an annual growth rate at a six-year high.
        3. Services also provide a substantial role in the international well-being of the U.S., creating a trade surplus in service sales to foreign markets for every year since 1970. Offshoring of service jobs may have the effect of reducing this surplus.
        4. The importance of the service industries grows out of demand for speed and convenience by consumers and the development of new technologies to satisfy those desires.
        5. Marketing is a major activity for most service firms because the growth of the potential markets for services represents a tremendous marketing opportunity and because

increased competition is forcing traditional service industries to differentiate themselves from their competitors.

IV. Classifying Goods and Services for Consumer and Business Markets – Consumer products are those destined for use by ultimate consumers while business, B2B, industrial, or organizational products – the terms are used interchangeably by many – contribute directly or indirectly to the output of other products for resale. Some products fall into both categories, being consumer goods under some circumstances, organizational goods under others.

A. Types of consumer products. Several classification systems divide consumer goods and services different ways. One differentiates between unsought products and sought products. The most common classification scheme divides consumer goods into groups based on customers' buying behavior.
   1. Convenience products: are goods and services that consumers want to buy frequently, immediately, and with minimum effort.
      a. Impulse goods and services are purchased on the spur of the moment, often without any pre-thought or planning at all, such as candy bars at the checkout of the supermarket.
      b. Staples are convenience goods and services that consumers constantly replenish to maintain a ready inventory; gasoline and bread are examples.
      c. Emergency goods and services are bought in response to unexpected and urgent needs – medical services after an automobile accident is an example.
   2. Shopping products are bought only after consumers compare competing offerings on such characteristics as price, quality, style, and color, and usually cost more than convenience goods.
      a. The features that distinguish shopping products are their physical attributes, service attributes such as warranties and after-sale service terms, prices, styling, and places of purchase.
      b. Buyers and marketers treat some shopping products, such as refrigerators and washing machines, as homogeneous products, that is, products for which one brand seems largely the same as another.
      c. Other products are considered heterogeneous because of the differences among them; the differences may be brand-related or may have to do with unique physical characteristics the products possess such as style, color, or fit.
   3. Specialty products offer unique characteristics that cause buyers to prize those particular brands, in many cases accepting no substitutes for the preferred brands.
      a. Purchasers of specialty goods and services know just what they want and are willing to pay accordingly.
      b. Both highly personalized service by sales associates and image advertising help marketers to promote specialty items.
      c. Some makers of specialty products have, in recent years, broadened their markets by selling some of their products through company-owned discount outlets.

B. Classifying Consumer Services is similar to classifying consumer goods. Service firms, however, may serve consumer markets, business markets, or both. They may also be classified based on whether they are equipment-based or people-based. Five questions aid in classifying services.
   1. What is the nature of the service?
   2. What type of relationship does the service firm have with its customers?

3. How much flexibility is there for customization and judgment on the part of the service provider?
4. Do demand and supply for the service fluctuate?
5. How is the service delivered?

C. Applying the consumer products classification system helps guide marketers in developing a marketing strategy. Consumer behavior patterns differ for the three classes of goods.
1. The system does possess some problems, however, because not all products neatly fit one or the other of the categories.
2. An automobile may be a specialty item for some people, an intensive shopping item for others.
3. Another problem is that consumers differ in how they buy the same item, some people buying from the first source that comes along, others explore the possibilities extensively before making a decision.

D. The types of business products reflect the uses to which business products are put. This results in six categories of business goods.
1. Installations are the specialty products of the business market, the classification including major capital investments for new factories and heavy machinery, and for communications systems.
   a. Since installations last a long time and their purchase involves large sums of money, their purchase is a major decision for an organization.
   b. Price does not typically dominate purchase decisions for installations.
   c. Installations are major investments often designed for the purchasers.
   d. Most installations are marketed directly from manufacturers to users.
2. Accessory equipment includes capital items that that typically cost less and last for shorter periods than installations.
   a. Quality and service exert important influences on purchase of accessory equipment, but price may significantly affect these purchasing decisions.
   b. Marketing these products requires continuous representation and dealing with the widespread geographic dispersion of purchasers.
   c. Advertising is an important component in the marketing mix for accessory equipment.
3. Component parts and materials are finished business products of one producer that actually become part of the final products of another producer.
   a. Purchasers of component parts and materials need regular, continuous supplies of uniform-quality products.
4. Raw materials include farm products such as cotton, eggs, milk, and soybeans, and natural products such as coal, iron ore, and lumber that ultimately become part of the buyers' final products.
   a. Most raw materials are graded according to set criteria, assuring purchasers of standardized products of uniform quality.
   b. Price is seldom a deciding factor in a raw materials purchase since terms are often set in central markets, determining virtually identical conditions of sale for competing sellers.
5. Supplies constitute the regular expense items that a firm buys for use in its daily operations.
   a. Supplies are also called MRO items because they comprise maintenance items, repair items, and operating supplies.

b. A purchasing manager regularly buys operating supplies as a routine job duty, often through wholesalers.

6. Business services include the intangible products that firms buy to facilitate their production and operating processes, including such items as legal services, insurance, and utilities.

   a. Organizations also buy adjunct services that are not essentially part of their final product to assist their operations.

   b. Price often strongly influences purchase decisions for business services.

   c. Purchase decision processes vary considerably for different types of business services.

   d. The buying and selling of business products often involves alliances among different types of firms to bring together their respective expertise in production of some product.

V. Quality as a product strategy involves issues of both product and service delivery. It is a key component of a firm's success in a competitive marketplace. A movement to create high-quality goods and services called "total quality management (TQM)" has developed that expects all employees of a firm commit themselves to continual improvement of products and work processes to achieve customer satisfaction and world-quality performance. The quality movement started in the U.S. during the 1920s as an attempt to improve product quality by improving the manufacturing process itself.

A. Worldwide quality programs, as far as the U.S. was concerned, became major issues in the early 1980s when American companies decided they had to improve product quality to win back market share they had lost to Japanese producers.

   1. As part of the ensuing national quality improvement program, Congress established the Malcolm Baldridge Award in 1987 to recognize excellence in quality management.

   2. In Europe, the quality movement is quite strong, with the ISO (International Standards Organization) 9002 standards describing international criteria.

   3. Many European companies require suppliers to complete ISO certification as a condition of doing business with them.

B. The role of benchmarking in quality is to develop a system of continuously measuring the performance of one's firm against the standards of performance set by outstanding examples to achieve superior performance that results in a competitive advantage in the marketplace.

   1. A typical benchmarking process involves three main activities:

      a. identifying processes that need improvement,

      b. comparing internal processes against similar processes of industry leaders, and

      c. implementing changes to improve quality.

   2. Benchmarking requires internal and external analyses of processes and operations.

C. Quality of Services is determined from the buyer's point of view during the "service encounter" – the point at which the customer and the service provider interact.

   1. Service quality refers to the expected and perceived quality of a service offering, and has a huge effect on the competitiveness of a company.

   2. Service quality is determined by five variables:

      a. Tangibles, or physical evidence.

      b. Reliability, or consistency of performance and dependability.

    c. Responsiveness, or the willingness and readiness of employees to provide service.

    d. Assurances, or the confidence communicated by the service provider.

    e. Empathy, or the service provider's efforts to understand the customer's needs and then individualize the service.

  3. The gap between the level of service that customers expect and the level they think they receive may be positive or negative. If it is favorable, the vendor's image is enhanced; unfavorable, the image suffers.

VI. Development of Product Lines has become the rule rather than the exception among American companies, a product line being a series of related products. By developing comprehensive product lines as opposed to concentrating solely on individual products, firms benefit in four ways.

  A. Desire to grow – A firm limits its growth potential when it concentrates on a single product, even though the company may have started that way, as did L. L. Bean with a single style of work boots.

  B. Enhancing the company's position in the market – A company with a line of products often makes itself more important to both consumers and marketing intermediaries than firm with only one product.

  C. Optimal use of company resources is improved by spreading the costs of its operations over a series of products, thus reducing the average production and marketing costs of each product.

VII. The Product Mix – The assortment of product lines and individual product offerings that the company sells is its product mix.

  A. Product mix width refers to the number of product lines the firm offers – more product lines means greater width.

  B. Product mix length defines the number of different products a firm sells, including all the products within each of its product lines.

  C. Product mix depth refers to the variations in each product the firm markets in its mix.
    1. Evaluation of a firm's product mix requires marketers to examine the three elements of width, length, and depth.

  D. Product mix decisions grow out of the need to examine the items in the firm's existing product line for additions or deletions. Many firms that expanded their product mixes without careful planning now find themselves with unprofitable lines and products which are candidates for elimination.
    1. Evaluation of the firm's product mix requires evaluation of the effectiveness of its depth, length, and width.
    2. One possibility for product mix expansion is to increase product line depth.
    3. An alternative is to offer a product variation that will attract a new segment.
    4. Some firms purchase product lines from other companies to expand their product mixes.

5. Yet another possibility is a line extension – an individual offering that appeals to a different market segment while relating closely to the existing product line.
6. The marketing environment plays a role in a marketer's evaluation of s firm's product mix. A shift in any of the environmental components can create a threat or an opportunity for a firm.
7. Examination of the firm's current product mix helps marketers to make decisions about brand management and new-product introductions.

VIII. The Product Life Cycle – This concept describes the progression of product innovations in an industry through four stages from the time they are first introduced until the time they are removed from the market.

A. Introductory stage – During this early stage of the product life cycle, the newly-introduced product's proprietor works to stimulate demand for the new market entry.
1. Heavy promotion is essential during this stage because the product is essentially unknown.
2. Technical problems and financial losses are common during the introductory stage because the firm is incurring heavy costs associated with promotion and research-and-development costs.

B. Growth stage – Sales volume rises rapidly during the growth stage as new customers make initial purchases and early buyers repurchase the product.
1. The growth stage may also bring new challenges for marketers as competitors rush to enter the market with similar offerings.

C. Maturity stage – Sales of the product continue to grow during the early part of this stage, but eventually level off as the backlog of potential customers diminishes.
1. Differences between competing products diminish as competitors discover the product and promotional characteristics most desired by customers.
2. Heavy promotional outlays emphasize any differences that still separate competing products and brand competition intensifies.
3. As competition intensifies, competitors tend to cut prices to attract new buyers, often causing retaliatory price cuts from other producers.

D. Decline stage – Innovations or shifts in consumer preferences bring about an absolute decline in industry sales.
1. As sales fall, profits for the product category decline, sometimes actually going negative.
2. The traditional product life cycle differs from fad cycles.
    a. Fashions and fads profoundly influence marketing strategies.
    b. Fashions are currently popular products that tend to follow recurring life cycles.
3. Fads are fashions with abbreviated life cycles, often of very short duration.

IX. Extending the Product Life Cycle – The product life cycle for a product is not immune to the effects of strength or weakness in the economy, increased competition, and technological innovation. In the introductory stage, marketing efforts should emphasize the stimulation of demand. The focus shifts to cultivating selective demand in the growth period. Segmentation helps maintain momentum during maturity, and during decline emphasis returns to increasing primary demand.

A. Extending the product life cycle can be successful if marketing action is taken early in the maturity stage. Several alternatives are available to extend indefinitely the length of the product life cycle.
   1. Increasing frequency of use by current customers during the maturity phase will result in increased sales even if no new buyers enter the market. Making seasonal products "in-demand" year round is a device to achieve this objective.
   2. Increasing the number of users seeks to increase overall market size by attracting new customers who previously have not used the product.
      a. Products may be in different stages of the product life cycle in different countries, thus creating new markets as older ones mature.
      b. Recently, the Walt Disney Company has targeted adults as customers for its theme parks, shifting the emphasis somewhat from children.
   3. Finding new uses for the product is an alternative cycle-extension strategy, involving such actions as promoting antacids as calcium supplements.
   4. Changing package sizes, labels, or product quality may open new markets for the product.
      a. The wine industry is an extensive user of packaging and labeling to attract consumers to its mature products.

B. Product deletion decisions are sometimes necessary when promising products do not achieve their potential. The decision usually must be made during the late maturity and early decline stages of the product life cycle.
   1. Firms may continue to carry an unprofitable item in order to provide a complete line for its customers.
   2. Shortages of raw materials sometimes prompt companies to discontinue marketing of previously profitable items.
   3. Interestingly, some firms delete profitable lines that don't fit their marketing mixes well, selling them to other firms that have success with them.

Name_____   Instructor_____

Section_____   Date_____

Key Concepts

The purpose of this section is to allow you to determine if you can match key concepts with the definitions of those concepts. It is essential that you know the definitions of the concepts prior to applying the concepts in later exercises in this chapter.

From the list of lettered terms, select the one that best fits in the blank of the numbered statement below. Write the letter of that choice in the space provided.

Key Terms

a. marketing mix
b. product
c. service
d. good
e. consumer product
f. business-to-business (B2B) product
g. convenience product
h. shopping product

i. specialty product
j. business services
k. total quality management (TQM)
l. service quality
m. product line
n. product mix
o. product life cycle

_____ 1. An intangible task that satisfies consumer or business user needs.

_____ 2. Product with unique characteristics that cause the buyer to prize it and make a special effort to obtain it.

_____ 3. Blend of four elements of a marketing strategy – product, price, distribution, and promotion.

_____ 4. Movement that asks all employees in a firm to continually improve products and work processes with the goal of achieving customer satisfaction and world-class performance.

_____ 5. Intangible products a firm buys to facilitate its production and operating processes.

_____ 6. Four stages through which a successful product passes: introduction, growth, maturity, and decline.

_____ 7. Product purchased after the consumer compares competing offerings from competing vendors on characteristics such as style, color, price, and quality.

_____ 8. A company's assortment of product lines and individual offerings.

_____ 9. Bundle of physical, service, and symbolic attributes designed to enhance buyer want satisfaction.

_____ 10. Good or service that the consumer wants to purchase frequently, immediately, and with a minimum of effort.

_____ 11. A series of related products offered by a company.

_____ 12. Tangible product that customers can see, hear, smell, taste, or touch.

_____ 13. Product designed for use by ultimate consumers.

_____ 14. Expected and perceived quality of a service offering.

_____ 15. Product that contributes directly or indirectly to the output of other products for resale; also called industrial or organizational product.

Name_____   Instructor_____

Section_____   Date_____

Self-Quiz

You should use these objective questions to test your understanding of the chapter material. You can check your answers with those provided at the end of the chapter.

While these questions cover most of the chapter topics, they are not intended to be the same as the test questions your instructor may use in an examination. A good understanding of all aspects of the course material is essential to good performance on any examination.

True/False

Write "T" for True or "F" for False for each of the following statements.

_____ 1. A narrow definition of the word <u>product</u> focuses on the physical or functional characteristics of a good or service rather than its want-satisfying capability.

_____ 2. Consumer perceptions of a service provider become their perceptions of the service itself because the service is inseparable from its provider.

_____ 3. Products marketed to consumers who may not yet recognize any need for them are called *sought* products.

_____ 4. Heterogeneous shopping products are shopping products whose brands the consumer considers essentially similar to each other.

_____ 5. Producers of specialty products often intentionally limit the number of retail outlets that carry their products.

_____ 6. Price and value are important factors in the purchase of heterogeneous shopping products, while style, color, and fit are more significant in the purchase of homogeneous shopping products.

_____ 7. One characteristic that distinguishes services from goods is the fact that buyers often play a role in the development and distribution of services.

_____ 8. The service sector of the U.S. economy now represents more than two-thirds of the economy as a whole.

_____ 9. The classification system for business products emphasizes product uses rather than consumer buying behavior.

_____ 10. <u>Raw materials</u> can be considered the convenience products of the business market.

_____ 11. Business Services are also known as MRO items because they are <u>mandatory required obligations</u> on the part of their users.

_____ 12. When bought by a firm, leasing and rental of equipment and vehicles, insurance, and legal counsel are examples of business services.

_____ 13. Component parts and materials never receive additional processing before becoming part of a finished good.

_____ 14. Supplies are often called MRO items because they include maintenance items, repair items, and operating supplies.

_____ 15. The consumer goods classification system works so well because consumers are so much alike in their buying patterns.

_____ 16. The product life-cycle concept applies to products or product categories in an industry, rather than individual product brands.

_____ 17. During the introduction phase of the product life cycle, large profits are common as the public becomes acquainted with the product's merits and begins to accept it.

_____ 18. The width of a product mix refers to the number of different products a firm sells.

_____ 19. One strategy for extending the product life cycle is to increase the overall market size by attracting new customers who previously have not used the product.

_____ 20. Marketers typically face the decision of pruning their product lines during the late growth and early maturity stages of the product life cycle.

_____ 21. Advertising is an important component in the marketing mix for accessory equipment in the business market.

_____ 22. Providing services to the international market is a drain on the U.S. economy because the country has suffered a trade deficit in services for every year since 1970.

_____ 23. Benchmarking requires only that a firm analyze its own activities to discover its strengths and weaknesses.

_____ 24. A line extension develops individual offerings that appeal to different market segments while remaining closely related to the existing product line – such as Coach's watches, shoes, hats, and sunglasses to accompany their well-known handbag line.

_____ 25. Price is often a deciding factor in the purchase of raw materials since it is negotiated on a purchase-by-purchase basis between buyer and seller.

Multiple Choice

Circle the letter of the word or phrase that best completes the sentence or best answers the question.

26. From a marketer's point of view, what people really buy when they purchase any product is
    a. a group of physical or functional characteristics.
    b. satisfaction of a want rather than a physical object.
    c. often nothing more than advice.
    d. something they cannot do for themselves.
    e. an absolute necessity for the maintenance of life and limb.

27. One of the characteristics that distinguishes services from goods is
    a. intangibility. Services cannot be seen, held, tasted, touched, and smelled prior to purchase.
    b. separability. It is the service, not the service provider, that is important to the buyer.
    c. imperishability. Services can be held in inventory.
    d. standardization. It's easier to standardize services than goods.
    e. stable quality. Once service quality levels have been set, they are easy to maintain.

28. Consumer products that are bought on the basis of basic differences in features between them, often involving style, color, and fit, would typically be
    a. homogeneous shopping products.
    b. impulse products.
    c. specialty products.
    d. demand products.
    e. heterogeneous shopping products.

29. Specialty products would typically include
    a. soft drinks and beer for a picnic.
    b. bread, milk, and gasoline, especially when you're running low on any of these.
    c. clothing, furniture, and appliances such as refrigerators and washing machines.
    d. Tiffany jewelry and Rolls Royce vehicles.
    e. candy, cigarettes, and newspapers.

30. Which of the following characteristics describes emergency goods?
    a. They are often purchased on the spur of the moment.
    b. Such items usually are bought in response to unexpected and urgent needs.
    c. They are bought only after extensive comparison of competing offerings.
    d. Location can make all the difference between the choice of one product and another.
    e. Buyers refuse to accept substitutes for the desired products and know exactly what they want.

31. The goods-services continuum provides
    a. information on the ignorance of the average consumer about the things he/she buys.
    b. a broader definition of the term "products."
    c. a means of visualizing the differences and similarities between goods and services.
    d. a measure of the tangibility of services.
    e. an estimate of the perceived value of a product.

32. Marketing these business products requires continuous representation and dealing with the widespread geographic dispersion of purchasers. They are
    a. installations.
    b. accessory equipment.
    c. raw materials.
    d. supplies.
    e. business services.

33. This term describes the stage of the product life cycle during which sales volumes rise rapidly as new customers begin to buy the product and previous users repurchase. Word of mouth, lowering prices, and mass advertising induce hesitant buyers to make trial purchases.
    a. experimentation.
    b. growth.
    c. introduction.
    d. maturity.
    e. decline.

34. The major obstacle to implementing the convenience, shopping, and specialty product classification of consumer goods is that
    a. many products are so different that they fall totally outside the scope of the classification.
    b. the system cannot be used in terms of the majority of buyers; it must be applied to a specific individual.
    c. some products fall into the gray areas between categories; they share the characteristics of more than one category.
    d. consumers differ in buying patterns; an item that's a shopping good for one person may be a specialty good for someone else.
    e. the system no longer works; human behavior has changed so much during the last decade that the system is out of date.

35. The category of industrial goods whose purchase may involve negotiations lasting over a period of several months, the participation of a large number of decision makers, and the provision of technical expertise by the selling company is
    a. installations.
    b. accessory equipment.
    c. raw materials.
    d. component parts and materials.
    e. supplies of various types.

36. The fact that customers of New York's Le Cirque restaurant and Pizza Hut experience considerably different cuisine, physical surroundings, prices, and service standards is exemplary of the
    a. inseparability of services from their supplier.
    b. essential intangibility of services.
    c. high level of service standardization.
    d. variation in service quality from vendor to vendor.
    e. blurring of the distinction between services and goods.

37. Operating supplies are often called "MRO items." The letters MRO stand for the words
    a. manufacturing, research, and organizational.
    b. multiple, random, and obvious.
    c. many, ridiculous, and outstanding.
    d. manual, required, and out-of-stock.
    e. maintenance, repair, and operating supply.

38. In the business market, operating supplies might be called the
    a. specialty products.
    b. shopping products.
    c. accessory equipment.
    d. convenience products.
    e. raw materials.

39. In the industrial market, finished goods of one producer that become part of the final product of another are called
    a. accessory equipment.
    b. mechanical attachments.
    c. maintenance items.
    d. repair items.
    e. component parts and materials.

40. The firm's objective in the growth stage of the product life cycle is to
    a. extend the cycle as long as possible.
    b. improve warranty terms and service availability.
    c. emphasize market segmentation rather than differentiation.
    d. compete effectively, perhaps changing and improving the product.
    e. price competitively, growing volume through lowered margins.

41. The highest national award for quality a U.S. company can receive is
    a. ISO 9002 certification.
    b. the Deming Award, only given every three years.
    c. the Malcolm Baldridge Award, established in 1987.
    d. the Shewhart Cup.
    e. America's Cup.

42. M&M/Mars Candy Company's production and sale of special-edition M&Ms for different holidays such as Easter and Halloween is an example of an attempt to extend the product life cycle by
    a. increasing frequency of use of the product.
    b. finding new uses for an existing product.
    c. increasing the number of users of Jell-O.
    d. changing package size, label, or product quality.
    e. physically modifying the product for a new market.

43. The dairy industry's "Got Milk" advertising campaign is designed to
    a. get people to drink more milk – in connection with the "Quart a Day" campaign.
    b. finding a new use for milk as a calcium and phosphorous supplement.
    c. convince people who have never drunk milk of its nutritional benefits.
    d. increasing the number of users of milk by broadening its consumer base to include all sorts of nontraditional milk drinkers.
    e. broadening the product line by offering a whole array of different package sizes right up to an 8 gallon drum for heavy users.

44. PepsiCo has two main product lines: soft drinks and snack foods. American Brands has five: tobacco products, distilled spirits, office products, home improvement items, and golf and leisure goods. From this information we can say that PepsiCo's product mix is
    a. narrower than American Brands'.
    b. longer than American Brands'.
    c. less consistent than American Brands'.
    d. the older of the two.
    e. deeper than American Brands'.

45. WD-40's survey that asked people to ask users from every state to submit their favorite uses for the product was an example of an effort to
    a. increase the product's frequency of use.
    b. increase the number of people who use the product.
    c. open the product up to the business market.
    d. create a new product service component for dairies.
    e. find new uses for the product.

46. One of the problems of having a very large – wide, long, and deep – product mix is that
    a. it becomes impossible to achieve economies of scale.
    b. there is no cushion to fall back on if one line in the mix fails.
    c. little choice is provided for consumers who want something different
    d. some valuable segments of the market may remain unserved.
    e. retailers may not carry the full range of products and consumers may be overwhelmed by the array of choices.

47. Introducing a new product that appeals to a different market segment while remaining closely related to the existing product line – like a coffee company's introduction of a caffeine-free product – would be
    a. cannibalization of the existing line.
    b. corporate diversification.
    c. line extension.
    d. product evaporation.
    e. line complementation.

48. Products such as life insurance and funeral services which are marketed to people who have not yet recognized any need for them may be categorized as
    a. specialty products.
    b. homeopathic shopping products.
    c. unsought products.
    d. convenience products.
    e. monolithic shopping products.

49. In the business market, accessory equipment
    a. is often sold through wholesalers called industrial distributors.
    b. ultimately becomes part of the finished product.
    c. is always marketed directly from manufacturers to users.
    d. is graded according to set criteria to facilitate purchase of products of known quality.
    e. is often referred to as mechanic technology.

50. A company with a line of products – as opposed to a single product – often
    a. suffers from a lack of identity because of the confusion about what it makes.
    b. makes itself more important to both consumers and marketing intermediaries.
    c. increases the average production and marketing costs of each product.
    d. reduces the firm's benefit from the expertise of its personnel.
    e. finds itself in exactly the same competitive position as a firm with a single product.

Name_____   Instructor_____

Section_____   Date_____

Applying Marketing Concepts

Elodie Martin was very busy. It was a nasty day outside, and the bad weather had stimulated her to analyze her company's sales records. She was both pleased and confused by what she saw there. Elodie's firm, Modular Products, Inc., manufactured products which were used by both consumers and industry. From their new plant in Springfield, Illinois they shipped "Basemount Hitches," a line of unique multi-purpose trailer hitches, all over the United States. The hitches were in such demand, Elodie knew, that people would literally drive a hundred miles to find a shop that would sell them one. The firm's other automotive line, a sturdy portable ramp widely supplied to industrial firms for use as a loading dock / truck body transition for loading equipment, had long been a satisfactory performer in the marketplace.

One of the firm's other lines, the Multiphasic Adjustable Office Chair, seemed to have fallen on hard times. Developed five years before, sales on this item had grown slowly for three years, then rapidly for another two years. Now, however, things were not so rosy. Competitors had begun to appear and Elodie felt that prices and profits from the chair were being squeezed by their activities. The other line in the Modular Products stable, the Anovese Precipitator, a device used to remove dust and grit from precision metal castings in manufacturing plants and used also by police forensic laboratories to extract dust samples from clothing, carpet, and similar locations to be tested as evidence in criminal cases, continued to do well. Elodie was glad she'd had the good luck to realize that police labs could use the precipitator just when the market among manufacturers for the thing seemed to be peaking out. She wondered if perhaps she could do the same thing with the office chair. So far, most chair sales had been made to office supply companies for resale to using firms, with an occasional large order being sold by Modular direct to a major using customer. Elodie knew that the chair could also be used as a therapeutic fixture for chiropractors and orthopedists because of all the adjustments that could be made to it. She began to think about the possibilities.

1. Into which category of consumer goods could "Basemount Hitches" best be placed?
    a. convenience
    b. homogeneous shopping
    c. heterogeneous shopping
    d. specialty
    e. impulse

2. Modular Products' line of portable ramps are probably treated by industry as
    a. installations.
    b. shopping goods.
    c. accessory equipment.
    d. supplies.
    e. raw materials.

3. The Multiphasic Office Chair is in which stage of the product life cycle?
    a. introduction
    b. growth
    c. maturity
    d. decline
    e. death

4. Elodie's deliberations about development of the Multiphasic Office Chair into a therapeutic device for chiropractors and orthopedists
    a. reveal her desperation; the idea is obviously ludicrous.
    b. have definite possibilities; it would extend the product life cycle by finding a new use for the product.
    c. would offer the possibility of extending the product life cycle by adding new users to the product's existing market.
    d. could conceivably extend the product life cycle by increasing the frequency with which the chair is used.

5. From Modular Products' point of view, their new Springfield plant is
    a. a specialty product.
    b. an installation.
    c. accessory equipment.
    d. a convenience product.
    e. none of the above.

6. Elodie's development of the police laboratory market for the Anovese Precipitator was
    a. a good example of extending the product life cycle by finding new users for the product.
    b. pure luck; she couldn't do that again in a thousand years.
    c. an example of product life cycle extension through a change in product packaging or quality.
    d. a very astute example of how a product can be changed from a shopping good to a specialty good by advertising.

Terry Thompson is a landscape architect who has been in practice some fifteen years. His clients are primarily large business firms, among them Regional Property Management Company (RPM), one of the nation's largest owners of beachfront rental properties and other vacation rental properties. Terry is somewhat concerned because his contract with RPM will expire soon, and he knows that he will be facing competition to continue the beautification program of the land surrounding the company's properties all over the Southeast. He knows that the executives of the company are very happy with his work, and he feels that they think of him as "their" landscaper. The other firms competing for the contract have sent in "sales teams" to try and convince RPM to do business with them, and each executive has mentioned to Terry what a turnoff the presentations have been, dealing primarily with costs and only marginally with aesthetics. This has made him feel better, because he knows his prices are competitive, and the plantings he has provided to RPM to carry out his designs have been only the best stock. Despite this, he knows he's going to have to be prepared to offer his very best as the renewal date approaches.

7. Clients who rent RPM's vacation properties are purchasing
   a. a pure service or something very close to it.
   b. something which is predominantly a service with some goods included.
   c. something which mixes products and services in roughly equal proportions.
   d. something which is predominantly a product with a somewhat smaller service component.
   e. a pure good.

8. Given that Mr. Thompson provides the plantings which are used in his work of beautifying RPM's properties, his position on the goods-services continuum is at the service end; what he does is a pure service.
   b. certainly not a pure service, though service is a large part of his product; he is dealing in goods as well.
   c. well toward the goods end of the continuum; his services are a minor part of the total offering he's providing.
   d. at the goods end; his product is purely goods.
   e. at both ends; the services he provides are totally separate from whatever goods may be involved.

9. Terry is hoping to retain the contract because he feels that he is in a position to provide the one thing that the other competitors don't seem to have,
   a. size and scale of operations.
   b. effective sales personnel who can really hammer home a concept.
   c. the ability to do the job the company wants done.
   d. the ability to cut costs at every opportunity, doing an acceptable job at the lowest expenditure.
   e. a personal relationship with company executives and their trust in his relationship with them.

10. Judging by what you know of Terry's clients, how would you categorize the nature of his services?
    a. They are directed toward the business market and are an adjunct service.
    b. They are directed to the consumer specialty-goods market.
    c. They are business oriented and provide personnel services.
    d. They are directed to the consumer shopping-goods market.
    e. They are consumer based and are performed by unskilled workers.

11. Terry's recognition that he's going to have to "be prepared to offer his very best" as the end of his current contract draws near implies that
    a. he feels he's going to have to bribe RPM officials to secure renewal of his relationship with them.
    b. he hopes to hit them with his very best designs just before his contract runs out.
    c. Terry knows that he's going to have to negotiate with the RPM people to secure a renewal of his contract.
    d. Terry feels there's little hope his contract will be renewed.
    e. that he hasn't done a very good job for RPM in the past.

This vignette is a little different. It asks you to think "outside the box." See if you have begun to grasp the materials you've seen in the last several chapters by reading the following and answering the questions.

Allison Parker, owner of Shop4U, Inc., is assessing the progress of her new business venture, shopping for people who don't have time to shop for themselves. A phone call to Shop4U with a request that a birthday present be bought for a six year old nephew and sent to the child's address can be fulfilled the same day the request is made. Allison is quite pleased; she has had to hire five additional shoppers to handle the avalanche of requests for things that people need to buy but can't find time to go out and get. The thirty percent surcharge over the cost of any merchandise purchased doesn't seem to bother many of the people who call to request the service, either.

12. Shop4U provides
    a. a consumer convenience service.
    b. a core task business service.
    c. a consumer specialty service.
    d. a business personnel service.
    e. an adjunct business service.

13. The need for a service like Shop4U grows out of changes in the
    a. economic environment.
    b. social/cultural environment.
    c. political/legal environment.
    d. technological environment.
    e. competitive environment.

14. Which of the following aspects of the political-legal environment do you think would have the greatest effect on Shop4U?
    a. State and local regulatory agencies
    b. Actions of the Securities and Exchange Commission
    c. The Federal Communications Commission
    d. Deregulation of freight rates by the railroad commission
    e. A change in customs rates and procedures

Name_____   Instructor_____

Section_____   Date_____

Surfing the Net

Keeping in mind that addresses change and what's on the Web now may have changed by the time you read this, let's take a look at some of the places on the Net that reflect aspects of product strategy. We are not endorsing or recommending any of these sources, merely making note of the information and services that people have elected to offer through the Internet.

There are so many Web sties that present product and service strategies that it has been extremely difficult to pick just a few for you to investigate. So I picked a lot of them for you to investigate!

Like ice cream? There's always Ben and Jerry's. Their Web site is at **http://www.benjerry.com** and is themed to the season or even the day if it's a major holiday. Duracell Batteries has an education-oriented site at **http://www.duracell.com.** Their major competitor, the Eveready Energizer, is at **http://www.energizer.com**, where you can order pink bunny stuff if you really like the durable little devil. For snack food junkies, Frito-Lay is out there at – yes, you guessed it – **http://www.fritolay.com**. If you're not fond of their products, check out the competition at **http://www.pringles.com** or that little chipster from Gramercy, Louisiana, makers of the Cajun Crawtater, Zapp's at **http://www.zapps.com.**

Sauce on the Web? It's Ragu at **http://eat.com.** For fun and games you might pick the Fox network at **http://www.fox.com** or Sega at **http://www.sega.com.** Magnavox lives at **http://www.magnavox.com,** but they're out for repairs today, so I suggest you try **http://www.funai-corp.com.** These people make Funai, Symphonic, Sylvania, and Emerson home entertainment products. For those Kodak moments, go for **http://www.kodak.com**.

Feeling active? The Professional Association of Diving Instructors can be reached at **http://www.padi.com**, New Balance Shoes at **http://www.newbalance.com or http://www.nike.com,** and Ping golf clubs at **http://www.pinggolf.com.**

Want to join? Information on membership in the American Business Women's Association is available at **http://www.abwa.org**. Alternatively, the American Astronomical Society can be reached at **http://www.aas.org.**

Thinking about getting an engineering degree overseas? Well, all sorts of interesting stuff about Bradford University in West Yorkshire (that's England, for those of you not into your shires) on their Web site at **http://www.brad.ac.uk.** It features an interesting overview of this school that began as a training institute for the textile industry 150 years ago. One of their more interesting programs is their "sandwich" degree – it's what we would call a co-op program. They're quite service oriented. Among the other foreign universities you might explore are the University of New South Wales, Australia, at **http://www.unsw.edu.au or** the Ludwig-Maximilians-Universität München, Munich, Germany at **http://www.uni-muenchen.de.**

New Orleans is my favorite city! And there's good stuff about it and Cajun Louisiana (also known as Acadiana) in the Gumbo Pages at **http://www.gumbopages.com**, although it seems some guy in Pasadena, California writes them! The best part of this site is the link to some good Cajun and Creole recipes that'll light up your life. Interested in current goings-on in the city itself? Try **http://www.nola.com** for a site run in collaboration with the *Times-Picayune* newspaper updated, as you might expect, daily.

Sites verified September 6, 2004.

Chapter 12
Category and Brand Management, Product Identification, and New Product Planning

Chapter Outline

You may want to use the following outline as a guide in taking notes.

I.   Chapter Overview

Brands play an enormous role in our lives. We choose them for all sorts of reasons and develop loyalty to some of them because of their quality, their price, or just because of habit. Companies must develop and manage products and product lines that they hope will become necessities to consumers. These are costly propositions so that both existing and new products must be carefully nurtured. Product planning and strategy has two critical elements. First, there is building and maintaining identity and competitive advantage for their product through branding. Then there is the new product planning and introduction process, often influenced greatly by a product or category manager.

II. Managing brands for competitive advantage involves creating and protecting a strong identity for products and product lines. Branding is the process of creating that identity. A brand is a name, term, sign, symbol, design, or some combination that identifies the products of a firm and differentiates them from competitors' offerings.

A. Brand loyalty is measured in three stages.
   1. Brand recognition is a company's first objective for newly introduced products.
      a. Advertising offers one way for increasing consumer awareness for a brand.
      b. Other strategies for creating brand recognition include offering free samples or discount coupons for purchases.
   2. At the second level of brand loyalty, brand preference, buyers rely on previous experiences with the product when choosing it, if available, over competitors' products.
   3. Brand insistence, the highest level of brand loyalty, leads consumers to refuse alternatives and search extensively for the desired merchandise, creating a monopoly for the product with its consumers. Luxury goods are more likely to achieve this status than are mass-marketed products.

B. The types of brands available for a firm to use can be classified in several ways. Some firms choose to sell their products without brands, in containers with plain labels and little or no advertising. Such products are called "generic products." The market for generic products grows during economic downturns but shrinks when times are good. Generic pharmaceuticals seem to have achieved some general level of acceptance, however.
   1. The competition between manufacturer's brands and private brands defines what was once called the "battle of the brands."
      a. Manufacturers' brands, also called *national brands*, are what most people think of when they think of a brand. A manufacturer's brand is a brand name owned by a manufacturer or other producer.
      b. Many large wholesalers and retailers place their own brands on the merchandise they market. These brands are called *private brands* or private labels, and are regarded as a way to reach additional market segments.

    c. Private brands and generic products expand the number of alternatives available to consumers.

    d. The growth of private brands in the U.S. has paralleled that of chain stores in the U.S. Many private brands are manufactured by large firms that also have their own manufacturer's brands in the market.

    e. One area of marketing in which private label branding is gaining new ground is the personal computer, with Best Buy and RadioShack selling PCs bearing their own labels.

C. Captive brands are national brands sold exclusively by a retail chain, such as K-Mart's Martha Stewart home furnishings and General Electric small appliances sold only through WalMart.

D. Family and individual branding are choices which must be made by a firm.

    1. A *family brand* is a brand name that identifies several related products such as Whirlpool appliances or Campbell Soups.

    2. A manufacturer may choose to market a product under an *individual brand*, which uniquely identifies a product itself, rather than promoting it under the name of the company or under an umbrella name covering several products.

        a. Individual brands cost more than family brands to market because each firm requires a new promotional campaign to introduce it to its target market.

        b. Alternatively, a promotional outlay for a family brand can benefit all the items in the line.

    3. Family brands should identify products of similar quality, of there is the possibility of damaging the firm's overall product image.

    4. Individual brand names should distinguish dissimilar products.

E. A strong brand identity backed by superior quality offers important strategic advantages for a firm. It increases the likelihood of brand recognition in the marketplace and contributes to consumers' perceptions of product quality. A strong brand can reinforce customer loyalty and repeat purchases and make it more likely that the brand will be sought on store visits.

    1. Brand equity is the added value that a certain brand name gives to a product in the marketplace.

    2. Globally, high brand equity often facilitates expansion into new markets. .

        a. Coca-Cola is the most valuable brand name in the world.

        b. A global brand is generally defined as one that sells at least 20 percent of its volume outside its home country.

    3. The global advertising agency Young and Rubicam has developed its *Brand Asset Valuator* using four dimensions of brand personality.

        a. Differentiation refers to a brand's ability to stand apart from competitors.

        b. Relevance refers to the real and perceived appropriateness of the brand to a big consumer segment.

        c. Esteem is a combination of perceived quality and consumer perceptions about the growing or declining popularity of a brand.

        d. Knowledge refers to the extent of customers' awareness of the brand and understanding of what a good or service stands for.

    4. Outside endorsers such as *Good Housekeeping Magazine* often assist a product in gaining equity.

    5. Brands with high equity can lose that equity for a number of reasons, such as real or perceived defects or problems in the courts.

  F. The roles of category and brand management to some extent have been chronologically sequential. Traditionally, companies have assigned the task of managing a brand's marketing strategies to a brand manager. Recently, companies have been re-evaluating the effectiveness of brand management.
    1. Major consumer goods companies have adopted a strategy called category management, in which a category manager oversees an entire product line.
    2. Kraft now uses a "customer manager" system in which each major grocery chain has its own representative from the company to handle its needs.

III. Product Identification usually involves the use of brand names, brand marks, and distinctive packaging.

  A. Brand names and brand marks are tools for identifying products.
    1. A brand name is the part of the brand consisting of words or letters that form a name that identifies and distinguishes the firm's offerings from those of its competitors, while a brand mark is a symbol or pictorial design that distinguishes a product.
    2. Effective brand names are easy to pronounce, recognize, and remember.
    3. A brand name should give buyers the correct connotation of the product's image.
    4. A brand name must qualify for legal protection as a registered trademark under the Lanham Act of 1946 (Title 15 U.S. Code).
    5. It has become increasingly difficult to coin effective brand names because of the large number of competitors attempting to effectively name their own products.
    6. When a class of products becomes generally known by the original brand name of a specific offering, the brand name may become a descriptive generic name and the original owner loses exclusive claim to the brand name.
    7. Marketers must distinguish between brand names that have become legally generic and those that only seem generic in many consumers' eyes.

  B. Trademarks are brands for which the owners claim exclusive legal protection. Trademark protection confers the exclusive legal right to use a brand name, brand mark, and any slogan or product name abbreviation.
    1. Trademark protection can be applied to words or phrases such as *Coke* for Coca-Cola or *the Met* for New York's Metropolitan Opera.
      a. It is also possible to receive trademark protection for packaging elements and packaging features such as shape, design, and typeface (trade dress).
      b. The next battlefield for trademark infringement cases may well be the Internet. Several significant cases of trademark infringement against pirates of well known brands have already been heard.
    2. Trade dress refers to visual cues used in branding to create an overall look for a product.
      a. Color selection, sizes, package and label shapes, and similar factors may all comprise parts of trade dress.
      b. Trade dress disputes have lead to many courtroom battles.

  C. Developing global brand names and trademarks is more complex than developing domestic ones. An excellent choice in one country may be inappropriate or unacceptable in another. The decision often breaks down into whether to use a single name in all countries or a name specifically chosen for each market.

D. Packaging can powerfully influence buyers' purchase decisions.
1. Firms are applying increasingly scientific methods to their packaging decisions, using computer graphics and other computer simulations to decide how the package should look and function.
2. Ultimately, packages serve three major functions
    a. Protection against damage, spoilage, and pilferage was the original objective of packaging.
        i.   In recent years, fear of product tampering has forced many firms to improve their package designs.
        ii. Many packages offer important safeguards for retailers against pilferage by being oversized or because they include devices to trigger alarms if carried through a sensing gate.
    b. Assistance in marketing the product is provided by packaging as a promotional tool.
        i.   Environmental friendliness is a feature of packaging that attracts a number of consumers.
        ii. Package design can be an important feature in attracting customer's attention, relating one item in a product line with the others, and creating a positive visual impression.
        iii. Packages can also enhance the convenience of using a product by making the package easier to open or the contents easier to dispense, for example.
        iv. Packages may possess extra value if they can be re-used, such as the jelly jar that doubles as a drinking glass.
3. Cost-effective packaging implies that packaging must not only do its job, but do it at reasonable cost. The number of materials that can be used for packaging is limited, and some are much less expensive than others – but will they do the job?
4. Labeling, though not one of the basic functions of packaging, has become an integral part of it.
    a. At one time, labels were a separate item – often a tag – that was attached to a package to carry the product's brand name or symbol, the name and address of the manufacturer or distributor, information about the physical aspects of the product, and recommended uses. Now labels are more permanently affixed to packages, often being printed on them.
    b. The Fair Packaging and Labeling Act requires that labels offer adequate information concerning package contents and that package design facilitate value comparisons.
    c. The Nutrition Labeling and Education Act of 1990 imposes a uniform format in which food manufacturers must disclose nutritional information about their products.
    d. Labeling requirements differ elsewhere in the world, so care must be taken to conform to local requirements.
    e. Finally, the Universal Product Code (UPC) is an aspect of labeling and packaging which has become extremely important since its introduction in 1974 as a method of cutting expenses in the supermarket industry because of its ability to identify specific products for database applications.

F. Brand extension is the strategy of attaching a popular brand to a new product in an unrelated product category.
1. Brand extension is NOT line extension, which is the practice of adding new sizes, styles, or related types to a pre-existing line of products.

      2. Introducing too many brand extensions can cause brand dilution, especially if a number of the extensions fail.

  G. Brand licensing occurs when a firm authorizes other companies to use its brand names, expanding its exposure in the marketplace.
      1. Major League Baseball is an excellent example of successful brand licensing over a period of many years.
      2. Brand licensing can present some problems because brands do not transfer well to all products.

IV. **New-Product Planning** is necessary because regular additions of new products to the firm's line helps to protect it from product obsolescence. New products are the basis of survival for the firm, some implementing new technological breakthroughs, others simply extending existing product lines.

  A. Product development strategies vary depending on the firm's existing product mix and the match between current offerings and the firm's overall marketing objectives, as well as the current market positions of its products.
      1. A *market penetration* strategy seeks to increase sales of existing products in existing markets.
         a. Companies may modify products, improve product quality, or promote new and different ways to use products.
         b. Product positioning refers to consumers' perceptions of a product's attributes, uses, quality, and advantages and disadvantages relative to competing brands.
      2. A *market development* strategy concentrates on finding new markets for existing products, typically using segmentation as a basis for the effort.
      3. *Product development* refers to the introduction of new products into identifiable or established markets.
         a. If a firm introduces new products into markets in which they already have a position in an effort to increase market share, those brands are called *flanker brands*.
      4. A *product diversification* strategy focuses on developing entirely new products for new markets.
      5. Regardless of the strategy chosen, firms must be careful to avoid investing resources in a new product introduction that will adversely affect sales of existing products – or *cannibalize* their sales.

  B. The consumer adoption process describes the series of stages consumers go through from first learning about new products to trying them and deciding whether to purchase them regularly or reject them. There are five stages in this process.
      1. <u>Awareness</u> occurs when people first learn about the new product but lack full information about it.
      2. <u>Interest</u> develops when potential buyers seek information about the new product.
      3. <u>Evaluation</u> occurs as consumers consider the likely benefits of the product.
      4. <u>Trial</u> involves potential consumers making trial purchases to determine the product's usefulness.
      5. <u>Adoption/Rejection</u> occurs if, after trial, use of the product produces satisfactory results (adoption) or not (rejection).
      6. Marketers must understand the adoption process to move potential consumers to the adoption stage.

C. Adopter categories categorize consumers on the basis of their likelihood to accept a new product earlier or later in the adoption process, or not at all.
1. Consumer innovators are people who purchase new products almost as soon as those products reach the market.
2. Early adopters, the early majority, late majority, and laggards represent the other adopting groups in terms of when in the process they decide to adopt the product.
3. The diffusion process brings acceptance of new goods and services by members of the community or social system.

D. Identifying early adopters of a new product can be vital to the product's success. Extensive research has established that early adopters tend to be younger, have higher social status, are better educated, and enjoy higher incomes than other consumers. They are more mobile than later adopters and change jobs and addresses more often. The early adopter uses impersonal promotion sources rather than word-of-mouth or company-generated promotion.
1. Rate of adoption determinants – There are five factors that influence the rate of adoption of an innovation.
   a. <u>Relative advantage</u>, the degree to which an innovation appears to be superior to previous ideas in terms of lower price, physical improvement, or ease of use increases its adoption rate.
   b. <u>Compatibility</u> is the measure of the innovation's consistency with the values and experiences of potential adopters; a high level of compatibility yields rapid adoption.
   c. <u>Complexity</u> is the relative difficulty of understanding the innovation; a high level of complexity slows adoption.
   d. <u>Possibility of trial use</u> such as a free or discounted trial of the product, reduces the risk of financial or social loss and increases the speed of adoption.
   e. <u>Observability</u> refers to the possibility of seeing the superiority of the innovation in concrete form; the more observable the value of the innovation is, the quicker it will be adopted.
2. Marketers who want to accelerate the rate of adoption can manipulate the five characteristics that determine the rate of product adoption at least to some extent through promotional efforts, good product design, free samples, in-home demonstrations, and conscious efforts to make products compatible with existing technology.

E. Organizing for new-product development must be accomplished in such a way that firm organization can stimulate and coordinate new product development. Some firms contract with independent design firms to develop new products, while others do it themselves using one or more of the four typical methods.
1. New product committees typically bring together experts in such areas as marketing, finance, manufacturing, engineering, research, and accounting to review and approve new product plans that arise elsewhere in the organization.
   a. Since members of a new product committee hold important jobs in the firm's functional areas, their support for any new product plan likely foreshadows approval for further development.
2. New product departments are separate, formally organized departments that generate and refine new product ideas as a permanent, full-time activity.

      3. Product managers are marketing professionals that support the marketing strategies of individual products or product lines.

        a. Product managers set prices, develop advertising and sales promotion programs, and work with sales representatives in the field.

        b. Recently, a number of large firms have modified the product manager structure or done away with it in favor of a category management structure based on small teams, rather than individuals.

      4. Venture teams consist of groups of specialists from different areas of the organization gathered to work together to develop new products, sometimes working together for a number of years.

        a. Some marketing organizations differentiate between venture teams and task forces, the task force being more of a coordinative operation rather than an originating effort.

        b. Unlike new product committees, venture teams do not disband after every meeting.

V. The New Product Development Process is time-consuming, risky, and expensive. Firms must examine dozens of product ideas to produce one successful product. A new product is more likely to be successful if the firm follows a six-step development process. Usually, the process is "phased," that is, followed in an orderly fashion from first step to last. Time pressure to get innovations to market, however, has argued for using "parallel" product development programs, in which team members work on the steps of the development process at the same time, speeding the development process significantly. Firms often use techniques – the Program Evaluation and Review Technique (PERT) and Critical Path Method (CPM) – developed by the Navy to expedite development efforts. Nike's recent introduction of golf clubs bearing its name called for a development budget and introductory promotional budget in excess of $135 million.

    A. Idea generation, the first step in new product development, begins with ideas from many sources – the sales force, suggestions from customers, research-and-development specialists, competing products, suppliers, retailers, and independent inventors.

    B. Screening separates ideas with commercial potential from those that cannot meet company objectives.

    C. Business analysis takes product ideas that have survived original screening and subjects them to a thorough analysis of their potential market, growth rate, and likely competitive strengths.

      1. Concept testing subjects the idea to additional study prior to its actual development.

      2. Screening and business analysis define the proposed product's target market and customer needs and wants and determine the product's financial and technical requirements.

    D. Development is the process of converting the idea into a physical product, an expensive proposition comprising a joint effort between the firm's development engineers and its marketers.

    E. Test marketing is an option that some firms use to gauge consumer reaction to their new products, determining whether the product delivers as promised under real-world conditions.

    F. Commercialization occurs when the product is ready for full-scale marketing and is offered to its target.

VI. Product Safety and Liability have become major issues in recent years. A product cannot satisfy consumer needs unless it is safe to operate. *Product liability* refers to the responsibility of manufacturers and marketers for injuries and damages caused by their products. Federal and state laws play a major role in regulating product safety. The Poison Prevention Packaging Act and the Consumer Product Safety Act are among the recent laws designed to assure that products are safe. The CPSC can ban products without court hearings, order recalls or redesigns of products, and inspect production facilities. The federal Food and Drug Administration must approve food, medications, and health-related devices such as wheelchairs. Product liability lawsuits have increased markedly in recent years, and their settlement costs can be very high. Regulatory activities and the increased number of claims have prompted companies to sponsor voluntary improvements in safety standards.

Name_____   Instructor_____

Section_____   Date_____

Key Concepts

The purpose of this section is to allow you to determine if you can match key concepts with their definitions. It is essential that you know the definitions of the concepts prior to applying the concepts in later exercises in this chapter.

From the list of lettered terms, select the one that best fits each of the numbered statements below. Write the letter of that choice in the space provided.

Key Terms

a. brand
b. brand recognition
c. brand preference
d. brand insistence
e. generic product
f. manufacturer's brand
g. family brand
h. brand equity

i. category management
j. brand name
k. trademark
l. brand extension
m. adoption process
n. consumer innovator
o. diffusion process

_____ 1. Brand that identifies several related products.

_____ 2. Stages that consumers go through in learning about a new product, trying it, and deciding whether to purchase it again.

_____ 3. Strategy of attaching a popular brand name to a new product in an unrelated product category.

_____ 4. A brand for which the owner claims exclusive legal protection.

_____ 5. Process by which new goods or services are accepted in the marketplace

_____ 6. Item characterized by a plain label, little or no advertising, and no brand name.

_____ 7. Added value that a certain brand name gives to a product.

_____ 8. People who purchase new products almost as soon as the products reach the market.

_____ 9. Name, term, sign, symbol, design, or some combination of these used to identify the products of a firm.

_____ 10. Stage of brand acceptance at which the customer refuses all alternatives and will search extensively for the desired good or service.

_____ 11. Part of a brand consisting of words or letters that form a name that identifies and distinguishes a firm's offerings from those of its competitors.

_____ 12. Product management system in which a manager who is responsible for profits and losses oversees a product line.

_____ 13. The stage of brand acceptance at which the customer is aware of a brand and can identify it.

_____ 14. Brand name owned by a manufacturer or other producer.

_____ 15. Consumer reliance on previous experiences with a product to choose that product again.

Name_____   Instructor_____

Section_____   Date_____

Self-Quiz

You should use these objective questions to test your understanding of the chapter material. You can check your answers with those provided at the end of the chapter.

While these questions cover most of the chapter topics, they are not intended to be the same as the test questions your instructor may use in an examination. A good understanding of all aspects of the course material is essential to good performance on any examination.

True/False

Write "T" for True or "F" for False for each of the following statements.

_____ 1. Branding is the process of creating and protecting a strong identity for products and product lines

_____ 2. A product's brand name should be easy to pronounce, recognize, and remember.

_____ 3. High brand equity may inhibit expansion into new markets because of the financial disadvantage the equity places on the product.

_____ 4. The unique shape of the bottle in which Coca-Cola has traditionally been sold constitutes part of its trade dress.

_____ 5. During the stage of brand acceptance called *brand insistence*, consumers will choose a product over its competitors if it is available; if it is not, they will accept a substitute.

_____ 6. Trade names and trademarks should not be confused; a trade name identifies a company while a trademark identifies a company's products.

_____ 7. Family brands cost more to market than individual brands because a new promotional campaign must be developed to introduce each new product to its target market.

_____ 8. Brand names which become generic, such as *aspirin* and *kerosene*, result in a strengthening of the original owner's exclusive claim to them.

_____ 9. In the Young and Rubicam *Brand Asset Valuator* approach to brand equity valuation, the term differentiation refers to a brand's ability to stand apart from competitors.

_____ 10. Captive brands are brands bearing a manufacturer's or designer's name which are available exclusively from a single retail chain such as K-Mart or Target.

_____ 11. In the past, the label was an integral part of a typical package. Today it has become a separate element that is applied to the package at a later date.

___ 12. The Fair Packaging and Labeling Act requires that nutritional labels on foods list the amounts of fat, sodium, dietary fiber, and calcium in typical servings.

___ 13. If a newly introduced product takes sales away from an existing product in the same line, it is said to be infiltrating the line.

___ 14. The Trademark Dilution Act of 1995 makes it more difficult to defend a trademark by requiring proof that a trademark violator knew it was in violation for a trademark owner to prevail in court.

___ 15. "Brand extension" refers to the strategy of attaching a popular brand name to a new product in an unrelated product category.

___ 16. The diffusion process focuses on individuals and the steps they go through in making the ultimate decision of whether to become repeat purchasers of a new product or to reject it as a failure to satisfy their needs.

___ 17. A market development strategy concentrates on finding new markets for existing products.

___ 18. In general, the more complex an innovative product is, the more slowly it will be adopted by consumers.

___ 19. In the new-product development process, the screening stage assesses the new product's potential market, growth rate, and likely competitive strengths.

___ 20. Before a company can develop a prototype of a new product, it should test market the product to gauge consumer reactions under normal conditions.

___ 21. Accelerated product development programs have been encouraged by the desire of many firms to keep pace with rapidly changing technologies and markets.

___ 22. New product committees tend to reach decisions rapidly and maintain liberal views, seldom compromising on important issues.

___ 23. In the adoption process, consumers must first become aware of the product before they can evaluate it.

___ 24. Packaging plays a very small role in providing safety through protection against tampering; after all, most products aren't used until after they have been removed from the package.

___ 25. Beyond making sure that their products will do the job they have been advertised to do, even if there is some risk of harm involved in that use, manufacturers and marketers have no responsibility for injuries and damages caused by their products.

Multiple Choice

Circle the letter of the word or phrase which best completes the sentence or answers the question.

26. Once a product has moved from the unknown to the category when buyers rely on previous experiences with the product when choosing it, if available, over competitive products, it can be said to have achieved brand
    a. recognition.
    b. visibility.
    c. preference.
    d. elevation.
    e. insistence.

27. When a company uses a unique brand name for each of the products in a line, it is practicing
    a. institutional branding.
    b. individual branding.
    c. national branding.
    d. private branding.
    e. family branding .

28. Which of the following is more true of family branding than of individual branding?
    a. A promotional outlay typically benefits only one product in the line at a time.
    b. It is more difficult to introduce a new product to retailers and consumers.
    c. The approach should be used for products which are dissimilar in use and share few market characteristics.
    d. These brands cost more to market because of the need to develop a new promotional campaign to introduce each new product.
    e. Users of this type of branding run the risk of harming overall product image if items are not of similar quality.

29. When a firm's product development orientation is toward developing entirely new products for new markets, it is practicing a strategy of
    a. product positioning.
    b. market penetration.
    c. product development.
    d. market development.
    e. product diversification.

30. When an individual, typically assisted by "analysts," sets product prices, develops advertising and sales promotion programs, works directly with the sales force, and is responsible for the profitabilty of a product line, you have a
    a. category management strategy in place.
    b. very volatile brand equity arrangement.
    c. product or brand manager structure for new-product development.
    d. distinct possibility of cannibalization by other products.
    e. product diversification strategy in place.

31. The most common organizational arrangement for new-product development is the
    a. new-product department.
    b. single-layer discovery system.
    c. new-product committee.
    d. the venture team arrangement.
    e. the idea-generation concept.

32. Which of the following is a good example of using a package to assist in marketing a product?
    a. packaging beer in brown or green bottles or cans of standard shapes and sizes
    b. providing tamper-resistant seals on food and medicine containers
    c. combining colors, sizes, shapes, graphics, and typefaces used in packaging to create a distinctive trade dress which sets the product apart from competitors.
    d. designing the package so that the product will not be deformed or crushed in shipment or damaged by high levels of humidity
    e. choosing from among alternative package designs the one which will adequately protect the contents at least cost

33. After a company has developed a prototype, it may decide to attempt to gauge consumer reactions to it under normal conditions. Such an activity is known as
    a. test marketing.
    b. competitive assessment.
    c. commercialization.
    d. analytical appraisal.
    e. semidomairevention.

34. The concept that manufacturers and marketers are responsible for injuries and damage caused by their products is called
    a. corporate social responsibility.
    b. the premise of extended warranty.
    c. customer relations.
    d. the rule of individual responsibility.
    e. product liability.

35. Brands owned by manufacturers and used to identify their products, such as Campbell's soups and Levi's jeans, are known as manufacturers' brands or
    a. national brands.
    b. private brands.
    c. individual brands..
    d. global brands.
    e. extended brands.

36. General Electric small appliances are available only at WalMart because
    a. General Electric Corporation is owned by WalMart.
    b. it's part of their trade dress.
    c. it's one of WalMart's captive brands.
    d. there is a co-branding contract between the two firms.
    e. GE is trying a brand extension strategy by introducing small appliances.

37. According to Young and Rubicam's *Brand Asset Valuator*, the dimension of a brand's personality that refers to the real and perceived appropriateness of the brand to a big consumer segment is
    a. stability.
    b. evaluation.
    c. esteem.
    d. relevance.
    e. knowledge.

38. Of the following proposed brand names, which would be most likely to receive trademark protection under U.S.Law?
    a. Grade A Milk
    b. Suntan Lotion
    c. Patrick O'Reilly's Irish Stew
    d. Grocery Store Foods
    e. 93 Octane Gasoline

39. Generic products
    a. often bear flamboyant brand names and flashy labels.
    b. increase their market share during economic downturns but subside when the economy improves.
    c. are designed to mimic brands with high consumer recognition and steal sales from them.
    d. were first made available in the U.S. in 1966 and have been successful ever since.
    e. account for over half the sales of certain types of goods.

40. The right of exclusive use granted to the owner of a brand by trademark registration
    a. includes any pictorial designs used in the brand.
    b. covers the brand name of the product.
    c. includes brand name abbreviations such as "Coke" for "Coca-Cola."
    d. preserves the brand owner's right to slogans such as "It's Miller Time."
    e. extends to all of the conditions mentioned in a through d.

41. The main purpose of oversized packaging, such as the plastic or paperboard trays in which prerecorded audio tapes and CDs are often displayed and sold, is to
    a. provide extra physical protection to the contents.
    b. prevent spoilage of the product by tampering.
    c. assist in the marketing of the product by providing convenience of access to it.
    d. reduce theft by making the product too bulky to fit conveniently into a pocket or purse.
    e. be a cost-effective way of facilitating goods handling.

42. That part of the product development process that is designed to separate ideas with commercial potential from those that stand little chance of meeting company objectives is called
    a. idea generation.
    b. concept testing.
    c. test marketing.
    d. business analysis.
    e. screening.

43. The stage of brand loyalty during which consumers refuse to accept substitutes for a desired brand, searching for it extensively if it is not immediately available, is called brand
    a. preference.
    b. insistence.
    c. aggravation.
    d. realization.
    e. recognition.

44. The Universal Product Code
    a. allows consumers to determine how long it has been since a product they are buying was produced.
    b. is a symbol displayed on many packages certifying that the product is manufactured to "universal standards."
    c. is a law that specifies that the labels on packages all over the world contain the same type and quantity of information.
    d. is a numerical bar code printed on packages and read by optical scanners that print the item's description and its price on the cash register receipt.
    e. is a standard of ethics for manufacturers of consumer goods that sets forth their customer relations policy.

45. The approach to new-product development which assigns teams of design, marketing, manufacturing, sales, and service people to carry out projects from idea generation all the way through to commercialization, often performing more than one step in the development process at a time, is
    a. phased development.
    b. the Critical Path Method.
    c. the Program Evaluation and Review Technique.
    d. parallel (accelerated) product development.
    e. sequential scheduling.

46. The original, historical objective of packaging was
    a. as a device to prevent the authorities from discovering smuggled goods.
    b. to provide physical protection for the product.
    c. to be cost-effective, the cheapest way to wrap the item.
    d. to establish an "identity" for the product.
    e. to provide convenience in storage, use, and disposal.

47. The federal agency created by this law has assumed jurisdiction over the safety of every consumer product category except food, drugs, and other products already regulated by other agencies. The law is
    a. the Alcohol, Tobacco, and Firearms Regulatory Act of 1934.
    b. the Fair Packaging and Labeling Act of 1966 as amended in 1989.
    c. the Omnibus Consumer Product Standards Act of 1987.
    d. the Consumer Product Safety Act of 1972.
    e. the Magnusson-Moss Consumer Products Warranty Act of 1973.

48. Among the industries that rely heavily on test marketing are firms that make
    a. snack foods, automobiles, and motion pictures.
    b. home appliances and technology products.
    c. women's fashion goods and cosmetics.
    d. industrial pumps and materials handling equipment.
    e. manufacturing equipment and assembly-line processes.

49. Which of the following was originally a brand name but has become generic through common usage over the years?
    a. Aspirin
    b. Jell-O
    c. Xerox
    d. Hoover
    e. Frigidaire

50. Creating a package which features a handy pour spout as an integral part of the design assists marketing of the product by
    a. producing a package that can be easily reused.
    b. making the product more convenient to use.
    c. establishing the product's identity through package design.
    d. producing a package which is cost-effective.
    e. protecting the product against damage, pilferage, or spoilage.

Name_____   Instructor_____

Section_____   Date_____

Applying Marketing Concepts

Wildermann Wisconsin Woolens has been in business for over sixty-five years. The company was founded in 1936 to manufacture and distribute the famous Wildermann Warm Winter Wear, a comprehensive line of incredibly comfortable clothing suited to the Mid North-American cold weather climate. Though not particularly stylish, the original line has stood the test of time and is still in production. Over the years, the company has added to its line of fashions, and now sells Wittle Woolies for Kids, smaller versions of the original line, Wildermann's Weatherproof Wonders, stylish adaptations of the company's basic product using other, more modern materials in addition to the original wool, and W-Ski Brand clothing for skiers and other cold-weather out-doorspeople.

Each item of Wildermann clothing bears the company's distinctive silver and blue brand symbol on the left sleeve.

1. The type of branding which Wildermann has traditionally used is
    a. individual branding.
    b. family branding.
    c. dealer branding.
    d. generic branding.
    e. indeterminate branding.

2. Just recently, Wildermann was approached by a large fashion chain that wants to buy Weatherproof Wonders to be marked with their brand and sold under the chain's name. The fashion chain's brand is a
    a. generic brand.
    b. national brand.
    c. individual brand.
    d. family brand.
    e. private brand.

3. Wildermann has received an offer from the Kawanishi Clothing Company of Tokyo. They want to produce clothing using Wildermann's designs and bearing Wildermann's brand in Japan, where a craze for "American look clothing" (sort of like the Sushi craze here) is under way. Wildermann courteously responds with a refusal and points out to the Kawanishi firm that the Wildermann brand belongs to them and any use of it by anyone else will result in legal action. Wildermann Wisconsin Woolens is
    a. asserting its trademark rights (under the International Trademark Convention).
    b. implemented a market penetration strategy.
    c. commencing a product positioning sequence.
    c. being obnoxious to the Japanese firm.
    d. actively pursuing market development.
    e. diversifying its product mix.

4. Though it is reasonably unlikely that such a thing would ever happen, suppose that some of the Wildermann Wonder items suddenly began bursting into flames while on store shelves and in consumers' homes – but not yet while being worn.   Which federal agency do you suppose would show the greatest interest?
   a. Federal Energy Regulatory Commission.
   b. Bureau of Alcohol, Tobacco, and Firearms.
   c. Consumer Product Safety Commission.
   d. Directorship of the Federal Reserve System.
   e. Nuclear Regulatory Commission.

5. If Wildermann decided to branch out into the production of swimwear and decided to create a new brand, such as "Dangerous When Wet," for that line, it would be
   a. developing a new family brand for the swimwear line.
   b. individually branding the swimwear.
   c. making a serious mistake; wearers of Wildermann clothing aren't going to be interested in swim wear.
   d. in violation of law; each clothing product must bear the brand name most closely associated with its maker.

"OK, people, settle down," Sam Kamenzuli called the group gathered in the conference room at Trunnion Industries to order. "We've got a lot to do today. This is our third meeting this year, and we've got four items on the agenda. First, as some of you know, Mel Oustalet will be replacing Leslie Hussman as our engineering member until Leslie gets back from leave. If you haven't heard, it's a boy! Leslie's just fine and so is the baby. Next, I've got three new concepts I want you to take with you and look over." He handed out large brown envelopes to six of the other seven people in the room. "You'll find the preliminary appraisal forms for each idea attached to their descriptions."

Gesturing toward the person who didn't get an envelope, he continued. "I'd like to introduce Mia Cascabel to all of you. She'll be responsible the New Era line when we introduce it next month. I've given her all the information we generated during our deliberations, but she may need to talk to some of you about details as we get closer to the intro date."

Everyone shook hands with Mia across the table and she excused herself to go back to her office. Sam started handing out slim volumes of paper bound in green to each person remaining. "Here are the preliminary results from Hannover City. As you can see, models K-30 and K-31 are doing well, but K-32 isn't really selling.

"Well, Sam, that's sort of what we expected from our earlier research, isn't it?" said a tall man halfway down the table.

"Yes, Jack," replied Sam.

"I'd be inclined to recommend we drop the K-32," said Jack, who was from manufacturing. "It's got too many bells and whistles, anyway."

"How do the rest of you feel?" asked Sam, scanning the table. Everyone was in agreement, as nodding heads indicated. "Good, then it's done. Our next meeting will be next week, same time, same place. Thank you all." And they filed from the room.

6. The above is most probably a transcript of a meeting of Trunnion Industries'
   a. flight products venture team.
   b. new product department.
   c. new product committee.
   d. separately funded delivery department.

7. The members of the group were given the documents in the brown envelopes so they could
   a. begin the process of idea generation.
   b. examine them and give their input to the screening process.
   c. do a business analysis on the information in the envelopes.
   d. test market the information in the envelopes.
   e. commercialize the information given them.

8. Mia Cascabel is very likely
   a. the category manager for the New Era line.
   b. a visitor to company headquarters.
   c. a research analyst whose work the firm has used.
   d. nobody important.
   e. somebody important, but why she's important is a secret.

9. The "results from Hannover City" probably had to do with
   a. some preliminary concept testing Trunnion was doing.
   b. a jury of executive opinion done at company headquarters.
   c. a survey of several thousand consumers.
   d. the results of test marketing a new product line.
   e. deciding whether or not to drop an old line.

Marcelin Rabelais didn't know whether to be happy or sad. "Oo-eee," he thought as he drove along the banks of Bayou Teche on his way home to Jeanerette, "so many things to do, so little time!" He wondered if he would ever have gotten into the fiberglass pirogue business if he had known how much work it was going to be. (A pirogue, for those of you not familiar with them, is a small, flat-bottomed boat, usually paddled or poled, uniquely suited to shallow water and widely used by fishermen and hunters in Louisiana – especially south Lousiana.)

Marcelin's product had been remarkably successful, not only because it was more durable than the traditional wooden pirogue, but also because he finished each boat in a special and unique camouflage pattern of his own design that had proven extremely effective in concealing them among swamp grass and hummocks. His name for the boats, "Un Petite Liberté" (A Small Freedom), and the associated artwork consisting of a picture of a duck and a redfish in silhouette against a white circle, both of which he applied to the bow of each craft, also set his product apart. He had just received news from his attorney (and cousin), Placide Bordelon, that his application for registration of all of these with the government had been approved. Alcide had also just received a letter from Hippolyte Couvillon, a resident of Thibodaux and owner of a large boat and motor store in Morgan City (and another cousin). Hippolyte proposed that Marcelin manufacture pirogues to Hippolyte's order, similar in most respects to the Petite Liberté except bearing Hippolyte's Eauvitesse nomenclature. Marcelin was also thinking about whether he should change the name of his company, New Iberia Fiberglass Works, to something related to boat building. Marcelin decided he would deal with these issues after he had a cup or two of café au lait and a beignet.

10. Marcelin's use of "Un Petite Liberté" in relation to his boats constitutes a
    a. brand mark.
    b. brand name.
    c. corporate name.
    d. generic name.
    e. trade suit.

11. The duck and redfish used by Mr. Rabelais to identify his boats is a
    a. trademark.
    b. brand name.
    c. dress name.
    d. generic mark.
    e. brand mark.

12. The combination of name, picture, and camouflage pattern for which Mr. Rabelais has se-
    cured registration would constitute
    a. a trade name.
    b. a brand name.
    c. a generic mark.
    d. a trademark.
    e. a brand mark.

13. Taken by itself, Marcelin's unique camouflage pattern is probably an example of
    a. trade dress.
    b. a generic mark.
    c. an infringement.
    d. a logotype.
    e. a type style.

14. The letter from Hippolyte Couvillon has to do with the idea of
    a. brand licensing.
    b. private branding.
    c. generic naming.
    d. collusion.
    e. brand management.

15. New Iberia Fiberglass Works is
    a. a trade name.
    b. a brand name.
    c. based on Alcide's wife's maiden name.
    d. a product identification.
    e. a measure of brand equity.

Name_____   Instructor_____

Section_____   Date_____

Surfing the Net

Keeping in mind that addresses change and what's on the Web now may have changed by the time you read this, let's take a look at some of the places on the Net that reflect aspects of new product introduction. We are not endorsing or recommending any of these sources, merely making note of the information and services that people have elected to offer through the Internet.

What's in a Cola – *Jolt* Cola, that is? Here's a product that's not yet available everywhere that you might want to look up. Why? Because its major selling point is that it's loaded with caffeine and compares itself with coffee, tea, and even caffeine tablets on this count. Go online with them at **http://www.joltcola.com** if the premise piques your curiosity. This site is a page of a larger site at **http://www.wetplanet.com** that features a number of novel soft drinks.

Interested in the pharmaceuticals market? There are a number of pharmaceuticals firms on the Net, both ethical houses (they make prescription medications) and proprietaries (they make over-the-counter products). Some announce new-product introductions though their Web sites. Pfizer (**http://www. pfizer.com),** Upjohn **(http://www.upjohn.com)** and Warner-Lambert **(http://warner-lambert.com)** have merged and any of the sites just noted take you to Pfizer's home page. Pfizer and Upjohn produced ethical (prescription) medications and Warner-Lambert was an over-the-counter maker before the merger. Bristol-Myers Squibb **(http://www.squibb. com)** owns a site showing its involvement with both ethical and proprietary products. Mergers such as these have been increasingly common in recent years in everything from banks to book publishing.

What's new in the automotive world? The auto makers would like us to believe everything is. Check it out for yourself! The following should be self-explanatory: **http://www.bmwusa.com; http://www.chrysler.com; http://www.ferrariworld.com; http://www.ford.com; http://www.isuzu.com; http://www.lexuscar.com; http://nissanusa.com; http://www.gm.com; http://www.toyota.com; http://hyundaicars.com;** and finally, **http://www.kia.com.** The Ford site is particularly interesting because it covers all their marques: Ford, Mercury, Lincoln, Mazda, Jaguar, Volvo, and Aston-Martin. If I've missed your favorite, I'm sorry. Lots of other car companies have Web sites that I didn't mention. See if you can ferret them out. Good luck!

Sites verified September 7, 2004

Part 4
Creating a Marketing Plan

Episode Four: Where Do We Go From Here?

As episode four begins, we find our fledgling entrepreneurs discussing their long-term plans for the company. They are examining their resources, and attempting to match the potential in the marketplace to their abilities and potentials. They have quickly recognized from their previous work that the potential for the kind of service they plan to offer is quite substantial. If the information they have is correct, then the potential in the local market could be as much as $78,000,000 this year, growing at a rate of somewhere between 14 and 33% per annum. Their resources, on the other hand, are limited to the $240,000 they have saved or borrowed, plus their own educations and talents.

Meanwhile, there are already 21 potentially active competitors in the market, with some 102 others who might someday pose a threat. On the other hand, many of these potential competitors displayed little marketing "savvy" to the partners when they had conducted their market survey.

Suzette was the first to speak. "Listen, guys," said she, "we have to set some kind of goals for ourselves or we won't have anything to work toward. What do you say we start with the long run and work our way back to the present? I figure that, if we play our cards right, we can get at least one percent of the market in five years. What do you think? That would be at least $1,131,000 in volume by then. Do you think we can get that big a market share? We'd have to do at least $375,000 this year and grow by at least 30 to 35 percent a year to get there in five years."

"Do you think that's aiming high enough?" asked Sandy. "We've got to get this operation going, which we know is going to cost at least $200,000 if we do it right. We're sure to lose money unless we get a pretty big chunk of the market pretty quick."

"On the other hand," said Mel, "if we aim too high and don't achieve our goals, we may think we've failed when we're really doing well. I figure that we'd be better off looking at bottom line profits rather than share of the market. I think we ought to look to make at least ten percent profit on sales."

"Okay," said Suzette, "I'll agree with both of you. I sure hope we can latch onto one percent of this market. I also hope we can make 10 percent on sales. But remember, we have to do this the customer's way. I think we should be available 24 hours a day, seven days a week. That should give us a real advantage over the other companies in the market. Sure, it'll cost a little more at first, but we'll build customer loyalty and probably generate more up-front money from maintenance contracts that way. Besides, I think we're all being too conservative. Remember, we're going after this market, not just giving it lip service.

We really should expect to lose money for the next couple of years. But we'll be offering people what they need, and it's sure to pay off in the long run."

Guidelines:

a. Where are Suzette, Sandy, and Mel getting the figures they are using in these discussions?

b. Remember that a lot of what happens depends on how actively our heroes pursue their business. Enthusiasm and dedication do count, if the market offers sufficient potential in the first place. Summarize their objectives and complete Parts II. A., II. B., and II. C. in your marketing plan.

Part 5
Distribution Decisions

Distribution strategy involves moving goods and services from producers to customers, and is an important marketing concern. Marketing channels and logistics processes are the two means by which this happens.

A marketing channel performs four functions: (1) it facilitates exchange by cutting the number of marketplace contacts needed to acquire goods; (2) it adjusts for discrepancies in the market's assortment of goods and services; (3) it standardizes exchange transactions; and (4) it facilitates searches by buyers and sellers. It may be short, simple, and direct or long, complex, and indirect. Some channels have no marketing intermediaries in them, others have several. Dual channels are often used to match product availability to the needs of users. "Reverse" channels have had to be developed to handle product recalls, warranty service, and returnable containers.

Channel strategy decisions begin with selection of a marketing channel. The selection is based on market factors, product factors, organizational factors, and competitive factors. Products may be made available through channels providing intensive, selective, or exclusive distribution. The battle for channel captaincy – a dominant position in the channel – has resulted in development and resolution of a number of types of channel conflicts including horizontal conflicts, vertical conflicts, and what has come to be called the grey market. In addition to the traditional, loosely organized channel, there are three classes of vertical marketing system (VMS) which can be used. These three types include the corporate, administered, and contractual VMSs.

Logistics is the mechanism which facilitates the operation of marketing channels. It is not enough that title is transferred from manufacturer to wholesaler to retailer, it is also necessary that product move from source to ultimate user. Logistics operates, usually through facilitating agencies, to move, store, and keep track of the product as it transits from producer through the channel of distribution to the ultimate user. These functions must be performed in a timely, efficient, and effective manner.

The objective of logistics is to achieve a stated level of customer service at least total overall cost. The physical distribution manager chooses from among alternative transportation, warehousing, inventory control, order processing, and packaging and materials handling methods to achieve this objective. Suboptimization – the minimization of the cost of individual physical distribution functions at the expense of the whole – is to be avoided.

The major modes of transportation are the railroads, motor carriers, pipelines, water carriage, and air carriage. Intermodal and multimodal arrangements add versatility to the system. A given carrier may be a common, contract, or private carrier. Each type of carrier survives because of certain unique capacities it has that no other carrier has. The last twenty years have seen a substantial deregulation of the transportation industry, resulting in greater flexibility in the choice of modes and carriers. Actual cargo carriers are assisted in their work by freight forwarders, firms that handle the paperwork of transportation, and supplemental carriers that serve the needs of certain specialized markets.

Warehousing has vastly increased its technological level. Automated warehouses have become common, and the study of warehouse location has changed the ways in which warehouses handle goods. The advent of practical, inexpensive computers and software packages for them has allowed two of the remaining elements of logistics – inventory control and order processing – to achieve a level of sophistication undreamt of just a few years ago. Finally, the development of

277

new, composite packaging materials and more sophisticated and gentler materials handling processes have reduced damage in the logistics stream.

Retailers sell goods and services to the ultimate consumer. Numerous types of retailers exist. Retailers may be classed on the basis of the form of their ownership, by the effort expended to shop at them, by the services they provide, and by the product lines they handle. Non-store retailing is a growing nontraditional form of retailing which includes direct marketing, telemarketing, Internet marketing, and automatics merchandising.

Retailing often changes in an evolutionary process called the "wheel of retailing" as products, institutional structures, and consumer buying habits change. After selecting a target market, a retailer must develop a merchandising strategy, customer service strategy, location-distribution strategy, promotional strategy, and pricing strategy and decide on the atmospherics that are going to be the signature of his or her store. Retailers are of many types; so many, in fact, that even the broadest efforts result in classifications based on form of ownership, shopping effort involved in using them, services provided, and product lines carried. Many recent trends in retailing are evidence of what is known as retail convergence wherein retailers become so similar because of scrambled merchandising – except for their pricing – that they are hard to categorize. Direct marketing includes direct mail, direct selling, direct response retailing, telemarketing, internet retailing, and automatic merchandising.

Wholesaling intermediaries create utility, provide services, and lower costs by limiting contacts between buyers and sellers. They include manufacturer-owned facilities, independent wholesaling intermediaries who may or may not take title to the goods they sell, and retailer-owned cooperatives and buying offices. Manufacturer-owned facilities include sales branches, sales offices, trade fairs, and merchandise marts. Among the independents, merchant wholesalers actually take title to the goods they intend to sell. They thus engage in speculative buying in the hope that purchasers will be found. Merchant wholesalers develop long-term relationships with manufacturers and retailers or industrial users. They include both full-function and limited-function examples. The full-function merchants may be industrial distributors or rack jobbers. The limited-function merchants include cash-and-carry wholesalers, truck wholesalers, drop shippers, and mail-order wholesalers. Agents and brokers are independent wholesaling middlemen who perform primarily a selling function. There are five types: commission merchants, auction houses, brokers, selling agents, and manufacturers' agents.

Chapter 13
Marketing Channels and Supply Chain Management

Chapter Outline

You may want to use the following outline as a guide in taking notes.

I. Chapter Overview

Distribution is an important marketing concern. Distribution strategy has two components: marketing channels which are organized systems of marketing institutions and their interrelationships that promote the physical flow and ownership of goods and services from producer to consumer or business user; and logistics and supply-chain management. Logistics is the process of coordinating the flow of information, goods, and services among members of the marketing channel. Supply-chain management is control of the activities of purchasing, processing, and delivery through which raw materials are transformed into products and made available to final consumers. Physical distribution is that part of logistics covering a broad range of activities aimed at efficient movement of finished goods from the end of the production line to the consumer. Physical distribution includes, but is not limited to, transportation. It includes customer service, inventory control, materials handling, order processing, protective packaging, warehousing and warehouse site selection. A well-planned distribution system provides ultimate users with convenient ways of obtaining the goods and services they desire.

II. The Role of Marketing Channels in Marketing Strategy – Distribution channels play an essential role in marketing strategy because they provide the means by which goods and services move from their point of production to ultimate users. First, they facilitate exchange by reducing the number of marketplace contacts necessary to make a sale. Second, distributors adjust for discrepancies in the market's assortment of goods and services by a process called sorting. Third, marketing channels serve to standardize exchanges by setting expectations for products and transfers themselves. Finally, marketing channels facilitate searches for products and services by both buyers and sellers. Literally hundreds of distribution channels carry products today, and no single channel best serves the needs of every company. In addition, the channel that works well today may become obsolete in the future.

III. Types of Marketing Channels – Channels must be chosen that best meet the needs of both sellers and buyers of the products to be distributed. Some channel possibilities involve several marketing intermediaries (or middlemen) that are organizations that operate between producers and consumers or business users. Retailers and wholesalers are both marketing intermediaries. Short marketing channels involve few intermediaries, while long channels involve many intermediaries.

A. Direct Selling occurs when a direct channel, that is a channel including only a producer and ultimate user, is used.
1. Direct selling plays a significant role in business-to-business marketing.
2. Direct selling is also important in retailing, that is, in consumer goods markets.
3. The party plan is a traditional direct selling strategy at retail, pioneered by the Tupperware Company.
4. Dell Computer uses a direct strategy, mainly Internet and telephone driven, for all its customers, be they business users, government entities, or consumers.

B. Channels using marketing intermediaries are numerous because the relationships between buyers and sellers differ from market segment to market segment. Some of the more common channels include the five discussed below.

1. Producer to wholesaler to retailer to consumer – This channel is the traditional channel for consumer goods and is based upon a market with many small producers serving large numbers of consumers, so that a lot of intermediation is necessary.

2. Producer to wholesaler to business user – Essentially similar in purpose to the channel above, this channel places one layer of intermediation (wholesalers called industrial distributors) between producer and business users.

3. Producer to agent to wholesaler to retailer to consumer – When producers are very small, agent intermediaries may be necessary to initiate the process of bringing buyers and sellers together.

4. Producer to agent to wholesaler to business user – Agents and similar intermediaries called brokers often intermediate in the B2B market. Sometimes agents serving the business market operate as *manufacturers' representatives*, serving as sales forces for small producers.

5. Producer to agent to business user – Ideally adapted to high unit sales where transportation costs are low, this arrangement provides the manufacturer or producer with a sales force at low cost.

IV. Dual Distribution refers to movement of products through more than one channel to reach the same target market. The strategy is usually designed to maximize market coverage or to improve cost effectiveness of the marketing effort. Though it is called "dual," there can be many alternative channels involved.

V. Reverse Channels are channels designed to return goods to their producers. They may be used to facilitate recycling, moving through the structure of the traditional distribution channel – only backwards – or the producer may set up collection centers for the products to be returned. Sometimes community action groups become a part of the channel structure. Reverse channels also handle product recalls and repairs.

VI. Channel Strategy Decisions involve selecting a channel to use, resolving issues of distribution intensity, the desirability of vertical marketing systems, and performance of existing intermediaries.

A. Selection of a marketing channel depends on a number of factors and how those factors impact the relationship between a marketer and its market.

1. Market factors reflect the needs of the product's intended markets, including their preferences. Other factors, such as market needs, geographical considerations, and average order size also have an impact.

2. Product factors include consideration of such concepts as the perishability – either real or fashion perishability – of products, how important convenience in purchase or use is for the product, and how complex the product is.

3. Organizational factors may include such considerations as the adequacy of financial, managerial, and marketing resources available to the firms involved in the channel, the breadth of the producer's product line, the manufacturer's desire for control over the marketing of its products, and the likelihood of antagonizing members of a current channel by investigating possible changes in distribution arrangements.

4. Competitive factors sometimes argue for the development by producers of alternate channels of distribution because present middlemen are not providing adequate promotion for their products.

B. Determining distribution intensity has to do with the decision of how many intermediaries are desirable at the various levels of the channel of distribution. The idea is to provide "adequate" distribution intensity of the product, though the definition of adequacy varies from product to product and firm to firm.

   1. Intensive distribution seeks to distribute the product through all available channels in a trade area. Intensive distribution is typical of convenience goods.

   2. Selective distribution is a distribution strategy in which the firm chooses only a limited number of retailers in a market area to handle its line. Such a strategy reduces distribution costs and allows greater control on the part of the manufacturer of the entire marketing effort.

   3. Exclusive distribution consists of choosing only one retailer in a market area who will be allowed to handle the manufacturer's line. The marketer gives up some market coverage using this strategy, but it is easier to maintain a quality, prestigious image when the option is chosen.

      a. Exclusive distribution may present some legal problems.

         i.   In an exclusive distribution strategy, some marketers try to enforce *exclusive dealing agreements* prohibiting marketing intermediaries from handling competing products. Such agreements may violate the Clayton Act if the producer or dealer holds a significant market share in the area and the result of the exclusive dealing agreement may bar competitors from the market.

         ii. Producers may set up *closed sales territories* to restrict their distributors to certain geographical areas. The legality of such arrangements depends on whether the result is a decrease in competition and whether the system imposes horizontal or vertical restrictions.

         iii. *Tying agreements* allow channel members to become exclusive dealers only if they also carry products other than those they want to sell. Such agreements are generally illegal under both the Sherman and the Clayton Act.

C. Who should perform channel functions? Some member of the channel of distribution must perform certain central marketing functions; these may be shifted from one channel member to another, but they cannot be eliminated. Independent intermediaries may earn profits in exchange for providing services to manufacturers and retailers. Those services must be done better than the manufacturers can do them for themselves, or the intermediaries become redundant. The Internet has provided "sites of opportunity" for firms such as pawn shops, which use the online markets to intermediate in transactions involving unusual or one-of-a-kind merchandise.

VII. Channel Management and Leadership – Distribution strategy does not end with the choice of a channel. Marketers manage channels in partnership with other channel members. The dominant and controlling member of a marketing channel is called the "channel captain." The channel captain's power may grow out of its power to reward or punish other channel members, or from contractual agreements, expert knowledge, or agreement among channel members about their best interests. Channel captaincy may shift – as for example from manufacturer to retailer – as the needs of the market place change.

A. Channel conflict creates substantial friction among the members and causes channels to become inefficient and rough-running. Two major types of conflict may hinder the normal functioning of a marketing channel.

1. Horizontal conflict may come about because of disagreements among channel members at the same level, such as two or more retailers or two or more wholesalers, or it may result when friction develops between different types of marketing intermediaries that handle similar products. When these conflicts arise, solution may be difficult but they must be attempted.

2. Vertical conflict occurs when friction develops between members at different levels of the marketing channel. Sometimes manufacturers attempt to bypass wholesalers and retailers and sell direct to consumers; on other occasions, retailers ask concessions from manufacturers the manufacturers believe to be unfair – such as slotting fees or slotting allowances, amounts demanded by retailers in return for stocking a manufacturer's products. Finally, the international market may generate problems when retailers sell "dumped" foreign goods at lower prices than domestic manufacturers can possibly charge.

3. The grey market describes the market for domestically-branded products sold under license outside the United States that are imported into the U. S. and sold in competition with domestically distributed and branded products. It is legal to import and sell such products, but to do so works against the interests of the domestic producer and creates friction between the domestic producer and its licensee and the importers that bring in the grey market product. Sometimes there are compelling reasons to allow this practice, such as when prescription drugs are imported or re-imported from Canada because the same drugs are less expensive there than in the United States.

B. Achieving channel cooperation requires that channel members learn how to cooperate effectively. All members of the channel should consider themselves to be part of a single organization. The channel captain takes a lead role in creating the desired levels of efficiency.

VIII. Vertical Marketing Systems are planned channel systems designed to improve distribution efficiency and cost effectiveness by integrating various functions throughout the distribution chain. The system can be integrated either forward or backward. Forward integration occurs when a firm attempts to control downstream distribution, as when a manufacturer absorbs its own wholesaling function or both wholesaling and retailing of its products. Backward integration is the situation that exists when a firm attempts to gain control of the members of the channel upstream of it. A manufacturer may attempt to acquire the suppliers of its raw materials or components, while a retailer might take over wholesaling or even manufacturing operations for the products it sells.

A. Corporate marketing systems are those in which a single owner runs organizations at each stage of the marketing channel. Administered marketing systems are created when a channel captain exercises its power over other members of the marketing channel, usually by controlling the inventories they make available to other members of the channel.

B. Contractual marketing systems coordinate distribution through formal agreements among channel members.
   1. Wholesaler-sponsored voluntary chains involve formal agreements between wholesalers and their independent retail customers who agree to use a common name, maintain standardized facilities, and purchase the wholesaler's products. The wholesalers undertake to advertise the system and pass along cost savings on purchases to the retailer members. Independent Grocers' Alliance (IGA) is a contractual system.

2. Retail cooperatives are similar to contractual systems except that they are owned by their retailer members who set up their own wholesaling operation and agree to buy a certain percentage of their merchandise from the cooperative wholesaler. Ace Hardware is a retail cooperative.

3. The franchise is an arrangement in which a franchisee agrees to meet the operating requirements of a franchiser. The vast majority of fast-food restaurants are franchise operations. Franchising has been a rapidly growing industry for three decades, and continues to grow today. Franchisees pay as little as a few thousand dollars to as much as many hundreds of thousands for a franchise. They may also have to pay a royalty to the franchiser for franchise rights. Major franchise chains justify the high cost of a franchise by stating that investment in a franchise allows the franchisee to buy into a winning team.

IX. Logistics and Supply Chain Management – Pier 1, the specialty home furnishings store, buys items from 600 suppliers in 55 countries and more than 80 percent of its sources are small firms. If deliveries are late or incorrect, the firm loses revenue. These facts point up the importance of logistics in distribution. Effective logistics requires proper management of the supply chain (also known as the value chain), which is the complete sequence of suppliers that contribute to the creation and delivery of merchandise. Logistical management plays a major role in giving customers what they need when they need it, hence a central role in the supply chain. The supply chain encompasses all activities that enhance the value of finished goods, including design, quality manufacturing, customer service, and delivery. Supply chain management looks in two directions: upstream and downstream. Upstream management involves managing raw materials, inbound logistics, and warehouse and storage facilities. Downstream management involves managing finished product storage, outbound logistics, marketing and sales, and customer service. Value-added service, another part of the supply chain, adds some improved or supplemental service that customers do not normally receive or expect.

A. Radio frequency identification (RFID) technology helps manage logistics. A tiny chip with identification information is placed on an item and read at a distance with a radio frequency scanner. The technology allows constant inventory analysis without physical contact with the items being scanned.

B. Enterprise resource planning systems use software to consolidate data from among the firm's units. Valuable though they are, such systems are not perfect and may cause mismatches between supply and demand.

C. Logistical cost control is important because distribution functions currently represent almost half of the typical firm's marketing costs. In the past, cost-cutting efforts have focused on economy in production, but conditions have changed so that today logistics offers possible cost savings. To reduce logistical costs, businesses are examining each link of their supply chains to identify and eliminate, reduce, or redesign activities that do not add value for customers.

1. Third party logistics firms specialize in handling logistical activities for their clients in the attempt to cut costs and offer value-added services. Outsourcing alliances bring producers and logistical service suppliers together to develop innovative, customized services that speed goods through manufacturing and distribution pipelines.

X. Physical Distribution – The physical distribution system is an organized group of components linked according to a plan for achieving specific distribution objectives. It has six components: customer service; transportation; inventory control; protective packaging and materials handling; order processing; and warehousing. All of these components function in an interrelated fashion. A reduction in transportation costs often results in an increase in warehousing costs, for example.

   A. Logistics managers must first decide on the level of customer service they are going to render and then seek to minimize the total cost of rendering that service. The problem of suboptimization arises when logistics managers attempt to minimize the cost of each of the components of the logistics system individually without regard to the effect each of them has upon the other. It is particularly likely when a new product is introduced that does not fit conveniently into its current distribution system. Effective management of physical distribution requires some cost trade-offs.

   B. Customer-service standards state goals and define acceptable performance for the quality of service that a firm expects to deliver to its customers. Designers of a physical distribution system begin by establishing acceptable levels of customer service, then assemble physical distribution components in a way that will achieve this standard at the lowest possible cost by working with the remaining five components of the physical distribution system.

   C. Transportation in the United States is provided by a largely deregulated industry. Typically adding 10 percent to the cost of a product, transportation and delivery represent the largest category of logistics costs for most firms. Many logistics managers have determined that the key to managing shipping costs is careful management of their relationships with shipping firms.
      1. Freight carriers set two basic kinds of rates.
         a. Class rates are standard rates for specific commodities moving between any origin-destination pair.
         b. Commodity rates, which are lower than class rates, are sometimes offered to favored shippers as rewards for regular business or a large-quantity shipment. These rates are also called special rates.
         c. The railroad and motor freight industries may also use contract or negotiated rates – a third type of rate agreed upon by a specific carrier and a specific shipper and made binding by contract.
      2. Freight carriers are classed as common, contract, or private
         a. Common carriers provide transportation services as for-hire carriers to the general public. Their rates and services are regulated and their operations require government approval.
         b. Contract carriers are for-hire transporters that enter into contracts with individual customers and operate exclusively to serve particular industries. They are most common in the motor freight industry.
         c. Private carriers are not for hire and transported only internally generated freight. They are largely unregulated, and under certain circumstances may be permitted to operate as common or contract carriers.
      3. There are five major transportation alternatives, each of which has its own unique characteristics.
         a. Railroads are the nation's leading transportation medium as measured in ton-miles (a ton-mile is a load of one ton carried for a distance of a mile). Railroads carry bulk commodities efficiently over long distances. The railroads have imple-

mented many innovative concepts such as unit trains, run-through trains, and intermodal or piggyback operations to improve service standards.

    i.   Unit trains run back and forth between a single loading point and a single destination carrying a single cargo such as coal, grain, or some other high-volume commodity.

    ii.   Run-through trains bypass intermediate terminals to accelerate schedules, often carrying a variety of products.

    iii.   In piggyback operations, highway trailers and containers ride on railroad flatcars, thus combining the long-haul capabilities of the train with the flexibility of motor haulers.

    iv.   Railroad service now has a high level of tracking and tracing capability effected through the implementation of Web access techniques and new software.

  b. Motor carriers carry about 80 percent of all goods in the United States at some point or another. Trucking is a rapidly-growing, flexible transportation medium. Technology has improved the efficiency of trucking, satellite communications and Web interaction being common. Some trucks serve as rolling factories, assembling products from component parts en route from one place to another.

  c. Water carriage includes inland service (barge lines) and oceangoing deepwater vessels. Slow moving, this medium is best used for bulky, low value commodities. Oceangoing ships have, of course, been the medium of choice for transoceanic shipping for thousands of years.

  d. Pipelines are specialized media of transportation but still rank third in volume after railroads and motor carriers. They are relatively slow and can only handle certain commodities.

  e. Air freight is becoming quite popular for domestic and international shipping because of the advantage in speed it offers. It is, however, more expensive than other media so much of the cargo carried is high value, time-sensitive stuff.

4. Freight forwarders are transportation intermediaries that consolidate shipments to gain lower rates for their customers. If a firm can ship an entire truckload or carload of a product, the rate per pound is usually much lower than if less than truckload or less than carload shipments are sent. Supplemental carriers, on the other hand, specialize in handling small shipments; they include firms such as United Parcel Service and Federal Express.

5. Transportation companies tend to specialize in serving certain kinds of customers, but sometimes they combine their services to give customers the advantages of each specialty. Intermodal coordination includes birdyback service – a motor freight and air freight combination; piggyback service – motor freight and rail transportation combined; and fishyback service – motor freight and barge or ship service together. These combinations give shippers faster service at lower cost than the single modes could deliver by themselves. Though originally multimodal services were originally created by different companies working together, there are now firms that offer multimodal services from their own resources alone.

D. Warehousing uses two types of facilities – storage warehouses and distribution warehouses. Storage warehouses hold goods for fairly long periods to balance supply with demand, while distribution warehouses assemble and redistribute goods, keeping them moving as much as possible. Break-bulk centers – central distribution centers that break down large shipments into smaller ones for delivery to individual customers in their area – have become popular as a means of saving money in the distribution process.

1. Logistics managers can cut distribution costs and improve customer service dramatically by automating their warehouse systems. Such systems save labor costs for high volume distributors while tracking sales and inventory levels of products handled.
2. In determining the number and locations of its storage facilities, a firm must consider two types of costs: warehousing and material handling costs; and delivery costs from warehouses to customers. These costs act in opposite directions, affecting ideal warehouse size and placement. Warehouse location also affects customer service.

E. Inventory control systems are designed to maintain enough inventory to meet customer demand without incurring unneeded costs for carrying excess inventory. Just-in-time production and vendor managed inventory systems both serve to keep inventory costs under control by shifting the responsibility for inventory maintenance to the supplier rather than the customer.

F. Order processing directly affects the firm's ability to meet its customer service standards because deficiencies in order processing may require use of high-cost shipping alternatives or large inventories to meet those standards. Order processing typically involves four activities:
   1. Conducting a credit check;
   2. keeping a record of the sale, including compensation records for the sales staff;
   3. making appropriate accounting entries;
   4. and locating orders.
      a. Stockouts occur when an ordered item in not available for shipment.
      b. Customers must be advised of stockouts and offered a choice of alternative actions.
   5. Technology has significantly improved efficiency in order processing.

G. Protective Packaging and Materials Handling comprise the arrangement and control of activities that move products within plants, warehouses, and transportation terminals.
   1. The process of unitizing combines as many packages as possible into each load that moves within or outside a facility. Unitizing creates a load that requires minimum labor to handle and minimizes pilferage and damage. The most common unitizing technique involves the use of pallets.
   2. Containerization is the combination of several unitized loads, usually into trailerloads or railcar loads. It reduces the loading and unloading time for ships.

Name_____   Instructor_____

Section_____   Date_____

Key Concepts

The purpose of this section is to allow you to determine if you can match key concepts with their definitions. It is essential that you know the definitions of the concepts prior to applying the concepts in later exercises in this chapter.

From the list of lettered terms, select the one that best fits each of the numbered statements below. Write the letter of that choice in the space provided.

Key Terms

a. distribution
b. marketing or distribution channel
c. logistics
d. supply-chain management
e. physical distribution
f. direct channel
g. dual distribution
h. intensive distribution

i. selective distribution
j. exclusive distribution
k. channel captain
l. vertical marketing system (VMS)
m. corporate marketing system
n. administered marketing system
o. contractual marketing system
p. radio frequency identification (RFID)

_____ 1. A marketing channel that moves goods directly from a producer to an ultimate user.

_____ 2. Network that moves products to a firm's target market through more than one channel.

_____ 3. Vertical marketing system that achieves channel coordination when a dominant channel member exercises its power.

_____ 4. Organized system of marketing institutions and their interrelationships that enhances the physical flow and ownership of goods and services from producer to consumer or industrial user.

_____ 5. Process which coordinates the flow of information, goods, and services among members of the distribution channel.

_____ 6. Vertical marketing system in which a single owner operates all levels of its marketing channel.

_____ 7. Vertical marketing system that coordinates channel activities through formal agreements among channel members.

_____ 8. A channel policy in which the vendor seeks to distribute a product through all available channels in a trade area.

_____ 9. A dominant and controlling member of a marketing channel.

_____ 10. Channel policy in which a firm grants exclusive rights to a single wholesaler or retailer to sell its products in a particular geographic area.

_____ 11. Movement of goods and services from producers to consumers.

_____ 12. Channel policy in which a firm chooses only a limited number of retailers to handle its product line.

_____ 13. Control of the activities of purchasing, processing, and delivery through which raw materials are transformed into products and made available to final consumers.

_____ 14. A planned channel system designed to improve distribution efficiency and cost effectiveness by integrating various functions throughout the distribution chain.

_____ 15. The broad range of activities aimed at efficient movement of finished goods from the end of the production line to the consumer.

_____ 16. Technology using a tiny chip with identification information that can be read by a scanner using radio waves from a distance.

Name_____   Instructor_____

Section_____   Date_____

Self-Quiz

You should use these questions to test your understanding of the chapter material. You can check your answers with those provided at the end of the chapter.

While these questions cover most of the chapter topics, they are not intended to be the same as the test questions your instructor may use in an examination. A good understanding of all aspects of the course material is essential to good performance on any examination.

True/False

Write "T" for True and "F" for False for each of the following statements.

_____   1.   Distributors adjust for discrepancies in the market's assortment of goods and services through a process known as sorting.

_____   2.   No single marketing channel best serves the needs of every company.

_____   3.   The producer to agent to business user channel is typically used when the product is sold in small quantities to each purchaser and the cost of product transportation is relatively high.

_____   4.   Dual distribution occurs only when a manufacturer uses more than one wholesaler or retailer in any given geographical market to reach the selected target market segment.

_____   5.   If the Zenith Corporation issued a recall for one of their television sets that offered a replacement unit when the original was returned to the store where it was bought – the dealer then to send the return to the manufacturer to receive reimbursement – a reverse channel of distribution would be created.

_____   6.   Horizontal conflict within a distribution channel occurs when members of the channel at the same level, such as two or more retailers, disagree.

_____   7.   A tying agreement is a contract between a manufacturer and a wholesaler or retailer which grants an exclusive territory but only if the retailer or wholesaler agrees to also carry products other than those they want to sell.

_____   8.   Retailers are prohibited from buying grey market goods from distributors because foreign licensees have no right to sell them outside the countries for which the license was granted.

_____   9.   A marketing intermediary can be a wholesaler, but not all wholesalers are marketing intermediaries

_____ 10.   Brokers are independent middlemen who may or may not take possession of the goods they sell, but never take title to them.

_____ 11.   The Internet provides a direct selling channel only for B2B purchases.

_____ 12.   Not all channel members wield equal power in the distribution chain. The dominant and controlling power in a marketing channel is called the channel captain.

_____ 13.   Decisions made in one area of a physical distribution system seldom affect efficiency in others.

_____ 14.   Downstream management of the supply chain involves managing finished product storage, outbound logistics, marketing and sales, and customer service.

_____ 15.   The technology that involves placing a tiny electronic chip with identification information on it that can be read at a distance by a radio frequency scanner on an item to help manage logistics is called radio frequency identification (RFID).

_____ 16.   Any increase in logistical costs should support progress toward the goal of maintaining customer-service standards.

_____ 17.   Contract carriers are for-hire transporters that do not offer their services to the general public; they establish contracts with individual customers and operate exclusively for particular industries.

_____ 18.   The largest category of logistics-related expenses for most firms, ordinarily amounting to about ten percent of total marketing cost, is the cost of inventory control systems.

_____ 19.   In transportation, negotiated rates are sometimes called special rates and are the standard rate for every commodity moving between any two places.

_____ 20.   Common carriers are for-hire carriers that serve the general public and whose rates and services are still regulated by government.

_____ 21.   Motor carriage suffers from the drawbacks of being only able to accommodate a small number of products and operating at low speed B only three to four miles per hour.

_____ 22.   Though many people are scarcely aware of its existence, the network of 214,000 miles of pipelines that crisscrosses the United States ranks third – after railroads and truck lines – in number of ton-miles of cargo transported per year.

_____ 23.   United Parcel Service, Federal Express, and the U. S. Postal Service are examples of supplemental carriers.

_____ 24.   Two categories of costs influence the number and locations of storage facilities used by a firm: (1) warehousing and materials-handling costs; and (2) delivery costs from suppliers to the firm.

_____ 25.   Order processing typically consists of four major activities: (1) check writing; (2) credit issuance; (3) correcting the order; and (4) locating the customer.

Multiple Choice

Circle the letter of the word or phrase that best completes the sentence or answers the question.

26. In the business market, most major installations and accessory equipment are sold
    a. by direct contact between producing firms and final buyers.
    b. to the ultimate user from the manufacturer through wholesalers.
    c. from the manufacturer through agents who sell to wholesalers who then sell to the ultimate user.
    d. by the manufacturer directly through agents to the ultimate user.
    e. by retailers direct to the ultimate user.

27. The so-called "traditional" channel of distribution for consumer products involves
    a. distribution by a producer through wholesalers and retailers to the consumer.
    b. distribution by a producer through retailers to the consumer.
    c. a producer selling directly to the ultimate user of the product.
    d. manufacturers, agents, insurers, wholesalers, and retailers.
    e. distribution by producers to the user through wholesalers and agents.

28. Which of the following would be a reverse channel of distribution?
    a. A manufacturer ships high-fashion clothing direct to a retailer.
    b. A supermarket receives returnable bottles from consumers and ships them back to the bottling plant to be sterilized and refilled.
    c. A manufacturer of industrial installations custom-designs a metal stamping plant for Kaiser Industries.
    d. The Electromatic Corporation supplies the State of Delaware with a complete traffic control system for the City of Wilmington.
    e. Your little brother sets up a stand in front of the house and, using lemons and sugar he's filched from the pantry, becomes a small businessman selling lemonade to passers by.

29. A dual distribution system is best exemplified by
    a. the use of insurance companies to absorb some of the risks of doing business.
    b. creation of a channel of distribution to handle the return of recyclable materials to factories for reprocessing.
    c. the practice by some social welfare agencies of opening neighborhood offices to be more convenient to their clients.
    d. the use of its own sales force and a parallel system of outside jobbers by a manufacturer of mechanics' tools.
    e. the action of an agent who brings together orange growers and wholesale grocers to create a market for fresh fruit.

30. In addition to their use as a device to facilitate recycling, reverse channels of distribution are often used
    a. for the distribution of services; intangible goods call for unique relationship between producer and ultimate user.
    b. in the industrial market for the distribution of high-tech products where a substantial degree of customization is required.
    c. for the handling of products which have been recalled by their maker or which must be returned to the factory for repairs.
    d. when a very short channel of distribution is called for by some characteristic of the product or the market.
    e. by facilitating agencies to facilitate the performance of the services they render.

31. Which of the following is an example of vertical channel conflict?
    a. conflict between two or more sporting-goods wholesalers
    b. conflict among a group of retail florists
    c. conflict among drug, variety, and discount retailers all of which sell the same branded products
    d. conflict between company-owned and independently-owned retail outlets in the same chain
    e. conflict between manufacturers and retailers which develops when the retailers develop private brands

32. The basic antidote to channel conflict is
    a. strict enforcement of all contractual provisions of the relationships among members of the channel.
    b. effective cooperation among channel members in well-organized efforts to achieve maximum operating efficiency.
    c. for members of the channel who don't agree with the way things are going to abandon that channel and start their own.
    d. creation of an integrated, single-company controlled channel from production to retail sale to prevent any conflict.
    e. dissolution of the channel by the channel captain; conflict can never be overcome, only contained.

33. Among the market factors which determine the structure of a distribution channel is
    a. the perishability of the product.
    b. the product's requirement for regular maintenance service.
    c. whether the product is designed for the consumer or the business market.
    d. the fact that a producer who is financially strong can hire its own sales force.
    e. that the single-product firm often discovers that direct selling is an unaffordable luxury.

34. Suboptimization occurs in physical distribution when
    a. inventory management fails, causing the system to run out of stock of important goods just when they're needed most.
    b. there is too much emphasis on customer service and not enough emphasis on reducing the cost of each physical distribution function.
    c. too ambitious a level of customer service is chosen as a standard, thereby driving up operations costs.
    d. each logistics activity is judged by its ability to minimize its own costs, but the impact of one task on the others leads to less than optimal results.
    e. firms find themselves operating out-dated, old-fashioned warehouses and can't afford to develop better, more efficient facilities.

35. Which of the following is most true of exclusive distribution?
    a. Some market coverage may be sacrificed by choosing this policy, but it often develops an image of quality and prestige for the product.
    b. Mass coverage and low unit prices make the use of wholesalers almost mandatory with this policy.
    c. The firm reduces total marketing costs and establishes better working relationships within the channel by choosing this policy.
    d. Adoption of this policy allows the consumer to buy the product with a minimum of effort.
    e. Cooperative advertising can be used for mutual benefit and marginal retailers can be avoided.

36. An exclusive-dealing agreement
    a. restricts the geographical territory of each of a producer's distributors.
    b. requires that a dealer who wishes to become the exclusive dealer for a producer's products also carry other products of that producer.
    c. is legal if the producer's or dealer's sales volume represents a substantial percentage of total sales in the market area.
    d. prohibits the distributors from opening new facilities or marketing the manufacturer's products outside their assigned territories.
    e. prohibits the marketing intermediary from handling competing products.

37. If a group of retailers were to start their own wholesaling operation, purchasing ownership shares in it and agreeing to buy a minimum percentage of their inventory from it, they would have created
    a. a corporate marketing system.
    b. a retail cooperative.
    c. a wholesaler-sponsored voluntary chain.
    d. an administered marketing system.
    e. a franchise system.

38. Which of the following statements best represents the position marketing managers should take with respect to distribution channel choices?
    a. Channels of distribution operate in such a way that it is virtually impossible to change the structure of an existing channel.
    b. When a particular member of a marketing channel is eliminated, the cost of channel operation is always reduced.
    c. Marketing managers must analyze alternative channels in light of consumer needs to determine the most appropriate channel or channels for the firm's goods and services.
    d. Eliminating independent wholesalers from a marketing channel should increase profit margins of other channel members by at least 10 percent.
    e. The structure of a marketing channel is such that changes in the structure often result in changes in the functions that must be performed.

39. Of the various levels of distribution intensity, the one which is most likely to present legal problems is
    a. intensive distribution.
    b. exclusive distribution.
    c. selective distribution.
    d. factory distribution.
    e. extra-heavy distribution.

40. Suboptimization in physical distribution is a problem because the overall objective of logistics managers is to
    a. deliver more goods faster and better than the competition.
    b. satisfy all the firm's customers all the time with the best quality products delivered fastest from a storage facility operated at the highest level of efficiency.
    c. develop the most modern, high-tech transportation network in the firm's marketplace so as to reduce competition and improve customer service.
    d. serve each manager with the minimum cost-profile of the distribution function under his supervision.
    e. achieve a specified level of customer service while minimizing the costs involved in physically moving and storing goods as they move from production point to ultimate users.

41. Which of the following would be a valid and realistic customer-service standard?
    a. All shipments will be sent motor freight.
    b. Shipment will be made open-account to firms D & B credit-rated BAA or better.
    c. Ninety percent of all orders are filled within twenty-four hours after receipt.
    d. Returns will be accepted only with prior approval by management.
    e. We dry-store merchandise ordered from us for seventy-two hours after we receive the order.

42. The largest single expense item in physical distribution for most firms is
    a. warehousing.
    b. materials handling.
    c. order processing.
    d. transportation and delivery.
    e. inventory maintenance.

43. The name of the transportation rate that is sometimes granted a favored shipper as a reward either for regular business or a large-quantity shipment is called a
    a. class rate
    b. negotiated rate.
    c. special rate.
    d. third-class rate.
    e. parametric rate.

44. Automated warehouses are capable of
    a. providing major savings for high-volume distributors such as grocery chains.
    b. reducing labor costs and worker injuries.
    c. lowering the amount of pilferage, fires, and breakage.
    d. all of the effects mentioned above.
    e. none of the things mentioned above.

45. If a freight carrier offers its services to the general public on a for-hire basis it is typically a
    a. contract carrier.
    b. designated carrier.
    c. private carrier.
    d. bulk carrier.
    e. common carrier.

46. Some firms feel compelled, for organizational reasons, to develop new distribution channels because
    a. they feel that independent marketing intermediaries do not adequately promote their offerings.
    b. there is such a small market for their offerings that intermediaries refuse to handle them.
    c. they wish to hold onto the lion's share of the profits from sales of their products.
    d. their products are so unique that no one exists to deal in them.
    e. they have such a bad reputation as suppliers that intermediaries will not handle their products.

47. Railroads continue to control the largest share of the freight business because they
    a. are capable of going places no other medium can reach.
    b. occupy a position to force other media to follow their rate schedules.
    c. move freight faster and better than any other medium.
    d. are the most efficient way to move bulky commodities over long distances.
    e. command over 90 percent of the long-haul volume.

48. For which of the following cargo lists would motor carriage be the most likely choice?
    a. finished lumber, automobiles, production machinery, industrial chemicals.
    b. clothing, food products, furniture and fixtures, machinery.
    c. grain, gravel, sand, and steel.
    d. natural gas, coal slurries, crude oil, jet fuel.
    e. cut flowers, microchips, medical instruments, precision tools

49. If you sought to ship a product domestically by the least-cost method, the obvious choice would be
    a. railroad.
    b. motor freight.
    c. pipeline.
    d. air freight.
    e. water carrier.

50. The warehouse most likely to be used by firms facing seasonal fluctuations in the supply of or demand for their products is
    a. a storage warehouse.
    b. a make-bulk center.
    c. an automated warehouse.
    d. a distribution warehouse.
    e. a break-bulk facility.

Name_____   Instructor_____

Section_____   Date_____

Applying Marketing Concepts

The Graumann Lebensmittel und Handlung Compagnie, KG, a general merchandise retailer located in Saarbrucken, Germany, is in the process of analyzing its relationships with its various suppliers and customers. Company management has discovered, as it expected, that most purchasing of soft goods (clothing, piece goods, towels) by the company is directly from the manufacturer of the item. Some of Graumann's other lines, however, are bought in a very different manner. Household electrics, if the quantity to be bought is large enough, can often be bought directly from the producer. If the order is small or if repair parts are needed, however, a local industrial distributor is often the source of products from the same manufacturers.

Graumann personnel also seem to be spending an inordinate amount of time handling goods which have been returned to the store for shipment back to manufacturers for repair under warranty or because a recall order was issued. The company also found that, in recent years, the furniture department, which has its own separate building and has always been somewhat autonomous in its operations, has gone heavily into office furniture and supplies, and sells more furniture, fixtures, and supplies to local businesses than it does household furnishings to the company's traditional customers.

Executives realize that times have changed, but are somewhat puzzled by all these relationships, and to top it all off, they have been approached by several other medium-sized retailers with the proposal that they all get together and set up their own captive wholesaling operation to sell to themselves so they can buy in larger overall quantities and save some money.

1. Graumann L and H typically purchases soft goods
    a. through a "traditional" consumer goods channel.
    b. through a channel direct from producer to retailer.
    c. wherever they can be gotten at the best price.
    d. only during peak seasons.
    e. from wholesalers specializing in soft goods.

2. Graumann L and H purchases of household electrics indicate the presence of
    a. collusion which probably violates the local antitrust laws.
    b. much confusion in their buying department.
    c. a dual distribution system for this class of product.
    d. the inadequacy of Graumann's inventory control system.
    e. a high level of demand for this merchandise in Saarbrucken.

3. The time which Graumann personnel are spending handling merchandise which is to be sent off for repair or other manufacturer adjustment should tell you that
   a. Graumann must handle very inferior goods; quality merchandise simply shouldn't be giving that much trouble.
   b. the channel of distribution from those manufacturers to Graumann must be somehow in disarray.
   c. times have changed a lot; in years past it would have been the retailer's responsibility to make good on these items.
   d. Graumann has become involved in reverse channels of distribution; these typically appear under these conditions.
   e. Graumann's Bonn buying group needs to be made aware of the deficiencies in the goods they are shipping.

4. Graumann's furniture department
   a. seems to have become a wholesale operation in office furnishings and supplies; it probably should be set up that way and the retail furniture and home furnishings department separated from it.
   b. seems to be one of the most efficient parts of the Graumann operation.
   c. is acting as a producer rather than as a marketing intermediary.
   d. is engaging in direct distribution, acting as agent for a broad range of manufacturers.
   e. serves primarily as the base for a reverse channel of business equipment and supplies.

5. If Graumann joins with the other retailers to create the wholesale operation they will have created a
   a. wholesaler-sponsored voluntary chain.
   b. franchise.
   c. corporate marketing system.
   d. administered marketing system.
   e. retail cooperative.

L'Especialités d'Auberges (LEDA) is a chain of retail stores catering to gourmet cooks. The company stocks everything the avid kitchen craftsman or craftswoman might need. Pots, pans, spoons, measuring devices, all the bells and whistles – you name it, they've got it. LEDA's history has been short but exciting. Founded only eight years ago as a small store in Petersburg, Virginia, the company now has over 250 stores nationwide. This rapid growth has brought not only profits but also problems. The main problem facing LEDA's founder and chief executive, Helmut Oberraeder, is the challenge of physical distribution.

The company has over 300 suppliers scattered all over the country. At present, each supplier receives orders from and ships directly to each LEDA store. Store managers are responsible for all shipping and materials-handling related to their stores. Mr. Oberraeder realizes that the system is causing problems. Suppliers charge more for small shipments to the stores than they would for large shipments to a company warehouse. Moreover, if LEDA buys in larger quantities, it can get the benefit of quantity discounts it is not now receiving.

There is also a problem with delivery; shipments are often late or simply don't arrive at the company's stores. Recently, store managers have begun to complain about having to inspect incoming shipments for defective merchandise, do paperwork on returns to suppliers, and handle special orders, all of which are very time-consuming. Personnel at company headquarters, meanwhile, are up in arms over their lack of control of buying activities at the local stores and their lack of information about inventory. To top it all off, sales are being lost because of too many stockouts in the retail stores.

Something must be done! Mr. Oberraeder has received several suggestions from other members of management, from lower-level employees who work in the affected areas of the company, and even from a certain number of irate customers. He has disregarded those suggestions that would have been too personally painful or physically impossible (leaping from high windows <u>does</u> hurt; let's not get into the physical impossibilities). Others he has given substantial thought. One of the more interesting suggestions involves setting up a central, automated warehouse to receive all supplier shipments. From that location, goods could be shipped to the stores by common carrier. A second suggestion is to set up several automated warehouses rather than one to cut down on delivery time.

Before a meaningful decision can be made, a number of questions must be answered and problems addressed.

_____ 6. LEDA should consider becoming a producer of some of the products they sell, thereby shortening the distribution chain and automatically making more money.

_____ 7. Because avoiding stockouts is so important to a firm like LEDA, vendor-managed inventory control would probably be a good choice for them.

_____ 8. Automated warehouses are probably quite feasible for the needs of a firm like LEDA.

_____ 9. Freight forwarders should be used by LEDA, especially if the company does buy a fleet of trucks.

_____ 10. A central distribution center might be a good choice for LEDA at this point in its existence.

11. What type of warehouse is the company thinking of installing?
    a. a storage warehouse
    b. a distribution warehouse
    c. a make-bulk facility
    d. a manufacturing warehouse
    e. a bonded warehouse

12. A key function of the warehouse the company is thinking of building is
    a. unitizing.
    b. containerizing.
    c. assembling and redistributing goods.
    d. long term storage.
    e. making bulk.

13. If the company uses a common carrier to deliver orders to the individual stores, what type of rate would do you expect it to be charged?
    a. a class rate
    b. a commodity rate
    c. a special rate
    d. a negotiated rate
    e. a flat rate

14. If LEDA were to install a physical distribution system, a basic systems orientation would require the inclusion of certain features. Others would remain optional. Which of the following would constitute an optional feature in such a system?
    a. order processing
    b. inventory control
    c. intermodal coordination
    d. customer service
    e. materials handling

15. If the company is losing sales due to stockouts in stores, then
    a. customer service standards are probably not being met.
    b. the stores are too far from the suppliers.
    c. the company needs to hire better store managers.
    d. customers are demanding too much; the company should take a "if we don't have it, you probably don't need it" posture.
    e. a careful analysis of the salesmen's activity sheets is in order; they're probably overselling some lines.

Name_____   Instructor_____

Section_____   Date_____

Surfing the Net

Keeping in mind that addresses change and what's on the Web now may have changed by the time you read this, let's take a look at some of the places on the Net that reflect aspects of distribution. We are not endorsing or recommending any of these sources, merely making note of the information and services that people have elected to offer through the Internet.

Services distributed over the Net? So it would seem, or at least they claim they're selling marketing services. This Web site says they are marketing planners. They really look more like Web site designers. Sometimes its very hard to tell. Try accessing them at **http://www.infinitehorizons.com**

Does the Net really cover the globe? Domestically, try **http://www.bestofnewengland.com** To see a selection of Italian products, access **http://made-in-italy.com**. Other online malls are the Swiss site at **http://www.markt.ch** (in German), which is now an auction site – sort of interesting because you bid in Swiss Francs – and another at **http://www.swissdir.ch/swisstrade.** At this latter mall you can take your pick from listings in English, French, Italian, and German and extensive lists of firms in Switzerland by industry, firm name, product lines, and so forth.

Got a hobby? You can probably find something to keep you happy on the Web. One general site is **http://www.ehobbies.com.** Collect baseball, comic, science fiction, basketball cards? Try **http://www.baseball-cards.com.** Fishing more your style? This site offers gear for all kinds of fishing aficionados (small rhyming pun intended). It's at **http://www.boatingstore.com.** You'll need to register and create a password so you can log in for this one.

Aw, go ahead, buy a car! They're on the Web at **http://www.autotrader.com; http://www.carbuyer.com;** and **http://www.cars.com.** Any make, model, or year is supposedly available from them at the above addresses. Alternatives include Dealernet at **http://www.dealernet.com**

Sites Verified September 7, 2004.

Chapter 14
Direct Marketing and Marketing Resellers:
Retailers and Wholesalers

Chapter Outline

You may wish to use the following outline as a guide for taking notes.

I. Chapter Overview

Retailing, wholesaling, and nonstore retailing, especially its direct marketing aspects, are integral components of the marketing channel. Direct marketing, which includes direct mail, telemarketing, direct-response advertising, infomercials, and Internet marketing, is a major form of nonstore retailing. Finally, there is automatic merchandising, selling carried out using vending machines.

II. Retailing – Retailers are the marketing intermediaries who are in direct contact with ultimate consumers. Retailing is the acts involved in selling merchandise to ultimate consumers. Retailers act as both customers and marketers in their channels, selling products to ultimate consumers and buying from wholesalers and manufacturers.

   A. The Evolution of Retailing illustrates the marketing concept in action, satisfying consumer wants and needs. Early North American retailing began with trading posts and pack peddlers that served settlements on the frontier, gradually developing through a number of institutional types until today Internet-enabled retailing has begun to assert itself.
      1. A key concept known as the wheel of retailing attempts to explain the pattern of change in retail institutions. Many major developments in the history of retailing appear to fit the wheel's pattern. Some exceptions disrupt the pattern, however.

III. Retailing Strategy – Retailers' strategies are based on the firm's goals and strategic plans. The two fundamental steps in the marketing strategy process are selecting a target market and developing a retailing mix to satisfy the chosen market, thus projecting the desired retail image.

   A. A retailer starts to define its strategy by selecting a target market. The importance of identifying and targeting the right market is illustrated by the erosion of department store retailing in favor of stores like Target. Deep discount stores like Family Dollar and Dollar General target lower-income shoppers. Hardware retailer Lowe's, Home Depot's most serious competitor, targets women. Marketing strategies must be developed in each case to attract the chosen customers to the stores.

   B. Merchandising strategy guides a retailer's decisions regarding the items it will offer. The retailer must decide on general merchandise categories, product lines, specific items within lines, and the depth and width of its assortments. To develop a successful merchandise mix, a retailer must weigh several priorities – the preferences and needs of its target market, how environment influences these choices, and the overall profitability of each product line and product category.
      1. Category management is a popular merchandising strategy in which a category manager oversees an entire product line and is responsible for the profitability of the

product group. Some firms find a target market of very small size and claim it as their own category – profitably.
2. In the battle for shelf space, Large-scale retailers are increasingly taking on the role of channel captain within many distribution networks, resulting in a shift of power from manufacturers of top-selling brands to the retailer who makes them available to customers.
    a. To identify items within a product line, retailers use a stockkeeping unit or SKU to identify each specific product offering.
    b. Because there are so many products now available, major retailers make demands on manufacturers in return for shelf space.
    c. Slotting allowances are payments made by manufacturers to get their products on the shelves of major retailers. Other fees manufacturers may be called upon to pay may include failure fees, renewal fees, trade allowances, and others.
3. Customer service strategy can be wrapped around heightened customer services for shoppers. The basic objective of all customer service focuses on attracting and retaining target customers, thus increasing sales and profits. A customer service strategy can also support efforts in building demand for a line of merchandise.

C. In pricing strategy, prices reflect a retailer's marketing objectives and policies.
1. The amount that a retailer adds to a product's cost to set the final selling price is the markup. The amount reflects the services performed by the retailer and the inventory turnover rate. A retailer's markup exerts an important influence on its image among present and potential customers. Marketers determine markups based partly on their judgments of the amounts that consumers will pay for a given product.
2. When buyers refuse to pay a product's stated price or when product improvements or fashion changes reduce the appeal of existing merchandise, a retailer must take a markdown – a reduction from the original price.

D. Location/distribution strategy is of significance in retailing. Retail experts often cite location as a potential determining strategy in the success or failure of a retail business. In recent years, many localities have become saturated with stores. Some retailers have been forced to close many stores, while others have experimented with nontraditional locations.
1. Planned shopping centers have drawn away much trade from downtown shopping areas. A group of retail stores designed, coordinated, and marketed as a unit to shoppers in a geographical trade area is a planned shopping center. There are five major types of planned shopping center.
    a. The neighborhood shopping center, the smallest of the five, most often consists of a supermarket and a group of smaller stores.
    b. Community shopping centers serve from 20,000 to 100,000 people and contain 10 to 30 stores, usually including a department store as the main tenant.
    c. Regional shopping centers serve at least 250,000 people and typically enclose 400,000 square feet or more of shopping space, with one or more major department stores as major tenants or "anchors."
    d. Power centers, usually located near large regional centers, include several huge specialty stores as stand-alone stores in a single trading area.
    e. Recently, a fifth type of shopping center has emerged, known as a lifestyle center and consisting of a combination of entertainment, shopping, and restaurant facilities in an attractive environment.
2. Retail analysts believe that America may have become saturated with shopping facilities.

E. A retailer's promotional strategy seeks to communicate to consumers information about its stores – locations, hours of operation, merchandise selections, and prices. Innovative promotions can pay off in unexpected ways, such as when IKEA used the interiors of elevators in Beijing apartment buildings to show how really <u>small</u> apartments could be tastefully decorated. National retail chains often purchase advertising space in newspapers, on radio, and on television, in Sunday newspapers, and even on the Internet. Retailers attempt to combine advertising with in-store merchandising techniques that influence decisions at the point of purchase. The retail salesperson plays a vital role in conveying a store image to consumers and in persuading them to buy. Sales personnel can "sell up" customers by persuading them to buy higher priced items than originally intended. In "suggestion selling," the sales representative seeks to broaden a customer's original purchase by adding related items, special promotional products, or holiday or seasonal merchandise. Poor service, on the other hand, also has an influence – a negative one – on customers' attitudes about a store. Finally, some retailers have attempted to use advertising to take the place of salespeople.

F. Store atmospherics are the physical characteristics and amenities that attract customers and satisfy their shopping needs. A store's exterior, including architectural design, window displays, signs, and entryways, helps to identify the retailer and attract its target market. Interior décor should also complement the retailer's image, respond to customers' interests, and induce shoppers to buy. Store designers must take into account that many people shop for reasons other than just purchasing needed products when they create the interior and exterior features of stores.

IV. The types of retailers continue to evolve in response to changes in demand so that a universal classification system has yet to be designed. Several schemes have been developed to define useful categories for purposes of definition, such as (1) form of ownership; (2) shopping effort expended by customers; (3) services provided to customers; product lines carried; and locations of retail transactions. These categories are non-exclusive – that is, a retail outlet can fall into more than one category.

A. Classification of retailers by form of ownership basically distinguishes between chain stores and independent retailers.
   1. Chain stores are groups of retail outlets that operate under central ownership and management and handle the same product lines.
   2. Independent retailers compete with the chains, each independent store being owned by a different individual or business. Independents are often members of wholesaler-sponsored voluntary chains, retail cooperatives, or franchise arrangements with other entities.

B. Classification by shopping effort breaks retailers down into the categories of convenience, shopping, or specialty retailers based on the types of goods they carry and how they operate.
   1. Convenience retailers feature accessible locations, long hours, quick checkout service, and adequate parking.
   2. Shopping stores, many of which are furniture, appliance, sporting goods, or clothing stores, base their appeal on advertising, window displays, in-store layout, and similar features to facilitate price, quality, and assortment

3. Specialty retailers attempt to create a reputation for carefully defined product lines, reputation, and service to convince consumers to spend considerable effort shopping at their stores.

C. Classification of retail stores on the basis of services provided yields three categories: the self-service, the self-selection, and the full-service retailer. The first two types deal in convenience goods purchased frequently with little assistance. The last features fashion-oriented merchandise backed by a broad array of customer services.

D. Classification by product lines is another way of identifying an array of stores and the strategies appropriate to them. The three types of stores that can be identified by the product lines they carry are the specialty store, the limited-line retailer, and the general merchandise retailer.

1. Specialty stores handle only a part of a product line, but handle it to some depth. Examples are grocery stores and women's shoe stores. Specialty stores should not be confused with specialty products.

2. Limited-line stores carry a large assortment of products within one product line or a few related lines, stocking a considerable assortment of items. Furniture stores and appliance stores are examples. A unique type of limited-line store is the "category killer," a store offering a huge selection of products at low prices within a single product line. Best Buy and Borders Books exemplify the category killer.

3. General merchandise retailers carry a wide variety of product lines that are all stocked in some depth. It is this feature that distinguishes them from the other two categories of stores classified in this manner. There are several different types of general merchandise retailers.

   a. Variety stores carry an extensive range and assortment of low-price merchandise. The classic example of such a store is Woolworth's. Such stores are less common now than was once the case, but they remain popular outside the United States.

   b. Department stores gather a series of limited-line and specialty stores under one roof. Marshall Field's of Chicago is a classic example, as is Dillard's in the South. Traditionally, department stores offered a wide variety of services such as charge accounts, gift wrapping, and liberal return policies. Over the past several decades, department stores have faced extensive competition from discount stores, catalog merchandisers, and hypermarkets. They have fought back by dropping certain product lines, adding bargain outlets, expanding parking facilities, and branching out into regional shopping centers. Some department store firms have, in effect, reinvented themselves by experimenting with new store layouts, merchandise assortments, and services.

   c. Mass merchandisers emphasize low prices for brand-name products, high product turnover, and limited services, often stocking a wider line of items than a department store but to less depth.

      i. Discount houses charge low prices and offer few services. By limiting services, they can keep prices 10 to 25 percent lower than those of the traditional department store. In recent years, discounters have moved upscale, becoming more like department stores. The <u>warehouse club</u>, of which Sam's and Costco are examples, are a growing form of the discount house.

      ii. Off-price retailers are another version of the discount house. They stock only designer labels or well-known brands of clothing at prices equal to or lower than wholesale. They are the cornerstones of the now-popular "outlet malls," shopping centers emphasizing off-price merchandise.

      iii. Hypermarkets and supercenters are two similar types of stores, giant one-stop shopping facilities that offer wide selections of grocery and general merchandise at discount prices. The essential difference between the two is size. Hypermarkets, at 200,000 square feet or more, are about a third larger than supercenters. Invented in France, where Carrefour and E. LeClerc are the market leaders, the hypermarket has only recently reached the U.S., where the Meijer stores of the upper mid-West are examples.

      iv. Showroom and warehouse retailers are essentially similar outlets that contact their customers by direct mail advertising and sell the advertised goods from showrooms that display samples.

E. Classifying retail transactions by location differentiates them on the basis of whether the transaction takes place in a store or not. Nonstore retailing not only generates orders, it also provides information to potential customers that may result in orders at a later time. "Direct marketing" is a concept that includes a number of varieties of nonstore retailing that will discussed later in this chapter.

F. Retail convergence and scrambled merchandising are causes of the difficulty marketers are having classifying retailers.

   1. Retail convergence, the term describes the availability of similar merchandise from multiple retail outlets distinguished mainly by price, is blurring the distinction between types of retailers and the merchandise they offer.

   2. Scrambled merchandising, which refers to retailers' combination of dissimilar lines in an attempt to boost sales volume, such as supermarkets offering bedding plants, motor oil, and even small appliances, also confuses the issue of what kind of store one may be talking about.

V. Wholesaling Intermediaries are firms whose primary function is to sell products to retailers or to other wholesaling intermediaries or business users. They may be firms called wholesalers, who take title to the goods they sell, or agents and brokers, who do not take title to the products they offer for sale.

A. Functions of wholesaling intermediaries include creating utility, providing services, and lowering costs by limiting the number of contacts between buyers and sellers.

   1. Creating utility involves making products available to consumers when they want them (time utility,) helping deliver goods and services for purchase at convenient locations (place utility,) and creating transactions that allow consumers use of products or services for their benefit (possession utility.)

   2. Providing services certainly provides the utilities mentioned above, and reflects the functions of marketing as well. Wholesaling intermediaries provide an array of services, and not all of them provide all possible services.

   3. Intermediaries, by representing many producers, cut the cost of buying and selling by reducing the number of interactions that have to take place between buyers and sellers for transactions to take place. An intermediary in a channel involving three producers and six ultimate users reduces the number of transactions necessary for all three buyers to purchase something from all six producers from 18 to 9.

B. Various types of wholesaling intermediaries operate in distribution channels. Some offer a broad array of products and services, while others are more specialized. In general, wholesalers may be classified by who owns them and further by how the title to goods flows through them. The three ownership possibilities are (1) manufacturer-owned, (2) independent wholesaling intermediaries, and (3) retailer-owned cooperatives and buying offices. Independent wholesaling intermediaries can be merchants, who take title to the goods they sell, and agents and brokers who do not.

1. Manufacturer-owned facilities exist because some products are perishable and need close control to maintain their quality; others require complex installation or servicing. Some require aggressive promotion, while yet others can profitably be sold by manufacturers direct to ultimate users.

   a. Sales branches carry inventories and process orders for customers from available stock.

   b. Sales offices do not carry inventories but serve as regional sales offices for manufacturers' sales personnel.

   c. Trade fairs are periodic shows at which manufacturers in a particular industry show their wares for visiting wholesalers and retailers.

   d. Merchandise marts provide space for permanent showrooms and exhibits that manufacturers rent to market their goods.

2. Independent wholesaling intermediaries may be either merchants or agents and brokers. Merchant wholesalers take title to the goods they sell, while agents and brokers do not.

   a. Full-function merchant wholesalers provide a complete assortment of services for retailers and business purchasers and are common in the drug, grocery, and hardware industries. In the business-goods markets, they are often called *industrial distributors*. Rack jobbers are full-function wholesalers that sell specialized lines to retailers, stocking the products, pricing the goods, and maintaining retail inventories.

   b. Limited-function merchant wholesalers have a traditional position in the marketplace, offering fewer services than do the full-function operators.

      i. Cash-and-carry wholesalers perform most wholesaling functions except financing and delivery and were once common in the grocery business.

      ii. Truck wholesalers (or truck jobbers) market perishable food items and products such as mechanics' tools, making regular deliveries to retailers or business users, performing sales and collection functions, and promoting product lines.

      iii. Drop shippers accept orders from customers and forward them to producers, who then ship the desired products to customers.

      iv. Mail-order wholesalers are limited-function merchant wholesalers who distribute catalogs (instead of sending sales representatives) to customers, who then purchase by mail or phone.

   c. Agents and brokers may or may not take possession of what they sell, but they never take title to the goods.

      i. Commission merchants, usually found in the agricultural goods markets, take possession of the goods they are charged with selling and receive a stipulated fee when sales are completed.

      ii. Auction houses gather buyers and sellers in one location and allow potential buyers to inspect merchandise before submitting offers to buy, receiving a percent of dollar sales for their efforts. A new venue for auction houses is the Internet, where eBay and similar firms have established a presence.

      iii. Brokers work mainly to bring together buyers and sellers, representing one of them but not both and receiving a commission from their client on completion of a sale. Brokers dealing in transactions between domestic vendors and foreign customers are called export brokers.

      iv. Selling agents essentially become the marketing department of their clients, exerting full authority over pricing and promotional activities, sometimes even lending money to their clients.

      v. Manufacturers' representatives exercise less authority over marketing activities than do selling agents, often working for a number of firms producing related but noncompeting products and receiving commissions on their sales.

   3. Retailer-owned cooperatives and buying offices are created in the attempt to reduce costs or provide special services. Some are set up as buying offices to purchase goods in quantity, some act more like traditional wholesalers captive to their retailer owners. Large chains often centralize large-order purchasing through such organizations.

VI. Direct marketing and other non-store retailing includes a large number of firms spending hundreds of billions of dollars a year.

   A. Direct mail, a major component of direct marketing, comes in many forms ranging from sales letters, postcards, brochures, booklets, catalogs, and house organs to video and audio cassettes. It offers several advantages such as the ability to select a narrow target market, achieve intensive coverage, and even personalize each mailing piece. Direst mail marketing relies on database technology to manage a segment mailing lists specific to a campaign. Catalogs are a popular direct mail device. New technologies are changing catalog marketing.

   B. Direct selling allows manufacturers to bypass retailers and wholesalers, setting up their own channels to sell directly to consumers.

   C. Direct-response retailing allows customers to order merchandise by mail or phone, by visiting a mail-order desk in a retail store, or by computer or fax machine. Many direct-response retailers rely on catalogs and other direct mail devices to create demand for products available in their stores. The Internet and unique catalogs are fast becoming popular devices for direct-response retailers. This technique also includes home shopping, including promotions on cable television and even advertising programs running thirty minutes on late-night television.

   D. Telemarketing is direct marketing conducted entirely by telephone. It is the most frequently used form of direct marketing. It will be discussed in detail in a later chapter.

   E. Internet retailing occurs when retailers sell directly to consumers via virtual storefronts on the Web. It has proven to be a risky form of retailing, working best when used in support of – rather than to replace – bricks-and-mortar stores.

   F. Automatic merchandising, which is essentially the use of vending machines, is responsible for some $25 billion in sales every year.

Name_____   Instructor_____

Section_____   Date_____

Key Concepts

The purpose of this section is to allow you to determine if you can match key concepts with their definitions. It is essential that you know the definitions of the concepts prior to applying the concepts in later exercises in this chapter. In this chapter, many terms appear similar at first glance. Be careful in making your matching choices.

From the list of lettered terms, select the one that best fits in the blank of the numbered statement below. Write the letter of that choice in the space provided.

Key Terms

a. retailing
b. wheel of retailing
c. stockkeeping unit (SKU)
d. markup
e. markdown
f. planned shopping center
g. retail convergence

h. scrambled merchandising
i. wholesaler
j. wholesaling intermediary
k. broker
l. manufacturers' representative
m. direct marketing

_____ 1. Channel intermediary that takes title to the goods it handles and distributes them to retailers, other distributors, or B2B customers.

_____ 2. Independent wholesaling intermediary who does not take title or possession of goods in the course of its primary function, which is to bring buyers and sellers together.

_____ 3. Distribution channel consisting of direct communication with a consumer or business user.

_____ 4. Group of retail stores planned, coordinated, and marketed as a unit.

_____ 5. All activities involved in selling goods and services to ultimate consumers.

_____ 6. A comprehensive term that describes wholesalers as well as agents and brokers.

_____ 7. Agent wholesaling intermediary who represents a number of manufacturers of related but noncompetitive products, receiving a commission on each sale.

_____ 8. Hypothesis that each new type of retailer gains a competitive foothold by offerings lower prices than current suppliers charge, maintaining profits by reducing or eliminating services.

_____ 9. Coming together of shoppers, goods, and prices, blurring the distinctions among types of retailers and the merchandise mixes they offer.

_____10. Amount by which a retailer reduces the original selling price of a product.

_____11. An amount that a retailer adds to the retailer's cost of the product to determine its selling price.

_____12. Retailing practice of combining dissimilar products to boost sales volume.

_____ 13. Specific offering within a product line such as a specific size of liquid detergent.

Name_____   Instructor_____

Section_____   Date_____

Self-Quiz

You should use these questions to test your understanding of the material in this chapter. You can check your answers with those provided at the end of the chapter.

While these questions cover most of the chapter topics, they are not intended to be the same as the test questions your instructor may use in an examination. A good understanding of all aspects of the course material is essential to good performance on any examination.

True/False

Write "T" for True or "F" for False for each of the following statements.

_____   1. Because of their critical role in marketing channels, retailers often perform an important feedback role by obtaining information from customers and transmitting it to manufacturers and other channel members.

_____   2. The development of retailing illustrates the marketing concept in action because the structure of retailing changes to satisfy changing consumer wants and needs.

_____   3. Suburban shopping centers, vending machines, and convenience food stores are good examples of the "wheel of retailing" in action.

_____   4. Slotting allowances are fees that retailers receive from manufacturers to secure shelf space for new products.

_____   5. Target stores have positioned themselves as upscale alternatives to WalMart by opening a chain of combination food and general merchandise stores called Super-Target.

_____   6. The basic objective of retail stores in providing services such as gift wrapping, alterations, bridal registries, and interior designers is to attract and retain target customers.

_____   7. A retailer's customer service strategy cannot support efforts to build demand for a specific line of merchandise.

_____   8. The amount of markup used by a retailer is typically determined solely by the range of services it offers.

_____   9. When improvements in other products or fashion changes reduce the appeal of current merchandise, a retailer might take an additional markup to assure the same profit from lower sales.

_____   10. A retail store that offers quality products at reasonable prices does not have to worry about location.

____ 11. Among the nontraditional retailing locations which have become attractive for firms such as McDonald's in recent years are hospitals, military bases, amusement parks, and gasoline stations.

____ 12. Planned shopping centers facilitate shopping by maintaining uniform hours of operation, including evening and weekend hours.

____ 13. "Lifestyle centers" are planned shopping centers that feature at least one major department store and as many as 200 other stores offering a wide array of goods within 30 minutes driving time of a population of 250,000 or more.

____ 14. The smallest type of planned shopping center is the community shopping center which usually contains only 5 to 15 stores serving a population ranging from 5,000 to 50,000 shoppers.

____ 15. Atmospherics are the physical characteristics and amenities of the interior of a store that are designed to attract customers and satisfy their shopping needs.

____ 16. If "selling up" is used with due consideration for customers' needs and they are sold something they really need, the potential for repeat sales dramatically diminishes.

____ 17. The stores known as "category killers," which include Borders Books and Home Depot, combine huge selections and low prices in a single product line.

____ 18. Merchandise assortments at off-price retailers change frequently because the off-price stores take advantage of special price offers from manufacturers selling excess merchandise.

____ 19. Retail convergence refers to the practice of locating goods strategically in the store to force consumers to ultimately end up at a certain display.

____ 20. When a retailer combines dissimilar product lines in an attempt to boost retail sales volume it is called "scrambled merchandising."

____ 21. Wholesaling intermediaries are involved in the production of three types of economic utility: form utility, place utility, and ownership (or possession) utility.

____ 22. The basic distinction between a manufacturer's sales office and a sales branch is that the sales branch carries inventory and the sales office does not.

____ 23. Full-function merchant wholesalers who operate in the business-goods market and sell machinery, inexpensive accessory equipment, and supplies are known as industrial distributors.

____ 24. Rack jobbers are limited-function merchant wholesalers because they have restricted their activities to certain specialized types of merchandise.

____ 25. Auction houses bring buyers and sellers together, operating in businesses such as frozen foods, real estate, and used machinery, where there are a large number of small suppliers and purchasers.

_____ 26. Drop shippers operate in industries such as coal and lumber where goods are bulky and customers make purchases in large lots.

_____ 27. Brokers can serve as a reliable channel for manufacturers seeking regular, continuing service because their ability to "make a market" places them in a unique position in the wholesale marketplace.

_____ 28. If a manufacturer decides to use a selling agent to handle its merchandise, it should realize that the selling agent will typically assume full control of pricing decisions and promotional outlays on its products.

_____ 29. Manufacturers' representatives differ from selling agents in that a manufacturer's representative takes the entire output of its principal while the selling agent usually is only one of a number of such intermediaries being used by that manufacturer.

_____ 30. Cash-and-carry wholesalers typically market perishable food items such as bread, tobacco, potato chips, and dairy products, making regular deliveries to retailers, performing sales and collection functions, and promoting product lines.

Multiple Choice

Circle the letter of the word or phrase that best completes the sentence or best answers the question.

31. The "wheel of retailing" concept
   a. postulates that new types of retailers succeed by entering the market at a fairly high price level and offering a complete service package.
   b. seems to describe well the development of such outlets as chain stores, discount stores, and supermarkets.
   c. applies most appropriately to the development of suburban shopping centers, convenience stores, and vending machines.
   d. theorizes that, after a new type of marketing institution has established itself in the market, it changes its ways of operating by reducing prices and services.
   e. relates best to the demise of the general store in the U.S.

32. A store or other retail outlet's "retail image" is
   a. the owner's perception of the store and the shopping experience it provides.
   b. its suppliers' perceptions of the store's operating philosophy, place in the market, and profitability.
   c. consumers' perceptions of the store and the shopping experience it provides.
   d. competitors' perceptions of the store and the market niche it occupies.
   e. always consistent with the expectations of the owner, competitors, and the shopping consumer.

33. The computerized diagram of how to exhibit selections of merchandise within a retail store is called a(n)
   a. stockkeeping unit (SKU)
   b. universal product configuration (UPC)
   c. planogram.
   d. floor plan.
   e. Automatic layout program (ALP).

34. The use of cable television networks to sell merchandise through telephone orders is
    a. the form of direct-response retailing known as home shopping.
    b. proving to be much less successful than was formerly hoped.
    c. a type of direct selling known as party selling.
    d. selling through an electronic catalog.
    e. catalog retailing.

35. If a retailer purchases a refrigerator from its supplier for $350 and offers it for sale for $650, subsequently reducing the price to $575 because few units sold at $650, the retailer has taken a markdown of
    a. $300
    b. $225
    c. $200
    d. $75
    e. $175

36. Vending machines
    a. have experienced strong resistance in many parts of the world such as Japan.
    b. are among the most profitable of all retailing institutions, averaging 8 percent profit on sales.
    c. are limited in growth potential by their inability to accept credit or debit cards.
    d. have now become a $25 billion a year industry in the United States.
    e. really got their start right after the First World War, selling books and magazines on the streets of Detroit.

37. The Sooper Market has gotten a deal. Cauliflower, for which they usually pay 70 cents a head and sell for 87 cents, is available in ample supply right now for 57 cents a head. Sooper has stocked up on some beautiful product and is offering it for 77 cents. The markup on this cauliflower is
    a. 20 percent of cost.
    b. 12.4 percent of selling price.
    c. 31 percent
    d. 17 cents.
    e. 20 cents.

38. A neighborhood shopping center is usually characterized by
    a. a market size of from 20,000 to 100,000 persons; the facility is usually anchored by a branch of a local department store or a large variety store.
    b. a size of from 5 to 15 stores serving 5,000 to 50,000 persons living nearby with convenience goods and some shopping goods.
    c. the presence of some professional offices such as those of physicians, dentists, and attorneys.
    d. a theme park on site somewhat like a mini Disney World.
    e. at least 400,000 square feet of shopping area.

39. When a salesperson in a store suggests that a new tie certainly would go well with that new shirt you just bought, he or she is practicing
    a. suggestion selling.
    b. selling up.
    c. use of atmospherics.
    d. franchising.
    e. simple selling.

40. When a store focuses its marketing efforts on accessible locations, long store hours, rapid checkout service, and ample parking, it would be reasonable to assume, considering classification by shopping effort, that it is a
    a. shopping store.
    b. variety store or specialty store.
    c. mass merchandiser like an off-price retailer.
    d. department store.
    e. convenience retailer.

41. Using classification by services provided as a base, a store that focuses on fashion-oriented merchandise backed by a complete array of customer services would most likely be a
    a. full-service retailer.
    b. self-service store.
    c. specialty store.
    d. limited-service store.
    e. convenience store.

42. Using product lines carried as the basis for classification, "category killers" are
    a. hardware stores.
    b. single-line stores.
    c. mixed merchandise marketers.
    d. limited-line stores.
    e. specialty stores.

43. A general merchandise retailer that offers an extensive range and assortment of low-priced merchandise is called a(n)
    a. variety store.
    b. department store.
    c. discount house.
    d. hypermarket.
    e. catalog retailer.

44. The most recent innovation in the discount house category is the
    a. factory-direct retail outlet.
    b. variety store.
    c. micromarket.
    d. mass merchandiser.
    e. hypermarket or supercenter.

45. Discount houses, off-price retailers, and hypermarkets are all examples of
    a. catalog retailers.
    b. department stores.
    c. mass merchandisers.
    d. specialty stores.
    e. small-scale independent retail merchants.

46. Mass merchandisers have made a place for themselves in the retail marketplace by emphasizing
    a. relatively low prices for not-so-well-known products, high turnover of goods, and limited services
    b. high prices for well-known brand name products, low turnover of goods, and a high level of quality service.
    c. relatively low prices for well-known brand name products, high turnover of goods, and limited services.
    d. relatively low prices for well-known brand name goods, high turnover of goods, and a high level of quality service.
    e. really low prices for well-known brand name goods, low inventory turnover, and a high level of quality service.

47. Department stores have been vulnerable to competition from mass merchandisers because
    a. of their refusal to modernize central city locations to provide the convenience factors people are looking for.
    b. they have been slow to adapt to conditions in the marketplace, often refusing to serve the need of urban residents from motives of tradition.
    c. their suburban locations isolated them from the real bases of their markets.
    d. their bare-bones approach to merchandising has turned a lot of people off to the way they do business.
    e. they have relatively high operating costs, averaging from 45 to 60 percent of sales.

48. The hypermarket
    a. originated in Germany and has spread throughout Europe and the Middle East.
    b. differs from a supermarket primarily in the merchandise carried and not so much in size and operating philosophy.
    c. is larger than the supercenter, usually featuring over 200,000 square feet of selling space stocked with a wide selection of grocery items and general merchandise at discount prices.
    d. has not as yet had marked success in any market in which it has thus far been introduced. It may be a blind alley in retail evolution.
    e. is just another name for the warehouse club type of retail store.

49. Maximiano Fanducci Tile Company just bought an odd lot of some really nice Italian ceramic tile. The tile cost 65 cents per square foot and Fanducci usually marks up its merchandise 35 percent on the selling price. What should be the asking price on this tile? (Rounded to the nearest cent)
    a. $0.88 per square foot.
    b. $1.00 per square foot.
    c. $1.22 per square foot.
    d. $1.64 per square foot.
    e. $2.00 per square foot.

50. Scrambled merchandising refers to
    a. the fact that most retailers are so disorganized that they do not know what their merchandise inventory includes, much less how much of each item is on hand.
    b. the practice of allowing merchandise normally housed in one department to be shifted to another department for a special sales event, thus "scrambling" the inventory.
    c. the practice of buying up stock from failed stores and mixing it in with fresh stock purchased for normal inventory, a questionable practice at best.
    d. the practice of carrying dissimilar lines in an attempt to generate additional sales volume.
    e. the habit which many consumers have gotten into of failing to replace merchandise which they have decided not to buy back on the proper shelves, dumping it instead any old place in the store, thus scrambling the merchandise.

51. Slotting allowances are most often paid
    a. by manufacturers to retailers to induce them to carry new, relatively unknown products.
    b. by retailers to manufacturers to prevent them from selling high-demand products to competitors.
    c. by retailers to manufacturers because they are so dependent on sales of a particular product that they'll pay a substantial premium to stock it.
    d. by manufacturers to wholesalers when the manufacturers are concerned that their permission to use a customer's warehouse space to store excess inventory will be revoked.
    e. when shelf space is shifted from one brand to another even though they both sell at the same price.

52. In the most technical sense, the term "wholesaler"
    a. should be applied only to merchant wholesaling intermediaries.
    b. applies across the board to all those institutions that are intermediaries in the channel of distribution.
    c. can be applied only to full-service marketing intermediaries.
    d. should be used only to describe a firm that deals in business goods.
    e. cannot be used to describe a firm that does not offer credit to its customers.

53. The marketing intermediary that predominates in markets for agricultural products, takes possession of such products when they are shipped to central markets for sale, acts as a producers' agent, and receives agreed-upon fees when it makes sales is the
    a. auction house
    b. commission merchant.
    c. selling agent.
    d. drop shipper.
    e. khalish basrahmi.

54. The marketing function being performed by wholesalers when they provide their customers with information about new products and report on competitors' activities and industry trends is
    a. buying.
    b. financing.
    c. risk taking.
    d. providing market information.
    e. reducing market contacts between manufacturers and end users.

55. A limited function merchant wholesaler that accepts orders from customers and forwards them to producers, who ship directly to the customers, is a(n)
    a. mail-order wholesaler.
    b. commission merchant.
    c. retailer-owned cooperative.
    d. industrial broker.
    e. drop shipper.

56. A manufacturer-owned facility that serves as a regional office for salespeople and processes customer orders from inventory on hand is a
    a. merchandise mart.
    b. sales branch.
    c. manufacturer's representative.
    d. brokerage house.
    e. sales office.

57. A permanent facility that provides space in which manufacturers rent space for showrooms and exhibits to market their goods is an example of a
    a. sales branch.
    b. trade fair.
    c. public warehouse.
    d. brokerage house.
    e. merchandise mart.

58. The gathering that takes place once a year at High Point, North Carolina, during which furniture manufacturers display their wares for visiting retail and wholesale buyers is an example of a
    a. manufacturer's agency.
    b. retail buying office.
    c. public market.
    d. trade fair.
    e. merchandise mart.

59. Which of the following is a full-function merchant wholesaler.
    a. a commission merchant.
    b. a rack jobber.
    c. an auction company.
    d. a truck wholesaler.
    e. a drop shipper.

60. Which of the following product assortments would you expect to find being handled by an auction company?
    a. bread, tobacco products, potato chips, candy
    b. hardware, cosmetics, jewelry, sporting goods
    c. tobacco, used cars, art works, livestock, furs
    d. health and beauty aids, housewares, paperback books, compact discs
    e. industrial chemicals, building materials

Name_____   Instructor_____

Section_____   Date_____

Applying Marketing Concepts

Pinsette, Inc., is an independently owned retail store that sells bowling balls, shoes, gloves, and appropriate clothing for men, women, and children. In addition, it offers a complete service department and its specialists can drill finger holes in and otherwise customize any ball – even old ones made of obsolete materials and in any color. Through an arrangement with a group of local professionals, lessons in the art of bowling are available for interested players.

_____ 1. Because of its combination of merchandise and services, Pinsette, Inc. can be said to practice scrambled merchandising.

_____ 2. Pinsette, Inc., is a not a good candidate to engage in direct selling.

_____ 3. Pinsette, Inc.'s product lines would be easy to market via teleshopping.

_____ 4. If the store added a line of hunting equipment, it would be engaging in scrambled merchandising.

_____ 5. In order to compete with the large chain stores, Pinsette, Inc., should carry exclusive lines, provide superior service, and stress their knowledge of local market conditions.

6. This store would be classed as a
   a. specialty store.
   b. general merchandise store.
   c. department store.
   d. limited-line store.
   e. discount house.

7. If a store like Pinsette, Inc., requires convenient access by at least 150,000 people to survive, which of the following locations would be most advantageous for it?
   a. neighborhood shopping center
   b. community shopping center
   c. suburban shopping center
   d. regional shopping center
   e. central business district

8. If this store sold only bowling balls, it would be an example of a
   a. specialty store.
   b. general merchandise store.
   c. department store.
   d. limited-line store.
   e. mass merchandiser.

9. If Pinsette, Inc., hired an interior designer to make the interior of the store resemble an old-fashioned neighborhood bowling alley or alternatively, a modern high-tech bowling facility, it would be attempting to use
   a. distribution to attract a target market.
   b. product/service strategy to attract buyers.
   c. retail image to attract a target market.
   d. location to attract customers.
   e. product/service strategy to attract new customers

10. Pinsette, Inc., is thinking about publishing a catalog and taking orders by phone and mail. They would send the ordered merchandise to the customer by mail or private carrier. What type of nonstore retailing would this be?
    a. personal retailing
    b. direct-response retailing
    c. automatic merchandising
    d. off-price retailing
    e. direct selling

Jerry and Rebecca Kulmbacher have operated Kulmbacher's Kosher Korner Market for over thirty years. During all that time, they have run their store the way they thought their customers would want them to. They open the doors at seven in the morning and close at ten at night, seven days a week. Their parking lot is large and well lighted, and they make sure there are never more than three people in line at the cash register. Employees are encouraged to remember the names of regular customers, and the Kulmbachers have managed to create a feeling of "family" among employees and customers as a group.

The Kulmbachers have always been very proud of the fact that their store kept away from what they referred to as "faddish merchandise" and stuck to the basics. They stock excellent quality meats, breads, and standard fruits and vegetables. Dairy products are sold in a separate part of the store. And everything in the store, without exception, is strictly Kosher for all Jews – Orthodox, Conservative, and Reformed. Of course, not all their clientele is Jewish, hence they can stay open on the Sabbath with the help of their non-Jewish employees.

11. In terms of the shopping effort required to shop at Kulmbacher's, the store is a
    a. shopping store.
    b. convenience store.
    c. specialty store.
    d. self-selection store.
    e. full-service retailer.

12. Looking at the product lines carried by Kulmbacher's we would have to come to the conclusion that the store was
    a. a specialty store.
    b. a limited-line store.
    c. a general merchandise store.
    d. a general store.
    e. a variety store.

13. Considering their pride in their resistance to carrying dissimilar lines of merchandise from the basics of grocerydom, it should be concluded that the Kulmbachers
    a. have resisted the temptation to go into scrambled merchandising.
    b. should move with the times and broaden their merchandise assortment.
    c. have accommodated themselves to the inevitable pressures of the need to make a profit by adding lines which scrambled their merchandise assortment.
    d. have successfully practiced selling up on their customers.
    e. know how to apply suggestion selling.

Upland Supply Company of Mont Tremblant sells hand and electric tools and supplies in several different ways. The company publishes a quarterly catalog it mails to any retailer with which it has done more than $500 in business during the three months before the mailing. It also operates a fleet of trucks that run weekly routes to regular customers (who have generated over $1,500 in business during the last three months) in its operating area. These trucks carry a selection of the most popular items in the company's line for immediate delivery, and the drivers take orders for any other items that are needed and deliver them on the next trip. Upland buys all its inventory from well-known and respected manufacturers.

If an account is sufficiently large ($10,000 in volume during the last three months), Upland Supply will even dispatch a truck to make immediate delivery of any order and will carry the balance owed on an open account for thirty days. Certain items in the Upland line are now handled by a special division of the company whose representatives visit all customers at least once a month and replenish their stock of "expendable items" – packaged screws, nuts, and washers; wiring devices, and very small tools like screwdrivers. They even put the merchandise on display for the customers and keep track of inventory as well. The company calls this division the "small stuff" department.

_____ 14. Even though it operates in several ways, Upland Supply remains a merchant wholesaler.

15. In serving its smaller customers (more that $500 but less than $1,500 in sales), the company acts like a
    a. drop shipper.
    b. cash-and-carry wholesaler.
    c. mail-order wholesaler.
    d. broker.
    e. rack jobber.

16. Upland handles its middle-sized accounts ($1,500 – $10,000) like a
    a. truck wholesaler.
    b. manufacturers' agent.
    c. drop shipper.
    d. commission merchant.
    e. selling agent.

17. Upland's large accounts are handled as if the company was a
    a. manufacturers' sales branch.
    b. full-function merchant wholesaler.
    c. limited-function wholesaler.
    d. drop shipper.
    e. commission merchant.

18. In terms of the way it operates, the "small stuff" division of Upland Supply is a
    a. trade fair.
    b. merchandise mart.
    c. drop shipper.
    d. rack jobber.
    e. public warehouse company.

Name_____   Instructor_____

Section_____   Date_____

Surfing the Net

Keeping in mind that addresses change and what's on the Web now may have changed by the time you read this, let's take a look at some of the places on the Net that reflect aspects of retailing. We are not endorsing or recommending any of these sources, merely making note of the information and services that people have elected to offer through the Internet.

What do you want to buy? The Internet is replete with retailing sites. Let's start with the biggies. WalMart is on the Net at **http://www.walmart.com**. Something a little more upscale? Nordstrom, the very customer service oriented department store, can be reached at **http://www2.nordstrom.com** The claim is that as they get to know a customer at this site, they e-mail you information about new items or special promotions that suit your tastes. Still looking for alternatives? Try the May Company (Famous-Barr) at **http://www2.shopmay.com** or Dillard's for those of you in the South at **http://www.dillards.com**. Alternatively, there's always Macy's at **http://www.macys.com**.

Any other major retailers on the Net? I guess we shouldn't leave out K-Mart. They're at **http://www.bluelight.com**. But I'd bet you would figure that one out yourself, sooner or later. In case you don't want to get involved in deep thought about that one, you can go with **http://www.kmart.com**.

Need copies? Kinko's can be reached at **http://www.fedexkinkos.com**. For other writing and study supplies, try the Office Max site at **http://www.officemax.com**. If there's no Officemax in your neighborhood, how about Office Depot at **http://www.officedepot.com**.

My kids have always said I had no intention of ever growing up. And they were right. The toy stores are on the Net and there's no harm in visiting. Sadly, FAO Schwarz, one of my favorites (remember the giant piano keyboard in the movie *BIG)* is no longer in business. There's always Toys 'R' Us. They're at **http://www.toysrus.com**. And if you're looking for toys for big people who need a functional excuse, try **http://www.harborfreight.com**, where you can find almost any kind of tool known to humankind.

Hungry? Just today I heard of a restaurant called the Red Ochre Grill with a really neat menu. It features Moreton Bay bug tails and Kangaroo sirloin, emu paté and wattleseed lavosh – native Australian cuisine, I'm informed – whatever it is. For a menu or reservations, try **http://www.redochregrill.com.au**. Of course, it's in Australia, so it may be a bit far from home for some of us. In my neighborhood, we like Commander's Palace – **http://www.commanderspalace.com**, Antoine's – **http://www.antoines.com**, and Redfish Grill – **http://www.redfishgrill.com**, all in New Orleans, of course.

Sites verified October 8, 2004

Part 5
Creating a Marketing Plan

The information that you will receive in this episode should allow you to complete Part III. C. of your marketing plan.

Episode 5: Let's Find a Place to Hang Our Hats

"If I ever have to look at another dump like that last one, I'll quit!" was Suzette's vehement comment after she and Mel drove away from the address the commercial real estate agent had given them. She and the guys knew what they needed: a place of about 2,000 square feet, part warehouse/service area, part office, located near the center of concentration of the businesses in New Blackpool. The problem seemed to be that the places they felt they could afford suffered from one or more fatal flaws, like inadequate wiring or lack of security in the form at least of some serious locks - after all, the place was going to be full of sophisticated electronic equipment, and they would have some proprietary software on hand that they didn't want copied or stolen.

"Let's try one more place, 'Suze' " said Mel the ever-optimistic. Now that we've established our credit with Cell Dynamics for unit circuit access, we can get going as soon as we get a place. It was rare luck that we were able to buy those two cars the police force ordered but never had delivered. I doubt that we could have found such nice machines anywhere else for the price. It's a good thing your uncle is in the automobile business and knew about them. I bet we'll be able to beat even Domino's on service calls. Those big V-8 engines certainly pack some get up and go, even if their gas economy isn't the best."

"That's true. I guess I can't expect everything to go smoothly all the time. Didn't you say you had seen an ad in today's paper for a place that it sounded like we could use?" asked Suzette.

"Yes," replied Mel, "it's right around the next corner. Let's take a look." And so saying, they turned the corner and parked next to nicely maintained concrete-block building. "I see there's someone here," said Suzette, pointing to a small van parked next to the open side door of the structure.

"Maybe we can get in and take a look," was Mel's reply, "or maybe whoever's there can tell us something about the place." They approached the open door.

Thirty minutes later they emerged in the company of an older man. "The place is just perfect, Mr. Landreneau. We'll have our attorney call yours tomorrow to iron out the details, but I think we've got a deal," said Suzette, shaking hands with the older man. "Very good, Ms. O'Malley," was his response, "I think you'll find the building and the location are perfect for your plans." Later, back at Suzette's house, where Sandy was waiting, the threesome sat down to organize their thoughts. Sandy passed out sheets of paper to the other two and said, "Well, I've talked to three people that we all know either from school or the Institute, and they've all agreed to come work with us. I guess in the beginning we'd all better hit the road and start making contact with the businesses that most need our services. We'll leave one person in the office to man the phones, while the rest of us go out and make ourselves known. The signmakers said they could have the sign hung by Monday afternoon and the stationery and business cards will be ready tomorrow. Since this is only Tuesday, we may be able to plead our case with a lot of people by the time the weekend rolls around."

"You know, I wonder if we really need that building," said Mel, thinking out loud. "I mean, it'll be great to have a real office to work in, but it's not like we have to have a place to store lots of inventory or anything." "I go with having the building," said Suzette. "We need a place to work, and we need a place where people can come to us. At some point, we're going to have to fine-tune what we're doing, and if potential customers can come to us and see what we're doing by watching demonstrations of the level of service quality our combination of hardware and software delivers on great big 25 inch monitors running in real-time right there in our equipment room, they'll know how exactly what they're buying. They can't see that if we make our presentations on Laptops or on their in-office machines."

"Too true," said Sandy. "If we become well-known, and I hope we do, people are going to come looking for us and are going to need a place to find us. It's like the 24 hour a day availability. We may discover we don't actually have to man the office on a 24/7 basis, but there's a lot of comfort to knowing your equipment can be replaced at a moment's notice, or repaired by somebody who knows how if something happens to it in the middle of the night. Communications availability has become crucial to a lot of businesses."

"I guess you're right" was Mel's reply.

"You guys get on home now," said Suzette, "and we'll meet again tomorrow morning to get the lease finalized with the lawyer."

Guidelines:

Review the requirements of Part III. C. of your Marketing Plan, and, using the information in this episode, complete that Part of the plan. Some materials in this episode will also be relevant to completion of Part III.D. of the Plan, as well.

Part 6
Promotional Decisions

Promotion is one of the most dynamic and severely criticized aspects of marketing. It is the marketing activity charged with informing, persuading, and influencing the consumer's purchase decision. Integrated marketing communications coordinate all promotion activities to produce a unified, customer-focused promotional message, often using extensive databases to identify potential customers. The essence of integrated marketing communications is coordination among the elements of the promotional program through teamwork and database management to reach the customers who are central to the firm's mission. Understanding the process of communication itself – the sender, message encoding, the message channel, decoding, response, and additional feedback – is quite important. Effective messages gain the receiver's attention, achieve understanding by both receiver and sender, and stimulate the receiver's needs, suggesting an appropriate method of satisfying them. Promotion objectives often include increasing demand, differentiating a product, accentuating a product's value, stabilizing sales, and providing information to consumers and others. The promotional mix includes personal selling and nonpersonal selling activities.

Recent years have seen tremendous growth in the promotional use of sponsorships, especially of various events in the sporting world. Sponsorships serve to integrate a promotional effort with an event or activity. Direct marketing has also grown markedly in the last twenty years as well, now including, in additional to the traditional direct mail, telemarketing, direct mail via TV, use of the Internet.

An optimal promotional mix considers the nature of the product, the nature of the market, the product's stage in its product life cycle, its price, and the funds available for promotional activities. Some promotional programs favor pushing strategies which promote to intermediaries to bring the product to market, while others promote to ultimate users in a pulling strategy. The objects of promotion determine the setting of a promotional budget. Traditional methods of allocating a promotional budget are percentage of sales, a fixed sum per unit, meeting the competition, and task-objective. Measurement of the effectiveness of promotion is difficult, pretesting and posttesting of advertising being the most common methods, but it is certain that promotion has social, business, and economic importance.

Nonpersonal promotional elements include advertising, sales promotion, direct marketing, and public relations. Advertising, any paid nonpersonal sales presentation carried by a medium and usually directed to a large number of potential customers, is an important part of modern business. Advertising may be product-based or institution-based, and can be designed to inform, persuade, or remind the receiving public. Advertising strategies include comparative, retail, and interactive advertising and celebrity testimonials. Creating ads is a multi-billion dollar industry, as is delivering them through TV, radio, newspapers, magazines, direct mail, and interactive and outdoor media.

Personal selling, a vital part of the promotional mix, has evolved from the role of the old-time peddler to today's professional sales practitioner who may use relationship, consultative, or team selling techniques. Sales channels include over-the-counter selling, field selling, telemarketing, and inside selling. Sales representatives may be called upon to process orders, sell creatively, or do missionary work.

New trends in personal selling include relationship selling, consultative selling, team selling, and sales-force automation. The sales process usually follows seven steps beginning with prospecting and qualifying. Then follow the approach and sales presentation. The content and emphasis of the sales presentation depend on whether the sales practitioner is responsible for order processing, creative selling, or missionary sales.   Then follow the demonstration and handling of objections. The sales rep then closes the sale and the whole process ends with follow-up after the sale has been made.

The existence of a personal sales force means there must be sales management. Someone must recruit, select, train, organize, supervise, motivate, pay, control, and evaluate sales practitioners and act in a boundary-spanning role between them and upper-level management.

Sales promotion is designed to stimulate consumer purchasing and dealer effectiveness. The basic types of sales promotion to consumers include coupons and refunds, contests, sweepstakes, samples, premiums, bonus packs, and specialty advertising. Trade-oriented promotions include trade allowances, point-of-purchase advertising, trade shows, dealer incentives, contests, and training programs. Both may also include other nonrecurrent, irregular selling efforts.

Public relations, a firm's communications and relationships with its publics, often supplements other promotional efforts in the marketing mix. Publicity, part of public relations, obtains favorable media coverage for a firm without payment to the media.

Ethical issues certainly form a part of the scope of the promotional responsibility and are probably best summed up simply by restating the marketing concept B find out what people want, offer it to them at a reasonable price, and make sure they are happy with it if they buy it.

Chapter 15
Integrated Marketing Communications

Chapter Outline

You may want to use the following outline as a guide in taking notes.

I. Chapter Overview

Promotion is the function of informing, persuading, and influencing the consumer's purchasing decisions. The elements of the promotion mix include personal selling and nonpersonal selling. These are assembled into a promotional mix that it is hoped will achieve the objectives of the firm. Promotion has business, economic, and social aspects. Nonpersonal promotion includes advertising, sales promotion, public relations, sponsorships, guerilla advertising, and publicity. The usual personal method of promotion is personal selling. Consumers receive marketing communications from a variety of media, including TV, magazines, and the Internet. Integrated marketing communications (IMC) coordinates all promotional media to produce a unified, customer-focused promotional message. IMC includes not only marketers but all other organizational units that interact with the consumer.

II. Integrated Marketing Communications strategy begins not with the organization's goods and services but with consumer wants and needs and works back to the product, brand, or organization. IMC looks at the elements of the promotional mix from the consumer's viewpoint: as information about the brand, company, or organization. Today's many markets and media create both opportunities and challenges. The opportunities involve reaching desirable market segments, the challenges relate to how it is to be accomplished. The increase in media options provides more ways to get information to consumers, but may also create information overload. A coordinated promotion may produce competitive advantage based on synergy and interdependence among the various elements of the promotion mix. IMC provides a more effective way to reach and serve target markets than less coordinated strategies.

A. Implementing a promotional strategy requires a big picture view of promotional planning that includes all marketing activities, not just promotion. Successful implementation of IMC requires that everyone involved in every aspect of promotion function as part of a team. The teamwork involves both in-house resources and outside vendors. IMC challenges the traditional role of the advertising agency, perhaps requiring more than one agency to fulfill all the desired communications requirements. .

B. The role of databases in effective IMC programs has vastly increased over the last ten years with the growth of the Internet. The move from mass marketing to customer-specific strategy requires not only a means of identifying and communicating with the firm's target market but also information about the important characteristics of each prospective customer. Direct sampling can be used to quickly obtain customer opinions about a firm's goods and services.

III. The Communications Process – The *sender* of a message acts as the source in the communications system, attempting to convey a *message* to a *receiver*. The message must be *encoded*, or translated into understandable terms, then transmitted through a communications *channel.* The receiver *decodes* the message to yield an interpretation of its content. The receiver's response, called *feedback*, completes the communication system.

A. An effective message (1) gains the receiver's attention, (2) achieves understanding by both receiver and sender, and (3) stimulates the receiver's needs and suggests an appropriate method of satisfying them.

B. The AIDA concept (attention-interest-desire-action) is related to this process, describing the steps consumers take in reaching a purchase decision. It is vital to both bricks-and-mortar and online marketers.

C. A marketing communication may originate with a sales manager who encodes it in the form of a sales presentation, advertisement, or other message. The channel can be a salesperson, advertising medium, or other medium. Decoding is often the most difficult part of the communications process because consumers do not always interpret messages the same way senders do.

D. Feedback provides a way for marketers to evaluate the effectiveness of a message and tailor responses accordingly. Feedback may be elicited by such devices as consumer contests to "find a new use for Product X," for example. Even nonpurchases – as a form of response -- can provide useful feedback to the sender of a message.

E. Noise represents interference at some stage of the communications process and can be especially problematical in international communications. Perhaps the most misunderstood language for U.S. marketers is English, dialects of which are spoken – differently – in 74 countries and different regions of the United States. (Just try explaining the proper grammatical use of "y'all" to a Yankee.)

IV. Objectives of Promotion – Generally, marketers identify five objectives for the promotions process.

A. Provide information to consumers and others. The traditional objective of promotion was to inform the market about the availability of a particular good or service, and a substantial amount of promotion is still designed to fulfill this objective. In addition to the traditional print and broadcasting media, marketers now distribute high-tech, low-cost tools such as video cassettes and CD-ROMs to give consumers product information.

B. Increase demand for a good or service. Some promotions seek to increase primary demand, the demand for a general product category, while others are aimed at increasing selective demand, the desire for a specific brand of a given product or service.

C. Differentiate the product. When consumers regard a firm's output as virtually identical to its competitors' products, the firm has virtually no control over variables such as price. Differentiation permits more flexibility in marketing strategy, such as price changes.

D. Accentuate the product's value. Promotion can explain the greater ownership utility of a product to buyers, thereby accentuating its value and justifying a higher price in the marketplace.

E. Stabilize sales. For most firms, sales are not uniform throughout the year, the variations occurring because of cyclical, seasonal, or irregular demand. Stabilizing these variations is often an objective of promotional strategy.

V. Elements of the Promotional Mix – The promotional mix requires a carefully designed blend of variables to satisfy the needs of a company's customers and achieve organizational objectives. The components of the promotional mix include personal selling and nonpersonal selling.

A. Personal selling is the oldest form of promotion and may be defined as a seller's promotional presentation conducted on a person-to-person basis with the buyer.

B. Nonpersonal selling includes advertising, sales promotion, direct marketing, and public relations. About one-third of expenditures in this category go for media advertising, with the rest being spent on trade and consumer sales promotion.
   1. Advertising is any paid, nonpersonal communication through various media about a business firm, not-for-profit organization, product, or idea by a sponsor identified in a message intended to inform or persuade members of a particular audience. Advertising primarily involves the mass media, such as newspapers, television, radio, magazines, and billboards, but also includes electronic media such as Web commercials, videotapes, and video screens in supermarkets.
   2. Product placement is a form of nonpersonal selling in which the marketer pays a motion picture or television program owner a fee to display his or her product prominently in the film or show.
   3. Sales promotion consists of marketing activities other than personal selling, advertising, and public relations that stimulate consumer purchasing and dealer effectiveness. It includes displays, trade shows, coupons, contests, samples, premiums, product demonstrations, and other nonrecurring, irregular selling efforts. Sales promotion geared to marketing intermediaries is called "trade promotion."
   4. Direct marketing is the use of direct communication to a consumer or a business recipient designed to generate a response in the form of an order, a request for further information, or a visit to a place of business to purchase specific goods or services.
   5. Public relations and publicity are a firm's communications with its various publics – customers, stockholders, suppliers, employees, the government, the general public, and society. Publicity, nonpersonal stimulation of demand for a good, service, person, cause, or organization through unpaid placement of significant news in a published medium or through favorable presentation of it on radio, television, or the stage, is an important part of an effective public relations program. Good publicity is highly desirable, bad publicity very undesirable – though sometimes unavoidable.
   6. Guerilla marketing is a relatively new approach to promotion used by marketers whose firms are underfunded for a full marketing program. It involves such firms creating innovative, low-cost ways to reach their target markets. Toyota elected to use guerilla marketing to introduce the new *Scion,* targeted to first-car buyers in their early twenties, while Reebok approached the same objective, introducing a new product, through the Internet. The results of guerilla marketing can be funny, outrageous, even offensive, but they are usually memorable.
   7. The different forms of promotion have their own advantages and shortcomings. Personal selling, though costly, is very effective. Advertising can create instant aware-

ness of a product and is fairly cheap per person reached, but closes fewer sales than personal selling. Good publicity is very desirable, but bad publicity can cause no end of difficulty.

VI. Sponsorships involve providing cash or in-kind resources to an event or activity in exchange for a direct association with the event or activity. The sponsor gets access to (1) the activity's audience and (2) the image associated with the activity.

A. Sponsorship spending in the U. S. has increased over the last ten years to $11 billion. Sports events are the dominant type of activity to be sponsored, followed by festivals, fairs, and touring attractions. Both big spenders and smaller firms are active in sponsorship.

B. Growth of sponsorships has been rapid over the last three decades. Restrictions on tobacco and alcohol advertising have led marketers to seek alternative promotional media, as has the escalating cost of traditional media and the additional opportunities for sponsorship growing out of diverse leisure activities and the increasing array of sporting events featured in the media. In addition, greater media coverage of sponsored events allows sponsors to gain greater exposure for the dollar, it is an effective way for global marketers to reach an international audience in a universally-understood manner, and the proven effectiveness of a properly planned and executed sponsorship can buy productive marketing contacts.

C. How sponsorship differs from advertising – Marketers have considerable control over the quantity and quality of market coverage when they advertise. Sponsors must rely on signs to present their message. Audiences react differently to sponsorship as a communications medium than to other media, usually regarding it more positively. This sometimes stimulates *ambush marketing*, in which a firm that is not an official sponsor tries to link itself to a major international event.

D. Assessing sponsorship results usually involves some of the same techniques used to measure advertising effectiveness, but due to the differences between advertising and sponsorship, other techniques are used as well. Despite the impressive visibility of special events, these events do not necessarily lead directly to increased sales.

VII. Direct Marketing – is one of the fastest growing elements of the promotional mix, with expenditures totaling more than $1.7 trillion per year. Direct marketing opens new international markets of unprecedented size. Direct marketing communications pursue goals beyond creating product awareness. The growth effect of marketing parallels the move toward integrated marketing communications in many ways.

A. Direct marketing communications channels use many different media forms because each works best for certain purposes.

B. Direct mail has become a viable channel for identifying a firm's best prospects and is a critical tool in creating effective direct-marketing campaigns. Direct mail can select a narrow target market, achieve intensive coverage, send messages quickly, choose from various formats, provide complete information, and personalize each mailing piece. Response rates are measurable and higher than other types of advertising, though costs are high and some consumers object to receiving "junk mail."

1. Catalogs have been a popular form of direct mail in the U.S. for over a century. Many companies built their businesses and created their images through catalogs. Many Americans still refuse to purchase from a catalog but others – especially those who live in rural areas or busy professional – depend on them for their shopping needs. Catalogs generate an average of $57 billion in consumer sales and $36 billion in B2B sales annually.

2. Telemarketing is direct marketing conducted entirely by telephone – either outbound or inbound. Though its use has been limited by "do not call" legislation, it remains the most frequently used form of direct marketing. Both B2C and B2B telemarketing are widely used. New technology has made telemarketing more efficient, and the exemption from the "do not call" rules of people already customers of the telemarketers, charities, opinion pollsters, and political candidates mean that the technique is not dead.

D. Direct mail via broadcast channels can take three forms: brief direct-response ads run on television or radio, home shopping channels, and infomercials. Direct-response ads may run 30, 60, or 90 seconds and include product descriptions and toll-free telephone numbers for ordering. Home shopping channels offer consumers a variety of products, including jewelry, clothing, skincare, home furnishings, and other products – much like an on-air catalog. Infomercials are 30 minute or longer product commercials resembling regular television programs.

E. Electronic direct marketing channels include Web advertising and electronic messaging. Electronic media deliver data near-instantly to direct marketers and help them to track consumer buying cycles quickly.

F. Other direct marketing channels include magazine ads with toll-free telephone numbers provided so the readers can contact the advertiser directly, reader-response cards placed in magazines, and special inserts targeting specific segments placed in all types of periodical publications. Kiosks provide another outlet for electronic sales.

VIII. Developing an Optimal Promotional Mix -- Blending advertising, personal selling, sales promotion, and public relations to achieve marketing objectives results in a promotional mix. Since measuring the effectiveness of each component quantitatively is impossible, the task of optimizing the mix is extra-ordinarily difficult. Five factors influence the effectiveness of the promotional mix.

A. Nature of the market – The marketer's target audience has a major impact on the choice of promotional methods. The number of buyers, their geographical dispersion, and the type of customer are all significant in the choice of methods. Whether the market for the product is new or mature also has a significant effect.

B. Nature of the product – The product itself affects the appropriateness of the promotional mix. Standardized products depend less on personal selling, for example, than to custom products with complex features or high maintenance requirements. Consumer products use more advertising than do business products. Within business products, installations are usually promoted using personal selling, while operating supplies are advertised.

C. Stage in the product life cycle – The promotional mix must be tailored to the product's stage in the product life cycle. Marketers of new products may need to work closely with customers to answer questions and adjust promotional mixes as needed. Growing products require relatively more advertising than products at earlier or later stages in the product life cycle. Products in the maturity phase of the cycle often require creative promotion to keep them in the minds of consumers.

D. Price of the good or service is the fourth factor that affects the choice of a promotional mix. Advertising dominates in the promotion of low-unit-value products. Big-ticket items, on the other hand, are best promoted using personal selling and high-tech media such as videocassettes, CD-ROMs, and glossy brochures.

E. Funds available for promotion define the limit of what can be done regardless of the choice of media or method. One cannot spend beyond one's budget, and many promotional budgets are relatively small.

IX. Pulling and Pushing Promotional Strategies are essentially two alternatives available to the marketer. A pulling strategy is a promotional effort by the seller to stimulate final-user demand that then exerts pressure on the distribution channel. By contrast, a pushing strategy relies more heavily on personal selling to promote the product to members of the marketing channel rather than to final users. Though they are spoken of as alternative methods, few firms depend entirely on either one. Timing is an additional factor that affects the choice of promotional strategies. Prior to actual sale, advertising is more useful than personal selling. Selling activities, however, are more important at the time of purchase than is advertising.

X. Budgeting for Promotional Strategy – Promotional budgets differ both in amount and in composition. B2B marketers tend to rely more on personal selling than advertising, while the opposite is true of consumer goods producers. Sales usually lag behind promotional expenditures for structural reasons – it takes time to fill shelves, boost low initial production, and supply buyers with knowledge. The ideal method of allocating promotional funds would increase the budget until the cost of each additional increment equaled the additional incremental revenue received – or to the point where marginal cost equaled marginal revenue. Since this is extraordinarily difficult, alternative methods have been developed.

A. Alternative methods of budgeting
1. The percentage-of-sales method is the most common way of establishing promotional budgets. It is simple but arbitrary, unrelated to promotional objectives.
2. The fixed-sum-per-unit method is similar to the percentage-of-sales method except that it allots a specific amount for promotion for each unit of sales or production.
3. Another approach is that of meeting competition. It does not help its user to get a competitive advantage, just to keep abreast.
4. The task-objective method bases the promotional budget on an evaluation of the firm's promotional objectives, thus attuning funds allocation to modern marketing objectives.
   a. First, realistic communications goals thet the firm desires to achieve must be set in a quantitative manner.
   b. Then, company marketers determine the amount and type of promotional activity required for each objective and combine them to determine the full budget amount.

    c. The underlying assumption of this approach is that the productivity of each promotion dollar can be measured.

   5. Promotional budgeting is not simple, and often requires difficult decisions.

XI. Measuring the Effectiveness of Promotion – Part of a firm's promotional effort is ineffective, but it is difficult to determine which part. Evaluating the effectiveness of promotion today is far different than it was even a few decades ago. Such measurements have evolved from store audits and warehouse withdrawal surveys through scanner-based records of actual sales data to Internet-enabled detailed data about the behavior of specific customers. Still, most marketers would prefer to use a direct sales results test to measure the effectiveness of promotion, but thus far such a measure has eluded them. Indirect evaluation helps researchers concentrate on quantifiable indicators of promotional effectiveness. Needless to say, marketers need to ask the right questions and understand what they are measuring.

   A. Measuring online promotions began with the measurement of hits (user requests for a file) and visits (pages read or downloaded in one session.) One way that online marketers measure the effectiveness of promotion is by incorporating some form of direct response into them. Two major ways of setting Internet advertising rates are now *cost per impression* and *cost per response (click-throughs)*. An impression occurs when someone sees an online ad. Cost per impression is how much an ad costs per person who views it. Cost per response measures the cost of an ad for each person who clicks on it.

XII. The Value of Marketing Communications is changing. New formats are transforming the idea of advertising and sales promotion. Promotional messages may appear anywhere, subtly or not-so-subtly displayed. Despite new tactics by advertisers, promotion has often been the target of criticism. New forms of promotion are considered even more insidious than those of the past because they do not look like paid advertisements. While promotion can certainly be criticized on many counts, it also plays a crucial role in modern society.

   A. Social importance of advertising is based on the fact that our society offers many choices and opportunities. The choices we make eventually determine acceptable practices in the marketplace. Criticisms of promotional messages as tasteless and lacking any contribution to society ignore the fact that our social system provides no commonly accepted set of standards for such judgments. Promotion is an important factor in campaigns aimed at achieving social objectives and performs an information and educational task crucial to the functioning of modern society.

   B. Business importance of promotion is well documented in the increase in funds spent on promotion over the years, testifying to management's faith in the ability of promotional efforts to encourage attitude change, brand loyalty, and additional sales. Nonbusinesses also recognize the importance of promotional efforts, the U. S. government alone spending $300 million per year on advertising.

   C. Economic importance of promotion is verified by the fact that it provides employment for large numbers of people. Promotional strategies increase the number of units of product sold and permit economies of scale in the production process, lowering production costs per unit, thus allowing lower prices. Advertising also supports the publication of magazines and newspapers and the activities of the broadcast media.

Name_____   Instructor_____

Section_____   Date_____

Key Concepts

The purpose of this section is to allow you to determine if you can match key concepts with their definitions. It is essential that you know the definitions of the concepts prior to applying the concepts in later exercises in this chapter.

From the list of lettered terms, select the one that best fits in the blank of the numbered statement below. Write the letter of that choice in the space provided.

Key Terms

a. promotion
b. marketing communications
c. integrated marketing
   communications (IMC)
d. AIDA concept
e. promotional mix
f. personal selling
g. nonpersonal selling
h. advertising

i. sales promotion
j. direct marketing
k. public relations
l. guerilla marketing
m. sponsorship
n. direct mail
o. pulling strategy
p. pushing strategy

_____ 1. Marketing activities other than personal selling, advertising, and publicity that stimulate consumer purchasing and dealer effectiveness.

_____ 2. Seller's promotional presentation conducted on a person-to-person basis with a prospective buyer.

_____ 3. Unconventional, innovative, low-cost marketing techniques designed to get consumers' attention in unusual ways.

_____ 4. Paid, nonpersonal communication through various media by an entity that is identified in the message and that hopes to inform or persuade members of a particular audience.

_____ 5. Firm's communications and relationships with its various publics.

_____ 6. Promotional effort by a seller to stimulate demand among final users who will exert pressure on the distribution channel to provide the good or service.

_____ 7. Blend of personal selling and nonpersonal selling created by marketers to achieve promotional objectives.

_____ 8. Provision of funds for a sporting or cultural event in exchange for a direct association with the event.

_____ 9. Acronym for the traditional explanation of the steps an individual must take to complete a purchase decision.

_____ 10. Function of informing, influencing, and persuading the consumer's purchase decision.

_____ 11. Direct communications other than personal sales contacts between buyer and seller designed to generate sales, information requests, or store or web site visits.

_____ 12. Promotional effort by a seller directed to members of the marketing channel rather than the final user to stimulate sales activities.

_____ 13. Coordination of all promotional activities to produce a unified promotional message that is customer-focused

_____ 14. Messages that deal with buyer-seller relationships.

_____ 15. Promotion that includes advertising, sales promotion, direct marketing, and public relations – all conducted without being face-to-face with the buyer.

_____ 16. Sales letters, postcards, catalogs, brochures, and the like, conveying messages directly from the marketer to the consumer.

Name_____   Instructor_____

Section_____ .   Date_____

Self-Quiz

You should use these questions to test your understanding of the material in this chapter. You can check your answers with those provided at the end of the chapter.

While these questions cover most of the chapter topics, they are not intended to be the same as the test questions your instructor may use in an examination. A good understanding of all aspects of the course material is necessary to good performance on any examination.

True/False

Write "T" for True and "F" for False for each of the following statements.

_____   1. Integrated marketing communications coordinates all promotional activities to produce a unified, customer-focused promotional message.

_____   2. The firm's product is at the heart of integrated marketing communications.

_____   3. Mass media such as TV ads, while still useful, are no longer the mainstays of marketing campaigns.

_____   4. In marketing communications, for a message to be effective, it must only gain the receiver's attention and be understood by both receiver and sender.

_____   5. E. K. Strong's "AIDA concept" pointed out that promotional messages had as their ultimate objective producing action in the form of a purchase or a more favorable attitude that might lead to future purchases.

_____   6. A classic example of noise in the communications process is the statement on a sign in a Bucharest hotel lobby: "The lift is being fixed for the next day. During that time, we regret you will be unbearable."

_____   7. Videocassettes containing promotional messages have proven to be relatively unsuccessful, research showing that only about 10 percent of recipients view them and response rates average only 4 percent.

_____   8.   While some promotions are aimed at increasing selective demand, more seek to increase primary demand.

_____   9. Under conditions of homogeneous demand, the firm has almost no control over marketing variables such as the price of its products.

_____ 10. While many people equate direct marketing with direct mail, it also includes telemarketing, direct response advertising, infomercials on TV and radio, direct-response print ads, and interactive electronic media.

_____ 11. Advertising, public relations, and sales promotion typically account for the bulk of a firm's promotional expenditures.

_____ 12. Sales promotion includes displays, trade shows, coupons, contests, samples, premiums, product demonstrations, and various nonrecurrent, irregular selling efforts.

_____ 13. Guerilla marketing can create instant awareness of a good, service, or idea; build brand equity; and deliver the marketer's message to mass audiences for a relatively low cost per contact.

_____ 14. A pushing promotional strategy relies heavily on personal selling to convince members of the channel of distribution to spend extra time and effort promoting the vendor's product.

_____ 15. Destabilizing fluctuations in sales that result from cyclical, seasonal, or irregular demand is often an objective of promotional strategy.

_____ 16. In the communications process, the message must be decoded before it can be transmitted through a communications channel.

_____ 17. The ideal method of allocating a promotional budget is to increase the budget until the cost of each additional increase equals the additional contribution to profit received.

_____ 18. Companies actually spend about two-thirds of their nonpersonal selling dollars on media advertising and consumer sales promotions.

_____ 19. Complaints levied against various form of promotional for being "tasteless" fail to recognize that what one group of people finds "tasteless" may be quite appealing to another group.

_____ 20. Probably the most common way to set promotional budgets, the "task-objective method" applies a predetermined money allocation to each unit of sales or production.

_____ 21. Direct mail offers advantages such as the fact that it allows advertisers to select a narrow target market, achieve intensive coverage, send messages quickly, and personalize each mailing piece.

_____ 22. Marketers have overcome the difficulty of isolating the effects of promotion from those of other marketing elements and outside environmental variables and can now use a direct sales results test to measure promotional effectiveness.

_____ 23. Among the indirect methods of evaluating the effectiveness of advertising are recall and readership measurements.

_____ 24. Successful integrated marketing communications programs deliver messages to intended audiences and also gather responses from them.

_____ 25. E-mail direct marketers have found that traditional practices used in print and broadcast media are difficult to adapt to electronic messaging.

Multiple Choice

Circle the letter of the phrase or sentence that best completes the sentence or best answers the question.

26. An effective message must
    a. be understood by the sender.
    b. stimulate the receiver's needs and suggest an appropriate means of satisfying them.
    c. be understood by the receiver.
    d. gain the receiver's attention.
    e. achieve all of the above objectives.

27. The AIDA concept, proposed over sixty years ago, explains the
    a. logic behind why Giuseppe Verdi named his famous opera in this peculiar fashion.
    b. steps by which an individual reaches a purchase decision.
    c. relationship among ability, intelligence, dedication, and activity in the marketing process.
    d. structural relationships among variables in the promotional mix.
    e. components of the promotion process: advertising, indoctrination, description, and acceptance.

28. In the communications process, attitude change, purchase, or nonpurchase are forms of
    a. encoding, reduction of the message to understandable terms.
    b. transmission, the use of the communications channel.
    c. feedback, and complete the communication system.
    d. decoding, interpretation of the message.
    e. noise, a continuous hazard to effective communication.

29. A firm's communications and relationships with its various publics is referred to as
    a. advertising.
    b. personal selling.
    c. sales promotion.
    d. public relations.
    e. direct marketing.

30. Of the following, which most correctly exemplifies noise in the marketing communications process?
    a. A viewer of a television commercial is distracted by the flipping of the TV picture and a loud buzzing sound coming from the speaker during the commercial.
    b. A viewer of the President's State of the Union message refuses to believe a word of it because he/she is a member of a different political party and is adamantly opposed to the president's policies and agenda.
    c. An individual isn't there when a promotional message appears on television.
    d. Visitors to a city in "tornado alley" laugh off a tornado alert because they've never been through a twister and don't believe in the danger.
    e. A commercial is presented at the right time to the right audience using an appropriate advertising medium.

31. A newspaper advertisement for a concert that speaks about the main performer, the time, and the place of the concert is designed primarily to
    a. differentiate the performance from competitive offerings in the same marketplace.
    b. increase primary demand for live entertainment.
    c. provide information to consumers and others.
    d. stabilize sales of tickets over a period of time.
    e. promote the theater rather than the performance itself.

32. A hotel which offers "weekend retreat" packages at lower rates than it rents those same rooms during the week is attempting to
    a. build brand image and equity for the hotel and stimulate selective demand.
    b. focus interest on their offering's novelty and demonstrate its superiority.
    c. provide product information for potential customers.
    d. supplement high occupancy during the week from business travelers and stabilize sales.
    e. differentiate their product and take control over its price.

33. Beyond the obvious goal of creating product awareness, other goals of direct marketing are typically
    a. yield large increases in sales volume for very small increases in cost.
    b. persuading people to place orders, request more information, or visit a store to make a purchase.
    c. to create instant awareness of a specific product and build brand equity before sales are made.
    d. to short-circuit competitive promotion and avoid claims made by other vendors.
    e. identify and target small, hard to reach local and domestic markets.

34. Nonpersonal stimulation of demand for a good, service, person, cause, or organization through unpaid placement of significant news about it in a published medium or through favorable presentation of it on radio, television, or stage is called
    a. publicity.
    b. public relations.
    c. advertising.
    d. sales promotion.
    e. personal selling.

35. Advertising, sales promotion, direct marketing, and public relations are all
    a. paid communications through various media that include identification of the sponsor and hope to inform or persuade members of a particular audience.
    b. examples of promotion through mass media such as newspapers, television, radio, magazines, and billboards.
    c. particularly appropriate methods of promoting products that rely on sending the same promotional message to large audiences.
    d. nonrecurrent personal promotional methods used on an irregular basis.
    e. forms of nonpersonal selling; advertising and sales promotion are usually regarded as the most important.

36. The original form of promotion, the one with the longest history, is
    a. advertising; advertising messages have even been found on the walls of the ruins of Pompeii.
    b. personal selling; presumably, the very first exchanges in trade were made by two individuals acting face-to-face.
    c. sponsorship; in Rome, competing businesses supported teams of gladiators who wore their sponsors' logos.
    d. public relations; the Phoenicians were careful to keep on good terms with their customers and competitors.
    e. publicity; Pepsi bottles at least three thousand years old have been found at stage level in the ruins of the Greek theater at Catharsis in the Pericardium.

37. Among the reasons for the growth of sponsorship over the past three decades has been the
    a. escalating cost of traditional advertising media having made commercial sponsorships cost-effective marketing tools.
    b. reduction in leisure time available for entertainment and fewer sporting events yielding larger attendance at entertainment productions and sporting events.
    c. lessening of government regulation on the advertising of liquor and tobacco allowing them to be more visible to the public as part of such activities as concerts and public stage performances.
    d. increased interest in medieval activities such as jousting that revived this traditional method of promotion.
    e. availability of cheap methods of production of practically every kind of promotional device that make sponsorship a simple, almost unplanned activity.

38. The fact that highly standardized products with minimal servicing requirements are less likely to depend on personal selling than are custom products that are technically complex is an example of the way the promotional mix can be influenced by
    a. the nature of the market.
    b. the product's stage of the product life cycle.
    c. the nature of the product itself.
    d. the product's price in the marketplace.
    e. the funds available for promotion.

39. The stage(s) of the product life cycle during which advertising gains relative importance in persuading consumers to make purchases
    a. is decline.
    b. is mid-growth.
    c. are early growth into mid-growth.
    d. are growth and maturity.
    e. is introduction.

40. If a manufacturer begins advertising a new product to consumers before that good has become available to marketing intermediaries in the channel of distribution, it is probably using a
    a. pushing strategy to secure distribution at the wholesale level of the channel.
    b. thrust-off promotion to get the product adopted by the members of the channel before the public becomes aware of it.
    c. mixed-bag strategy designed to create the proper atmosphere for product introduction to the consumer market.
    d. pulling strategy to develop end-user demand so that final consumers will put pressure on intermediaries to stock the product.
    e. forced-choice to make channel members decide which of two competing products they're going to stock.

41. Which of the following statements is most true of direct marketing?
    a. Direct marketing is limited to the use of only a few similar media forms.
    b. Because direct marketing is interactive, marketers can tailor individual responses to meet consumers' needs.
    c. Use of direct marketing is not expected to lead directly to orders, sales leads, store traffic, or increased sales.
    d. Direct marketing now accounts for over half of total U.S. advertising expenditures – over $2.85 trillion per year.
    e. Direct marketing suffers from a rate of growth slower than that of most other promotional alternatives.

42. The two major techniques for setting Internet advertising rates are
    a. number of hits per day and recall measurements of how much members of the target remember of their use of the site.
    b. number of visits to the site and readership of site content.
    c. cost per impression and cost-per-response (click-throughs).
    d. indirect measurement of scanner data.
    e. store audits and customer counts.

43. The method of allocating a promotional budget based on a sound evaluation of the firm's promotional objectives is the
    a. percentage of sales method.
    b. fixed-sum-per-unit method
    c. the task-objective method.
    d. method of meeting competition.
    e. method of allocating a fixed sum for advertising: when it's gone, it's gone.

44. The most common way of establishing promotional budgets is most likely the
    a. marginal analysis method advocated by Alfred Marshall.
    b. percentage-of-sales method whether past-period or future-period based.
    c. fixed amount available method used by the federal government.
    d. fixed-sum-per-unit method advocated by auto manufacturers.
    e. method described by Alois Svoboda in *Alligators and Advertising*.

45. Effective use of marginal analysis for promotional budgeting requires
    a. carefully hoarding money from one year to the next until it can be most effectively spent.
    b. having available a very large sum of uncommitted funds to support the promotional program.
    c. understanding the necessity for a concentration of funds on advertising and the lesser importance of personal selling.
    d. retarding the promotional expenditure flow until results are apparent.
    e. identifying the optimal point, which requires a precise balance between marginal expenses for promotion and resulting marginal receipts.

46. Personal selling is usually considered to work better than advertising under which set of conditions?
    a. when the target market is made up of industrial purchasers or retail or wholesale intermediaries
    b. when the product is being promoted to the ultimate consumer and is an over-the-counter drug
    c. when the market is composed of a large number of small-volume buyers scattered over a large geographic area
    d. when the product is a highly standardized, non-technical item available almost everywhere
    e. when the product is of low unit value

47. Given the capacity to control for other variables operating in the marketplace, most marketers would prefer to measure promotional effectiveness using
    a. standard statistical tools such as mean difference testing.
    b. sales inquiries and studies of customer attitude change caused by promotion.
    c. indirect evaluation of effectiveness using such devices as recall and readership analysis.
    d. direct-sales-results tests which would reveal the impact on sales of every dollar spent on promotion.
    e. traditional methods based on the expertise of company executives.

48. Promotion has assumed a degree of economic importance if for no other reason than that
    a. government decisions eventually determine what is acceptable practice in the marketplace.
    b. most modern business institutions cannot survive in the long run without promotion.
    c. business enterprises recognize the importance of promotional efforts.
    d. many television commercials contribute to cultural pollution.
    e. it provides employment for millions of people.

49. Comments such as "Advertising is almost always in bad taste" or "They shouldn't be allowed to advertise that – it's not good for you" relate to
    a. the importance of advertising to the economic well-being of the country.
    b. advertising's role in perpetuating undesirable stereotypes.
    c. advertising's importance as a business phenomenon.
    d. relationships we've all noticed between advertising and mental capacity.
    e. perceptions of advertising relating to its social importance and freedom of customer choice.

50. Promotion can be said to have business importance because
    a. most modern institutions simply cannot survive in the log run without promotion.
    b. it reduces sales volume, thus increasing per-unit cost.
    c. it subsidizes the communications media.
    d. it performs all of the functions outlined above.
    e. None of the above constitutes a valid reason to call promotion "important."

Name_____   Instructor_____

Section_____   Date_____

Applying Marketing Concepts

It's always a little rough to report for work at a new place for the first time, and Malcolm Carmichael admitted to himself that he felt uneasy about his new job at Heindorf Chemie, one of Schwabisch-Gmund's best known makers of essential chemicals. Replacing a promotions manager who had been there for twenty-five years was not an enviable task. Malcolm was especially sensitive because, though his German was near-perfect because of his many years of residence in that country, he was still of Scots birth and ancestry and looked it, with the red hair and freckles associated by many with Scots. But, taking the bull by the horns, so to speak, Malcolm soon got acclimated and settled down to a long, close look at the company's promotional program.

Some things were pretty much as he expected them to be. As an industrial supplier, largely to the pharmaceuticals industry, Heindorf followed fairly conventional advertising and personal selling practices. John was disturbed, however, when he discovered that there was no mechanism by which the comments and actions of customers were reported back to his department. He also observed that many of the company's promotional pieces--advertisements, catalogs, and mailers--were badly written and hard to understand – especially those directed to foreign customers. He also noticed that a large number of items which had been mailed to customers and prospective customers were returned by the post office as undeliverable.

Malcolm felt he had cause to worry about the company's relationship with the local community. Fences surrounding the Heindorf plant bore signs saying "No Trespassing--Keep Out" and the main gate, which was guarded by armed security personnel, was even more intimidating with its "Stop--Show Identification--Authorized Personnel Only" sign. Such isolation seemed a bit much to John, as did the fact that Heindorf had no athletic teams playing in the local junior or adult football (soccer) leagues in a city where the game was only slightly less important than politics.

1. Heindorf's promotional program, given their nature as a manufacturer, probably
    a. puts more emphasis on personal selling than on advertising.
    b. puts more emphasis on advertising than on personal selling.
    c. emphasizes personal selling and advertising about equally.
    d. uses neither personal selling nor advertising.
    e. relies on publicity to carry the burden of promotion.

2. Malcolm's concern about the lack of a way for him to get to know customers' comments and actions indicates he was distressed
    a. with the effectiveness of his sales promotion program.
    b. with the degree to which his advertising money was being wasted on fancy artwork by the layout department.
    c. that feedback from the marketplace was not being used to make adjustments to the company's programs and practices.
    d. that his position in the company was isolated from the decision makers at headquarters.
    e. that salesmen weren't doing their jobs in the field properly.

3. The large number of returns of mailed material, if they are not the post office's fault, probably result from
   a. uncorrected errors in the database from which the mailings are compiled.
   b. refusals by recipients because they don't like Heindorf.
   c. a problem with noise in the communications process.
   d. difficulties with decoding by recipients of the mailings.
   e. interference with the mail by the vampires who are rampant in Schwabisch-Gmund.

4. Difficulty in understanding an advertising message, a catalog entry, or the vocabulary of a mailer means
   a. that Heindorf Chemie must be on the verge of failure.
   b. very little; these sorts of things are used merely to get the customer's attention.
   c. that someone in the production department probably wrote the catalogs.
   d. there is danger that noise will be created in the communications channel that will defeat the intent of the communication.
   e. that someone has probably been trying to do two jobs at once: write advertising and learn to read.

5. Heindorf Chemie's seeming isolation from the local community is probably evidence
   a. of good legal thinking; the company doesn't want to have to worry about paying for injuries to unauthorized persons on its grounds. It's better to shoot them for trespassing before they can hurt themselves.
   b. of the fact that they've got something evil to hide at their plant location.
   c. that the president of the company really did say "Bah, humbug!" last Christmas when approached by the local Church Fund.
   d. of the low level of competitiveness in the chemical market these days.
   e. of a serious weakness in their public relations program.

High Density Memory Modules Company [HDM(2)C], a manufacturer of memory sticks for computers (also known as "flashdrives" or "jumpdrives"), sells 256 megabyte USB compatible sticks to wholesalers in units of twelve to a case, which is the standard unit for sales and cost analysis purposes. Alexcis te Kanewha, the promotions manager for HDM(2)C, is concerned that intermediaries are not making a strong effort to tell ultimate users about the benefits of memory sticks. She is considering mounting a promotion campaign aimed directly at her ultimate target market rather than promoting to the intermediaries and leaving promotion to ultimate users primarily in their hands, as is presently the case.

Alexcis is also concerned about how money for promotional activities is budgeted. At present, she is allotted $50 per case of disks shipped to use for promotional purposes. Corporate goals are to increase HDM(2)C's market share from the present 8 percent to 15 percent in three years. Alexcis doesn't see how she can do that with the money that's been budgeted.

6. Alexcis' concern with the efforts of the intermediaries reflects her doubt about the effectiveness of the present
   a. waffling strategy being used by HDM(2)C.
   b. pushing strategy used by the company.
   c. running strategy in place.
   d. "smoking gun" approach to promotion.
   e. pulling strategy favored by management.

7. Conversion to a promotion strategy that called for HDM(2)C to promote directly to ultimate users would result in a
   a. timing approach to promotion.
   b. strong pushing effect by intermediaries.
   c. great deal of confusion about where to buy HDM(2)C memory sticks.
   d. pulling strategy for the HDM(2)C memory sticks.
   e. lawsuit by competitors; you can't do it that way

8. Which of the following promotional budgeting techniques is HDM(2)C using now?
   a. percentage of sales
   b. task-objective method
   c. fixed sum per unit
   d. meeting competition
   e. spend what you have

9. If ten percent of total sales had been the promotional allocating rule, the method would have then been
   a. percentage of sales.
   b. fixed sum per unit.
   c. meeting competition.
   d. task-objective method.
   e. marginal analysis method.

10. If Alexcis can convince management that she needs to spend $15 million over the next three years to achieve the desired market share, regardless of how many units are shipped during the period, she will have converted them to which of the following budgeting approaches?
    a. meeting competition
    b. arbitrary allocation
    c. task-objective method
    d. marginal revenue approach
    e. perfect world method.

Name_____ Instructor_____

Section_____ Date_____

Surfing the Net

Keeping in mind that addresses change and what's on the Web now may have changed by the time you read this, let's take a look at some of the places on the Net that reflect aspects of integrated promotion. We are not endorsing or recommending any of these sources, merely making note of the information and services that people have elected to offer through the Internet.

Looking to sell your home? There are several sites that feature *Sale by Owner* areas, places that list and describe homes offered by their owners. Two of these advertising vehicles may be found at: **http://www.AbetterFSBO.com** and **http://www.virtualfsbo.com**

Direct Marketing On-Line? Try the *Online Shopping Mall* at **http://www.onlineshopping.net** or *Downtown Anywhere*, "conveniently located in central cyberspace" at **http://awa.com**. Alternatives include **http://www.shopping.msn.com** on Microsoft Network. These sites feature retail merchandise.

If you're concerned about the security of your use of the Internet for shopping, see the American Bar Association's site, **http://www.safeshopping.com,** that discusses how to be a safe shopper on the net.

Need a bear? Teddy, that is. The Vermont Teddy Bear Company at **http://www.vtbear.com** manufactures Teddy Bears and sells on the Net. Even this small firm has found the Internet a vehicle for its message.

Need photographs for your ads, brochures, and other promotional materials? The National Press Photographers' Association at **http://metalab.unc.edu/nppa,** can put you in touch with a photographer or a photo library that should be able to help you out.

How about some people to do the work? Well, we've got public relations firms at **http://www.prfirms.org,** their trade organization Web site, and advertising agencies (for the UK, anyway) at **http://www.adassoc.org.uk.** I was somewhat surprised not to find a Web site for the American Association of Advertising Agencies, but I could have missed it. I did find a site that lists the members of the American Advertising Federation that themselves are listed on the Internet. It's at **http://www.siu.edu/~aaf/agency.html**.

Sites verified February 2, 2003

Chapter 16
Advertising and Public Relations

Chapter Outline

You may wish to use the outline that follows as a guide in taking notes.

I. Chapter Overview

The Nonpersonal Elements of Promotion include advertising and public relations. Advertising is the most visible form of nonpersonal promotion, and marketers often use it and sales promotion together to create effective promotional campaigns. This chapter discusses advertising and then considers alternative advertising strategies and the process of creating an advertisement. Advertising media channels are examined. Public relations, publicity, and cross promotion in e-commerce are dealt with. Alternative methods of measuring the effectiveness of online and offline nonpersonal selling are examined. Finally, there is a discussion of current ethical issues related to nonpersonal selling.

II. Advertising involves paid nonpersonal communication through various media with the purpose of informing or persuading members of a particular audience. Most of the world's leading advertisers are domiciled in the United States. In an industry on which over $200 billion is spent annually, spending varies among industries as well as companies. The emergence of the marketing concept and implementation of integrated marketing communications expanded the role of advertising.

A. Types of advertising include <u>product advertising</u>, nonpersonal selling of a good or service, and <u>institutional advertising</u>, promotion of a concept, an idea, a philosophy, or the goodwill of an industry, company, organization, person, geographical location, or government agency. Institutional advertising is often closely linked to the public relations function of the enterprise.

B. Objectives of advertising are to inform, to persuade, and to remind, either one of these at a time or in combination.
   1. Informative advertising attempts to increase initial demand for a good, service, organization, person, place, idea, or cause. It works best during the early stages of the product life cycle.
   2. Persuasive advertising attempts to increase demand for an existing good, service, organization, person, place, idea, or cause. It is best used during the later stages of the product life cycle.
   3. Reminder advertising strives to reinforce previous promotional activity by keeping the name of – you guessed it – a good, service, organization, person, place, idea, or cause before the public. If well handled, this type of advertising is effective during the entire product life cycle.
   4. Advertising is presently viewed as a way to achieve communications objectives as outlined directly above, ultimately resulting in favorable viewpoints toward a promotional message.

III. Advertising Strategies are designed to inform, persuade, or remind consumers by developing a message that best positions the firm's product in the audience's mind.

A. Comparative advertising is a promotional strategy that emphasizes advertising messages with direct or indirect comparisons with dominant brands in the industry. Leaders in the industry generally do not use such tactics. Comparative advertising has become the norm only in recently because regulators who once discouraged it now view it as pro-competitive.

B. Celebrity testimonials are a popular technique for increasing advertising readership in a cluttered market. Both the number of celebrity ads and the money spent for them have increased in recent years.
1. Association with big-name personalities improves product recognition in a promotional environment filled with hundreds of competing commercials.
2. Another advantage to using celebrities is that they have significant impact on consumers of other cultures.
3. Celebrity testimonials generally have the greatest impact when the celebrity is a credible source of information about the product being promoted. A celebrity who endorses too many products may create confusion in the marketplace, as do those whose personal problems become issues in the press.
4. To avoid problems brought on by the variable behavior of humans, some advertisers use cartoon characters as endorsers. For many firms, celebrity endorsers are now considered marketing partners rather than just pretty or famous faces that sell goods and services.

C. Retail advertising is all advertising by retail stores that sell goods or services directly to the consuming public. Many retailers think of advertising as a secondary activity, though that attitude is changing. Retailers often share the cost of advertising with a manufacturer in the technique called "cooperative advertising."

D. Interactive advertising involves two-way promotional messages transmitted through communications channels that induce message recipients to participate actively in the promotional effort. Such advertising changes the balance between marketers and consumers, adding value to the interaction by offering the viewer more than just product-related information. Most firms deliver their interactive advertising messages through proprietary online services and through the Web.

IV. Creating an Advertisement begins with research to pinpoint goals the ad needs to accomplish, guiding the design of the ad. About $300 billion per year is spent on advertising campaigns in the U.S. alone. Because they are expensive to create, ads must be effective and memorable or money will have been wasted. Marketers sometimes face special challenges when they develop advertising objectives for services.

A. Translating advertising objectives into advertising plans requires first that the firm define the objectives for its advertising campaign. Marketing research helps guide choices in areas such as budgeting, copy writing, scheduling, and media selection. Positioning involves developing a marketing strategy that achieves a desired position in a prospective buyer's mind.

B. Advertising messages must carry an appropriate communication to consumers using both visual and verbal components. Meaningful, believable, and distinctive appeals are necessary to stand out from the clutter. Ads are not created individually but as part of specific campaigns. Advertisers must decide how to communicate their marketing message – should, for example, the focus be on an appeal such as price or should it evoke an emotional response of fear, humor, or fantasy.

1. Fear appeals have become more common in recent years than was the case before. Such appeals are appropriate for products used to avert negative outcomes, such as insurance. But fear appeals can backfire, with people tuning them out.
2. Humorous ads seek to create a positive mood related to a product. Humor may improve audience awareness and enhance the consumer's favorable image of a product. Not everyone, however, has the same sense of humor.
3. Ads using sex appeal as a basis attract attention, but work at building product recall only when the appeal is consistent with the product being advertised

C. Developing and preparing ads should flow logically from the promotional theme selected. Ads should be designed to (1) gain attention and interest, (2) inform and/or persuade, and (3) eventually lead to a purchase or other desired action.
1. Gaining attention and generating interest – cutting through clutter – can be a formidable task.
2. Print advertisements have four major elements: the headline, illustration, body copy, and signature. These should work together to generate the desired interest and attention.
3. The steps in producing an ad include developing the idea that it is desired to communicate; then a rough layout is produced; this is then refined until the final version of the advertisement is produced. It is an evolutionary process.
4. Advances in technology allow advertisers to create novel, eye-catching advertisements, often using computer software.

D. Creating interactive ads should recognize that the Internet's major advantages are its ability to act speedily, provide information, exchange input through two-way communication, provide self-directed information, and allow personal choice. The many new ways to advertise on the Internet testify to the rapidly changing environment on the Web and in e-commerce in general.
1. Banners, advertisements on a Web page that link to an advertiser's site, are the most common type of advertising on the net. Banners have evolved into missiles, target-specific messages that appear on the computer screen at just the right moment. Keyword ads are an outcropping of banner ads, appearing in search engines on the results page of a search, specific to the term being searched.
2. Advertorials are banner ads that have evolved so that they are similar to the ads in the telephone Yellow Pages. Some of these have been developed into "interstitials," ads appearing between Web pages of related content.
3. There are several other types of ads found on the Internet, most related to the pop-up.

V. Media Selection requires choosing appropriate media to carry a firm's message to its audience. Research is used to identify the ad's target market to determine its size and characteristics. Advertisers match the target market characteristics with appropriate media and determine which selection of media is most cost-effective. Each medium has its advantages and disadvantages.

A. Television, including both network and cable, accounts for almost one in four advertising dollars spent in the U.S. In the past ten years, cable television's share of ad spending and revenues has grown tremendously. As cable audiences grow, programming improves, and ratings rise, advertisers will be compelled to commit more of their advertising dollars to this medium. Television advertising has powerful impact, mass coverage, repetition of messages, flexibility, and prestige. It should be noted, however, that some types of products are banned from television advertising and it is expensive, temporary, and lacks selectivity.

B. Radio has always been a popular medium for news reporting and targeting advertising to local audiences, but in recent years has shown accelerated growth as a source of immediate information and entertainment. Radio ad revenues in the U.S. are slightly greater than those for cable television. Radio is noted as a medium of enormous variety. It is also cheap, flexible, and mobile. Most radio listening is done at home, in cars, or with headset-equipped portables, but technology has given birth to radio on the Net.

C. Newspapers continue to dominate local markets, accounting for $44 billion of annual advertising expenditures. Newspapers are a flexible medium because advertising can vary from one location to another. It is a prestige medium because people recognize newspapers' deep impact on the community. Newspaper ad coverage can be intense. According to the Newspaper Association of America, consumers rely on newspapers as their source of advertising information for a variety of goods and services. The disadvantages of newspaper advertising include short life span, hasty reading, and relatively poor reproduction quality.

D. Magazines fall into two broad categories: consumer magazines and business magazines. Magazines may also be classed according to whether they are published monthly or weekly.
    1. The primary advantages of magazine advertising are that they are selective in reaching precise target markets, reproduction quality is high, they have long life, some are quite prestigious, and many offer an array of special services.
    2. Media buyers look at circulation numbers and demographics to choose placement opportunities and negotiate rates.

E. Direct mail offers the advantages of selectivity, intensive coverage, formal flexibility, completeness of information, and personalization. Its disadvantages are high cost per reader, dependence on the quality of mailing lists, and some consumers' resistance to it. Direct mail is so widely used because of its advantages. The downside of direct mail is clutter – better known as junk mail.

F. Outdoor advertising represents only two percent of total advertising spending, and traditionally consists of billboards, painted bulletins or displays, electric spectaculars, and the occasional animated sign or display. Newer varieties include stenciled messages on the backs of park benches (a guerilla tactic), cleanup of a section of highway with a sign noting who the good Samaritan was, for the brave of heart and desperate of pocket book, advertising tattoos on their bodies, and similar devices.
    1. The advantages of outdoor advertising include immediate communication of simple ideas, repeated exposure to a message, and strong promotion for locally available products. It is particularly effective in heavily-traveled areas.
    2. The drawbacks of outdoor relate, first, to clutter. It is also subject from brevity of exposure and distraction on the part of motorists who have other things on their minds. In addition, the public is concerned over aesthetics and there are those who consider outdoor advertising unattractive.

3. New technologies are reviving outdoor advertising. Animation, sculpture, laser images, digital displays, and even TV-like picture stories are enlivening the medium.

G. Interactive media are growing up. Consumers like to find out about new products online, and almost half think online advertising is rich in information and helps them decide what products to buy. As a result, budgets for interactive advertising are growing.

H. Other advertising media include a wealth of alternative and lesser-known media. Transit advertising includes ads interior to and on the exterior of buses, subway and commuter trains, and terminals and stations. Ads also appear on taxicabs, bus stop shelters and benches, and entertainment and sporting event turnstiles, in public restrooms, and on parking meters. Advertising in motion picture theaters is becoming quite common. In addition, ads appear on T-shirts, inlaid in store flooring, and in numerous other venues.

VI. Media Scheduling is the setting of the timing and sequence of a series of advertisements. Sales patterns, repurchase cycles, and competitors' activities are the most important factors affecting this activity. Advertisers use the concepts of reach, frequency, and gross rating points to measure the effectiveness of media scheduling plans. Reach is the number of different people or households exposed to an ad at least once during a specified time period, usually four weeks. Frequency is the number of times an individual person is exposed to an advertisement during a specified time period, also usually four weeks. Multiplying reach by frequency yields the total "weight" of the media effort, the campaign's gross rating points. Marketers have begun to question the effectiveness of reach and frequency to measure ad success online. The actual media schedule specifies which ads will be run how often and where across the whole spectrum of the chosen media choices they will appear.

VII. Organization of the Advertising Function differs from one organization to another. Advertising is usually organized as a staff department reporting to the vice president or director of marketing. The advertising director is an executive position with responsibility for the functional activity of advertising. His or her major responsibilities include supervision of advertising research, design, copy writing, media analysis, and sometimes sales and trade promotions.

A. Advertising agencies are firms whose marketing specialists assist advertisers to plan and prepare advertisements. The major functions of advertising agencies may be classified as creative services; account services; marketing services, which include media services, marketing research, and sales promotion; and finance and management

VIII. Public Relations has been defined as the firm's communications and relationships with its various publics – customers,   employees, stockholder, suppliers, government agencies, and society. It is an efficient, indirect communications channel through which a firm can promote products although its objectives are usually broader than those of the other components of promotional strategy. About 160,000 people work in public relations in the U.S. The industry is in a period of major growth because of the increasing importance of ethical conduct and environmental and international issues. The public relations department links the firm and the media. A PR plan is developed in much the same way as is an advertising plan, and the presence of the Internet has had an effect on how such planning is accomplished.

A. Marketing and nonmarketing public relations address two different audiences in two different ways. Nonmarketing public relations refers to a company's messages about general management issues, and is directed more or less at any or all of the firm's publics. Marketing public relations, on the other hand, refers to narrowly focused public relations activities that directly support marketing goals. Marketing public relations may be proactive, in which case the marketer actively seeks out opportunities to promote the firm's products, or reactive, in which the marketer responds to external threats to the firm's image or well-being.

B. Publicity, which is nonpersonal stimulation of demand for a good, service, place, idea, person, or organization by unpaid placement of significant news about the product in a print or broadcast medium, is the aspect of public relations most closely related to promoting a firm's products. It is low in cost, but not free. Firms often pursue publicity to promote their images or viewpoints, or to make organizational activities known. Publicity has, in the minds of some, the advantage of not appearing to be an advertisement, hence being more credible.

IX. Cross Promotion occurs when marketing partners share the expense of a promotional campaign that meets their mutual needs. The entertainment industry is one of the most prominent users of cross promotion, often with movie studios partnering with fast-food chains.

X. Measuring Promotional Effectiveness is important because advertising is typically sold on the basis of the cost to deliver the message to viewers. This is usually expressed as "cost-per-thousand," and by this measure billboards are cheapest with television and some newspapers the most expensive. Firms need to determine whether their campaigns accomplish appropriate promotional objectives. By measuring promotional effectiveness, organizations can evaluate different strategies, prevent mistakes before spending money on specific programs, and improve their overall promotional program.

A. Measuring advertising effectiveness is a difficult and costly process, but essential to the success of any marketing plan. Media research assesses how well a particular medium delivers the advertiser's message, where and when to place the advertisement, and the size of the audience. Message research tests consumer reactions to an advertisement's creative message.

   1. Pretesting employs a variety of evaluation methods to assess an advertisement's likely effectiveness before it actually appears in the chosen medium. One advertising agency doctors magazines, inserting prerelease copies of ads in current magazines and measuring the impact of those ads on people who receive free copies of the doctored magazines. Another uses a sales conviction test to evaluate magazine ads, asking consumers which of two ads would be more likely to convince them to buy the advertised item. People are exposed to TV and radio ads and asked to react positively or negatively to them in another test, and in some cases they are offered a free product if they return a card using proposed ad copy by mail. The greater the number of returned cards, the better it is concluded the ad copy is. Blind product tests ask readers to select unidentified products based on proposed ad copy. Finally, mechanical devices are sometimes used to measure eye movement or changes in skin resistance of people exposed to test ads.

2. Posttesting assesses advertising copy after it has appeared in the selected medium. Readership tests are used to determine if people remember reading ads they are known to have seen in magazines. The magazines are used as interviewing aids. Unaided recall tests are similar to readership tests except the respondents do not see copies of the magazine after the initial reading. Inquiry tests offer gifts to people who respond to them, using the cost per request as a measure of ad effectiveness. Finally, split runs allow the advertiser to insert different versions of the same ad in the same vehicle – newspaper, magazine, even TV program on cable – to determine the effectiveness of ads using inquiries or recall and recognition tests.

B. Measuring sales promotion effectiveness is relatively easy because sales promotions often result in direct consumer responses. The effectiveness of sampling in the consumer market, for example, has been measured. It is also true that trade promotions such as allowances, contest, and dealer incentives, for example, give easily measurable results such as sales increases or heavier store traffic. The results of trade shows and training programs, on the other hand, are not so easily determined.

C. Measuring public relations effectiveness must be undertaken in the context of the objectives of the PR program as a whole and for specific activities. The simplest and least costly level of assessment consists of measuring the outputs of the PR program. To analyze PR effectiveness more deeply a firm can conduct focus groups, interview opinion leaders, or conduct detailed opinion polls.

D. Evaluating interactive media involves the use of several methods. Hits (user requests for a file) and clickthroughs (when a user clicks on an ad to get more information) are among the more common. Ad banners are sold on a cost-per-thousand basis. There is not yet a standard measurement system for interactive media, but a number of firms offer Web tracking and counting systems and two firms that audit audience reports for the medium are currently in operation.

XI. Ethics in Nonpersonal Selling can best be examined by viewing the status of the three most significant functions of this aspect of promotion – advertising, sales promotion, and public relations.

A. Advertising ethics must first recognize that advertising is permitted by law, but not necessarily encouraged. A number of areas of advertising are under scrutiny by concerned individuals and government entities. Among these is advertising aimed at children, which is often confected to resemble entertainment rather than advertising. Liquor advertising, especially on television, is another area under scrutiny. Finally, cyberspace advertising presents the problem of the difficulty of determining what is advertising and what editorial matter. A second problem related to the same area is the issue of *cookies*, small text files sent to one's computer every time a Web site is accessed. Are they invasions of privacy?

1. Puffery and deception differ slightly. Puffery is exaggeration about a product's superiority or the use of subjective or vague statements that may not be literally true. Exaggeration is not new, nor is it unexpected in advertising. The issue is, when does it become an implied guarantee? The Uniform Commercial Code allows puffery but frowns upon outright deception, so this question is quite significant, and the answer to it remains unclear.

B. Ethics in public relations may also raise issues. Can it be ethical to represent a tobacco company or to defend an unsafe product? Is response to negative publicity ethical if the publicity is true? The PR Society's Code of Professional Standards in general prohibits such actions.

Name_____ Instructor_____

Section_____ Date_____

Key Concepts

The purpose of this section is to allow you to determine if you can match key concepts with their definitions. It is essential that you know the definitions of the concepts before applying the concepts in later exercises in this chapter.

From the list of lettered terms, select the one that best fits in the blank of the numbered statement below. Write the letter of that choice in the space provided.

Key Terms

a. advertising
b. product advertising
c. institutional advertising
d. informative advertising
e. persuasive advertising
f. reminder advertising

g. comparative advertising
h. cooperative advertising
i. advertising campaign
j. advertising agency
k. publicity
l. cross promotion

_____ 1. Nonpersonal selling effort that makes direct or indirect promotional comparisons with competing brands.

_____ 2. Nonpersonal selling of a particular good or service.

_____ 3. Promotion seeking to reinforce previous promotional activity by keeping the name of the good, service, organization, person, place, idea, or cause in front of the public.

_____ 4. Promotion that attempts to increase demand for an existing good, service, organization, person, place, idea, or cause.

_____ 5. Promoting a concept, an idea, a philosophy, or the goodwill of an industry, company, organization, place, person, or government agency.

_____ 6. Paid, nonpersonal communication through various media with the purpose of informing or persuading members of a particular audience.

_____ 7. Sharing of advertising costs between the manufacturer and the retailer of a good or service.

_____ 8. Marketing specialist firm that assists advertisers in planning and implementing advertising programs.

_____ 9. Promotion that seeks to develop initial demand for a good, service, organization, person, place, idea, or cause.

_____ 10. Stimulation of demand for a good, service, place, idea, person, or organization by disseminating commercially significant news or obtaining favorable media presentation not paid for by the sponsor.

_____ 11. Series of different but related ads that use a single theme and appear in different media within a specified time period.

_____ 12. Promotional technique in which marketing partners share the cost of a promotional campaign that meets their mutual needs.

Name_____ Instructor_____

Section_____ Date_____

Self Quiz

You should use these questions to test your understanding of the chapter material. You can check your answers with those provided at the end of the chapter.

While these questions cover most of the chapter topics, they are not intended to be the same as the test questions your instructor may use in an examination. A good understanding of all aspects of the course material is essential to good performance on any examination.

True/False

Write "T" for True and "F" for False for each of the following statements.

_____ 1. The term institutional advertising is broader in meaning than the term corporate advertising, though they both refer to nonproduct promotion.

_____ 2. General Motors, Time Warner, Procter and Gamble, Pfizer, and Ford Motor Company, all headquartered in the United States, are five of the top advertisers in the world.

_____ 3. One would expect to find persuasive advertising being used in the introductory stage of the product life cycle.

_____ 4. Ultimately, the three primary objectives of advertising are to inform, to persuade, and to remind their target – either individually or in conjunction with each other – of something.

_____ 5. Web advertisements that appear in a separate browser window while the Web user waits for a Web page to download are called *intermedials*.

_____ 6. The secret to success in choosing the best advertising strategy is to develop a message that best positions a firm's product in the audience's mind.

_____ 7. Interactive media differ from traditional advertising by providing brief, entertaining, attention-getting messages rather than helping the consumer through the purchase and consumption processes.

_____ 8. Institutional advertising is the type of promotion that comes to the average person's mind when advertising is the topic of conversation.

_____ 9. Cartoon characters delivering celebrity testimonials are seldom used by advertisers because they lack credibility – after all, who's really going to believe a cartoon character uses a product.

_____ 10. Corporate advertising is another name for institutional advertising sponsored by a specific firm.

_____ 11. The objective of media selection is to obtain adequate media coverage without advertising beyond the identifiable limits of the potential market.

_____ 12. Most newspaper advertising revenues come from national advertisers, while television derives the bulk of its revenues from local sources.

_____ 13. In the past decade, cable television's share of advertising revenues has grown tremendously, while the traditional networks – NBC, CBS, ABC, Fox , and Warner Bros. – have had to refocus their advertising strategies due to declining ratings and soaring costs.

_____ 14. Among the disadvantages of television advertising are its lack of impact, inflexibility, and low prestige rating.

_____ 15. Radio – thanks to the Internet – now allows customers to widen their listening times, distances, and choices through their computers.

_____ 16. Magazines are divided into three basic categories – consumer, farm, and business publications.

_____ 17. Outdoor advertising as a promotional medium is particularly effective along rural highways and in other low-traffic areas.

_____ 18. Interactive media like the Internet is growing rapidly, with a growing number of firms budgeting increasing amounts to support their use of it.

_____ 19. Advertising agencies are often used by large advertisers because, among other reasons, they employ highly qualified specialists who provide a degree of creativity and objectivity that is difficult to sustain in a corporate advertising department.

_____ 20. Pretesting is generally more desirable that posttesting of advertising because of the potential cost savings – avoiding placing ineffective ads.

_____ 21. A firm's use of "puffery" creates a warranty of the truth of the claims being made on the part of the advertiser which is enforceable in state and federal courts.

_____ 22. In a given company, the public relations department is the linkage between the firm and its suppliers.

_____ 23. Nonmarketing public relations refers to narrowly focused activities that directly support marketing goals.

_____ 24. Public relations is an efficient indirect communications channel for promoting products, although its objectives are broader than those of other components of promotional strategy.

_____ 25. Relationship marketing programs like co-branding and co-marketing are forms of cross promotion.

Multiple Choice

Circle the letter of the word or phrase that best completes the sentence or best answers the question.

26. An advertisement which emphasizes the superiority of one product over another – and names the products – is a(n)
    a. reminder advertisement.
    b. comparative advertisement.
    c. institutional advertisement.
    d. creative advertisement.
    e. illegal advertisement.

27. About one in five (20 percent) of U.S. ads and 80 percent of Japanese ads include
    a. celebrities.
    b. price comparisons.
    c. puffery.
    d. appeals to patriotism.
    e. musical references.

28. The dominant advertising medium in the United States, in terms of dollars spent on its use, is
    a. television, taking network and cable television together.
    b. radio, because of the tremendous flexibility it offers.
    c. the newspaper, though cable television has come to rival this choice.
    d. magazines, because everybody reads them.
    e. direct mail because no one has time to shop any more.

29. Advertising the purpose of which is to develop initial demand for a good, service, organization, person, place, idea, or cause is called
    a. product advertising.
    b. persuasive advertising.
    c. informative advertising.
    d. reminder advertising.
    e. comparative advertising.

30. Advertising that strives to reinforce previous promotional activity by keeping the name of the advertised thing or concept before the public is called
    a. selective advertising.
    b. reminder advertising.
    c. informative advertising.
    d. selective advertising.
    e. persuasive information.

31. If an advertisement by the National Fisheries Council were to appear that featured that idea that it is a good thing to eat lots and lots of any kind of fish B because fish is a good source of vitamins and minerals not found elsewhere – we could categorize that ad as
    a. product advertising.
    b. persuasive advertising.
    c. reminder advertising.
    d. political advertising.
    e. institutional advertising.

32. Radio advertising has become "the fastest growing media alternative" in recent years because
    a. of its quality reproduction, long life, ease of carriage, and prestige.
    b. it possesses formal flexibility, completeness of information, and personalization.
    c. it is quite popular in rural areas where other media are not available.
    d. as more and more people find they have less time, it provides immediate information and entertainment almost anywhere – including anywhere the Internet is available.
    e. it has powerful multisensory impact, mass coverage, flexibility, and repetition of message.

33. Which advertising medium offers the advantages of selectivity, intensive coverage, speed, completeness of information, and personalization, among others?
    a. radio
    b. television
    c. newspapers
    d. magazines
    e. direct mail

34. Some of the disadvantages of using the newspaper medium as an advertising vehicle are
    a. lack of flexibility found in other media, long lead time between ad placement and appearance.
    b. short life span, relatively poor reproduction quality, and haste in reading.
    c. high cost, loss of control of the promotional message, and public distrust of the medium.
    d. consumer resistance to the medium and high per-person acquisition cost.
    e. the necessity for an extremely brief message and lack of aesthetics in the eyes of the public.

35. Interactive media
    a. enhances two-way communication but discourages audience participation.
    b. supplements messages delivered traditionally, causing confusion among its viewers.
    c. offers two-way communication, flexibility, and is a link to self-directed entertainment.
    d. suffers from a low-level of consumer involvement, with e-mail responses around one percent.
    e. is too expensive right now to be considered a viable medium.

36. Outdoor advertising is particularly effective
    a. in rural locations where the message can be seen at a great distance.
    b. along lightly traveled streets so that people can pay more attention to the advertising and less to driving.
    c. when fairly large blocks of print are used to communicate the desired information.
    d. when placed along metropolitan streets and in other high-traffic areas.
    e. when placed so that foot traffic is forced to detour around the billboards to get where it's going.

37. Within most businesses, the advertising function is usually set up as
    a. a staff department reporting to the vice-president or director of marketing.
    b. a line department reporting directly to the chief executive officer of the company.
    c. a home-office department housed in the engineering division.
    d. a staff department with responsibility directly to the president of the firm.
    e. a functional division of the company with its own vice-president and an equal voice in company policymaking with all other divisions.

38. The world's largest advertising agency in terms of worldwide gross income
    a. is the Japanese agency Dentsu.
    b. has become Moscow-based NovoRuss Information.
    c. is the London-based WPP Group.
    d. is New York's McCann-Erickson Worldwide.
    e. is Madrid-based Publicidad Generale de Espana.

39. The final step in the advertising process is
    a. choice of a medium to carry the message.
    b. definition of a target market to which to appeal.
    c. retention of an advertising agency to develop the program.
    d. development and production of an actual advertisement.
    e. measurement of the effect of the advertisement.

40. When the marketer takes the initiative and seeks out opportunities to promote the firm's product using public relations techniques, that marketer is most likely using
    a. nonmarketing public relations.
    b. publicity generation.
    c. reactive marketing public relations.
    d. proactive marketing public relations.
    e. guerilla public relations.

41. The form of nonpersonal promotion that generates minimal costs compared with other forms of nonpersonal promotion is
    a. newspaper advertising.
    b. short-wave radio advertising
    c. publicity.
    d. live advertising.
    e. cross promotion.

42. The number of times an individual is exposed to an advertisement during a certain time period, usually of four weeks, is called
    a. reach.
    b. frequency.
    c. gross rating points.
    d. net rating points.
    e. advertising effectiveness.

43. Which of the following is an advantage of newspaper advertising?
    a. It has a short life span.
    b. It is read rapidly by most readers.
    c. Reproduction quality is improving.
    d. It is faced with clutter.
    e. It can vary from one locality to the next.

44. A company's communication with its various publics about general management issues are
    a. public relations activities that support marketing goals.
    b. reactive MPR.
    c. proactive MPR.
    d. nonmarketing public relations.
    e. publicity.

45. When a manufacturer shares the cost of a retailer's advertising its products, it is practicing
    a. demonstrative advertising.
    b. comparative advertising.
    c. retailer-sponsored advertising.
    d. testimonial advertising.
    e. cooperative advertising.

46. When interviewers from McCann-Erickson ask heavy users of a product which of two alternative advertisements would convince them to purchase it, they are conducting a
    a. sales conviction test.
    b. blind product test.
    c. dummy ad test.
    d. recognition pretest.
    e. aided recall test.

47. The post-test of advertising effectiveness in which interviewers ask people who have read selected magazines whether they observed various ads in them, using the magazines as interviewing aids, is
    a. Burke's *Day-After Interview System*.
    b. the Gallup and Robinson *Unaided Recall Test*.
    c. the *Starch Readership Report*.
    d. *AdWatch*, a joint venture of the Gallup Organization and *Advertising Age*.
    e. Inquiry Corporation's *Split Runs*.

48. Looked at from the point of view of dollars spent on advertising activity, the one of the following media that is least popular in the U.S. is
    a. network television.
    b. newspapers.
    c. outdoor.
    d. direct mail.
    e. radio.

49. Created by production of special events, holding press conferences, and preparing news releases and media kits, this aspect of promotion is
    a. point-of-purchase promotion.
    b. sampling.
    c. trade show promotion.
    d. publicity.
    e. specialty advertising.

50. A national television ad informs us that that the new Matsushita Hi-Def Giant Screen TV is now available in the U.S. at Best Buy and only at Best Buy. The best definition of this type of advertising is
    a. institutional.
    b. as cross-promotion.
    c. as a celebrity testimonial.
    d. that it is interactive.
    e. as a continuing promotional device.

Name_____ Instructor_____

Section_____ Date_____

Applying Marketing Concepts

Your job as national advertising manager for Bubba's "Get the Dirt" Truck Wash, a product of the Bubba Chemical Company of Scooba, Mississippi, has become a source of great frustration to you. You know that your product is superior to any other vehicle cleaner on the market and that the addition of genuine 4,3-iso-diethyl-methyl stearate (in effect, a serious degreaser and road gunk dissolver) makes your product an excellent vehicle cleaner and deodorizer. It is also a totally natural product, containing only organically produced ingredients. But your firm is so small (less than one percent of the market) that you can't afford to buy advertising like Prestone, Du-Pont, Turtle Shell, or any of the others "big boys" of the industry. Faced with this problem, you are considering how best to use your rather modest advertising budget.

1. Convinced that your small share of the market is due to the fact that the majority of the population doesn't know of your product, you feel that you must use your advertising to tell them who and what you are. The type of advertising to use in this instance would be
   a. product advertising.
   b. persuasive advertising.
   c. outdoor advertising.
   d. reminder advertising.
   e. informative advertising.

2. Very aware that your unique selling proposition requires the use of an advertising medium that will be highly selective, speedy in effect, highly personalized, and capable of delivering a complete message, you choose as your major medium
   a. local newspapers.
   b. direct mail.
   c. specialty magazines.
   d. outdoor advertising.
   e. radio.

3. Reasoning that part of the explanation of why your market share is so small is because very few people have ever tried your product, you authorize your local representatives to approach the local playground of their choice and offer to sponsor a baseball or soccer team in the park league. Each player will receive a uniform with a jersey emblazoned with the Bubba's Truck Wash logo. Your agent will be allowed to put up a fence sign with the Bubba's name and their name on it. This promotional technique is
   a. the form of publicity known as sampling.
   b. point-of-purchase advertising.
   c. an advertising pretest
   d. part of your public relations effort.
   e. interactive advertising.

4. Upon reflection, you decide that one way to improve your competitive position would be by advertising your product in such a way as to point out its obvious superiority to Tough Stuff, Gulf Wash, IndustraKlean, and other well-known truck washes, each of which would be mentioned by name. This type of advertising is called
   a. competitive advertising.
   b. compulsive advertising.
   c. comparative advertising.
   d. "cause" advertising.
   e. corporate advertising.

5. Further thought – you think a lot – convinces you that making a frontal attack on all your major competitors might not be the best way to develop Bubba's product market. You consider, however, creating for Bubba's an advertising program in which you will pay part of the cost of advertising featuring your product placed in local newspapers by retailers that stock it. Such an arrangement is called
   a. comparative advertising.
   b. cooperative advertising.
   c. free spending promotion.
   d. performance advertising.
   e. product promotion.

6. You decide to try and get the most "bang for your buck" by placing small two and three column-inch ads in local newspapers that include no illustration, only the single phrase "Don't Forget to Buy Bubba's Truck Wash!" Such ads would be considered to be a(n)
   a. persuasive ad.
   b. reminder ad.
   c. informative ad.
   d. institutional ad.
   e. corporate ad.

Melanie Castrogiovanni has the task of creating her firm's advertising plan for the next fiscal year. She has reviewed all the information she was able to gather very carefully. Her Firm, Baldwin Better Bearings, Inc., a major international trader in ball, spindle, and roller bearings and related products from Europe and the Far East, spent over $1 million on advertising last year, but Melanie isn't sure what happened to the money. Top management at BBBI set no specific promotional objectives, though they did spend a lot on audience analysis reports and research aimed at identifying the characteristics of the readers of the ads for the company's products. Invoices from research suppliers also note that a substantial sum was paid to McCann-Erickson for some pretesting of ads, and a firm called Midwestern Interactive Advertising received monthly payments for Site Maintenance (Promotional). Another large sum was paid to the European Friction Reduction Foundation, Inc., for "Exhibit at Commercial FrictionFest 2005." Finally, there appear to have been quarterly mailings of several thousand "catalog updates" to the firm's largest customers.

7. The quarterly mailings of catalogs would be categorized as
   a. direct mail advertising.
   b. magazine advertising.
   c. public relations.
   d. interactive promotion.
   e. outdoor advertising.

8. Ms. Castrogiovanni will probably be unable to come to any conclusions concerning the success of last year's advertising program because
   a. no audience analysis was undertaken.
   b. no objectives were set.
   c. pretesting was done incorrectly.
   d. media choices were improperly made.
   e. the budget was too small for analysis.

9. The research which was done to identify the characteristics of the firm's audience was
   a. a pretest of the company's advertising.
   b. a wise use of a portion of the advertising budget.
   c. budgeted as a test of the achievement of advertising objectives.
   d. a posttest of an aspect of the advertising's effectiveness.
   e. the perfect test of the validity of promotional objectives.

10. The money paid to McCann-Erickson for ad pretesting probably went for
    a. galvanic skin response measurements.
    b. the use of a hidden camera to photograph eye movement of ad readers.
    c. studio screening of ads for selected consumers.
    d. blind product tests.
    e. sales conviction tests.

11. The money paid to Midwestern Interactive Advertising was probably for
    a. work they did keeping the company's Web site current and correct.
    b. participation in industrial and consumer trade shows.
    c. production of materials to be used in company sales contests.
    d. manufacture of miniature samples of company products to be given as inducements to buyers.
    e. bribes paid to obscure European officials to sign permits allowing the exportation of bearings, bolts, and other products.

12. The check to FrictionFest 2005 was probably for
    a. participation in the yearly bearing makers and distributors trade show in Pilsen, Czech Republic.
    b. medical treatment for BBBI employees who, in the course of their labors, were bounced by browned-off bearings.
    c. advertisement in a technical publication celebrating the glories of the friction-reducing bearings.
    d. design fees to a famous boutique bearing designer to upgrade the aesthetic quality of BBBI's products.
    e. rental for outdoor ads all over Europe showing bearings in attractive, useful-appearing poses.

Name_____   Instructor_____

Section_____   Date_____

Surfing the Net

Keeping in mind that addresses change and what's on the Web now may have changed by the time you read this, let's take a look at some of the places on the Net that offer insights into advertising, sales promotion, and public relations. We are not endorsing or recommending any of these sources, merely making note of the information and services that people have elected to offer through the Internet.

Need to sell a textbook? You can advertise it in the online textbook exchange (or see what other people want for the textbooks they've got) at **http://www.studentmkt.com/**. You can also buy all sorts of stuff aimed at college students at this site.

Want to get the scoop on your favorite packaged food maker's offerings? First, check the pantry and see what YOUR cans and boxes say. That's the stuff YOU like. I checked mine and discovered that I could communicate with Tony the Tiger at **http://www.kelloggs.com** or drop an e-mail line to another major cereal maker at a product-specific site: **http://www.cheerios.com**. I also discovered that Quaker Oats was there – we can't leave the hot cereal people out, can we – at **http://www.quakeroats.com** It took a bit more work to find, but for us deep Southerners Falls Mills, out of Belvidere, Tennessee, maintains the site du jour of hot cereal. Give it a look at **http://www.grits.com** Having discovered this rather interesting nom de site, I wondered what would happen if I tried **http://www.mayonnaise.com**. Why don't you have a go at it and see who's there? You might also try **http://www.moutarde.com/english**; it's and interesting site about REAL Dijon. And finally, to round out the condiments, try **http://www.heinz.com** for ketchup. (I tried **http://www.mustard.com** and was very surprised. The site doesn't seem to have much to do with mustard)

Curious about the way public relations works? Check some of the press release databases on the net, like PR Newswire's "Company News on Call" feature at **http://www.prnewswire.com**. That's just one of several services offered at this website. An alternative source for company news is Business Wire at **http://www.businesswire.com**.

Into trade shows and conferences? Welcome to Trade Show Central at **http://www.tscentral.com**. It's all about where to get stuff to put on a trade show.

As you might expect. the big boys of advertising all have sites. It shouldn't be too hard for you to figure out who's located at **http://www.mccann.com, http://www.ddb.com, http://www.grey.com/frontpage**, or **http://www.burke.com**, if you've read this chapter.

Sites verified October 8, 2004.

Chapter 17
Personal Selling and Sales Promotion

Chapter Outline

You may want to use the following outline as a guide in taking notes.

I. Chapter Overview

In exploring personal selling and sales promotion strategies, this chapter gives special attention to the relationship-building opportunities the selling situation presents. Personal selling is the process of a seller's person-to-person promotional presentation to a buyer. The sales process is essentially interpersonal and is basic to any enterprise. Personal selling is a primary component of a firm's promotional mix in six well-defined situations. These are (1) when customers are geographically concentrated; (2) when the dollar amounts of individual orders are large; (3) when the firm markets goods and services that are expensive, technically complex, or require special handling; (4) when trade-ins are involved; (5) when products move through short channels; or (6) the firm markets to relatively few potential customers. Sales promotion, the other major topic of this chapter, includes all those marketing activities other than personal selling, advertising, and public relations that enhance consumer purchasing and dealer effectiveness.

II. The Evolution of Personal Selling covers a span of several thousand years. Selling is far different today than it was even forty or fifty years ago. Today's sales representative is a highly-trained professional. Selling is a vital, vibrant, dynamic process which has transitioned from a transactions-based to a relationship-based philosophy along with the other aspects of the marketing discipline. In fact, personal selling is an attractive career choice for today's college and university students.

III. The Four Sales Channels available to marketers each have their own positive and negative aspects. Telemarketing and online selling are cheaper than field selling and over-the counter sales, but their lack of personal contact with prospective make them somewhat less effective.

A. Over-the-counter selling is the most frequently-used sales channel, typical of selling in retail and some wholesale situations. Customers come to the stores of their choice to select products or services appropriate to their needs. Before the advent of the big chain retailers, it was not unusual for local retailers to know their customers by name and be familiar with their tastes and preferences. Some firms are attempting to recreate this relationship in the old-fashioned way. Other firms are trying to recreate the personalized one-on-one experience of over the counter selling over the Internet, but so far, success has been elusive. Best Buy's "CARE Plus" program stands as an example of an in-house selling philosophy which seems to work quite well.

B. Field selling involves making sales calls on prospective and existing customers at their businesses or homes. Considerable creative effort and technical expertise may be required. Selling new Boeing 7E7 Dreamliners calls for considerable technical knowledge, for example. Field selling is considerably more expensive than other selling options largely because of the travel required. In fairly routine selling situations, the field sales representative may basically act as an order taker who processes regular customers' orders. Some field selling may have a local focus, or it may require many days and nights away from home calling on distant customers. Thousands of smaller businesses now rely on network marketing, selling in peoples' homes in imitation of Avon, Mary Kay, and Tupperware. The implementation of the national "Do Not Call" registry appears also to have increased the volume of door-to-door sales effort recorded.

C. Telemarketing is a sales channel in which the selling process is conducted by phone, provides sales and services to the business-to-business and direct-to-customer markets. Outbound telemarketing involves a sales force that relies on the phone to contact customers, reducing the substantial costs of personal visits to personal visits to customers' homes or businesses. A major drawback to outbound telemarketing is that is that the majority of customers don't like it. There are both federal and state laws (in twenty-three states) restricting the use of telemarketing. So why is outbound telemarketing such a popular sales technique? It is cost-effective and it works. Inbound telemarketing usually involves a toll-free number that customers call to obtain information, make reservations, and purchase goods and services.

D. Inside selling is a combination of field selling techniques applied through inbound and outbound telemarketing channels with a strong customer orientation. A successful inside sales force relies on close working relationships with field representatives to solidify customer relationships. Their function is to turn opportunities into actual sales and to support technicians and purchasers with current solutions.

E. Integrating selling channels involves blending alternative sales channels to create a successful cost-effective sales organization. All of the types of selling outlined above may be used to complement each other in one situation or another.

IV. Recent Trends in Personal Selling reflect current conditions that call for different strategies than salespeople used in the past. Team selling, technical capacity and a technological vocabulary and patience are requirements the modern sales representative is more likely to need than his or her predecessors. Companies rely on four major personal selling approaches to address these concerns, which together are changing the sales function.

A. Relationship selling is a technique for building a mutually beneficial relationship with a customer through regular contacts over an extended period. The success of tomorrow's marketers depends on the relationships they build today in both the consumer and B2B markets.

B. Consultative selling involves meeting customer needs by listening to customers, understanding and caring about their problems, paying attention to details, and following through after the sale. It builds customer loyalty by working hand in hand with relationship selling to build customer loyalty. The rapid pace of technology drives business at unprecedented speed, and the need for sales representatives to possess engineering educations has become a serious one in many industries. Online companies use consultative selling models to create long-term customers. *Cross-selling* is a technique that capitalizes on a firm's strengths by offering multiple products or services to the same customer.

C. Team selling joins sales representatives with specialists from other functional areas of the firm to complete the selling process. In situations where selling involves detailed knowledge of new, complex, and ever-changing technology, team selling offers a distinct competitive edge in meeting customers' needs. On occasion, team selling may involve bringing in help from outside the company. In any team selling situation, preparation is the key to selling well.

D. Sales force automation is the application of new technologies to the selling process. It may be broadly defined to mean the use of pagers, Web-browsing cell phones, voice and electronic mail, and laptop and notebook computers. Alternatively, it may be narrowly interpreted to mean the use of computers by salespeople for activities beyond the use of word processors, spreadsheets, and connections to order-entry systems. Using these tools, both small and large firms can increase efficiency and spend more time on client acquisition and retention. Some firms have integrated UPC scanning and order generation to expedite order processing, while other have integrated telephony with the Internet as part of their selling effort. SFA usage differs sharply from industry to industry. Food, beverage, and pharmaceutical firms have been using sophisticated systems for a number of years, while apparel companies have been reluctant to shift from their traditional methods.

V. Sales Tasks today are oriented toward establishing long-term buyer-seller relationships and with helping customers select the best products to meet their needs rather than simply selling what is available. Not all selling activities are alike, but all them seem to involve three basic tasks: order processing, creative selling, and missionary sales. Most sales personnel do not fall into a single category, but perform all three of these to some extent. Improving the productivity of the sales force is a major consideration for most firms.

A. Order processing, which both field selling and telemarketing may perform, is most often found at the wholesale and retail levels. Order processing involves three steps: (1) identifying customer needs; (2) pointing out the need to the customer; (3) completing (writing up) the order. Order processing is part of most selling positions. Sales force automation is easing order-processing tasks.

B. Creative selling is generally used to develop new business by adding new customers or by introducing new goods and services. The technique involves identifying the customer's problems and needs and proposing a solution in the form of the good or service being offered. As more and more companies consolidate their operations and the number of buyers for a product or service shrinks, creative selling becomes increasingly important to make the sale.

C. Missionary selling is an indirect approach to sales. Salespeople sell the firm's good will and provide customers with information and technical or operational assistance. Missionary sales may involve both field selling and telemarketing. Many aspects of team selling also fit the definition of missionary work.

VI. The Sales Process involves seven steps in a sequence. The steps follow the AIDA concept of Attention – Interest – Desire – Action previously discussed. Sales personnel modify the steps in the process to match their customers' buying processes. The seven steps are explained below.

A. Prospecting and qualifying are two activities which go together. Prospecting is the process of identifying potential customers while qualifying is determining that the prospect really is a potential customer. New sales personnel may find that prospecting is frustrating because there is generally no immediate payback from the work. Recently, sales representatives have turned to the Internet for prospects. Qualifying can be a two-way street, with the sales representative determining that the prospect has the authority and resources to make the purchase decision and the prospect agreeing that he or she is a candidate for the goods or services being offered.

B. Approach is the sales representative's initial contact with the prospective customer. Based on all the relevant information available about a qualified prospect – precall planning – allows the sales representative to contact the prospect armed with knowledge about the prospect's purchasing habits, attitudes, activities, and opinions. Retail salespeople usually cannot do much precall planning, but they can compensate by asking leading questions during the actual approach process.

C. Presentation is when the sales representative gives the prospective customer the actual sales message. The presentation should be clear, concise, well-organized, and it should emphasize the positive issues on the table. The degree of preparation and the depth of presentation depend on the circumstances of the situation. Increasingly, presentations are going high-tech.

D. Demonstration of a product or service is the real thing. Photographs of the product in action or even a video of the service being rendered are not the same as actually experiencing the event. The involvement created by a demonstration awakens customer interest in a way that no amount of verbal presentation can. Most firms use new technologies to make their demonstrations more effective, often using full-color video and stereo sound as part of the process. The key to a good demonstration is planning.

E. Handling Objections is a vital part of the selling process. Objections are expressions of sales resistance by the prospect – and it is only reasonable to expect them to occur. They may involve the product's features, its price, and services to be provided by the vendor. During this stage of the selling process, sales representatives are often confronted with objections concerning a <u>competitor's</u> product. It is best not to criticize the competition. Overcoming objections starts with a "we can do it" attitude and the superior features of the firm's product – it's not that the competitor's product is bad, it's just not as good for the particular purpose of this customer.

F. Closing is the moment of truth in selling – the point at which the sales representative asks the prospect for the order. Some sales representatives find it difficult to do this, however. To be effective, sales people must learn when and how to close a sale. There are several fairly standard methods which might be used.
    1. The "If I can show you . . ." technique identifies the prospect's major cause for concern and then offers convincing evidence of the offering's ability to solve the problem.
    2. The alternative-decision technique poses choices for the prospect either of which is favorable to the sales rep.
    3. The SRO (or standing-room-only) technique warns the prospect that a sales agreement should be concluded now because the product may not be available at such favorable terms later on or that an important feature will soon be changed.
    4. Silence is often an effective close because it puts the prospect in the position of having to take some action – either positive or negative.
    5. An extra-inducement close offers the prospect special incentives designed to motivate a positive buyer response.

G. Follow-up includes those activities designed to reinforce the customer's purchase decision and make sure that the company delivers high-quality goods or services on schedule. These post-sales activities often determine whether the current buyer will become a repeat customer. Follow-up helps strengthen the bond salespeople try to build with customers in relationship selling.

VII. Managing the Sales Effort – the overall direction and control of the personal selling effort, are in the hands of sales managers, who are organized hierarchically. Sales managers perform a **boundary-spanning** role in that they link the sales force to other elements of the environment. The sales manager's job requires a unique blend of administrative and sales skills depending on the specific level of the sales hierarchy. Personal selling requires effective planning and strategic objectives. Sales-force management is the administrative channel for sales personnel, linking individual salespeople to general management. Women account for almost half of U. S. professional sales people, but only about a quarter of B2B sales representatives. Sales managers perform seven basic managerial functions. These functions are as follows:

A. Recruitment and Selection of successful salespeople are, together, one of the sales manager's greatest challenges. One of the difficulties lies in the reluctance of many high-school guidance counselors and colleges to promote the advantages of a sales career to students. Careful selection of salespeople is important because (1) the process involves substantial amounts of money and management time and (2) selection mistakes damage customer relations and create costly-to-correct performance problems.
1. A successful sales career, however, satisfies all of the following five areas that many people think of as important in the choice of a profession.
a. Opportunity for advancement is ample in sales. Sales representatives advance rapidly in most firms.
b. High earnings are typical in sales; a top-level consumer sales representative typically earns more than $75,000 a year.
c. Personal satisfaction is achieved by performing successfully in a competitive environment and by helping customers satisfy their needs and wants.
d. Job security in the selling profession is high. Economic downturns affect sales personnel less than other employees and there is a continuing need for good sales personnel.
e. Independence of action and a variety of experiences are typical of sales positions.
2. A seven step process is typically used in the selection of sales personnel. It typically includes application, a screening interview, in-depth interview, testing, reference checks, a physical examination, and analysis followed by a hiring decision.

B. Training of sales representatives may be accomplished by on-the-job methods, individual instruction, in-house classes, and external seminars. Techniques applied include instructional videotapes, lectures, role-playing exercises, slides, films, and interactive computer programs. Simulations may also be used. Ongoing sales training is important for veteran salespeople as well as for individuals new to the professions. Mentoring is a key training tool in many organizations.

C. Organization of the sales force is the responsibility of sales management. The most common schemes used to organize the sales force are geography, products, types of customers, or some combination of these. A product sales organization should have specialized sales forces for each of the major categories of the firm's products. Firms that market similar products throughout large territories often specialize geographically. Customer-oriented organizations use different sales strategies for each major type of customer they serve. Among firms organizing by customer type, a growing trend is the national accounts organization, an arrangement where sales managers or sales teams are assigned to major accounts in each of the firm's markets. As companies expand their market coverage across national borders, they may elect to use a variant of the national accounts organization. Individual sales managers may adapt the strategies described to suit the specific needs of the areas under their control.

D. Supervision of the sales function varies in amount and type depending on the nature of the marketplace and selling task. It is difficult to say how much and what type of supervision works best in general, but the concept of span of control does give some idea. This concept states that the number of sales representatives that can be handled by a first-level manager varies with the complexity of the selling task, the ability of the individual sales manager, the interdependence among the various sales reps, and the training each of them receives.

E. Motivation is an important component of the management of the sales force. Satisfaction of emotional needs is involved, as is provision of financial incentives. Incentives may include, as well as basic monetary compensation, leisure trips or travel, gifts, recognition dinners, plaques, awards, and cash. Not all incentive programs, however, are successful in motivating employees. Sales managers can improve sales-force productivity by understanding what motivates individual salespeople. Experience theory relates motivation to the employee's appraisal of his or her ability to do the job and how performance relates to achieving awards.

F. Compensation of sales personnel may be done using a commission plan, a straight-salary plan, or some combination of these options. Bonuses based on end-of-year total results are another popular means of compensation. Commissions are payments tied directly to the sales or profits a sales representative achieves. Salaries are fixed payments made periodically to an employee. Because good sales personnel are hard to find and expensive to train, sales managers want to make every effort to retain productive workers. Compensating new people fairly while recognizing the productivity of longer-term workers is one of the problems faced by sales managers. The typical U.S. sales representative is well compensated, earning about $80,000 a year.

G. Evaluation and control of sales performance is one of the more difficult tasks of sales management. The process typically includes sales quotas – specified sales or profit targets that the firm expects its sales representatives to achieve – but many other factors can come into play, such as customer satisfaction, profit contribution, share of product-category sales, and customer retention. Regardless of the elements in the evaluation program, the sales manager must follow a formal system of decision rules. First, individual performance must be compared to a set of standards. Second, the strong points of the person being ranked must be considered. And finally, the weaknesses or negative aspects of the individual's performance must be examined. The evaluation is summarized following a set procedure that weighs and evaluates all the components of the evaluation process. Areas of weakness or deficiency should be pointed out, and a program for correcting the deficiencies implemented.

VIII. Ethical Issues in Sales are significant because selling as a profession has a negative image in the minds of many people. Television, movies, and literature have tended to create and perpetuate this point of view. Today's highly paid, professional sales representative knows that success is based on building and maintaining relationships with clients. Some people believe   that ethical problems are inevitable because making sales benefits the person making them, therefore how can such a person be unbiased or work for the benefit of the client? Thousands of companies are working to overcome the stigma associated   with sales careers to promote ethical behavior have become a part of the central philosophy of many firms.

A. Despite management efforts to foster ethical behavior, sales personnel do sometimes find themselves in situations with their employers, fellow employees, and customers that involve ethical dilemmas. Among the ethical breaches that occur between sales people and their employers are improper use of company property and stealing. Sexual harassment is another problem faced by sales representatives – of both sexes. Another issue is that of using bribes to secure a sale. Some customers demand kickbacks to do business with a particular firm. In all such cases, the alternatives of going along with the unethical request, ignoring it, confronting the individual who suggests the behavior, or reporting it are essential options. Generally speaking, the worst course is to succumb to the unethical proposal. Experts recommend that the sales representative tell the person who suggests the unethical behavior that they prefer to gain the business on its merits without unethical conduct. If that doesn't solve the problem, it is recommended that the sales representative report the situation to his or her supervisor, who should then take it up with the other company's purchasing supervisor.

IX. Sales Promotion, marketing activities other than personal selling, advertising, and publicity that enhance consumer purchasing   and dealer effectiveness, accounts for $250 billion per year in expenditures. Sales Promotion techniques, originally intended as short-term incentives aimed at producing immediate buying responses, are now integral parts of many marketing plans. Both retailers and manufacturers use sales promotions to offer consumers extra incentives to buy. An entire industry exists to offer expert assistance in the use of sales promotion. Sales promotion complements other types of promotion and some of the best promotional programs combine several. Sales promotions have their positive features, but also possess limitations.

A. Consumer-oriented sales promotions include games, contests, sweepstakes, and coupons to persuade customers to try their products. Sales promotions must be used selectively because if they are used too much, consumers begin to expect price discounts, diminishing brand equity.
1. Coupons and refunds, the most widely used form of sales promotion, offer discounts on the purchase price of goods and services. Coupons are typically distributed through the mail, in magazines, through package insertions, and most recently, via the Internet. Refunds (or rebates) offer cash back to consumers who send in proof of purchase of the offering firm's products.
2. Samples, bonus packs, and premiums are three different applications of the "try it, you'll like it" approach to customer solicitation.
   a. Sampling is the free distribution of a product in an attempt to obtain future sales. It produces a higher response rate than most other promotions, but it is a high cost proposition because not only is product being given away, but until the samples are used up consumers will not be buying the product.

    b. Bonus packs are specially designed packages that give the consumer a larger quantity of product for the regular price.

    c. Premiums are items given free or at reduced cost with purchases of other products.

  3. Contests and sweepstakes are two approaches to introducing new goods and services and attracting additional customers.

    a. Contests require entrants to solve problems or write essays, and may also require proof of purchase of the sponsor's products.

    b. Sweepstakes choose their winners by chance, so no product purchase is necessary.

    c. The advent of the Internet has created more sophisticated and creative contests and sweepstakes.

  4. Specialty advertising, which traces its roots back several hundred years, is a sales promotion technique that places the advertiser's name, address, and advertising message on useful articles that are then distributed to target consumers. Advertising specialties help reinforce previous or future advertising and sales messages.

B. Trade-oriented promotion (often referred to as trade promotion) is sales promotion that appeals to marketing intermediaries rather than to consumers. It offers financial incentives to retailers and wholesalers and should return quick results and improve sales.

  1. Trade allowances are special financial incentives offered to wholesalers and retailers that purchase or promote specific products.

    a. Buying allowances give retailers discounts on goods. They include "off-invoice" allowances that allow the deduction of specific amounts from dealer invoices re the receipt of free goods when they order certain quantities. In promotional allowances, the manufacturer agrees to pay a part of the cost of special promotions or advertising that features the manufacturer's products.

    b. Some retailers require vendors to pay them a slotting allowance before they will stock that vendor's goods. This practice is considered to be questionable by some, and may ultimately become the subject of judicial review.

  2. Point-of-purchase advertising describes displays or other promotion located near the site of actual buying. POP promotions often appear at the ends of shopping aisles.

  3. Trade shows, often organized by industry trade associations, bring together vendors who serve the industry to display their products or services for association members. Trade shows give especially effective opportunities to introduce new products and generate sales leads. Some trade shows also reach the ultimate consumer, as well.

  4. Dealer incentives, contests, and training programs are, for the most part, designed to induce retailers and their sales people to increase sales and promote products. The rewards for success may include major prizes or cash, of which "push money" is an example. For more expensive and technical products, training programs improve the retail sales representative's likelihood of successfully selling the product.

Name_____ Instructor_____

Section_____ Date_____

Key Concepts

The purpose of this section is to allow you to determine if you can match key concepts in the chapter with their definitions. It is essential that you know the definitions of the concepts before using the concepts in later exercises in this chapter.

From the list of lettered terms, select the one that best fits the numbered statement below. Write the letter of that choice in the space provided.

Key Terms

a. personal selling
b. over-the-counter selling
c. field selling
d. telemarketing
e. inside selling
f. relationship selling
g. consultative selling
h. team selling

i. sales force automation (SFA)
j. order processing
k. creative selling
l. missionary selling
m. sales promotion
n. specialty advertising
o. trade promotion
p. point of purchase (POP) advertising

_____ 1. Application of computer and other technology to improve the efficiency and competitiveness of the sales function.

_____ 2. Sales presentations made at prospective customers' locations on a face-to-face basis

_____ 3. Selling by phone, mail, and electronic commerce.

_____ 4. Indirect selling in which specialized salespeople promote the firm's goodwill among indirect customers, often by assisting in product use.

_____ 5. Personal selling conducted in retail and in some wholesale locations in which customers come to the seller's place of business.

_____ 6. Interpersonal influence process involving a seller's promotional presentation on a person-to-person basis with the buyer.

_____ 7. Meeting customer needs by listening to them, understanding – and caring about в their problems, paying attention to details, and following through after the sale.

_____ 8. Promotional presentation involving the use of the telephone on a outbound basis by sales reps or on an inbound basis by customers who initiate calls to obtain information and place orders.

_____ 9. Personal selling situations in which buyers must undertake considerable analytical decision making, creating a need for skillful vendor proposals of solutions for customer needs.

_____ 10. Sales promotion technique that places the advertiser's name, address, and advertising message on useful articles that are then distributed to target customers.

_____ 11. Regular contacts between sales reps and customers over an extended period to establish a sustained seller-buyer relationship.

_____ 12. Sales promotion that appeals to marketing intermediaries rather than to consumers.

_____ 13. Display or other promotion placed near the site of the actual buying decision.

_____ 14. Marketing activities other than personal selling, advertising, and publicity that enhance consumer purchasing and dealer effectiveness.

_____ 15. Selling situation in which several sales associates or other members of the organization are recruited to assist the lead sales rep in reaching all those who influence the purchase decision.

_____ 16. Selling, mostly at wholesale and retail levels, that involves identifying customer needs, pointing them out to customers, and completing orders.

Name_____ Instructor_____

Section_____ Date_____

Self-Quiz

You should use these questions to test your understanding of the material in this chapter. You can check your answers with those provided at the end of the chapter.

While these questions cover most of the chapter topics, they are nor intended to be the same as the test questions your instructor may use in an examination. A good understanding of all aspects of the source material is essential to good performance on any examination.

True/False

Write "T" for True and "F" for False for each of the following statements.

_____ 1. While the average U.S. firm's advertising expenses represent from 1 to 3 percent of total sales, personal selling expenses are likely to equal 20 to 25 percent.

_____ 2. Rather than selling one-on-one as was once traditional, in B2B settings it is now customary to sell to teams of corporate representatives who make up the client firm's decision-making units.

_____ 3. In team selling, a single sales practitioner seeks to build a mutually beneficial relationship with a large customer on a regular basis over an extended period.

_____ 4. Approximately 60 percent of college marketing graduates choose sales as their first marketing position, in part because of the attractive salaries and career potentials.

_____ 5. Order processing, as a sales activity, becomes the primary task in situations where needs cannot be readily identified and are not acknowledged by the customer.

_____ 6. A sales representative whose job is to answer the phone and take orders or answer customers' questions is involved in outbound telemarketing.

_____ 7. Consultative selling works hand-in-hand with relationship selling to build customer loyalty.

_____ 8. A virtual sales team is a network of strategic partners, trade associations, suppliers, and others who are qualified and willing to recommend a firm's goods or services.

_____ 9. Order processing is an indirect approach to sales, in which sales people sell the firm's goodwill and provide their customers with information and technical or operational assistance.

_____ 10. New products often require creative selling because the salesperson must identify the customer's problems and needs and then propose a solution in the form of the good or service being offered.

_____ 11. Many aspects of team selling can also be seen as missionary sales, as when technical support personnel help design, install, and maintain equipment.

_____ 12. The first step in the selling process is making the approach to the prospective customer.

_____ 13. Though prospecting may involve hours, days, or weeks of effort, it is a necessary step in the sales process.

_____ 14. Effective pre-call planning gives the salesperson relevant information about the prospect's purchasing habits, attitudes, activities, and opinions.

_____ 15. The seller's objective in a features-benefits presentation is to talk about the technical features of a good or service, rather than explaining benefits the buyer might receive from their use.

_____ 16. Objections raised by sales prospects should be treated as a cue for providing additional information to the potential customer.

_____ 17. The moment of truth in selling is the closing – the point at which the sales representative asks the prospect for an order.

_____ 18. The "If-I-can-show-you . . ." closing technique warns the prospect that a sales agreement should be concluded now because some important feature of the deal being offered, such as price or availability, will soon be changed.

_____ 19. One of the problems with successfully recruiting people to become sales practitioners is the low degree of job security offered by this kind of employment.

_____ 20. Sales promotions replace other types of promotion and often produce their best results when used alone.

_____ 21. Much ongoing sales training, an important feature of the job even for veteran sales personnel, is conducted by sales managers in an informal manner.

_____ 22. About three-quarters of the consumers who receive samples try them, particularly if they have requested them.

_____ 23. Trade allowances are special financial incentives offered to wholesalers and retailers that purchase or promote specific products.

_____ 24. Compensating sales representatives by commission combines maximum selling incentive with ample reason to perform nonselling activities such as completing sales reports, delivering sales promotional materials, and normal account servicing.

_____ 25. Contests, as forms of sales promotion, require entrants to complete a task such as solving a puzzle or answering questions in a trivia quiz.

Multiple Choice

Circle the letter of the word or phrase that best completes the sentence or best answers the question.

26. The percentage of sales the average firm spends on personal selling activities is most likely to fall into which of the following
    ranges?
    a. 1 up to 3 percent
    b. 3 up to 5 percent
    c. 5 up to 10 percent
    d. 10 up to 15 percent
    e. 15 percent or more

27. If, in a field selling situation, the sales practitioner is joined by specialists from other functional areas of the firm to assist with
    the sales process,
    a. relationship selling is taking place.
    b. team selling is probably taking place.
    c. confusion can result because of all the points of view that have to be reconciled.
    d. expectancy theory is being applied to the selling process.
    e. a major accounts organization is probably in place.

28. A sales practitioner whose job involves selling in a retail or wholesale situation where customers typically visit the seller's location on their own initiative is engaged in
    a. creative sales.
    b. over-the-counter sales.
    c. field selling.
    d. missionary work.
    e. demand selling.

29. A selling approach in which the sales force relies on use of the telephone to contact customers is best known as
    a. inbound telemarketing.
    b. under-the-counter selling.
    c. creative selling.
    d. rule-bound order processing.
    e. outbound telemarketing.

30. Sales practitioners engaged in inside selling
    a. turn opportunities into sales and support technicians and purchasers with current solutions.
    b. provide maximum convenience for customers who initiate the sales process.
    c. regularly visit local stores and businesses calling on established customers.
    d. typically work in teams of ten or twelve to give the impression of competence.
    e. go for the "good old boy" sales style in a big way.

31. When a sales practitioner meets customer needs by listening to customers, understanding and caring about their problems, paying attention to details, and following through after the sale, the sales practitioner is
    a. practicing consultative selling.
    b. completing a creative selling assignment.
    c. engaged in sales engineering.
    d. acting as a missionary to that customer.
    e. functioning as a "drummer" in the classic sense of the word.

32. Which of the following statements is true concerning the sales activity of prospecting?
    a. Leads about prospects seldom come from previous customers of the company.
    b. Prospecting is difficult work involving many hours of diligent effort.
    c. Prospecting is exciting to new sales personnel because it is easy and fun.
    d. Once a good client base has been established, the sales practitioner can stop prospecting; sales will come from the referrals existing clients will provide.
    e. Trade show exhibits and social contacts seldom yield good sales prospects.

33. The process of qualifying a sales prospect
    a. involves gathering relevant information about the prospect to make initial contact go more smoothly.
    b. is the task of making sure that the prospect has the authority and resources to make purchase decisions and securing agreement from the prospect that he/she is a candidate for the goods or services being offered.
    c. is used less frequently by retail sales practitioners than it is by wholesalers' and manufacturers' sales representatives.
    d. involves making the initial personal contact with the prospect.
    e. is considered by many sales management experts to be the very essence of the sales process.

34. One important advantage of personal selling over most advertising is its ability to
    a. represent accurately the appearance of the product.
    b. describe and itemize the product's significant features.
    c. gain the customer's attention and develop interest.
    d. present a standardized treatment of the product to all prospects.
    e. actually demonstrate the product to the potential buyer.

35. The most widely used form of sales promotion is
    a. sampling, the free distribution of a product in an attempt to obtain future sales.
    b. the "never-take-no-for-an-answer" approach; the name of this approach really says it all.
    c. premiums, items given free or at reduced cost with purchase of other products.
    d. coupons that offer discounts on the purchase price of goods and services.
    e. specialty advertising, the technique that places the advertiser's name, address, and advertising message on useful articles distributed to target consumers.

36. The key to a successful product demonstration is
    a. impact; the demonstration must be really impressive.
    b. planning; the salesperson should check and recheck every aspect of the demonstration before its delivery.
    c. novelty; the prospect should be shown the product in a new and different way.
    d. effect; some practitioners say that the demonstration should sell the product all by itself.
    e. detail; the demonstration should show the product in every possible use or application.

37. Sales promotions that appeal to marketing intermediaries rather than to final consumers are called
    a. trade promotions
    b. rebates and refunds.
    c. contests and sweepstakes.
    d. sampling plans.
    e. premiums.

38. Broadly used, this term refers to the use of everything from pagers and cellular phones, to voice and electronic mail, to laptop and notebook computers in personal selling. It is
    a. the technology revolution.
    b. the electronic evolution.
    c. sales force automation.
    d. the era of technical wonder.
    e. the nerd phenomenon.

39. Trade allowances are trade promotions that are
    a. special financial incentives offered to wholesalers and retailers that purchase or promote specific products.
    b. displays or other promotions located near the site of an actual buying decision.
    c. items given free or at a reduced cost with purchases of other products.
    d. involved with offering cash back to consumers who send in proofs of purchase of one or more products.
    e. backed by free distribution of a product in an attempt to produce future sales.

40. The successful sales practitioner seeks to ensure that today's customers will be future customers through effective
    a. handling of prospect objections; a convinced customer is a repeat customer.
    b. sales presentations; a customer well-sold is a repeat customer.
    c. closing techniques; a customer who believes it was all his or her own idea will come back again.
    d. follow-up; this post-sales activity often determines whether a person will become a repeat customer.
    e. prospecting; a customer from the beginning is a customer for life.

41. In sales promotion, a specially packaged item that gives the purchaser a larger quantity at the regular price is known as a
    a. premium.
    b. sweepstake
    c. coupon return.
    d. refund.
    e. bonus pack.

42. The first step and one of the sales manager's greatest challenges in building an effective sales force is
    a. organizing the sales practitioners in a format consistent with the firm's needs.
    b. training sales personnel in correct selling techniques.
    c. motivating sales personnel to persist in their selling efforts.
    d. compensating sales personnel fairly and equitably.
    e. recruiting and selecting a group of qualified personnel.

43. Which of the following statements concerning selling as a profession is true?
    a. Advancement laterally to a more responsible position in some other functional area of the firm seldom happens to sales personnel.
    b. Economic downturns affect personnel in sales more than they do people in most other employment areas.
    c. The earnings of successful sales practitioners compare favorably with those of successful people in other professions.
    d. Sales practitioners seldom operate as "independent" business people but usually as part of a selling team.
    e. Sales practitioners derive satisfaction in their profession largely from their incomes and seldom from helping customers satisfy their wants and needs.

44. In the selection of sales personnel, which of the following is often the step before the applicant is sent to the assessment center for testing?
    a. a screening interview
    b. a physical examination
    c. an in-depth interview
    d. reference checks
    e. filling out the application

45. A firm whose sales organization markets large numbers of similar but separate products of a very technical or complex nature sold through an array of marketing channels should probably be organized
    a. geographically.
    b. along customer lines.
    c. using engineering specialties as a base.
    d. by product category.
    e. according to the sizes of the various customers of the firm.

46. The method of compensating sales practitioners that is based directly on the sales or profits that person achieves is
    a. a plan involving salary, bonuses, commissions, and other incentives.
    b. straight salary, no commission.
    c. a salary-plus-bonus plan.
    d. a salary-plus-commission program.
    e. straight commission, no salary.

47. Simulations are often elements of
    a. the training program for new sales personnel.
    b. a cover-up when sales managers make mistakes and have to be transferred.
    c. the testing program for potential recruits for sales positions.
    d. the motivational structure to impel sales personnel to higher achievement.
    e. the compensation program for sales personnel.

48. Each aspect of sales performance for which a standard exists should be measured separately. This helps to prevent
    a. evaluation of the process of selling rather than the achievements of the sales operative
    b. confusion on the part of the evaluated individual as to how the evaluation was conducted.
    c. the halo effect in which the rating on one factor is carried over to other performance variables.
    d. personalities becoming the basis for evaluation, rather than performance.
    e. the bad news being transmitted back to the sales employee through unauthorized channels.

49. Motivation of sales personnel
    a. is not a complex process because of the simplicity of the work.
    b. seldom appeals to ego needs, peer acceptance, or recognition.
    c. usually takes the form of debriefings, information sharing, and financial and psychological encouragement.
    d. requires tight supervision and constant monitoring of the work of the sales force.
    e. seldom involves monetary awards or fringe benefits such as club memberships.

50. The compensation plan giving management the greatest control over how sales personnel allocate their efforts but least incentive to expand sales volume is
    a. straight commission.
    b. salary plus bonus.
    c. commission with bonus.
    d. straight salary.
    e. salary with commission.

Name_____   Instructor_____

Section_____   Date_____

Applying Marketing Concepts

Whew! Vendamille Tourascent finally realized she was going to make it. She really was going to graduate from college! Armed with the happy knowledge that she had made it to her last semester, she went to East North Central State's placement office to sign up for interviews with firms seeking people with her qualifications. She was surprised to discover that there were quite a few positions available with local companies that called for sales skills involving strong interest in problem-solving and customer service but indicated that no outside work or travel would be required. A number of other positions called for degrees in finance or marketing, and showed that "business development" was the area for which personnel were being sought. A little investigation revealed that the accounting firms and financial institutions listing these positions were among the most aggressive in the area, seeking new commercial accounts in an active fashion. She signed up for several of these interviews, and was somewhat surprised when she was told that a number of the companies specified that potential applicants must have had certain courses before they could even be interviewed.

Either because of good planning or dumb luck, Vendamille had taken and done well in all the required courses, and was able to interview with a number of these firms. They all required a seemingly endless stream of paperwork. First, there was the placement office form to fill out, then each company seemed to want her to fill out a "personal data sheet," and finally there was the interview. She wondered who the people who were interviewing her were. They seemed to know the company and its products quite well, and indicated that if she were to be chosen to fill an open position, she would be working for them. After her third interview in two days, she decided to go somewhere quiet and think about this whole process. It seemed very detailed and confusing.

1. The positions with local wholesalers calling for selling and problem-solving skills and but no outside work were probably
    a. missionary sales positions.
    b. positions as sales trainers.
    c. inside selling positions.
    d. creative selling positions.
    e. field sales positions.

2. The positions with the accounting firms and financial institutions were most likely
    a. portfolio analysts' positions.
    b. openings for staff accountants in the auditing division.
    c. related to sector analysis or loan profitability.
    d. field sales positions in the commercial accounts area.
    e. missionary sales positions designed to build public image.

3. If the interviewing process is looked at as a sales opportunity for the companies interviewing (selling the idea of working for them), then their requirement that Vendamille have a degree in a particular major and/or have taken particular courses would be part of the
   a. prospecting and qualifying process.
   b. approach to the prospect.
   c. presentation of company advantages.
   d. preapproach planning.
   e. followup step in sales.

4. If one of the firms with whom Vendamille interviewed was interested in her, what do you suppose would happen next?
   a. She would be asked to report to a doctor's office for a physical examination.
   b. She would be called in for a second interview.
   c. The company would make her take a battery of placement tests.
   d. She would be hired immediately.
   e. They would keep her on the hook for a while, then make her an offer.

5. The people with whom Vendamille had her first interview were probably
   a. professional interviewers who do this sort of thing all the time.
   b. people who occupied the same position she would and had been told to find a successor so they could be transferred.
   c. sales managers for the companies in the local area, doing part of their job.
   d. representatives of her college filling in for people who worked for the interviewing companies.
   e. staff people from the interviewing companies who had nothing better to do.

Flux Density (that's his Web and Rave name – his real name is John O'Hara) recently went to a nearby store to buy a new DVD of video cuts by his favorite musical group, the Shrieking Blue Herons. Brenda (aka Gold), a helpful salesperson, assisted him to find the DVD he wanted and he was in the process of walking with her to the cash register to pay for it when she stopped at a display of DVD storage boxes and asked if he had the same problem she did storing her videos neatly and conveniently. Though Flux said he'd never had such a problem – his old shoe box worked just fine – Gold showed him how a particular storage container had little partitions in it that separated the DVDs and that it could even be locked to keep out the curious and light-fingered. Flux was impressed – the container was functional and Gold was cute and well-informed – so he added a storage container to his order. His scintillant personality and purple hair also got him Gold's e-mail address and phone number – it seems they had similar enter-tainment interests – she too was an SBH fan.

6. Gold's demonstration of the storage container is an example of
   a. order processing.
   b. creative selling.
   c. telemarketing.
   d. closing.
   e. prospecting.

7. Gold's assistance of Flux in finding the DVD that met his needs and ringing up the sale is an example of retail
   a. order processing.
   b. creative selling.
   c. missionary selling.
   d. passive selling.
   e. qualifying.

8. Gold's job category would be stated in terms of
   a. field selling.
   b. missionary selling.
   c. telemarketing.
   d. over-the-counter sales.
   e. merchandising.

The sales force at Formulario Bologna, S.p.A. (FB), a major Italian maker and distributor of high-tech fuel additives, is divided into three groups: the consumer products group, the major accounts group, and the industrial products group. Sales people in the consumer products group are paid a base salary plus ten percent of their gross sales after they have met a minimum sales volume requirement for the month. The requirement is set on a month-by-month basis. In other words, next month's payment amount and rate-of-pay is based on this month's sales performance.

The industrial sales force is also salaried, but they receive an additional payment each month based on the new account activity they generate. The amount is based on the number of new accounts each sales representative opens weighted by management's estimate of the ultimate volume each account will generate. The amount the sales representative sold the account on opening does not matter.

The members of the major accounts group are not thought of as sales representatives. They number among themselves work-design specialists, process engineers, materials specialists, and even a group of fuel chemists. A delegation from FB will often visit one of the major accounts as a group, each member prepared to deal with customer interaction in his or her own specialty. They try to develop the customers' confidence in their ability to solve his or her firm's problems better than anyone else.

9. The sales force at FB is organized along
   a. product lines.
   b. customer lines.
   c. geographical lines.
   d. a combination of geographical and customer lines.
   e. a combination of product and geographical lines.

10. Sales representatives in the consumer products group are compensated on a
   a. straight salary basis.
   b. salary plus commission basis.
   c. salary plus bonus basis.
   d. straight commission basis.
   e. basis no one understands.

11. Sales representatives in the industrial products group are paid
    a. a straight commission.
    b. salary plus commission.
    c. straight salary.
    d. salary plus bonus based on new business.
    e. commission plus bonus.

12. If we identify the members of the major accounts group as members of the sales force, how might we best characterize their working together in groups to fill customer needs?
    a. telemarketing
    b. consultative selling
    c. team selling
    d. sales force automation
    e. field selling

13. Whether the members of the major accounts group are classed individually as sales representatives or not, their efforts to develop customer confidence in their ability to solve the customer's problems (a long-term outlook) is an example of
    a. a "take the money and run" approach.
    b. follow-up as part of the selling process.
    c. boundary-spanning.
    d. relationship marketing.
    e. an ethical issue in sales organization.

Name_____   Instructor_____

Section_____   Date_____

Surfing the Net

Keeping in mind that addresses change and what's on the Web now may have changed by the time you read this, let's take a look at some of the places on the Net that reflect aspects of personal selling and sales management. We are not endorsing or recommending any of these sources, merely making note of the information and services that people have elected to offer through the Internet.

What a wreck! No, this really doesn't have much to do with anything, but selling and sales management sites are sort of thin on the ground on the Web, so I thought I'd just plug my old alma mater and let you know that the Georgia Tech student radio station has a Web site at **http://cyberbuzz.gatech.edu/wrek/.** So does tech itself. Try **http://www.gatech.edu.**

But seriously, folks, there are some interesting Web sites that have a bearing on the field of sales. One that, at this writing, looks promising, is CommerceNet. This service is designed to provide an interactive forum for business. At this site you can get detailed product information, make product comparisons, and make purchases. Take a look at **http://www.commerce.net** and its associated links.

J. P. Morgan and Company, a name that should be familiar to many of you, has a Web site that provides a daily list of risk rates in the financial market. But this investment banking firm also has digital recruiting brochures to attract new talent to the investments field. Check it out at **http://www.jpmorgan.com.**

Employment opportunities and Resumé Postings server may be the place to find that sales job. This location on the Net links with a number of sites where job opportunities are listed. Try them at **http://www.careerbuilder.com/cm/home.html.**

Really looking for a job? There are several employment agencies on the Web that claim to offer sales opportunities. You might try **http://www.monster.com** or **http://www.jobbroadcasting.com**, or this last one which I was surprised to discover is located in tiny (but rather pretty) Daphne, Alabama, just across Mobile Bay from the city of he same name. This certainly illustrates how the Internet frees business from having to locate in major cities. The site is **http://www.industrial-sales.com**. They apparently place sale personnel in the bearing and transmission parts industries.

Sites verified October 10, 2004

Part 6
Creating a Marketing Plan

Episode Seven is designed to provide you with information that will let you complete Part III. D. of your marketing plan.

Episode Six: Now Let's Get the Message Out – We're Here!

When we left our intrepid entrepreneurs (say those last two words real fast three times), they were in the process of arranging for quarters into which to move their new business. It is now several weeks later, and most of the mechanics of set-up have been accomplished. The firm now has a business address, all of the appropriate licenses and permits, a work space equipped with excellent communications testing equipment and equipment for repairing their customers' field units when service problems develop, and two rather nice cars – Ford Crown Vics with Police Interceptor Packages – for business use.

The problem now is to let people know that the firm exists, and that it is eager to provide the high-quality service its owners have made as their objective. The three partners have met to discuss the promotional means they're going to use to get their message across.

"Well, I think it's obvious that we need a display ad in the Yellow Pages," said Sandy. "As I said before, there are all these other firms which have listings, but only a very few ads. I think we need something to tell our target market we're out there to serve them."

"Good thought," replied Mel, "but the next edition of the Yellow Pages doesn't come out for four months. What are we going to do in the meantime? I propose we advertise in the business section of the newspaper; just a small ad once a week, and we can offer a free "communications analysis" as a get-acquainted deal."

"Now I know why you wanted those stickers with our name, address, phone number and "communications systems service and maintenance" printed on them," commented Suzette, "you plan on sticking those on any piece of equipment we get our hands on!"

"And on any other logical surface that would give us a shot at being the first firm they think of when the idea of a wireless digital communications system occurs to those that don't have them or something happens to the equipment of those that do," laughed Mel. "Better than that. I propose that, for the time being, we all keep acting as a sales force and get out there dropping off business cards and stickers at every business whose door we can get through. How about it?"

"Real good," remarked Suzette, "but I've been thinking; why just try to let these people know who we are. Why not generate cash flow as soon as possible by selling them maintenance service right off the bat. I've written up a little promotional piece that we can drop off along with our business cards when we call on people. See, it tells them a little about the three of us – let's face it, we've got pretty good credentials and if we don't toot our own horn who's going to toot it for us – along with some information on the cost of lost business that can crop up when you don't maintain and update your equipment regularly. Having access to people who know how to do the job right – and fast – is very important and having a maintenance contract for their communications equipment is very important to these firms. I think we can generate some business that way. I've even had the back page of the flier printed with some important equipment facts and failure symptoms that will let them spot problems they can correct without calling us. That may keep them from throwing the brochure away."

"Super job!" was Sandy's comment, "and though it may be a little bit off the track, let me volunteer to do something which may seem a little strange but I think will do us a world of good. I'm going to hire my niece – she's your cousin Salvinia, Mel (aren't big families wonderful) – to come over on Saturday mornings and work on the grass and shrubs around this building. Have you noticed what dumps most of our competitors' facilities are? I don't see any reason why we shouldn't have a good-looking place. And I think we should spend time keeping the inside neat, too."

"Not off the track at all, Sandy," said Suzette, "people do react to the appearance of a place, and we have to expect our customers to come by here to talk with us and see what we're doing for them. They might as well get a good impression of us from our store as well as from our work. Besides, this isn't a bad neighborhood for a commercial street. We might as well get along with our neighbors, too. I know Salvinia loves to work in the yard. Maybe we can get her to plant some of those flowering shrubs she put in around your aunt's house."

Guidelines:

Examine the suggestions the partners have made and use them and your own ideas to complete Part. III. D. of the marketing plan.

Part 7
Pricing Decisions

Price is whatever a product can be exchanged for in the marketplace. In the modern society, price is usually stated in terms of monetary units, but commodities such as wheat are still sometimes used as media of exchange. Prices are difficult to set and dynamic in nature. Ultimately, a fair price is one that yields a profit and is justifiable.

Price is the component of the marketing mix most universally affected by the legal environment. Tariffs, taxes on imported goods, often serve to allow local producers to price their output above world market levels. Antitrust legislation provides the basic foundation for domestic regulation of price in the United States, amplified by the Robinson-Patman Act that prohibits a broad range of price-discriminatory actions. At the state level, unfair-trade laws (also called Unfair Trade Practices Acts) also have an effect on price-setting.

Pricing objectives can be related to profitability, sales volume, meeting competition, and creating a prestige image for one's product or firm. The PIMS studies determined that product quality and market share are major contributors to firm profitability. Pricing objectives for not-for-profit organizations differ somewhat from those of for-profits. The not-for-profits sometimes seek to maximize profit, but may also seek simply to recover costs, create market incentives, or suppress consumption of a product.

Elasticity of demand with respect to price is another factor which must be considered in the pricing of a product. Economic theory and actual costs provide the rational framework for pricing. Economic theory is relatively seldom used in the setting of actual prices. Cost, on the other hand, is the most commonly used basis for setting prices today. The typical cost-plus approach to pricing attempts to set a price for the product which will recover the cost of producing and distributing it and allow for some margin of profit. Two methods of applying cost-plus pricing exist, the full-cost method and the incremental cost method.

Breakeven analysis is a technique which is often used to help marketing executives decide whether required sales levels to achieve profitability are a realistic goal. A modified breakeven model which superimposes an estimated demand curve over the cost and revenue curves of the breakeven chart helps identify the range of feasible prices and provide a more realistic base for deciding on the price to actually ask in the marketplace. Yield management has become a practicable pricing strategy in industries where demand fluctuates widely. In the global market, prices may be subject to factors which change somewhat the way in which they are formulated.

The making of pricing decisions is a two-step process which involves (1) setting prices and (2) administering the pricing structure. Alternative pricing strategies include a skimming strategy, a penetration pricing strategy, and competitive pricing. Competitive conditions have a significant effect on which of these strategies is chosen by a particular firm.

There are numerous influences on price quotes, among them being a firm's costs and policies as well as discounts and allowances which may prevail in a particular industry. Shipping costs generated because of geographical separation of buyer and seller often represent a part of price, and it is important to know whether they will be paid by purchaser or vendor. Pricing policies include psychological pricing including odd and unit pricing, product line pricing, promotional pricing, and flexible pricing. Price limits often relate the price/quality relationship in the consumer's mind.

Prices in the industrial market are often subject to negotiation or may be based on competitive bids. In large corporations, the necessity to set transfer prices when goods are transferred among profit centers of the same firm is a major decision problem. The market globalization which expresses itself in part in the online market has resulted in changes in traditional global pricing policies.

Pricing products to be sold online should involve consideration of the likelihood of cannibalization, competing with one's own products on a price basis on the Internet. In addition, the Internet features the availability of shopbots, search programs that seek out specific products and report on those with the lowest price.

Chapter 18
Price Concepts and Approaches

Chapter Outline

You may want to use the following outline as a guide in taking notes.

I. Chapter Overview

    How much does a product cost? The price is the exchange value of a good or service –
    whatever that product can be exchanged for in the marketplace. In this millennium, the price
    usually refers to a sum of money rather than some alternative such as a certain number of
    bushels of wheat, though wheat and similar commodities are sometimes used as media of
    exchange. Prices are difficult to set and dynamic – that is, changeable – with market condi-
    tions. A fair price is one that is profitable but justifiable, thus fair.

II. Pricing and the Law – Setting prices is influenced by a number of legal constraints imposed
    by federal, state, and local governments. Tariffs – taxes on imported products – often make
    it possible for local producers to set prices for domestic products higher than world market
    levels. Tariffs may also be used to remedy dumping – the selling of foreign-produced goods
    below their domestic prices in the U.S. market. Other countries can, of course, use tariffs for
    the same purposes. Not every regulatory price increase is a tax. When government man-
    dates certain actions by businesses, they may recover the costs of those fees by passing
    them on to their customers. Scalping of sports ticket has also become a legal issue in recent
    years. Pricing can be affected by lawsuits filed against product producers. Even if blame-
    less, firms that must defend themselves against suits have to pay the costs and pass them
    along to their customers. Finally, pricing is regulated by the general terms of U.S. antitrust
    legislation.

    A. The Robinson-Patman Act (1936) is a Depression era law that was inspired by price
        competition triggered by the rise of grocery store chains.
        1. Technically and amendment to the Clayton Act (1914), which had outlawed price dis-
            crimination between geographic areas that injured local sellers, the Robinson-
            Patman Act prohibits price discrimination in sales to wholesalers, retailers, and other
            producers, but <u>not</u> consumers.
            a. Differences in price must reflect cost differentials.
            b. The law prohibits selling at unreasonably low prices in order to drive competitors
                out of business.
        2. Price discrimination, where some customers pay more than others for the same
            products, dates back to the very beginnings of trade and commerce
            a. Technology has added to the frequency and complexity of price discrimination.
            b. As long as discounts and promotional allowances do not restrict competition, they
                avoid the penalties of the Robinson-Patman Act.
        3. Firms accused of price discrimination often argue that they set price differentials to
            meet competitors' prices and that cost differences justify variations in prices.
        4. A defense based on cost differentials works only if the price differentials do not ex-
            ceed the cost differences resulting from selling to various classes of buyers.

B. Unfair-trade laws – often called Unfair Trade Practices Acts – supplement federal legislation at the state level. These state laws require sellers to maintain minimum prices for comparable merchandise. Nearly forgotten for many years, these laws have been getting a workout in recent years as large retailers have begun to be accused of selling products below cost.

C. Fair-trade laws, which became invalid with the passage of the Consumer Goods Pricing Act (1975), allowed manufacturers to stipulate minimum retail prices for their products and to require dealers to sign contracts agreeing to abide by these prices.
    1. The fair trade laws asserted that a product's image, determined in part by its price, was a property right of the manufacturer.
    2. Fair trade legislation had its roots in the Great Depression.
    3. After fair trade laws were invalidated by a Supreme Court decision, Congress passed the Miller-Tydings Act (1937) exempting such laws from federal anti-trust provisions.
    4. The popularity of these laws declined over the years until they were invalidated by superseding federal legislation in the mid-1970s.
    5. A new semantic interpretation of the term "fair trade" has led some retailers to charge higher than market prices for some products in an attempt to help farmers in poor countries make a living wage.

III. Pricing Objectives and the Marketing Mix – The extent to which any or all of the four factors of production – natural resources, capital, human resources, and entrepreneurship – are used depends on the prices that those factors command. A firm's goals and objectives ultimately determine the prices it sets for its output. Price affects and is affected by the other elements of the marketing mix – product, promotion, and distribution. While pricing objectives vary from firm to firm, they can be categorized into four groups.

A. Profitability objectives are necessary because a firm, whether operated for profit or not-for-profit, must cover its costs and provide a financial cushion to cover unforeseen needs and expenses.
    1. Economic theory is based on the two theories that, first, firms will behave rationally, and second, that rational behavior will result in an effort to maximize gains and minimize losses.
    2. Marketers should evaluate and adjust prices continually to accommodate changes in the environment.
    3. Intense price competition often results when rival manufacturers battle for leadership positions in new product categories.
    4. Profits are a function of revenue and expenses: Profits = Revenue – Expenses; and revenues are determined by the product's selling price and the number of units sold: Total revenue = Price x Quantity Sold. A profit maximizing price is the price at which further increases will cause disproportionate decreases in the number of units sold.
    5. The above approach is referred to as *marginal analysis,* and identifies profit maximization as the point at which the addition to total revenue is just balanced by the increase in total cost.
    6. Since marginal analysis is seldom possible in practice, marketers commonly set target-return objectives that are short-run or long-run goals usually stated as percentages of sales or investment.

B. Volume objectives are served when marketers set a minimum acceptable profit level and then seek to maximize sales subject to this profit constraint in the belief that increased sales are more important than immediate high profits to the long-run competitive picture.

1. Sales maximization can also result from nonprice factors such as service and quality.
2. Another volume-related pricing objective is the market-share objective – the goal set for controlling a portion of the market for a firm's good or service.
    a. The Profit Impact of Market Strategies (PIMS) project, an extensive study by the Marketing Science Institute, revealed that two of the most important factors influencing profitability were product quality and market share.
    b. The PIMS data revealed that firms with market shares above forty percent averaged 32 percent return on investment.
    c. The relationship between market share and return on investment also applied to a firm's individual brands.
    d. Marketers have developed an underlying explanation of the positive relationship between profitability and market share: firms with large shares accumulate greater operating experience and lower costs relative to competitors with smaller market shares.
3. Meeting competition objectives are those that simply aim to meet competitors' prices.
    a. Price is a pivotal factor in the ongoing competition between long-distance telephone services and wireless carriers.
    b. Pricing objectives tied directly to meeting prices charged by major competitors deemphasize the price element of the marketing mix and focus more strongly on nonprice variables.
    c. Lands' End, the Sears subsidiary, focuses on non-price elements of the marketing mix, promoting its products' benefits, colors and styles, the company's excellence in customer service, and its easy-ordering system – in addition to price. Airlines, where ticket prices have become extremely competitive, have taken a similar position, emphasizing convenient schedules, comfortable seating, and other non-price incentives.
4. When discounts become normal elements of a competitive marketplace, other marketing mix elements gain importance in purchase decisions. A new strategy called value pricing has emerged that emphasizes the benefits a product provides in comparison to the price and quality levels of competing offerings.
    a. Laundry detergents are good examples of value pricing.
    b. Value-priced products generally cost less than premium brands, but marketers point out that value does not necessarily mean inexpensive.
    c. Value pricing is currently best seen in the personal computer industry.

C. Prestige objectives establish a relatively high price for a product to develop and maintain an image of quality and exclusiveness that appeals to status-conscious consumers.
    1. Tiffany jewelry lives at the high end of the price spectrum.
    2. In contrast to the low-price strategies used by marketers of economy cars, Jaguar ads promote exclusivity and are aimed at wealthy prospects.
    3. Having a corporate jet confers a prestige image on a firm, but the cost may be prohibitive; the alternative of fractional ownership imparts the required prestige at lower cost.

IV. Pricing objectives of not-for-profit organizations fall into four well-defined classes.

A. Profit maximization for not for profits often consists of their attempts to maximize the return on a single event or a series of events.

B. Cost recovery is an objective of some not-for-profit organizations that attempt to recover only the actual cost of operating the unit.

C. Market incentives are used by some not-for-profits when they price their products below cost or offer them for free to encourage use of the product or service. The downtown shuttle buses operating in a number of communities are examples of implementing this sort of objective.

D. Market suppression is a pricing objective that seeks to raise the price of "undesirable" gods so high that people will significantly reduce their consumption of the products. High taxes on alcohol and tobacco, parking ticket penalties, and bridge tolls are examples.

V. Methods for Determining Prices – Two basic methods for determining prices exist – applying the theoretical concepts of supply and demand and, alternatively, completing cost-oriented analyses.

   A. Often neglected in the discussions of this subject is another concept of price determination – one based on the impact of custom and tradition.
      1. Customary prices are retail prices that consumers expect as a result of tradition and social habit, such as 25 cents for a pack of chewing gum.
      2. Initial prices must be set for all products, and the prices must be reviewed and adjusted from time to time as needed as cost and competitive conditions change.

VI. Price Determination in Economic Theory is based on the idea that profit-maximization is the objective of business. Prices are set in the marketplace by comparing supply and demand. The analytical base is quite detailed and complex.

   A. Definitions
      1. *Demand* refers to a schedule of the amounts of a firm's product that consumers will purchase at different prices during a specified period.
      2. *Supply* is a schedule of the amounts of a good or service that will be offered for sale at different prices during a specified time period.
      3. *Pure competition* is a market structure with so many buyers and sellers that no single participant can significantly affect price.
      4. *Monopolistic Competition* is typical of retailing and features large numbers of buyers and sellers exchanging heterogeneous, well differentiated products.
      5. *Oligopoly* is a marketplace in which there are few sellers of a largely undifferentiated product.
      6. A *monopoly* is a market structure in which there is only one seller of a product or service for which there are no close substitutes.

   B. Cost and revenue curves are important because understanding them allows for an analysis of revenue versus expense.
      1. Types of costs
         a. Variable costs change with the level of production (like manufacturing labor and raw materials costs.)
         b. Fixed costs remain stable at any production level within a certain range (such as lease payments or executive salaries.)
         c. Average total costs are the result of dividing the sum of variable and fixed costs by the number of units produced.
         d. Marginal cost is the change in total cost that results from producing an additional unit of output.

    2. Revenue calculations
       a. Average revenue is calculated by dividing total revenue by the quantity of product associated with the revenue. It is the demand curve for the firm.
       b. Marginal revenue is the change in total revenue that results from selling an additional unit of output.
    3. Profit maximization occurs when marginal costs equals marginal revenues.

C. The concept of elasticity in pricing strategy explains why the impact of changes in price on sales varies greatly.
    1. Elasticity is the measure of responsiveness of purchasers and suppliers to price changes.
       a. Price elasticity of demand is the percentage change in the quantity of the good or service demanded divided by the percentage change in its price.
          i. When this ratio is greater than 1, demand is said to be elastic. A change in price results in a proportionately larger change in quantity demanded.
          ii. When the ratio is less than 1, demand is inelastic. A change in price results in a proportionately smaller change in quantity demanded.
       b. Elasticity is determined by several factors.
          i. Availability of substitutes for or complements of the product affect its elasticity.
          ii. The product's Internet presence; this has broadened the availability of similar products at a broad range of prices, creating a situation of demand elasticity for any one product.
          iii. Elasticity of demand also depends on whether a product is perceived to be a necessity or a luxury.
          iv. Products may change how they are perceived over time or with changes in the economy; necessities may, in tight economies, move into the luxury category and vice versa.
          v. Elasticity also depends on the portion of a person's budget he or she spends on the good or service.
          vi. Demand often shows less elasticity in the long run than in the short run because of consumers' time perspectives.
    2. Elasticity and revenue are explicitly related. A product with elastic demand will show a decrease in revenue with an increase in price whereas a product with inelastic demand will produce more revenue with an increase in price. The opposite is also true.

D. Practical problems of price theory exist, despite a high level of understanding of the concepts. For example, some firms don't attempt to maximize profits; it is also difficult to estimate demand curves.

VII. Price Determination in Practice – Price theory's practical limitations have forced marketers to turn to other techniques to set price. The most common method is cost-plus pricing, that uses a base-cost figure per unit and adds a markup to cover unassigned costs and provide a profit. The main differences among the many cost-plus techniques are the relative sophistication of the costing procedures involved. The procedures used by a small retail store are usually much simpler than those used by a manufacturer. Cost-plus pricing usually works well for a firm that keeps its costs low, letting it keep prices low and still make adequate returns.

A. Alternative pricing procedures, both cost-oriented, are the full-cost method and the incremental-cost method.
1. Full-cost pricing uses all relevant variable costs in setting a product's price and allocates those fixed costs that cannot be directly attributed to the production of the specific item being priced.
a. The full-cost approach has two deficiencies.
i. There is no consideration of competition or demand for the item.
ii. Any method for allocating overhead (fixed costs) is arbitrary and may be unrealistic.
2. Incremental cost pricing attempts to use only those costs directly attributable to a specific output in setting price for that output.

B. Breakeven analysis is a means of determining the number of goods or services that must be sold at a given price to generate sufficient revenue to cover total costs. The total cost curve for the product is calculated as is the revenue curve for that product at a given price. The intersection of the two curves – where total cost equals total revenue – describes the breakeven point for that product at that price.
1. Once the breakeven point has been reached, sufficient revenues will have been earned from sales to cover all fixed costs.
a. Target returns may be factored into the breakeven analysis by adding total fixed cost to the profit objective and dividing by the per unit contribution to revenue (excess of price over variable cost).
2. Breakeven analysis is an effective tool for marketers in assessing the sales required for covering costs and achieving specified profit levels.
3. The problems with breakeven analysis are three in number.
a. First, the model assumes that costs can be divided into fixed and variable components, which may not be true.
b. Second, the model assumes that per-unit variable costs do not change at different levels of operation, which also may not be true.
c. Finally, the basic breakeven model does not take into account demand, being a cost-based model.

VIII. Toward Realistic Pricing – Economic theory calls for balancing the effects of supply and demand at the point of equilibrium. Most pricing approaches are cost oriented. Since such an approach violates the marketing concept, modifications are called for to add demand analysis to the pricing decision.

A. The Modified Breakeven Concept is a model that brings demand into the equation started with the breakeven model. The analysis determines by consumer research how many units of product will be sold at a series of proposed prices. This information is added to the information contained in a basic breakeven analysis to determine which price offers the greatest potential profit. It may also reveal that none of the proposed prices offers the likelihood of an acceptable amount of profit.

B. Yield management strategies allow marketers to vary product prices based on such factors as demand, even though the cost of providing those goods or services remain the same. The logic is to adjust prices during the course of the day, week, or season so as to yield the greatest stream of revenue. When demand is high, prices are adjusted upward; when demand slackens, prices are adjusted downward. Airline tickets are a prime example of yield management. If one buys one's ticket early – or sometimes, late – enough, it is often possible to travel extraordinarily cheaply by air.

IX. Global Issues in Price Determination – Firms engaging in global marketing must use pricing strategies that reflect their overall marketing strategy. Five pricing objectives are useable by firms operating in the global market; four are similar to objectives available in the domestic market. The fifth is unique to international marketing. Marketers may choose profitability objectives if their company is a price leader that tends to establish international prices or if they are a low-cost producer. Volume objectives are especially important in situations where nations lower their trade barriers to expose domestic markets to foreign competition. Meeting competitors' prices has become important in Europe because of increased competition. Prestige is a valid pricing objective in international marketing when products are associated with intangible benefits such as high quality, exclusiveness, or attractive design. Finally, the pricing objective unique to international marketing, price stability, is desirable though difficult to achieve. National and international conflict, both economic and political, change policies and alter prices. Price stability is especially important for producers of commodities – products with easily accessible substitutes that other nations can quickly supply. Countries that export value-added products, on the other hand, tend to retain a level of price stability higher than that of commodity producers.

Name_____   Instructor_____

Section_____   Date_____

Key Concepts

The purpose of this section is to let you determine if you can match key concepts with their definitions. It is essential that you know the definitions of the concepts prior to applying the concepts in later exercises in this chapter.

From the list of lettered terms, select the one that best fits each of the numbered statements below. Write the letter of that choice in the space provided.

Key Terms

a. price
b. Robinson-Patman Act
c. unfair-trade laws
d. fair-trade laws
e. profit maximization
f. target return objective
g. Profit Impact of Market
    Strategies (PIMS) Project

h. value pricing
i. customary prices
j. elasticity
k. breakeven analysis
l. modified breakeven analysis
m. yield management

_____ 1. Point at which the additional revenue gained by increasing the price of a product equals the increase in total costs.

_____ 2. Pricing strategy emphasizing benefits a product provides in comparison to the price and quality levels of competing   offerings.

_____ 3. Pricing technique that evaluates consumer demand by comparing the quantities that a firm must sell at a variety of prices in order to cover total cost with estimates of expected sales at those prices.

_____ 4. In pricing strategy, the traditional amounts that customers expect to pay for certain goods or services.

_____ 5. Pricing technique that determines the number of products that must be sold at a specified price in order to generate sufficient revenue to cover total cost.

_____ 6. Federal legislation prohibiting price discrimination that is not based on a cost differential; this law also prohibits selling at an unreasonably low price to eliminate competition.

_____ 7. Short-run or long-run pricing practice intended to achieve a specified return on either sales or investment.

_____ 0. Pricing strategies designed to maximize revenues in situations such as air fares and theater tickets where costs are fixed.

_____ 9. Exchange value of a good or service.

_____ 10. Statutes once enacted in most states that permitted manufacturers to stipulate minimum retail prices for their products.

_____ 11. Major research study that discovered a strong positive relationship between a firm's market share and its return on investment.

_____ 12. State law requiring sellers to maintain minimum prices for comparable merchandise.

_____ 13. Measure of the responsiveness of purchasers and suppliers to a change in price.

Name_____   Instructor_____

Section_____   Date_____

Self-Quiz

You should use these objectives to test your understanding of the chapter material. You can check your answers with those provided at the end of the chapter.

While these questions cover most of the chapter topics, they are not intended to be the same as the test questions your instructor may use in an examination. A good understanding of all aspects of the course material is essential to good performance on any examination.

True/False

Write "T" for True and "F" for False for each of the following statements.

_____   1.   The Robinson-Patman Act (or Anti-Chain Act) often permits firms to set prices on domestically produced goods well above world market levels.

_____   2.   The price of an item is what it can be exchanged for in the market place. Price does not necessarily involve money.

_____   3.   The basic argument for the passage of fair-trade laws was that a product's image, which is determined in part by its price, is a property right of the manufacturer who should have the right to protect it.

_____   4.   The Robinson-Patman Act is sometimes called the "Anti-P & G Act," because it was designed to curb pricing abuses by large consumer-goods manufacturers like Proctor and Gamble.

_____   5.   The Robinson-Patman Act prohibits price discrimination in sales to wholesalers, retailers, and other producers; cost differentials, however, may constitute a defense for differences in the prices charged to different customers.

_____   6.   Unfair-trade laws are federal laws requiring sellers to maintain mandated minimum prices for comparable merchandise.

_____   7.   The Miller-Tydings Resale Price Maintenance Act of 1937 exempted interstate fair-trade contracts from compliance with antitrust requirements, allowing the various states to continue their fair-trade acts in place.

_____   8.   Product decisions, promotional plans, and distribution choices have little or no effect on the price of a good or service.

_____   9.   Classical economic theory assumes that firms will behave rationally and that this will result in an effort to maximize gains and minimize losses.

_____   10.   Target return pricing objectives satisfy the desire to generate maximum profits as judged by management, stockholders, and the public.

_____ 11. Many firms set a minimum acceptable sales level as their objective and then seek to maximize profits subject to the sales constraint in the belief that increased sales will generate immediate higher profits.

_____ 12. If the price of a product increases 10 percent and sales of the product decrease 8 percent, that product can be said to have elastic demand with respect to price (price elasticity of demand.)

_____ 13. The demand for a product for which there are a large number of close substitutes will tend to be elastic.

_____ 14. In marginal analysis, profit maximization is achieved when the addition to total revenue caused by selling an additional unit equals the increase in total cost caused by offering that unit.

_____ 15. Value priced products generally cost less than premium brands, but marketers point out that "value" doesn't necessarily mean "inexpensive."

_____ 16. Economic theory postulates that businesses strive to maximize sales; the truth is that many of them seek to maximize profits, perceived to be a more realizable goal.

_____ 17. PIMS data reveals that firms with a 40 percent or greater market share earn an average of 32 percent on investment, while those with a less than 10 percent share earn an average of only 13 percent.

_____ 18. The PIMS study revealed that two of the most important factors influencing a firm's profitability are its product quality and market share.

_____ 19. Pricing objectives tied directly to meeting prices charged by major competitors tend to overemphasize the price element of the marketing mix and focus more strongly on competitive variables.

_____ 20. Segmentation strategies designed to secure small shares of large markets rather than those seeking to gain large shares of small markets might be the better choice if PIMS data is correct.

_____ 21. The advertisement for Joy Perfume that states that the product is the "costliest perfume in the world" placed in very upscale magazines indicates that its maker is seeking to achieve a prestige image and pricing objective for this product.

_____ 22. Since not-for-profit organizations, by definition, do not have profitability as a goal, they never seek to maximize profits.

_____ 23. Modified competition is a market structure with relatively few sellers in which pricing decisions by each seller are likely to affect the market but no single seller controls it.

_____ 24. A product that is perceived to be a necessity will have greater elasticity of demand than one that is perceived to be a luxury.

_____ 25. Full-cost pricing uses all relevant variable costs in setting a product's price. In addition, it allocates those fixed costs that cannot be attributed directly to production of the item being priced.

Multiple Choice

Circle the letter of the word or phrase that best completes the sentence or best answers the question.

26. The federal law passed in 1936 which was inspired by price competition from developing grocery store chains and prohibits price discrimination in sales to wholesalers, retailers, and other producers is the
    a. Sherman Act.
    b. Miller-Tydings Act.
    c. Celler-Kefauver Anti-merger Act.
    d. Consumer Goods Pricing Act.
    e. Robinson-Patman Act.

27. A defense may be made against a charge of violating the price discrimination provisions of the Robinson-Patman Act if the accused can show that
    a. another firm violated the Act in the same fashion and wasn't caught.
    b. nobody in the firm is competent to understand the meaning of the law.
    c. competitors engage in similar behavior on a regular basis.
    d. the firm's price discounts are justified by cost differences in serving the different customers.
    e. the company has been doing this sort of thing for years.

28. A firm using value pricing for a good or service might promote that product using a slogan such as:
    a. "The resort hotel of incomparable service."
    b. "Be the envy of your friends and the talk of your neighborhood."
    c. "Among the most expensive wines in the world."
    d. "The highest quality available – if you have to ask how much it costs, you can't afford it."
    e. "Great performance at a reasonable price."

29. Which of the following is a target-return pricing objective?
    a. attempting to assure specific total unit sales in the current year
    b. matching the prices of the established industry price leader
    c. establishing relatively high prices to maintain an image of quality and exclusiveness
    d. seeking to capture and retain a specific market share percentage
    e. attempting to maintain a 7 percent net profit as a percent of sales

30. Marginal analysis is the approach used to determine price when a firm's pricing objective is
    a. maximizing sales volume.
    b. maximum profit.
    c. meeting competition.
    d. creating prestige.
    e. market leadership.

31. Value pricing is a pricing strategy that
    a. emphasizes the benefits a product provides in comparison to the price and quality levels of competing products.
    b. requires a more complex analytical process of determination than other pricing methods.
    c. seeks maximization of profits at the expense of image creation, functionality, and prestige.
    d. creates an image of quality and exclusiveness to the detriment of revenue.
    e. earns higher market share for its product at the expense of real long-term earnings.

32. Which of the following would be more likely to be a pricing objective of a not-for-profit organization than of a for-profit one?
    a. meeting competitors' prices
    b. achieving a target return on investment
    c. generating a specific dollar sales volume
    d. discouraging consumption of a product
    e. maximizing overall unit sales volume

33. The producer of which of the following products most likely follows a prestige pricing policy?
    a. Sacher Chocolate, "By Appointment to the Imperial Household of Austria-Hungary"
    b. Timex watches, "Stylish, Inexpensive Timepieces Everyone Loves."
    c. Schaefer beer, "The Beer to Have When You're Having More than One."
    d. Ken-l Ration for dogs, "Rover Will Love It."
    e. Coca-Cola, "The Pause that Refreshes."

34. One of the most significant studies of pricing strategies and objectives of the last twenty years was the PIMS project. For what does the acronym PIMS stand?
    a. Project to Initiate Marketing Selection
    b. Pennsylvania Institute of Marketing Studies
    c. Profit Impact of Marketing Strategies
    d. (Etude de) Produits Interieur du Marché Superieur
    e. Palomar Investigation of Marketplace Situations

35. When a nonprofit organization attempts to get prices on certain products reduced in the hope that such an action will increase consumption of those products, it is probably driven by the objective of
    a. cost recovery pricing.
    b. market suppression.
    c. profit maximization.
    d. seeking a target return on investment.
    e. providing market incentives.

36. Retail prices that customers have come to expect as a result of tradition or social habit are called
    a. residual prices.
    b. customary prices.
    c. day-to-day prices.
    d. unusual in today's market.
    e. controlled prices.

37. A schedule of the amounts of a product or service that consumers will purchase at different prices during a specified time period is
    a. a demand schedule.
    b. a competitive volume schedule.
    c. a description of market structure
    d. a supply schedule.
    e. an equilibrium schedule.

38. A market structure characterized by a large number of buyer and sellers exchanging hetero-geneous, relatively well-differentiated products, giving marketers some control over prices, is called
    a. nominal competition.
    b. monopolistic competition.
    c. oligopoly.
    d. monopoly.
    e. perfect competition.

39. The market structure with so many buyers and sellers that no single participant can signifi-cantly influence price is
    a. perfect competition.
    b. modified competition.
    c. pure competition.
    d. oligopolistic competition.
    c. monopolistic competition.

40. The average total cost of producing a product may be computed by
    a. computing the change in total cost resulting from producing an additional unit of output and dividing by total output.
    b. determining the amounts of costs that change with level of production and dividing by gross revenue.
    c. dividing the sum of total variable and fixed costs by the number of units produced.
    d. dividing revenue by number of units sold and subtracting variable cost.
    e. determining the change in total revenue resulting from selling one more unit of output.

41. Monopoly exists when
    a. there exists only one seller of a product for which there are no close substitutes.
    b. sellers in the market are few but large and product is undifferentiated.
    c. there are few buyers in a market, and sellers have to scramble to keep them supplied.
    d. there are numerous buyers and sellers in the market but communication among them is imperfect.
    e. buyers refuse to purchase what sellers have to offer.

42. Costs which remain stable regardless of the level of production achieved are called
    a. variable costs.
    b. fixed costs.
    c. average total costs.
    d. marginal costs.
    e. average revenue.

43. In the traditional economic model based on analysis of revenue and cost curves, profit maximization occurs when
    a. average total cost equals average revenue.
    b. marginal cost equals average revenue.
    c. average revenue equals average total cost.
    d. marginal cost equals marginal revenue.
    e. average total cost equals marginal cost.

44. The most popular method of price determination used today is
    a. marginal analysis pricing.
    b. incremental-cost pricing
    c. full-cost recovery pricing.
    d. cost-plus pricing.
    e. breakeven pricing.

45. When most of a firm's costs are fixed over a wide range of outputs and the primary determinant of profitability is the revenue produced by sales, it is appropriate to use
    a. full-cost pricing.
    b. incremental-cost pricing.
    c. yield management to set prices.
    d. cost-plus pricing.
    e. the MPMC model as the price setter.

46. Modified breakeven analysis differs from traditional breakeven analysis in that
    a. breakeven occurs when total revenue equals marginal revenue, instead of when average revenue equals total cost.
    b. no consideration is given to the required profit when making the analysis of costs and revenues.
    c. calculations are made using computer programs as the mechanism, rather than manually.
    d. breakeven no longer occurs when total profit equals total variable cost, but rather when total variable cost equals marginal revenue.
    e. consideration is given to evaluation of consumer demand as well as analysis of prices and costs.

47. Basic breakeven analysis
    a. is useless as a pricing tool because it is based on assumptions which are always untrue.
    b. identifies when a company's costs will equal its revenues at some price for the product, assuming that costs can be assumed to be divisible into fixed and variable parts.
    c. has become less sophisticated in recent years because there has been a tendency to abandon it in favor of more useful tools.
    d. is an effective way of recognizing marketplace variables and preparing for them beforehand.
    e. is not described by any of the above choices.

48. In the global market, producers of commodities – products such as bananas and sugar cane – may find this pricing objective more important than do producers of value-oriented products. The objective is
    a. profitability.
    b. market share.
    c. meeting competition.
    d. price stability.
    e. prestige image.

49. The continued development of on-line marketing affects the elasticity of product demand by
    a. making people aware of the availability of different models and prices, thus creating greater demand elasticity.
    b. providing greater price stability, hence less elasticity, because everyone will know what market conditions are like.
    c. allowing larger profit margins for retailers as they increase prices and reduce demand elasticity.
    d. letting vendors charge higher prices of consumers because they are vulnerable to supply manipulation.
    e. fostering chaos and the ultimate collapse of the economy as we know it.

50. The Morton Manufacturing Company makes iron castings for the plumbing industry. They are planning to introduce a new high-style manhole-cover assembly targeted at upscale neighborhoods and are wondering how many units they'll have to sell to break even on the deal. Fixed costs to tool up to make this assembly have been $150,000. Variable costs for each unit produced will be $20. At a price of $50 per assembly, how many units must be sold to break even?
    a. 2,500
    b. 4,000
    c. 5,000
    d. 8,000
    e. 7,500

Name_____　Instructor_____

Section_____　Date_____

Key Concepts

Applying Marketing Concepts

Eastern Shore Baking Company bakes and sells specialty breads, all of which are based on either a single or a blend of several entirely whole grain flours under the "Whole Grain Best" label. Elvin Catamaran, director of marketing for the company, was planning a speech to be delivered before the student marketing club at nearby Memphremagog University. Elvin knew the students would want to know about his company's marketing mix in general, and he also knew that pricing was sure to be an exceptionally hot issue because of a big price-fixing case in another industry that had been heavily covered by the press lately. It would be difficult to explain Eastern Shore's pricing policies because the firm did not aggressively use price to generate sales. As one of three firms dealing in this rather unique class of product in a five-state area, ESBC was satisfied with its third of the market and really didn't want to rock the boat unnecessarily. Prices were set at the beginning of the selling year based on the result of contract negotiations with suppliers of the flours and in some cases whole grains that ESBC ground themselves and from which the breads were made. Those prices were then maintained till the next year, subject only to special promotional activities.

In general, prices were set as follows: The cost of buying, milling (if needed), blending, baking and packaging each of the various breads ESBC made was computed. Costs that could not be assigned to a particular item were not included in the calculations. Once costs were determined, an amount sufficient to cover selling expenses and apportioned fixed costs and provide a reasonable profit was added to determine shelf (list) price. Since the other two firms in the area used the same method of determining price, initial prices were usually quite close, and were often identical. Differences that existed in the early part of the season "ironed themselves out" by midyear.

_____ 1.　Eastern Shore's pricing objective would be classified as profit maximization.

_____ 2.　The company would benefit from using modified break-even analysis.

_____ 3.　ESBC is constrained by customary prices and thus cannot change prices from year to year.

_____ 4.　ESBC's prices do not take into account demand for their products.

_____ 5.　If Mr. Catamaran were to apply modified breakeven analysis to his problem, he would have to use a method that assumes that variable cost would be a constant amount per unit.

6. Eastern Shore Baking Company's pricing objective is
   a. profit maximization.
   b. to maximize sales.
   c. a target rate of return on investment.
   d. meeting competition.
   e. to secure market share.

7. Mr. Catamaran's talk is really about setting prices in a(n)
   a. purely competitive market.
   b. oligopolistic market.
   c. monopolistically competitive market.
   d. monopsonistic market.
   e. market characterized by highly differentiated products.

8. The pricing mechanism which the company uses is
   a. the cost-plus approach.
   b. based on breakeven analysis.
   c. basically a modified breakeven process.
   d. based on analysis of demand elasticity.
   e. probably aimed at arriving at a customary price.

9. Mr. Catamaran's method of determining costs for pricing purposes was to apply
   a. full costing.
   b. breakeven analysis.
   c. markup on selling price.
   d. differential costing.
   e. incremental costing.

10. If we had been told that the "Whole Grain Best" brand was strongly preferred over competing brands in two of the five states where it was sold, we could have concluded that, in those states, Whole Grain Best's market was probably
    a. purely competitive.
    b. monopolistically competitive.
    c. oligopolistic.
    d. poligopolistic.
    e. monopolistic.

Hans-Gunther Horstschuler is in an enviable position. A graduate of the French National Engineering University at Metz (civil engineering), Technische Hochschüle der Baukunst von München (architecture), and the Parsons School of Design (interior design), he is in such demand as both designer and contractor of office buildings that he can literally name his own price. There are even reports of people hiring "hit" men to eliminate others who sought to use his services. Mr. Horstschuler realizes that popularity like his won't last forever and has stated in public that his fees are going to be high enough so that when things taper off he, his wife, and their six children will be able to live comfortably for many, many years.

The cost of a Horstschuler-built structure is now about $375 per square foot. The average office building in the area costs around $60 per square foot. Though apoplectic with envy, other contractors continue to build and successfully sell conventional structures at average prices because, even though they would love to be able to, not many firms can afford a building that costs $375 per square foot.

11. Mr. Horstschuler is well aware that his work possesses an image of quality and exclusiveness that appeals to status-conscious firms, and is pricing according to
    a. a volume objective.
    b. a target return objective.
    c. a prestige objective.
    d. an objective of meeting competition.
    e. an objective of maximizing sales.

12. The structure of the supply side of the building market in Mr. Horstschuler's part of the country right now is probably
    a. purely competitive.
    b. oligopolistic.
    c. a monopoly.
    d. monopolistically competitive.
    e. monogamous.

13. If we assume that the actual cost of construction of a Horstschuler-built structure is no greater than that of a building built by a "lesser" contractor and we take seriously his comments about "living comfortably for many, many years," we might conclude that his pricing objective has a component of
    a. securing market share.
    b. profit maximization.
    c. meeting competition.
    d. target return on investment.
    e. serving a selected market segment.

14. If Mr. Horstschuler collects money from his clients by submitting to them the invoices from his subcontractors and suppliers to which he adds a (rather large) percentage for his own costs and efforts, then the pricing method he is using is
    a. breakeven pricing.
    b. incremental cost pricing.
    c. modified breakeven pricing.
    d. customary pricing.
    e. cost-plus pricing.

Name_____   Instructor_____

Section_____   Date_____

Surfing the Net

Keeping in mind that addresses change and what's on the Web now may have changed by the time you read this, let's take a look at some of the places on the Net that reflect aspects of price determination. We are not endorsing or recommending any of these sources, merely making note of the information and services that people have elected to offer through the Internet.

Finding good Web sites to exemplify price determination was not easy. Typically, people's sites give you the results of their pricing decisions, not the logic behind them. On the other hand, where there's a will, there is often a way.

Looking for price determination at its most direct? Check out one or more of the auctions we've discovered. At an auction, the price is determined by direct interaction of supply and demand. If you've never been to an auction, you really should go to one – but leave your money at home. Auctions can be addictive. Some on-line auctions and their specialties include **http://www.oldandsold.com** that features all sorts of antiques, **http:/www.auctionarms.com** which specializes in firearms and related collectables, for the wine connoisseurs among you, there's **http://www.zachys.com** for auctions of wines of various sorts, and finally, for everything you could ever imagine and a lot of things you probably can't, there's always **http://www.ebay.com**.

Another example of direct interaction setting prices is in the stock market. A good entree to that market is the CNN Financial Network's financial markets service at **http://money.cnn.com.** This site has links to a number of other stock and bond market oriented sites. Alternatively, you might try Corporate Financial Online at **http://www.cfonews.com** for more detailed analysis of recent activity in the market and other links to important sites.

Finally, you might give some thought to what you're worth – at work, that is – at the JobNet Web site. This site compiles listings of available jobs from a number of sources, with trends in employment and employment statistics built in. Try it at **http://www.westga.edu/~coop/.** If you don't care for what you see there, there's always **http://www. careers.msn.com** or the related site **http://www.monster.com**. If you need more, try **http://www. hotjobs.com.**

Sites verified October 16, 2004.

Chapter 19
Managing the Pricing Function

Chapter Outline

You may want to use the following outline as a guide in taking notes.

I. Chapter Overview

Pricing is a dynamic, continuous process. Pricing decisions require that someone accept responsibility for making them and administering the resulting price structure. But someone must also set the overall pricing structure – basic prices and appropriate discounts for channel members, quantity purchases, and geographic and promotional considerations. The decision to make price adjustments is directly related to demand. In the retail gasoline and airline industries, significant price changes occur as "step outs" – a move by one firm that then waits to see if anyone else will follow its lead. Businesses tend to react slowly to movements in demand either up or down. Many price changes are cost-driven. This chapter examines pricing strategies and price structures, primary pricing policies, competitive and negotiated prices, and transfer pricing.

II. Pricing Strategies grow out of the marketing strategies firms formulate to accomplish overall organizational objectives.

    A. Skimming pricing, with its name derived from the term "skimming the cream," is also known as "market-plus" pricing, with prices being set relatively high with respect to the prices of competing products.

        1. A company can practice a skimming strategy in setting a market-entry price when it introduces a distinctive good or service with little or no competition.

        2. Improvements in existing products may allow firms to change from other pricing structures to a skimming structure.

        3. Skimming strategies are often used by marketers of high-end goods and services.

        4. In some cases a firm may maintain a skimming strategy throughout most stages of a product's life cycle – jewelry is an excellent example of such a situation.

        5. Sometimes maintaining a high price through the product's life cycle works and sometimes it does not.

        6. Despite the risk of backlash, a slimming strategy offers several benefits.

            a. It allows a manufacturer to quickly recover its research and development costs.

            b. It allows a firm to maximize revenue from a new product before competitors enter the field.

            c. Skimming is a useful tool for segmenting a product's overall market on price.

            d. Skimming permits marketers to control demand in the introductory stages of a product's life cycle and then adjust productive capacity to match changing demand.

        7. During the late growth and early maturity stages of its life cycle, a product's price typically falls for two reasons

            a. the pressure of competition causes price downturns and

            b. the product's marketers desire to expand its market.

        8. A skimming strategy has one chief disadvantage: It attracts competition because it is such a lucrative strategy.

B. Penetration pricing strategy sets a low price as a major marketing weapon. Low prices are often used when firms enter a new industry characterized by dozens of competing brands.
   1. Penetration pricing is also known as "market-minus" pricing when it is used to move a new-coming brand from the status of an unknown to the stage of brand recognition – or even preference.
   2. Marketers introducing new products using this strategy often find that competitors that perceive them to be a threat often match their prices.
   3. Firms that find that competitors match their prices – such as the discount air carriers – often compete by combining attractive airs fares, high customer service levels, and routes that other carriers do not serve. Thanks to the presence of casinos and service provided by Southwest and other airlines, the once sleepy little regional airport in Gulfport, Mississippi is now Gulfport International.
   4. Retailers use penetration pricing to lure customers to new stores.
   5. Penetration pricing works best for products for which demand is highly elastic.
   6. Everyday low pricing is closely related to penetration pricing, except that the strategic philosophy is to set and maintain low prices on a continuous basis rather than relying on short-term price reductions.
      a. In many cases, the EDLP strategy is used by manufacturers in dealing with channel members to stabilize wholesale prices.
      b. Some retailers oppose EDLP strategies, while others advocate them.
   7. It is a myth that a low price is a "sure sell" – price elasticity must be significant or low prices will result in lower revenue industry-wide because lower prices will not result in higher sales.

C. Competitive pricing is a strategy that depends on reducing the emphasis on price competition by simply matching competitors' prices, relying on the product, promotion, and distribution components of the marketing mix to provide the needed differentiation.
   1. Home Depot and Lowe's both use price-matching strategies, meeting and even beating competitors' prices.
   2. Even when the products being sold are heterogeneous, firms monitor the prices of major competitive offerings to be sure that their firms do not differ markedly in price.
   3. Under competitive pricing, a price reduction by one firm has financial effects throughout the industry as other firms match the reduction.
   4. Even WalMart is not immune from competitive pricing – especially from the so-called "dollar stores."
   5. When they price products at the general level of competitive offerings, firms largely negate the price variable in their marketing strategies and must find alternative incentives to induce customers to buy from them.

III. Price Quotations – A firm's choice of how to quote the prices of its offerings is based on industry conditions including competitive trends, cost structures, and traditional practices, as well as the firms' own policies. Most price structures are built around *list prices*, the prices normally quoted to potential buyers.

A. Reductions from list price – The actual price a consumer pays for a product (the market price) may but often does not equal the list price. The list price merely represents a starting point from which reductions are subtracted to determine what one will actually pay.
   1. Cash discounts are price reductions received for the prompt payment of bills and are a traditional pricing practice in many industries. Many business students are familiar with cash discounts of the form 2/10, net 30.

2. Trade discounts are payments to channel members for performing marketing functions; these are also known as functional discounts.
   a. Trade discounts initially reflected the operating expenses of each class of intermediary in a channel of distribution, but have now become more or less customary for many industries.
   b. Trade discounts are usually applied "in sequence," that is, the retailer's discount is subtracted from the list price and the resulting amount is the basis from which the wholesaler's discount is subtracted.
3. Quantity discounts are reductions in price granted for quantity purchases.
   a. Quantity discounts may be either cumulative, an arrangement in which discounts are granted based on purchases over a stated time period, or noncumulative, providing a one-time reduction in price.
   b. Many businesses have come to expect quantity discounts from suppliers, and the firm that does not offer them runs the risk of losing substantial amounts of business.
   c. Marketers typically favor combinations of cash, trade, and quantity (volume) discounts.
4. Allowances are deductions in price that resemble discounts yet are different.
   a. Trade-ins, often used in the sale of durable goods such as automobiles, consist of the vendor's accepting used merchandise, typically of the same kind as that being bought, as part of the selling price of a new good.
   b. Promotional allowances reduce the price of goods to members of the distribution channel in return for their participation in promotion of a manufacturer's products in the form of advertising and sales support.
      i. The recent release by *Consumer Reports* of information concerning the hidden allowances given retail automobile dealers but included in the prices of automobiles sold at retail has given additional information on which consumers can base their bargaining strategy in new car purchases.
      ii. For years, the price of music CDs has been artificially high because of the presence of promotional allowances tied to retailers' agreements not to sell products below a minimum advertised price.
5. Rebates are the refund of a portion of the purchase price paid for a product and are usually used when sales are slow and manufacturers want to reduce inventories without permanently cutting prices.
   a. Rebates may be paid in cash or as contributions to savings arrangements such as prepaid college tuition plans, or they are sometimes applied to the purchase price of a product by the retail vendor.

B. Geographic considerations – In pricing, these considerations generally have to do with costs related to transportation of goods by members of a distribution channel. Such costs may be handle one of three ways: the vendor pays all the costs; the buyer pays all the costs; or the vendor and the buyer split the costs between tbem.
1. FOB (free on board) plant, also known as FOB origin, involves vendors pricing goods to include no shipping charges. Shipping charges become the responsibility of the buyer at the time the goods are placed aboard the transportation carrier of the buyer's choice.
   a. An alternative to FOB origin pricing is FOB origin-freight allowed, in which buyers are allowed to subtract the cost of shipping from their bills. The amount received by the vendor thus varies with the amount of the shipping costs.

2. Uniform delivered pricing (sometimes called postage-stamp pricing) is in force when the vendor quotes all buyers the same price, including freight charges. Buyers near the vendor's plant pay what is called "phantom freight" or more for the actual goods because of their proximity to the source.

3. Zone pricing modifies the uniform delivered price concept by dividing the overall market into zones within which the same freight costs are paid by all buyers.
    a. Zone pricing can result in situations where a two or three-mile trip to buy certain goods is worth it to the ultimate consumer because retailers have to pay higher costs of transportation in one nearby location than in another.

4. Basing point pricing is a scheme in which the price of a good includes the list price of the product at the factory plus shipping charges from the basing point – which may not be the location from which the item is actually shipped – nearest the buyer. This system is designed to level the competitive playing field among vendors because they all quote identical transportation rates. Such systems are quite rare today.

IV. Pricing Policies – These general guidelines reflect marketing objectives and influence specific pricing decisions. Pricing policies form the basis for more practical price-structure decisions. Specific policies deal with various competitive situations, the final choice depending on the environment within which the decisions must be made.

A. Psychological pricing is based on the belief that certain prices or price ranges make products more appealing to buyers than others. Prestige pricing, discussed elsewhere, is one of the three available choices.
    1. Odd pricing, which began life as a cash-control device and is sometimes called "off-even" pricing, has become entrenched in retail pricing because many people believe that pricing products just below the next even increment – like $4.98 rather than $5.00 – somehow induces customers to think of the product as selling for $4.00 plus a few cents.
    2. Unit pricing states prices in terms of some standard unit of measurement such as ounces, pounds, or even number of items in the package and is supposed to facilitate price comparisons among products sold in packages of different sizes.

B. Price flexibility may or may not be a policy of a vendor. Flexible pricing exists when sellers permit different prices for different customers. Most mass-marketing programs operate on a single-price basis, with flexible pricing being characteristic of programs based on individual bargaining.
    1. Traditionally, automobiles have been sold on a flexible-price basis, but Saturn pioneered the single-price concept for new automobiles on its introduction as a brand.
    2. The telecommunications industry has moved away from its traditionally extraordinarily complex tariff schedules to something more like a fixed-price schedule, but not sufficiently rapidly to prevent many people from abandoning hard-wired phones for a cellular alternative.
    3. Variable pricing may be an effective policy in some circumstances, but when applied above the retail level in the channel of distribution, such policies may run afoul of the provisions of the Robinson-Patman Act.

C. Product line pricing is the practice of setting a limited number of prices for a selection or merchandise, rather than pricing items individually.
    1. If a retailer offers neckties at only three prices – say $12.95, $16.95, and $21.95 – it becomes much simpler to decide which tie to buy than if the ties were priced at twelve or fifteen different prices in that same approximately nine-dollar range.

2. Product line pricing is very popular among retailers because it offers benefits both to them and to their customers.
3. Many airlines divide their seating areas on international flights according to product-line pricing into as many as four classes – discount, coach, business-class, and first-class.
4. A potential problem with product-line pricing is that once a limited number of price points has been decided upon, firms may have difficulty changing the prices of individual items.

D. Promotional pricing uses a lower-than normal price as a temporary ingredient in a firm's selling strategy.
   1. Leader pricing and loss leaders are two varieties of promotional pricing very popular among retailers.
      a. Loss leaders are products priced below cost to attract customers who will, it is hoped, buy other, regularly priced merchandise.
      b. Leader-priced merchandise is priced slightly above cost to avoid violating unfair-trade laws and generate some contribution to return on promotional sales.
      c. The most common practitioners of loss leader and leader pricing are supermarkets and mass merchandisers such as WalMart and Target.
      d. Leader pricing has even reached the personal computer industry in the form of a price war that has driven prices down to levels that make profit margins razor-thin. Indeed, the prices of brand-new computers have tumbled from as much as $5,000 to as little as $400 – and the $400 units are technologically far advanced from the $5,000 units of 1990.
   2. Promotional pricing has two pitfalls that may affect those who choose to use it.
      a. Some buyers are not attracted by promotional pricing.
      b. If the promotional price remains in place too long, customers may come to regard the promotional price as the customary price of the product and resist price increases.

E. Price-quality relationships are one of the most thoroughly researched aspects of pricing. Price can serve as an important indicator of a product's quality to potential purchasers.
   1. The relationship between price and perceived quality is a widely used tool for marketers. The names Rolex, Bentley, and Sulzer, in their respective industries, are perceived as "top of the line" products.
   2. Premium products, that is, products that have established a positive relationship between their quality and the price at which they are sold, have proven able to withstand the ups and downs of economic activity.
   3. Price limits define the concept of the price-quality connection quite well: consumers define certain limits within which their quality perceptions vary directly with price.
   4. Hyperinflation, the condition where the rate of monetary inflation goes into high two-digit or even three-digit percentages, destroys the perceived relationship between price and quality because it becomes almost impossible to decide what something "should" cost because a product bought by a vendor last week and offered for sale today will cost fewer units of currency than the same thing bought today and offered for sale tomorrow. In other words, prices for the same thing keep going up because the value of the money – not the quality of the product keeps declining.

V. Competitive Bidding and Negotiated Prices – Many government and organizational procurement departments do not pay set prices for their purchases, particularly when they are buying very large quantities. Prices are determined, instead, by a process of competitive bidding. Some firms are very good at meeting the specifications called for by government bidding rules at good prices, which is why 85 percent of all U.S. police cars (and those used by the police of Moscow) are Ford Crown Victorias.

A. Negotiating prices online starts with the realization that auctions are the purest form of negotiated pricing; hence, the presence of the many auctions such as eBay.com, Tickets.com, and Priceline.com certify to the negotiated nature of many prices on line.

VI. The Transfer Pricing Dilemma – This is a pricing problem unique to large firms that have to decide how much to charge themselves for products being moved between profit centers in their own organization. Profit centers are parts of the organization to which revenue and controllable costs can be assigned – such as a department. Decentralized firms are those that tend to have the largest number of profit centers. In a large firm, profit centers might secure many needed resources from sellers within the firm. Transfer pricing can be complicated, especially when the firm is a multinational. Multinational transactions between divisions of the same firm offer the opportunity to avoid paying taxes on profits. In some cases, such arrangements allow the manipulative firm to arrange its intrafirm (that is, within itself) pricing so that all its profit is made in the country with the lowest tax rates.

VII. Global Considerations and Online Pricing – The presence of the Internet has had and will continue to have a profound effect on pricing. Since every online marketer is a global marketer – whether by intent or not – internal and external conditions growing out if its involvement with Internet vending affect it and what it does. Internally, its objectives and aspirations may change as the Internet opens up new vistas to it, while externally, conditions in international markets, regulatory limitations, trade restrictions, competitive actions, economic events, and the status of the industry globally will all have an effect.

A. Traditional global pricing policies include a standard worldwide price, dual pricing, or market-differentiated pricing. A standard worldwide price can be successful if foreign marketing costs remain low enough so that they do not affect overall costs or if prices reflect average unit costs. Dual pricing sets one price for domestic sales of the product, another for foreign sales. Such a pricing policy guarantees a profit on every product sold, but may make it difficult to sell any product because prices exceed those charged by competitors. Dual pricing may be made somewhat flexible by using cost-plus schemes that allow discounts or prices that can change with changes in local competitive conditions. Market-differentiated pricing allows even greater flexibility in pricing, closely tracking local conditions and pricing accordingly.

B. Characteristics of online pricing include new applications of old techniques of price adjustment, such as on-line coupons that allow busy shoppers to avail themselves of temporary discounts on desirable products.
1. Cannibalization is a problem for online vendors who find themselves creating situations where they engage in price competition with their own products. It is not unusual to find vendors offering products at one price to people who physically visit their stores, but at other, lower prices for those who shop with them on the Internet.
2. Another situation characteristic of Internet pricing is the use by consumers of shopbots, special search programs that act as comparison shopping agents, finding and

reporting the vendors with the lowest prices. Newer bots also solicit input from shoppers concerning their perceptions of other factors of vendor performance such as service quality and customer support.

C. Bundle pricing is an Internet-common pricing policy in which the base product comes with an array of additional products or services at no additional cost. Bundling is part of a strategy to increase the long-term use of the bundled products, typically services, offered with a base product such as a computer, cable or satellite TV service, or telephone access.

Name_____   Instructor_____

Section_____   Date_____

Key Concepts

The purpose of this section is to allow you to determine if you can match key concepts with their definitions. It is essential that you know the definitions of the concepts prior to applying the concepts in later exercises in this chapter.

From the list of lettered terms, select the one that best fits each of the numbered statements below. Write the letter of that choice in the space provided.

Key Terms

a.   skimming price strategy
b.   penetration pricing strategy
c.   competitive pricing strategy
d.   allowance
e.   FOB (free on board) plant (FOB Origin)
f.   FOB origin-freight allowed (freight absorbed)
g.   uniform-delivered pricing

h.   zone pricing
i   psychological pricing
j.   promotional pricing
k.   loss leader
l.   cannibalization
m.   bundle pricing

_____   1.   Pricing policy based on the belief that certain prices or price ranges make a good more appealing than others to buyers.

_____   2.   Pricing strategy involving the use of a relatively low entry price as compared with competitive offerings; designed to help secure initial market acceptance.

_____   3.   System that handles transportation costs by allowing the buyer to deduct shipping expenses from the cost of the goods.

_____   4.   Offering two or more complementary products and selling them for a single price.

_____   5.   Pricing strategy designed to de-emphasize price as a competitive variable by pricing a product at the general level of comparable offerings.

_____   6.   Price quotation that does not include shipping charges.

_____   7.   Securing additional sales through lower prices that take sales away from the marketer's other products.

_____   8.   System that handles transportation costs by dividing the market into geographic regions and setting a different price in each region.

_____   9.   Price-setting system that handles transportation costs by quoting all buyers the same price, including transportation expenses.

_____   10.   Pricing strategy involving the use of a high price relative to competitive offerings.

_____ 11.   Pricing policy in which a lower than normal price is used as a temporary ingredient in a firm's marketing strategy.

_____ 12.   A specified deduction from list price, including trade-in and promotional versions.

_____ 13.   Product offered to consumers at less than cost to attract them to stores in the hope they will buy other merchandise at regular prices.

Name_____   Instructor_____

Section_____   Date_____

Self-Quiz

You should use these objective questions to test your understanding of the chapter material. You can check your answers with those provided at the end of the chapter.

While these questions cover most of the chapter topics, they are not intended to be the same as the test questions your instructor may use in an examination. A good understanding of all aspects of the course material is essential to good performance on any examination.

True/False

Write "T" for True and "F" for False for each of the following statements.

_____ 1. In some cases, such as that of fine jewelry, a firm may maintain a skimming pricing strategy throughout most of the stages of a product's life cycle.

_____ 2. Many firms begin a penetration pricing strategy with the intention of maintaining that price for a substantial length of time, so that success of the strategy cannot be measured in terms of trial purchases.

_____ 3. During the late growth and early maturity stages of the product life cycle, a product that was originally introduced using a skimming pricing strategy is typically increased in price to compensate for the pressure of competition and the desire to expand its market.

_____ 4. One advantage of a skimming strategy is that it permits the marketer to control demand in the introductory stages of the product life cycle and then adjust productive capacity to meet changing demand.

_____ 5. One of the forms of everyday low pricing involves retailers like WalMart and Lowe's that compete by offering consumers consistently low prices on a broad range of items.

_____ 6. Penetration pricing works best when a good or service possesses highly elastic demand.

_____ 7. Retailers universally oppose everyday low pricing strategies because of their use of "high-low" strategies that depend on frequent specials and promotions.

_____ 8. When a competitive pricing strategy is in place, a price reduction has few financial effects on the entire industry because other firms seldom match the first firm's drop.

_____ 9. Price-matching strategies such as those used by Lowe's and Home Depot are examples of competitive pricing strategies.

_____ 10. When marketers only occasionally price their products at the general levels of competitive offerings, they largely negate the price variable as an element of their marketing strategy.

_____ 11. Marketers typically avoid combinations of cash, trade, and quantity discounts, tending to use one or the other of them exclusively.

_____ 12. Trade discounts initially reflected the operating costs of members of a channel of distribution, but they have become more or less "customary practices" in some industries.

_____ 13. If a trade discount were quoted as "35 percent, 15 percent off list price" for wholesalers, this would mean that wholesalers would pay the manufacturer of the good the list price less the 35 percent that they were to discount the list price to retailers, less another 15 percent of the discounted price to compensate them for their costs, profits, and services.

_____ 14. A vendor who offers a price reduction of 4 percent to customers who record annual purchases of at least $30,000 with that vendor in a given year is offering a noncumulative quantity discount.

_____ 15. The major categories of allowances are price adjustments and trade-outs.

_____ 16. When "FOB origin" pricing is used, the buyer pays only the cost of loading the merchandise aboard the carrier selected by the seller.

_____ 17. "Uniform-delivered pricing" is sometimes also known as *postage-stamp pricing*, and might be considered to be the exact opposite of FOB origin pricing.

_____ 18. The often-used term "FOB" is really an abbreviation for "Foreign Overload Batching."

_____ 19. Both zone and uniform delivered pricing have the drawback that some customers will be paying *phantom freight*.

_____ 20. Originally, odd pricing was used as a cash-control device, forcing clerks to make change, but remains as a common feature of today's price quotes.

_____ 21. Unit pricing – pricing goods in terms of some recognized unit of measure or by standard numerical count – has significantly improved the shopping habits of low-income consumers by allowing them to make more meaningful price comparisons.

_____ 22. One-price policies characterize situations in which individual bargaining between vendor and potential purchaser is employed, whereas variable pricing is used where mass selling marketing programs are typical.

_____ 23. Product-line pricing offers the shopper the advantage of picking a price range and then devoting his or her attention to the non-price features of the product such as color, style, material, or other relevant features.

_____ 24. Loss-leader pricing is prohibited in those states with unfair-trade laws.

_____ 25. Hyperinflation such as has existed in some South American and Asian countries in recent years sharpens the relationship in consumers' perceptions between the price and quality of products.

Multiple Choice

Circle the letter of the word or phrase that best completes the sentence or best answers the question.

26. Canon's new S600 printer that featured individual ink tanks that allow the user to replenish a single color without disposing of the entire ink cartridge was introduced using a
   a. skimming pricing strategy.
   b. penetration pricing strategy.
   c. competitive pricing strategy.
   d. "market-minus" price strategy.
   e. functional strategy.

27. Which of the following is one of the advantages of a penetration pricing strategy?
   a. It allows the firm to quickly recover its research and development costs.
   b. It is effective in segmenting the overall market on a price basis.
   c. Large numbers of highly price-conscious consumers pay close attention to the appeal of penetration pricing.
   d. It permits the marketer to control demand in the introductory stages of the product's life cycle and to adjust productive capacity to meet demand.
   e. It largely negates the price variable in the marketing strategy.

28. When a skimming strategy is used, the product's price is typically reduced during the late growth and early maturity stages of the product life cycle because
   a. volume of production is sufficiently high to allow reductions in the per-unit cost of the product.
   b. successive price declines may expand the firm's market size and meet challenges posed by new competitors.
   c. the profits earned during the introductory and early growth stages of the cycle may be plowed into new productive technology, making lower prices possible.
   d. competition has been effectively stifled and the product can now be allowed to sell at its "natural" price.
   e. the product's proprietors have achieved their target objective and can now afford to take less "off the top" for contribution to profit and overhead.

29. Though the one chief disadvantage of a skimming pricing policy is its tendency to attract competition, it may still be used effectively for a relatively long period if
   a. financial pressure can be placed on potential competitors which will prevent them from entering the market.
   b. research and development costs are quite small and can be recovered very early in the product life cycle.
   c. production facilities are able to satisfy all potential demand which may develop.
   d. patent protection or some other unique proprietary ability – like a trade secret B can keep out competition.
   e. inventories of goods are kept larger than any demand for the product which may develop.

30. When a penetration pricing strategy is used,
    a. prices are set at a level well above the prices of existing competing products.
    b. the price of the product is adjusted as necessary to keep it competitive with similar products in the market.
    c. the product is usually already in the decline stage of its life cycle and price manipulation is a normal feature of this stage.
    d. it is necessary that there be no pre-existing competition; otherwise, the strategy won't work.
    e. new products or services are initially priced noticeably lower than competing offerings in industries with many competing brands.

31. A penetration pricing policy is likely to be most successful when
    a. few consumers are sensitive to price.
    b. many suppliers are price-sensitive.
    c. some suppliers are price-sensitive.
    d. demand for the product is highly elastic.
    e. supply for the product is highly elastic.

32. In industries with relatively homogeneous products,
    a. competitors must match each other's price reductions to maintain market share and competitive position.
    b. skimming pricing is often used as a differentiating tool among producers of what are essentially commodities.
    c. penetration pricing may provide the consumer advantage necessary for success.
    d. pricing based solely on costs is almost mandatory.
    e. market-plus pricing offers the advantage of high short-term return with little down-side risk.

33. Using a competitive pricing strategy
    a. creates the situation of segmenting the overall market on a price basis.
    b. conveys an image of distinction and appeal to buyers who are less sensitive to price.
    c. shifts the marketing emphasis to nonprice competition in product, distribution, and promotional areas.
    d. is useful to introduce new products in industries where there are large numbers of competing brands.
    e. discourages competition, since the attractive financial returns associated with skimming are not usually present.

34. Which of the following most closely represents the list price of a product?
    a. the amount of money you and your next door neighbor's son both agree is fair to pay him to cut your lawn
    b. the amount of money you ask for when you decide to sell your 1994 Mitsubishi Montero
    c. the manufacturer's suggested retail price (MSRP) on a new GE television set
    d. the advertised price of a home offered "for sale by owner" in a classified newspaper advertisement
    e. the price you paid for your new set of tires after all discounts and allowances were subtracted from the original price

35. Reductions in price offered for prompt payment of bills B usually specifying the exact time period involved B are known as
    a. trade discounts.
    b. cash discounts.
    c. quantity discounts.
    d. cutback discounts.
    e. "off price" discounts.

36 If the payment terms on an invoice are shown as 4/10, net 60, then
    a. the full amount must be paid within ten days and legal action will be taken after 60.
    b. the full amount is due in 60 days but if you pay the invoice in ten days you can deduct four percent from the total.
    c. four percent of the invoice must be paid in ten days, and the rest in 60 days.
    d. ten percent of the amount due must be paid in four days, with the rest due at the end of 60 days.
    e. four-tenths of the amount billed is due in 60 days.

37. Payments to channel members for performing marketing functions are known as
    a. cash or seasonal discounts.
    b. seasonal or cumulative discounts.
    c. incremental or decremental discounts.
    d. trade or functional discounts.
    e. noncumulative quantity discounts.

38. If a trade discount stated as "50 percent, 15 percent off list" were offered to a wholesaler by a manufacturer, then the wholesaler would pay which of the following prices for a good whose usual retail price to the consumer was $100?
    a. $32.50
    b. $35.00
    c. $37.50
    d. $41.00
    e. $42.50

39. A discount that depends only on the number of units or dollar value of product bought in a single transaction is a
    a. noncumulative quantity discount.
    b. cumulative quantity discount.
    c. promotional quality discount.
    d. cash or standard discount.
    e. market position status discount.

40. Allowances are similar to discounts in that they
    a. provide that larger customers pay less per unit for the things they buy.
    b. are based on the operating expenses of each level in the channel of distribution.
    c. specify deductions from the list price of a product.
    d. alter the financing rates normally quoted to potential buyers.
    e. are used uniformly across the consumer and industrial segments of the market.

41. Trade-ins accepted by the vendors of consumer durables such as automobiles are
    a. trade discounts.
    b. rebates.
    c. market pricing.
    d. allowances.
    e. variable pricing.

42. A means of handling transportation expenses in which only the seller pays the shipping charges is
    a. FOB plant pricing.
    b. uniform delivered pricing.
    c. zone pricing.
    d. all-for-one pricing.
    e. freight absorption.

43. When a lower-than-normal price is used as a temporary ingredient in a firm's selling strategy,
    a. it is called predatory pricing.
    b. "market-up" pricing may result.
    c. pass-through pricing is the policy.
    d. "market-down" conditions may result.
    e. it is called promotional pricing.

44. Pittsburgh-plus pricing was
    a. a variety of zone pricing once used in the Chicago meat packing industry.
    b. the basing-point system of quoting prices in the American steel industry in the early part of the twentieth century.
    c. widely used by manufacturers of parts for automobiles during the 1960's and 1970's.
    d. a type of FOB origin-freight allowed pricing typical in the fresh produce (fruits, vegetables, and like goods) industry in the western United States.
    e. a method of determining how much it would cost to ship anything to Pittsburgh.

45. When a retailer prices products in terms of some standard numerical count (by the dozen or the hundred or the gross), that retailer is using
    a. unit pricing.
    b. promotional pricing.
    c. odd pricing.
    d. psychological pricing.
    e. average-cost pricing.

46. The use of a variable price policy by a seller
    a. facilitates mass marketing programs where the customer does not expect to negotiate the price.
    b. creates the possibility of haggling between buyer and seller over the price of every item in the store.
    c. can often be recognized by the preponderance of prices ending in 5, 8, or 9.
    d. is quite common in large-scale department store retailing, where variable pricing is the rule.
    e. may result in retaliatory pricing by competitors.

47. When a retail firm prices goods slightly above cost to avoid violating minimum-markup regulations and to earn some return on promotional sales, it is using
    a. bait and pull pricing.
    b. bull and bear pricing.
    c. leader pricing.
    d. product-line pricing.
    e. multiple-unit pricing.

48. The concept of <u>price limits</u> basically says that
    a. people consciously limit their spending to goods which do not affect their consumption patterns.
    b. a firm may encounter legal opposition if the prices of its products exceed certain limits.
    c. the relationship between price and sales volume is limited to values greater than 2.
    d. consumer have limits within which their product-quality perceptions vary directly with price.
    e. individuals expect to be able to limit spending to necessities and a few luxuries, even in bad times.

49. In the governmental and industrial markets, when there is only one supplier of a good or service or where extensive research and development work is called for by a contract,
    a. competitive bidding may nonetheless be required by law.
    b. negotiation is likely to be the basis on which the contract is awarded.
    c. an escalator clause is typically included in the contract to protect the buyer from price increases.
    d. transfer pricing may be used to reduce the process of contracting to a comprehensible level.
    e. specifications must be especially carefully written so that breach or abrogation of the contract will be easy to prove in court.

50. FOB origin-freight allowed pricing is also known as
    a. postage-stamp pricing.
    b. pricing to the market.
    c. zone pricing.
    d. basing point pricing.
    e. freight absorption.

Name_____   Instructor_____

Section_____   Date_____

Applying Marketing Concepts

Adastra High Definition Television Corporation manufactures a line of HDTV sets that are distributed throughout the United States. Sold primarily through specialty outlets, Adastra products are recognized as leaders in their field. Sales volume and profits have increased dramatically over the last five years. Adastra sells to retailers through its own sales force, but in those parts of the country where sales volume isn't large enough to justify maintaining a company sales representative, it uses electronics wholesalers.

Adastra is a respected name in its industry. Retailers often feature the company's line in their advertising. The company encourages this and gives dealers who advertise their relationship price reductions on Adastra products to help them pay their advertising costs. They also have a somewhat unusual approach to pricing for an electronics manufacturer. Prices on Adastra products are the same, including transportation, to any dealer anywhere in the country.

The company's product line includes three ranges of HDTV set. The "stellar" units have a 15 by 25 inch picture tube and sell in the $525 to $700 range, depending on special features. The "Galactic" models are somewhat larger with 21 by 35 inch pictures. These units sell for $950 to $1200. The top of the line "Universality" models feature a very nice 27 by 45 inch picture and sell for $1800 to $2200. Adastra publishes manufacturer's suggested retail prices (MSRP's) whose dollar amounts always end in a 98 (like $1098) and encourages dealers to stick with that ending even if they discount the product off the MSRP. It is management's belief that the 98 ending helps sales.

_____ 1. Adastra's pricing policies encourage retailers to sell their products as loss leaders.

_____ 2. Since Adastra quotes the same price to all buyers of its products it is using a unit pricing policy.

_____ 3. The company is encouraging its retailers to use psychological pricing.

_____ 4. If Adastra were to institute a trade-in program, it would be suggesting that retailers sell the company's products at less than list price.

_____ 5. By pricing its products in different ranges, the company is attempting to define important product characteristics that differentiate the product lines and contribute to customer choices to trade up or trade down.

6. The discount that Adastra gives wholesalers who sell to retailers is called a
   a. cash discount.
   b. trade discount.
   c. quantity discount.
   d. promotional discount.
   e. rebate.

7. What kind of allowance does Adastra currently grant its distributors?
   a. a rebate
   b. a trade-in
   c. a promotional allowance
   d. an allowance for returned goods
   e. a sales representative's field allowance.

8. Adastra's geographic pricing policy is
   a. FOB plant.
   b. FOB plant–freight allowed.
   c. zone pricing.
   d. basing point pricing.
   e. uniform delivered pricing.

9. The company's general pricing policy is one of
   a. product line pricing.
   b. unit pricing.
   c. skimming pricing.
   d. penetration pricing.
   e. price fixing.

10. The firm encourages its retailers to engage in
   a. skimming pricing.
   b. penetration pricing.
   c. unit pricing.
   d. odd pricing.
   e. unusual pricing.

Sendlinger Office Machines Company is a sells computers and related products dealership in Jamestown, New York. The company sells two domestic brands – Hewlett-Packard and IBM, one German make, Mannesman, two Japanese lines, Panasonic and Toshiba, and one computer made in Spain, La Independencia. Advertising strongly suggests that potential computer buyers "Watch Sendlinger send down computer prices," but specific prices are never advertised and each retail customer bargains with the company for his or her own purchase price on a specific computer.

The company is also on the state's "bid list," so it periodically receives requests to bid on providing computers for the highway patrol, employees' benefits program, and other state agencies. These bid requests are carefully read, and if what is needed is described clearly enough, the company may enter a bid. Occasionally, the government market manager will have to call the State capitol in Albany to find out exactly what is meant by certain wording in the request sent out by the state agency.

All computers sold by the Sendlinger Company are sold delivered to the buyer in Jamestown. If the buyer doesn't want to take delivery In Jamestown, the company can make arrangements to have the computer delivered to them by another dealer from his stock for the additional amount of money it would cost to ship the computer from Jamestown to that vendor.

When asked about his pricing policies, Mr. Sendlinger said, "One thing we know is that we never want to be the cheapest dealer around nor do we want to be the highest priced. People don't like you to be either one of those things. We just want to sell computers at a reasonable price that people think represents good value for the money."

____11. Though all consumer prices are subject to negotiation at Sendlinger's, the evidence provided suggests that their pricing strategy is a competitive one.

____12. When a supplier such as Sendlinger's enters a bid on a state request for bids, they are really opening the process of negotiation to supply those computers.

13. Sendlinger's basic pricing policy appears to be a
   a. fixed-price policy
   b. variable price policy.
   c. list price policy.
   d. product line policy.
   e. zone pricing policy.

14. When the government market manager calls Albany to get additional information on bid requests, he is probably trying to clarify the bid request's product
   a. specifications.
   b. end-use.
   c. price limits.
   d. function.
   e. user name.

15. The geographical pricing policy the company uses for delivery of computers distant from Jamestown is
   a. zone delivered pricing.
   b. freight absorption pricing.
   c. postage-stamp pricing.
   d. basing point pricing.
   e. FOB Jamestown.

16. Mr. Sendlinger's comments about not wanting to be too cheap nor too expensive suggest that he is aware of
   a. how fickle the consumer can really be.
   b. the concept of price limits.
   c. the uses of odd pricing.
   d. the essence of the computer-buying experience.
   e. how difficult it is to make money.

Name_____   Instructor_____

Section_____   Date_____

Surfing the Net

Keeping in mind that addresses change and what's on the Web now may have changed by the time you read this, let's take a look at some of the places on the Net that reflect aspects of managing the pricing function. We are not recommending any of these sources, merely making note of the information and services that people have elected to offer through the Internet.

Prices aren't always under anybody's control, and the stock market is an interesting example of how a completely open market works. The following is a very interesting Web site in this connection, which, though rather lengthy to access, lets you look at graphs of the ups and downs of prices of a number of stock issues. Try **http://www.stockmaster.com** or **http://redherring.com** and take a look.

To compare prices of Internet service in various places, there are a number of sites you might care to explore. Lade's of Cape Coral, Florida, is an Internet service provider in that area that can be reached at **http://www.boblade.com,** while in Yarmouth on Cape Cod, Massachusetts, Diversified Technologies can be accessed at **http://www.divtech.net.** In the west, the local Internet service provider for Broken Arrow, Oklahoma (and most of the rest of the state), can be reached at **http://www.okpride.net,** while if you're interested in getting hooked up in Sydney or Melbourne (Australia), you should contact **http://www.spln.net.au**. Make sure you type in the .au tag on this one, or you'll get a totally different domestic site. In Hamilton, Ontario, Canada, try **http://www.ispnet.ca** to access the local ISP, and finally, in the UK, a local Internet service provider can be reached at **http://www.demon.net**.

Some sites with information about pricing of telephone communication services include **http://www.cellone.com** for Cellular One, while **http://www.sbc.com** belongs to SBC Communications (formerly Pacific Bell Telephone Company), and Sprint may be found at **http://www.sprintlink.net.** Any interest in Ma Bell? American Telephone and Telegraph offers Internet service through their site at **http://www.att.net.** There are Internet service providers in practically every city in the U.S. and elsewhere.

Ever wonder why insurance costs what it does? Take a look at the Web site of the American Risk and Insurance Association at **http://www.aria.org**   There you'll find an explanation of risk theory, the risk management profession, and other neat stuff about this organization.

A most interesting group of sites somewhat different from the one above, but still insurance-related, are the following **http://www.geico.com**; **http://www.progressive.com**; **http://www.allstate.com**; and **http://www.statefarm.com**. Using them, you can get rate quotes, compare coverage, and get a feel for how each of these firms operates. The comparison is easy and even possibly worthwhile. Some of these firms offer broad ranges of coverage, while others are somewhat more limited.

Sites verified January 14, 2003

Part 7
Creating a Marketing Plan

The information contained in this episode will help you complete Parts III. A. and III. B. of your marketing plan for Logeto Enterprises. You may wish to review the material in Part Four of the text to refresh your memory before attempting to complete Part III. A.

Episode Seven: How Much Is Too Much? (And How Little Is Not Enough?)

"OK," said Sandy, "let me get this straight. We're going to offer 'minimum turnaround' commercial digital wireless maintenance and repair service aimed primarily at business users here in the New Blackpool area. We're going to be open 24 hours a day, and we'll serve anyone who is willing to pay our prices. We're going to offer maintenance contracts as well, and that ties in explicitly with the for-a-fee alternative. In other words, we don't care whether we start a relationship with a customer as a repair specialist or in a maintenance role. A customer is, after all, a customer. I see. That makes me happy. What about you, Mel?"

"I'm fine, too, Sandy," Mel said, "I can see where I'm going to be spending a lot of time doing preventive maintenance for people whose equipment gets a lot of hard use. You know, I'll bet we're one of the few firms in town with people who know how to create the right diagnostics to anticipate failure before the components quit and prevent damage before it happens. It should be fun!"

"Right, fellas," spoke up Suzette, "but you know we've got to get down to brass tacks on price sooner or later. You guys have fun just going out there and playing around with all that sophisticated equipment, but if we don't make some money around here, it's not going to be long before we won't be able to pay the rent. Service work and maintenance contracts are another story and we need to tell it. Come look at these figures I've put together. They outline some price information I got my hands on." And so saying, she handed to Mel and Sandy a copy of the information contained in Table P7-1.

"Very interesting," muttered Sandy, reading the charts he had been handed, "we've really got a wide range of prices here, don't we. It looks like the most common local price for repair service is either 60 or 50 dollars per hour when you work it out."

"Yes," replied Mel, "but there are 5 firms charging only $50. I wonder if they know something we don't know – or maybe it's that we know something they don't – (laughing) like how to do the job right!"

"Well," smiled Suzette, "I've run some figures and if they are right, we can make money according to our expectations at any rate equal to or greater than $50 per hour. That price would put us in a very competitive position as far as the other places that offer these kinds of services are concerned."

"Yes, that's true," answered Sandy, "but it's still the next-to-the bottom price for the market. I think we're better than that. I think we should ask at least $60 per hour for our services, and there should be a three-hour minimum."

"I'll buy the three-hour minimum," spoke up Mel, "but the average I see in these figures is $61.00 and change per hour. Why don't we want to charge something like that?"

"Let's put that decision off for now," commented Suzette, "if we offer maintenance contracts, you know, we're going to have to price them as well. How do you propose we do that?"

Table P7-1: New Essex Area Maintenance Price Data
(From a Survey of 21 Firms)

Repair Charge Per Hour	Number	Percent Reporting
$100	2	9.5%
$ 75	2	9.5%
$ 67.50	2	9.5%
$ 60	5	23.8%
$ 53	4	19.0%
$ 50	5	23.8%
$ 40	1	4.7%

Mean per hour charge: $61.08
Median per hour charge: $60.00
Modal per hour charge: $50.00/60.00

Table P7-2: Installation and Maintenance Time for
Typical Commercial Digital Wireless Equipment

Unit Type	Initial Time (Install)	Time for Rework (About Every 90 Days)	Average Units Per Site
High-power Roving System	6 Hrs.	0.75 Hrs.	1
Video Reference/Scan Unit	10 Hrs.	1.0 Hrs.	3
Field Unit	3 Hrs.	0.50 Hrs.	20
Pocket Portable	2 Hrs.	0.25 Hrs.	2
Total Time (Time x Units)	100 Hrs.	57.00 Hrs.	

"I've got that one solved for you, Suzette," responded Sandy. "An article I read last night gave some actuarial figures and some prices for maintenance contracts and it said that maintenance contracts that sell cost approximately as much yearly as reworking a site.

"You mean a contract that involves every unit on the site?" asked Mel.

"Yes," answered Sandy, "and it looks like that sort of thing costs about thirty-eight percent, on average, of what all new equipment would cost. I think our maintenance contracts should be priced at around thirty-eight percent of the cost of a new site to the client."

Lori entered the conversation at this point to announce "Good thinking, Sandy; I've seen that article and I think you're right. Let's work on that sort of price for maintenance contracts. Now let's get back to the per hour price for our service call business. What price do you think we should set? Let's vote on it."

Guidelines:

a. Outline the company's product/service strategy in your planning notebook. Refer back to the information provided in the earlier parts of this exercise for items which may expand on what you learned in this part. Recognize how this strategy developed to serve the needs of the market and of our entrepreneurial trio.

b. What sort of price structure do you favor for Sumesa Enterprises? Should their hourly rate be $50, $55, $60 or some other amount? This time, the decision is yours to make, but you should be able to justify it if called upon to do so.

c. Approximately how much money would you charge for a yearly maintenance contract (on average)? How would the price be adjusted for different customers?

Part 8
Creating a Marketing Plan

The material provided in this episode should allow you to complete section III. E. of your marketing plan.

Episode Eight: So When Do We Start To Get Rich?"

The three partners, having incorporated their business, have themselves each bought 20,000 shares of the authorized 80,000 shares of Subchapter S common stock for one dollar apiece. They were able to borrow $90,000 from family and friends and have also secured a $90,000 bank loan, both at a rate of 9.5%, the whole to be repaid over five years in monthly installments of $3781.80.

Pro Forma Income Statements for the first three years of operation have been prepared and are included in Table P8-1.

Table P8-1: Pro Forma Income Statements for Years 1, 2, and 3 Sumesa Enterprises, Inc.

Year	One	Two	Three
Revenue	$291,460	$346,752	$408,294
Allowances	8,000	9,600	11,448
Net Sales	283,640	337,152	396,846
Internal Services	48,210	49,350	49,840
Employee Wages+	90,000	105,000	120,000
Gross Margin	145,430	182,802	227,004
Operating Expenses	209,718	130,298	126,740
Marketing Expense*	28,718	60,062	64,778
Operating Income(Loss)	$(93,006)	$ (7,558)	$ 35,486

*Includes Sales Commissions, Sales Staff Salaries, and Advertising.
+Compensation to three hired employees not members of the corporation.

The threesome, Sandy, Mel, and Suzette, will have collected separate commissions and salaries not included in "employee wages" as compensation during the first three years. Those amounts are summarized in Table P8-2.

Table P8-2: Amounts Paid Incorporators, First Three Years Sumesa Enterprises, Inc.

Year	One	Two	Three
Administrative Salaries	$ 60,000	$ 60,000	$ 60,000
Service Salaries	38,400	38,400	38,400
Sales Commissions	13,490	24,494	29,210
Sales Salaries	22,800	22,800	22,800
Total Amounts	$134,690	$145,694	$150,410

The amounts above were paid share and share alike to each of the three corporate members. They are, of course, due any dividends which they may elect to pay themselves from profits earned in years three and subsequent years.

Guidelines:

Use this information to prepare Part III. E. of your marketing plan. Note that, since this is a startup business, projections have been made pro forma for a period of three years. Impact of the trio's efforts will be evidenced by the degree to which the projections and reality are similar.

Question:

Will it all have been worth it? Considering the future of the company, will the three partners have gotten out of it what they expected to, in your opinion? Remember, the psychic reward of entrepreneurship has some value.

Chapter Solutions

Chapter 1

Key Terms

1. F	6. J	11. B	16. Q	21. R
2. S	7. N	12. A	17. I	
3. L	8. E	13. O	18. K	
4. P	9. H	14. D	19. M	
5. T	10. C	15. U	20. G	

Self-Quiz

1. T	11. F	21. F	31. c	41. e
2. F	12. F	22. F	32. b	42. e
3. T	13. T	23. T	33. a	43. d
4. F	14. T	24. F	34. b	44. c
5. T	15. F	25. T	35. e	45. d
6. F	16. F	26. b	36. a	46. e
7. T	17. F	27. d	37. c	47. c
8. F	18. T	28. c	38. a	48. a
9. T	19. T	29. a	39. d	49. e
10. T	20. T	30. d	40. b	50. b

Applying Marketing Concepts

1. T	6. B	11. B
2. T	7. B	12. C
3. F	8. C	13. A
4. F	9. C	14. C
5. A	10. D	

Chapter 2

Key Concepts

1. b	6. g	11. j	16. m
2. k	7. n	12. q	17. i
3. c	8. a	13. p	
4. e	9. o	14. h	
5. l	10. f	15. d	

Self-Quiz

1.	F	11.	F	21.	F	31.	c	41.	a
2.	F	12.	T	22.	F	32.	e	42.	c
3.	F	13.	T	23.	T	33.	d	43.	b
4.	T	14.	T	24.	T	34.	a	44.	e
5.	F	15.	F	25.	T	35.	a	45.	d
6.	T	16.	F	26.	d	36.	d	46.	a
7.	F	17.	F	27.	b	37.	c	47.	c
8.	T	18.	T	28.	c	38.	d	48.	e
9.	T	19.	T	29.	e	39.	a	49.	b
10.	T	20.	F	30.	b	40.	b	50.	e

Applying Marketing Concepts

1.	a	6.	c	11.	b
2.	b	7.	a	12.	d
3.	a	8.	d		
4.	c	9.	b		
5.	b	10.	c		

Chapter 3

Key Concepts

1.	e	6.	j	11.	m
2.	l	7.	d	12.	h
3.	n	8.	i	13.	a
4.	g	9.	c	14.	k
5.	b	10.	f		

Self-Quiz

1.	F	11.	T	21.	T	31.	e	41.	c
2.	T	12.	F	22.	T	32.	c	42.	d
3.	T	13.	T	23.	F	33.	c	43.	b
4.	T	14.	F	24.	T	34.	d	44.	a
5.	F	15.	T	25.	T	35.	e	45.	c
6.	T	16.	T	26.	c	36.	e	46.	b
7.	F	17.	F	27.	a	37.	a	47.	d
8.	F	18.	F	28.	a	38.	e	48.	b
9.	F	19.	F	29.	d	39.	b	49.	d
10.	T	20.	F	30.	b	40.	e	50.	a

Applying Marketing Concepts

1.	F	6.	e	11.	b
2.	T	7.	a	12.	d
3.	T	8.	e	13.	a
4.	F	9.	c	14.	b
5.	T	10.	b		

Chapter 4

Key Concepts

1. j	6. f	11 n	16. l	21. q
2. h	7. b	12. r	17. v	22. t
3. m	8. c	13. k	18. g	
4. i	9. a	14. u	19. o	
5. e	10. s	15. d	20. p	

Self-Quiz

1. T	11. F	21. F	31. c	41. b
2. F	12. T	22. T	32. d	42. e
3. T	13. F	23. F	33. b	43. b
4. T	14. F	24. F	34. e	44. a
5. F	15. T	25. F	35. a	45. c
6. F	16. F	26. a	36. b	46. a
7. T	17. T	27. c	37. d	47. e
8. T	18. T	28. e	38. e	48. c
9. T	19. F	29. d	39. d	49. d
10. F	20. T	30. a	40. c	50. b

Applying Marketing Concepts

1. c	6. a	11. a
2. d	7. c	12. d
3. b	8. b	13. c
4. b	9. a	
5. d	10. b	

Chapter 5

Key Concepts

1. m	5. i	9. h	13. p	17. f
2. a	6. n	10. r	14. g	18. k
3. q	7. b	11. c	15. o	
4. e	8. j	12. d	16. l	

Self-Quiz

1. F	11. T	21. F	31. d	41. d
2. F	12. F	22. T	32. a	42. b
3. T	13. T	23. F	33. a	43. b
4. T	14. T	24. F	34. c	44. b
5. F	15. T	25. T	35. e	45. c
6. F	16. F	26. e	36. e	46. c
7. T	17. F	27. c	37. a	47. b
8. T	18. F	28. e	38. d	48. a
9. T	19. T	29. d	39. c	49. a
10. T	20. F	30. b	40. e	50. d

Applying Marketing Concepts

1. T	6. T	11. d
2. b	7. F	12. b
3. d	8. F	13. a
4. a	9. T	14. a
5. F	10. d	

Chapter 6

Key Concepts

1. c	6. g	11. a
2. j	7. f	12. m
3. e	8. b	13. o
4. h	9. i	14. d
5. l	10. n	15. k

Self-Quiz

1. T	11. T	21. T	31. a	41. a
2. F	12. T	22. T	32. d	42. c
3. F	13. T	23. F	33. e	43. e
4. F	14. T	24. F	34. e	44. c
5. T	15. F	25. T	35. a	45. a
6. F	16. T	26. b	36. b	46. e
7. T	17. T	27. d	37. e	47. d
8. T	18. T	28. a	38. c	48. e
9. F	19. F	29. c	39. b	49. a
10. F	20. F	30. c	40. a	50. c

Applying Marketing Concepts

1. T	6. b	11. T
2. T	7. c	12. F
3. b	8. c	13. T
4. e	9. a	14. F
5. a	10. c	

Chapter 7

Key Concepts

1. h	5. a	9. m	13. r	17. g
2. c	6. e	10. d	14. f	18. k
3. i	7. q	11. o	15. l	
4. b	8. n	12. j	16. p	

Self-Quiz

1. T	11. T	21. T	31. a	41. c
2. F	12. F	22. F	32. a	42. d
3. T	13. T	23. T	33. d	43. b
4. F	14. T	24. F	34. b	44. b
5. T	15. F	25. T	35. c	45. a
6. F	16. T	26. d	36. e	46. d
7. F	17. F	27. a	37. c	47. b
8. T	18. F	28. e	38. c	48. a
9. T	19. T	29. b	39. e	49. d
10. F	20. T	30. e	40. e	50. e

Applying Marketing Concepts

1. c	6. d	11. T
2. d	7. a	12. F
3. a	8. c	13. F
4. c	9. T	14. F
5. b	10. F	

Chapter 8

Key Concepts

1. c	6. k	11. b	16. j
2. g	7. n	12. o	
3. d	8. a	13. l	
4. i	9. e	14. p	
5. f	10. m	15. h	

Self-Quiz

1. F	11. F	21. T	31. e	41. e
2. T	12. F	22. T	32. a	42. c
3. T	13. T	23. F	33. b	43. a
4. T	14. T	24. F	34. a	44. c
5. F	15. F	25. T	35. e	45. b
6. F	16. T	26. b	36. d	46. c
7. T	17. F	27. c	37. b	47. d
8. F	18. T	28. e	38. d	48. d
9. T	19. F	29. c	39. a	49. e
10. T	20. F	30. d	40. a	50. b

Applying Marketing Concepts

1. T	6. b	11. F	16. d
2. T	7. c	12. T	17. a
3. F	8. a	13. F	
4. F	9. c	14. b	
5. F	10. a	15. c	

Chapter 9

Key Concepts

1. m	4. a	7. k	10. e	13. g
2. d	5. f	8. n	11. c	14. d
3. b	6. j	9. h	12. i	15. l

Self-Quiz

1. T	11. T	21. T	31. c	41. e
2. F	12. F	22. F	32. b	42. b
3. T	13. T	23. T	33. a	43. d
4. T	14. T	24. T	34. d	44. c
5. F	15. F	25. F	35. c	45. b
6. F	16. F	26. b	36. e	46. b
7. F	17. T	27. a	37. d	47. c
8. T	18. T	28. c	38. d	48. b
9. F	19. F	29. e	39. e	49. b
10. T	20. F	30. a	40. d	50. e

Applying Marketing Concepts

1. F	6. c
2. T	7. e
3. F	8. b
4. b	9. d
5. c	10. c

Chapter 10

Key Concepts

1. e	6. h	11. m
2. f	7. o	12. c
3. l	8. d	13. i
4. a	9. b	14. g
5. j	10. n	15. k

Self-Quiz

1. F	11. T	21. T	31. b	41. c
2. T	12. F	22. F	32. c	42. a
3. F	13. T	23. T	33. b	43. a
4. T	14. T	24. F	34. d	44. d
5. F	15. F	25. T	35. a	45. d
6. T	16. F	26. e	36. e	46. b
7. F	17. T	27. a	37. b	47. e
8. F	18. F	28. b	38. a	48. d
9. T	19. F	29. d	39. c	49. c
10. T	20. T	30. c	40. e	50. e

Applying Marketing Concepts

1.	b	6.	b
2.	a	7.	d
3.	e	8.	c
4.	a	9.	a
5.	a	10.	b

Chapter 11

Key Concepts

1.	c	6.	o	11.	m
2.	i	7.	h	12.	d
3.	a	8.	n	13.	e
4.	k	9.	b	14.	l
5.	j	10.	g		

Self-Quiz

1.	T	11.	F	21.	T	31.	c	41.	c
2.	T	12.	T	22.	F	32.	b	42.	a
3.	F	13.	F	23.	F	33.	b	43.	d
4.	F	14.	T	24.	T	34.	c	44.	a
5.	T	15.	F	25.	F	35.	a	45.	e
6.	F	16.	T	26.	b	36.	d	46.	e
7.	T	17.	F	27.	a	37.	e	47.	c
8.	T	18.	F	28.	e	38.	d	48.	c
9.	T	19.	T	29.	d	39.	e	49.	a
10.	F	20.	F	30.	b	40.	d	50.	b

Applying Marketing Concepts

1.	d	6.	a	11.	c
2.	d	7.	a	12.	a
3.	c	8.	b	13.	b
4.	c	9.	e	14.	a
5.	b	10.	a		

Chapter 12

Key Concepts

1.	g	6.	e	11.	j
2.	m	7.	h	12.	i
3.	l	8.	n	13.	b
4.	k	9.	a	14.	f
5.	o	10.	d	15.	c

Self-Quiz

1. T	11. F	21. T	31. c	41. d
2. T	12. T	22. F	32. c	42. e
3. F	13. F	23. T	33. a	43. b
4. T	14. F	24. F	34. e	44. d
5. F	15. T	25. F	35. a	45. d
6. T	16. F	26. c	36. c	46. b
7. F	17. T	27. b	37. d	47. d
8. F	18. T	28. e	38. c	48. a
9. T	19. F	29. e	39. b	49. a
10. T	20. F	30. a	40. e	50. b

Applying Marketing Concepts

1. b	6. c	11. e
2. e	7. b	12. d
3. a	8. a	13. a
4. c	9. d	14. b
5. a	10. b	15. a

Chapter 13

Key Concepts

1. f	6. m	11. a	16. p
2. g	7. o	12. i	
3. n	8. h	13. d	
4. b	9. k	14. l	
5. c	10. j	15. e	

Self-Quiz

1. T	11. F	21. F	31. e	41. c
2. T	12. T	22. T	32. b	42. d
3. F	13. F	23. T	33. c	43. c
4. F	14. T	24. F	34. d	44. d
5. T	15. T	25. F	35. a	45. e
6. T	16. F	26. a	36. e	46. a
7. T	17. T	27. a	37. b	47. d
8. F	18. F	28. b	38. c	48. b
9. F	19. F	29. d	39. b	49. e
10. T	20. T	30. c	40. e	50. a

Applying Marketing Concepts

1. b	6. F	11. b
2. c	7. T	12. c
3. d	8. F	13. a
4. a	9. F	14. c
5. e	10. T	15. a

Chapter 14

Key Concepts

1. i	6. j	11. d	
2. k	7. l	12. h	
3. m	8. b	13. c	
4. f	9. g		
5. a	10. e		

Self-Quiz

1. T	11. T	21. F	31. b	41. a	51. a
2. F	12. T	22. T	32. c	42. d	52. a
3. F	13. F	23. T	33. c	43. a	53. b
4. T	14. T	24. F	34. a	44. e	54. d
5. T	15. F	25. F	35. d	45. c	55. e
6. T	16. F	26. T	36. d	46. c	56. b
7. F	17. T	27. F	37. e	47. e	57. e
8. F	18. T	28. T	38. b	48. c	58. d
9. F	19. F	29. F	39. a	49. b	59. b
10. F	20. T	30. F	40. e	50. d	60. c

Applying Marketing Concepts

1. F	6. d	11. b	16. a
2. F	7. d	12. b	17. b
3. F	8. a	13. a	18. d
4. T	9. d	14. T	
5. T	10. b	15. c	

Chapter 15

Key Concepts

1. i	6. o	11. j	16. n
2. f	7. e	12. p	
3. l	8. m	13. c	
4. h	9. d	14. b	
5. k	10. a	15. g	

Self-Quiz

1. T	11. F	21. T	31. c	41. b
2. F	12. T	22. F	32. d	42. c
3. T	13. F	23. T	33. b	43. c
4. F	14. T	24. T	34. a	44. b
5. T	15. F	25. F	35. e	45. e
6. T	16. F	26. e	36. b	46. a
7. F	17. T	27. b	37. a	47. d
8. F	18. T	28. c	38. c	48. e
9. T	19. T	29. d	39. d	49. e
10. T	20. F	30. a	40. d	50. a

Applying Marketing Concepts

1.	a	6.	b
2.	c	7.	d
3.	a	8.	c
4.	d	9.	a
5.	e	10.	c

Chapter 16

Key Concepts

1.	g	6.	a	11.	e
2.	b	7.	h	12.	h
3.	f	8.	j		
4.	e	9.	d		
5.	c	10.	k		

Self-Quiz

1.	T	11.	T	21.	F	31.	e	41.	c
2.	T	12.	F	22.	F	32.	d	42.	b
3.	F	13.	T	23.	F	33.	e	43.	e
4.	T	14.	F	24.	T	34.	b	44.	d
5.	F	15.	T	25.	T	35.	c	45.	e
6.	T	16.	F	26.	b	36.	d	46.	a
7.	F	17.	F	27.	a	37.	a	47.	c
8.	F	18.	T	28.	a	38.	a	48.	c
9.	F	19.	T	29.	c	39.	e	49.	d
10.	T	20.	T	30.	b	40.	d	50.	b

Applying Marketing Concepts

1.	e	6.	b	11.	a
2.	b	7.	a	12.	a
3.	d	8.	b		
4.	c	9.	d		
5.	b	10.	e		

Chapter 17

Key Concepts

1.	i	6.	a	11.	f	16.	j
2.	c	7.	g	12.	o		
3.	e	8.	d	13.	p		
4.	l	9.	k	14.	m		
5.	b	10.	n	15.	h		

Self-Quiz

1. F	11. T	21. T	31. a	41. e
2. T	12. F	22. T	32. b	42. e
3. F	13. T	23. T	33. b	43. c
4. T	14. T	24. F	34. e	44. c
5. F	15. F	25. T	35. d	45. d
6. F	16. T	26. d	36. b	46. e
7. T	17. T	27. b	37. a	47. a
8. T	18. F	28. b	38. c	48. c
9. F	19. F	29. e	39. e	49. c
10. T	20. F	30. a	40. d	50. d

Applying Marketing Concepts

1. c	6. b	11. d
2. d	7. a	12. c
3. a	8. d	13. d
4. b	9. b	
5. c	10. b	

Chapter 18

Key Concepts

1. e	4. i	7. f	10. d	13. j
2. h	5. k	8. m	11. g	
3. l	6. b	9. a	12. c	

Self-Quiz

1. F	11. F	21. T	31. a	41. a
2. T	12. F	22. F	32. d	42. b
3. T	13. F	23. F	33. a	43. d
4. F	14. T	24. T	34. c	44. b
5. T	15. T	25. F	35. b	45. c
6. F	16. F	26. e	36. e	46. e
7. T	17. T	27. d	37. a	47. b
8. F	18. F	28. a	38. b	48. d
9. T	19. T	29. a	39. c	49. a
10. T	20. F	30. b	40. c	50. c

Applying Marketing Concepts

1. F	6. c	11. c
2. T	7. b	12. d
3. F	8. a	13. b
4. T	9. a	14. e
5. T	10. b	

Chapter 19

Key Concepts

1.	i	5.	o	9.	c	13.	f	17. l
2.	b	6.	q	10.	d	14.	h	
3.	j	7.	n	11.	p	15.	m	
4.	e	8.	k	12.	g	16.	a	

Self-Quiz

1.	T	11.	F	21.	F	31.	d	41.	d
2.	F	12.	T	22.	F	32.	a	42.	e
3.	F	13.	T	23.	T	33.	c	43.	e
4.	T	14.	F	24.	T	34.	c	44.	b
5.	T	15.	F	25.	F	35.	b	45.	a
6.	F	16.	F	26.	a	36.	b	46.	b
7.	F	17.	T	27.	c	37.	d	47.	c
8.	T	18.	F	28.	d	38.	e	48.	d
9.	T	19.	T	29.	a	39.	a	49.	b
10.	T	20.	T	30.	b	40.	c	50.	e

Applying Marketing Concepts

1.	F	6.	b	11.	T	16.	b
2.	F	7.	c	12.	F		
3.	T	8.	e	13.	b		
4.	F	9.	a	14.	a		
5.	T	10.	d	15.	d		

Solutions for Creating a Marketing Plan

Episode Two

a. The firm's nature is becoming fairly clear in episode two. It is to be a firm specializing in commercial communications using digital wireless equipment and technology. It will be located in the as yet unnamed home town of the three people who have decided to start it, and they have about $240,000 available to them to get under way. Thus, their geographical scope and their financial resources are limited.

    The company is to be a corporation, appropriately licensed and conforming to the constraints of the various environments impinging on it. It has no sales and profits history as yet, just cash on hand and considerable expertise in digital wireless technology and practice.

b. The data provided are designed to lead our heroes to choose to create a firm, which will develop digital wireless communications alternatives with particular appeal to the business user. While there are some 175,875 <u>households</u> in the area that own cell phones, and 11.0 percent of those (6,985 households) which use a commercial form of digital wireless service, and it is dubious if they use non-household members to maintain their systems. Under other conditions, it might be desirable to do extensive research into the household market for Web site development, but with the limited resources on hand, the business market for Sumesa's services seems far more accessible and the potential much greater.

    The 25,895 business firms in the area offer a market with a use level of 35 percent at present, and it is likely that a substantial number of the remainder will need sites soon in the future. It appears as well that the smaller firms have lagged the larger ones in making their presence known as commercial digital wireless communicators. One reason for this may have been their fear of having to do their own maintenance, exactly the kind of thing Sumesa is prepared to do. Moreover, the predicted rate of growth for the maintenance segment of the relevant market is estimated at 33 percent, over twice the rate of growth of other interactive wireless products and services.

Episode Three

Sumesa's analysis of competitive conditions in New Blackpool involves analysis of three aspects of that environment. First, the firm must consider direct competition from firms specializing in commercial digital wireless communications service. Of these, there are 21 who are potentially active competitors of Sumesa Enterprises. Second sources of possible competition are the firms who engage primarily in providing personal communications service, but who also do commercial-related work (or say they do). Of these there are 102 who <u>might</u> be active competitors, but a very interesting statistic in this regard is the fact that only 29 firms indicated that they did this sort of work for any but their "regular customers." What, exactly, is a "regular customer?" Sumesa will be organized to serve commercial "always-on" digital wireless customers, so the level of competition with these firms will not be as direct or as intense as with the other firms whose main business is commercial service. From a marketing planning point of view, the commercial digital wireless service firms appear to be first-line competitors with the personal cellular service firms constituting a second line of far less serious importance.

The third aspect of the analysis is provided by the subjective comments offered by Suzette and Sandy. It appears as though the potential competition is not very effective in defining its mission or in communicating that mission within its own organization or to the using public. A firm whose employee contact with the community via the telephone doesn't even know whether it offers a particular service -much less 8 of them out of 60 - indicates that there is a lack of clarity in the firms' statements of their missions and their orientation to the marketplace. One might even say that their consciousness of the process of segmentation is limited, and it is quite likely that one would be right. It is certainly true that firms that deal with high-tech equipment tend to be started and operated by people who are themselves technologists, not marketers, and often suffer from a lack of skills in human interaction as a result. There is obviously weakness among the competition, and they certainly are not very aggressive, as the two display ads from among 21 *Yellow Pages* listings would tend to indicate.

Lacking information on market share, further analysis of the intensity of local competition cannot be undertaken, but it is quite unlikely that such information would be available in a local market situation.

Episode Four

a. The partners are getting their figures from the data given in this episode as well as information from previous episodes. Their estimate of a commercial digital wireless service market of $78,000,000 in the local area was based on the $15 billion estimate for the national market multiplied by New Blackpool's proportion of that population, some 0.52% (slightly more than one-half of one percent). The $1,131,000 projection for one percent of the market five years hence was arrived at by compounding $780,000 (currently one percent of the market) at 14 percent for five years, the current year being uncompounded. This is a very lowball or conservative estimate of market potential, as using the projected rate of growth for the industry would generate a volume prediction in excess of $2,000,000 for the fifth year hence. Suzette's comment about doing $375,000 this year and growing at a rate of 30 to 35 percent to achieve the $1,131,000 volume derives from one source: her assumption of $375,000 in volume this year and $1,131,000 in five years.

b. It appears that our heroes have decided that their objectives are to be one percent of the market in five years and a rate of profitability of 10 percent on sales at the end of that time. They recognize that, in the meantime, they are likely to lose money for a few years to come, but they are prepared to do so in order for their firm ultimately to succeed. Their business philosophy seems very marketing oriented, with a twenty-four hour a day operation envisioned. They want their customers to be happy with their service and hope to build customer loyalty, which will ultimately result in the writing of a lot of maintenance contracts. Later information may call for revision of the objectives and policies set at this point in the plan.

Episode Five

Sumesa Enterprises, as a service organization, occupies a somewhat unusual position in the distribution channel. They are providers of a business service, so their channel of distribution will be direct. As participants in the business-to-business market, their initial sales efforts will probably include a lot more personal selling than advertising. At any rate, Sumesa will be participating in a marketing channel in which they will be acting as a direct provider of services.

The proprietors have already acquired most of the physical distribution facilities they are going to need: two automobiles in which to make sales and emergency calls and a combination shop/warehouse/office. They are probably also going to need some manual materials-handling equipment, like a carry cart and possibly a hand truck for some of the heavier and bulkier test and analysis equipment which they will be moving to use in performing their service functions.

Their location was chosen to make them physically convenient to the greatest number of businesses. Obviously, they took some care in the choice. They are certainly aware of the need for a secure location, a particular consideration for firms that own expensive and sometimes hard-to-replace equipment or which produce intellectual property, which can be of great damage if it falls into the wrong hands.

Their major physical distribution characteristics, in my estimation, should be accessibility, speed of service, and a high level of accuracy filling each customer's order. Mistakes, though inevitable, are very undesirable for a firm in this position. They should also offer flexibility of scheduling в at their customers "convenience" though this feature is perhaps redundant to mention in this context. It is important to remember that their operating philosophy is "minimum waiting time" for their customers. Moreover, I think it is significant that one of the things they were looking for was a building that wasn't a "dump." While physical beauty is not a <u>necessary</u> attribute of a facility devoted to this sort of activity, it sure doesn't hurt to produce an attractive appearance when customers come to see what kind of work you're doing for them. I can think of several instances when business service firms have lost their credibility with me when I discovered their office was "less than attractive," especially when the condition could have been avoided. More will be said on this under promotion.

Episode Six

In this episode, Mel, Sandy, and Suzette reveal a rather complex but fairly well thought out promotional plan. They will be using Yellow Pages advertising and newspaper advertising, sales promotional stickers and business cards, personal selling, and even public relations to develop a positive image for their firm. It might be very interesting to attempt to explicitly differentiate among the various forms of promotion, which the entrepreneurs plan to use. Are the stickers, for example, advertising or are they sales promotion? My view would be that they are a variety of point-of-purchase advertising, a sales promotion tool. When does personal selling end and sales promotion begin in those instances when one of the selling partners hands a prospect a promotional brochure? A discussion of "supportive literature" could be very beneficial at this point. And let us not forget the importance of the business card. Many of these are saved and filed on the chance that the person who gave it to the recipient will someday be needed in a professional capacity. For the small businessman they are almost literally worth their weight in gold. I am also a big fan of *Yellow Pages* advertising, but not necessarily in the form of major display ads. Certainly a listing is absolutely necessary, and you get that when you subscribe to commercial phone service, but a small, well-written copy box to highlight the business and set it off (differentiation) can be both promotionally and cost effective.

A very fruitful discussion hinges on the idea of keeping the building clean, neat, and presentable, if only because so many service firms don't bother to do this. If neatness and attractiveness count in a retail environment, why is it that they seem not to be important at wholesale or for service firms? The answer, of course, is that they do count for every business that the public can see. All other things being equal, a neat, tidy operation has the advantage over one, which is kept, in a less attractive state. Indeed, the neatness may be reflected in the firm's fire and liability insurance premiums because a neat area is usually a safe area. Some businesses are inherently dirtier than others auto repair shops, for example, create more than their share of oily, greasy dirt just because they are what they are. And foundries – well, best we not get into the nature of foundries. Let us just note that the floors of foundries are made of dirt – and they're usually the cleanest parts of the building. But even these kinds of places can be kept neater than they usually are with a little extra effort that pays big dividends in customer satisfaction.

Students should feel free to suggest alternative means of promotion, which Sumesa Enterprises could use. They should, however, be warned, should they suggest using radio or TV ads, that experience has taught us that using these media for this kind of service is generally ineffective for two reasons: (1) the ad is often lost in the clutter of other advertising unless the service is needed right now, and (2) such advertising tends to create generic demand for the service, seldom specific demand for the services of a specific firm.

Episode Seven

a. It should be well enough established by now that Sumesa Enterprises intends to provide twenty-four hour a day, seven-day a week commercial digital wireless repair and site maintenance service directed primarily at the business market such that further elucidation would be unnecessary, but one can never be sure. This is, however, the first time the term "minimum turnaround" has been used to describe the firm's mission, and that may be significant in allowing students to differentiate between personal cellular phone users and business communications users. Personal users do not usually view them exclusively as money-making tools which cost money when they are out of service, and hence will tolerate a certain amount of lost access time and "out-of-service" on their equipment. If a business communication system goes down or loses service time, people cannot get their work done, orders can't be placed, and the company loses money. There is a substantial situational difference here that can be explored at length if it is desired to do so.

b. For their other activities, the corporate moguls have any number of prices available to them. We know that $50 per hour for equipment service is their bottom line minimum price below which they cannot go and achieve their stated objectives of volume and profitability. The data also show that there is quite a lot of clustering at the price levels around $50 and $60. As a new firm entering a fairly competitive market, it is probably unwise to try and adopt a skimming policy even though the quality of their product is ultimately going to be higher than that of the competition. Their potential customers don't know that, and right now probably wouldn't care, anyway. A penetration pricing strategy would be the best choice in this case. My personal leanings are toward $60 per hour with a three-hour minimum. This places them almost 15 percent below the average price in the market and twenty dollars below the median price, and still offers profit potential better than they have indicated they need in order to be satisfied. The three-hour minimum is reasonable because it is almost impossible to do anything substantive in a single hour.

c. Using the information given, a typical maintenance contract would run between $2850 and $3500 per year, depending on whether they decide to use $50 or $60 per hour as their base hourly rate. Obviously, each contract would have to be pegged to the number and type of unit operated by the client and the average time involved in working on such equipment in the average year. Their pricing of maintenance contracts will be in line with industry practice, and though it may be low when compared with the total cost of setting up a system, being based on their per-hour price, it must be discounted in recognition of the fact that the money is received up front and the work is done later – and then, may be less than the contract postulates. (Of course, it may also be more than that, but that's why maintenance contracts exist. They are, after all a form of insurance and the insurer and insured are betting against each other.)

It is always well to remember that prices are not etched in stone. If Sumesa's quality service develops for them a satisfactory volume of business, price can be adjusted upward or downward to satisfy the goals of the entrepreneurs. We might judge, from some of their discussions, that they really aren't in it just for the money, anyway, and that the desire for profit is the desire to put bread on the table as needed, but also to have a good time while doing it.

Episode Eight

Completing this section of the marketing plan completes the entire plan. The crucial question arising out of the projections of sales, costs, and revenues given in this section is meant to be "Will it be worth it?" On first blush, the income figures for these three fairly well educated people may seem a little low: An average of $50,000 per year after three years of hard work, if it all works out!

On the other hand, some would say they have been very generous with themselves. They have drawn three classes of salaries plus commissions while this firm was struggling to get off the ground. What would things have looked like if some of those monies had been left in the business? Let's give Mel, Sandy, and Suzette just their administrative and sales salaries and plow the rest into the business. Well, the first year's loss of $93,006 would have been reduced to $56,710, the second year's loss of $7,558 would have been a profit of $39,736, and the third year's profit would have been $87,496. Of course, it's their money to do with as they will, and they've weathered the worst of it and are now making a profit even after paying themselves reasonably well.

One can but wonder, on the other hand, what happened to the $375,000 in the first year, growing at a rate of 30+ percent per year? Obviously, the original projection of one percent of a market of grand scope was a bit overly optimistic c but the business has become profitable, nonetheless.

But there is more to it than may appear just in the raw figures. There is the equity, or sellout value in the company once it gets to be a going concern. There is the stream of profits, which will just be starting to accrue at the end of that third year. There is the possibility of turning some of the day-to-day operations of the company over to hired employees and taking a little (or a lot) of time off. And, of course, there is the idea of working for yourself, rather than for someone else, which may itself be the motivation to start any small business. Some more dedicated students may attempt to project the income of this firm out for a longer period. If they do, advise them to pick a relatively conservative rate of growth, as was done in the model (20% per year). They may assume that gross margin will stabilize at about 80% of net sales, and total expenses at about 70% of net sales, quite possibly declining slightly as fixed costs become a somewhat smaller percentage of the total.

At the end of five years, if projections are fulfilled, this firm should be grossing in excess of $415,000 and earning a net yearly profit of something in the neighborhood of $50,000 or more, after all expenses and salaries are paid. The question of the worth of that kind of return remains up in the air, and can only be answered in terms of the worth to the three entrepreneurs of being entrepreneurs. Somehow, I think they'll be happy with it.